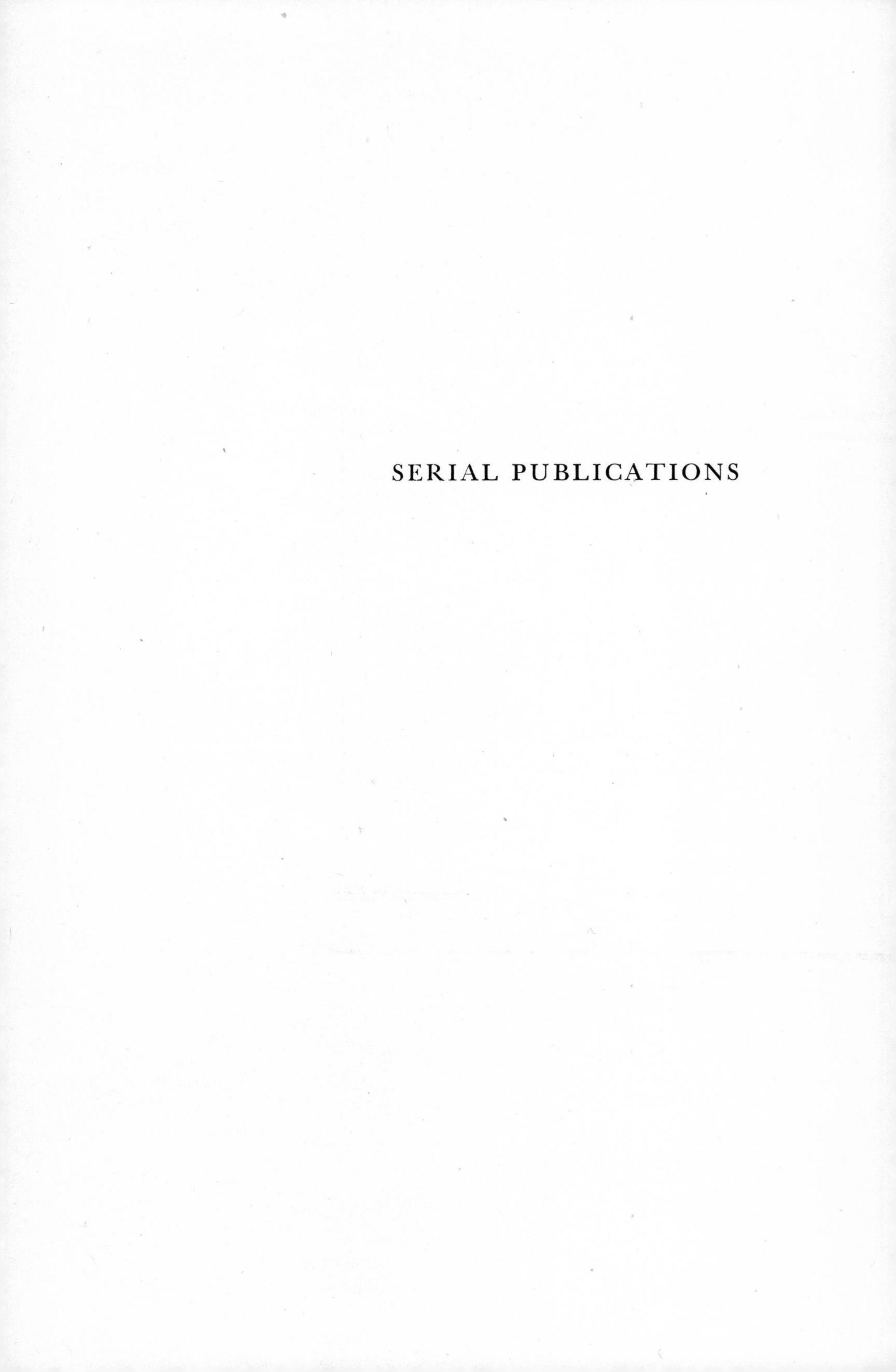

SERIAL PUBLICATIONS

ANDREW D. OSBORN
Harvard University

Serial Publications

Their Place and Treatment
in Libraries

CHICAGO • 1955
American Library Association

Manufactured in the United States of America
Library of Congress catalog card number 55-7353

To my old chief, colleague, and friend

KENNETH BINNS

Formerly Librarian of the Commonwealth National Library

Canberra, Australia

with esteem and affection

Preface

THIS BOOK has been designed as a theoretical and practical introduction to the library aspects of serial publications. These publications are now so profuse and at the same time so significant for library purposes that librarians generally should have a good grasp of their nature and of the modes of controlling them. Like rare books, serials give rise to frequent and sometimes intricate technicalities with which not only specialists but also head librarians, department heads, and others should be acquainted since serials are part and parcel of the workaday library. At all times throughout the text I have tried to present these technicalities in such a way that both the specialist and the non-specialist can comprehend and benefit by the discussion.

Theory has been emphasized because libraries ought to base their practice on sound principles. When they do, local practice can be individualistic in many respects; for which reason the book does not attempt to codify practices, but instead refers to representative libraries from time to time.

The working hypotheses I have followed in developing and organizing the book may be summarized as follows:

Serials are an indispensable feature of most library programs by virtue of their informational and research value.

Serials of all types should be accorded equal status. No main type should be discriminated against. This principle applies most particularly to government documents, which all too often have been set apart from the classified collection and given substandard treatment in their cataloging, classification, current housing, and binding.

Specialized serial records should as a rule be developed for control purposes and economy of effort. Primarily these include the visible index, the shelf list, the *Union List of Serials,* and *New Serial Titles* (or other appropriate union lists).

For all parts of a library the specialized records should to the fullest extent be regarded as a joint concern, no matter in which department they may be located.

The specialized records should serve clearly defined ends, and the serial entries in the general card catalog should be complementary to them.

Recognition of this principle is essential if duplication of effort is to be avoided.

The rules for serial cataloging require revision to allow fully for the contributions made by the visible index, the *Union List of Serials,* and *New Serial Titles.*

Serial functions, notably those connected with processing and current servicing, should when practicable be in the hands of specialists: partly because of the unpredictable nature of serials and partly because of the technicalities which must endlessly be faced in larger collections.

On both the local and the national level, extensive cooperation between libraries is a prerequisite for the sound development of serial resources.

Indexing and abstracting mediums, as well as union lists, must be promoted on a larger scale than heretofore. They should be more comprehensive and less duplicative in their coverage.

Microreproduction and other copying devices must play an ever-increasing role in the rounding out and preserving of serial files, as well as in making them widely available; but the microreproduction program should be carefully planned, because some forms of serial micropublication give rise to major service problems.

In terms of library economy, serial publications will really come into their own in the comparatively near future when libraries of all kinds are linked up in national networks of television facsimile reproduction machines.

Special libraries have been taken into account equally with general libraries. Though these two types are in some ways distinctive, each has much of value for the other to study. Perhaps because of their intense preoccupation with serials, special libraries have somewhat more to offer general libraries than the other way around. It is certainly true that general libraries can often benefit by investigating the ways in which special libraries learn of new titles of worth and by examining the businesslike methods of control which they adopt. This text is in keeping with special library traditions when it argues for enterprising, economical, and efficient procedures.

I owe an immense debt of gratitude to those colleagues who have supplied information or illustrative material and to those who have read through part or all of the manuscript. The contribution of the Library of Congress has been truly notable; there I am specially grateful to C. Sumner Spalding, Chief of the Serial Record Division, for all the help and advice he has given. For assistance in various ways I want to express my deep appreciation to Eleanor S. Cavanaugh, Librarian of Standard and Poor's Corporation Library; F. Bernice Field, Assistant Head of the Catalogue Department, Yale University Library; Elizabeth Kientzle, Gifts and Exchange Librarian, John Crerar Library, and Editor of *Serial Slants;* Robert E. Kingery, Chief of the Preparation Division, New York Public Library; A. Ethelyn Markley, Associate Professor, University of California School of Librarianship;

Bella E. Shachtman, Chief of the Catalog and Records Section, Department of Agriculture Library; Beatrice V. Simon, Assistant University Librarian, McGill University; and Vernon D. Tate, Director of Libraries, Massachusetts Institute of Technology. Also I want particularly to thank my colleagues at Harvard, above all Susan M. Haskins who helped especially with the bibliography, William A. Jackson who contributed much to the chapter on rarities, and the staff of the Serial Division.

Special thanks are due to those who have given permission to quote from their publications, including a number of those mentioned in the previous paragraph. Grateful acknowledgment is also made to the following: Dr. William Warner Bishop *(The Backs of Books, and Other Essays in Librarianship);* Catholic University of America Press (Bernard M. Fry, *Library Organization and Management of Technical Reports Literature);* Columbia University Press (Alice I. Bryan, *The Public Librarian,* and James L. McCamy, *Government Publications for the Citizen);* Cresap, McCormick and Paget *(Survey of Preparation Procedures, Reference Department, New York Public Library);* Dr. John F. Fulton (Dr. Harvey Cushing, *Consecratio Medici, and Other Papers);* Harcourt, Brace and Company (William S. Learned, *The American Public Library and the Diffusion of Knowledge);* Margery C. Quigley *(Portrait of a Library);* the Special Libraries Association *(Technical Libraries, Their Organization and Management);* and the University of Minnesota Press (John L. Lawler, *The H. W. Wilson Company).*

Finally I wish to express my thanks to the Publishing Department of the American Library Association. Upon completion of the manuscript, it is a pleasure to look back upon the friendly advice and help of so many people.

Andrew D. Osborn

Widener Library
Cambridge, Massachusetts
January 8, 1955

Contents

❦ List of Illustrations

The visible index in the Serial Record Division at the Library of Congress. The largest library installation in the world.

Introduction

SERIALS, which are indispensable for research and information, the twin aims of the modern library, are in the main a recent form of publication. However, some forms of serials, such as almanacs, news-pamphlets, and newssheets, go back to the comparatively early days of printing. The Romans had their *acta diurna,* while Henry Fischer, in referring to the thousandth anniversary of a Chinese newspaper, took the story much further back into history:

> According to the French investigator, Professor Eugene Revillout, the London *Morning Post* and the *Times,* respectively, represent no higher type of newspaper than was the *Official Gazette,* published 1,700 years before Christ in Egypt. Late explorations in Egyptian tombs show, according to the authority named, that the *Official Gazette* of Egypt was a newspaper in every sense of the word . . .
>
> *King-Choo,* the Pekin daily newspaper, likewise official in character, appeared first A.D. 911, at the beginning of the year, and its every issue since then is on file at the Chinese State Department. Typographically, in make-up, style and grade of paper, *King-Choo* has not changed in a thousand years.[1]

The first American newspaper appeared in Boston on September 25, 1690. It was entitled *Publick Occurrences* and was suppressed after a single issue. The first American periodicals, both published in 1741, were Andrew Bradford's *American Magazine,* which survived for three monthly issues, and Benjamin Franklin's *General Magazine,* whose first number appeared three days after Bradford's but which ran for six monthly issues.

The European prototypes were published several generations earlier than these. It is generally accepted that the first real newspapers were issued in Germany in 1609. The first periodicals came in 1665 when the *Journal des savants* and the *Philosophical Transactions* of the Royal Society of London appeared. Even so, this was a late start; but by now serials have more than made up for lost time, while their

[1] Henry W. Fischer, "Newspapers 3,609 Years Old," *The Inland Printer* 43:244, 1909.

growth in the twentieth century has been nothing short of phenomenal.

The history of serial publications falls into four main periods.[2]

1. To 1700, the so-called incunabula period of serial publications
2. 1700-1825, rise of the literary periodical, the "gentleman's" magazine, the learned society journal, and the newspaper; also legal, religious, and general scientific periodicals; plus serials of other types: government publications, law reports, etc.
3. 1825-1890, period of expansion through technical advances in printing and from 1870 the prevalence of wood pulp paper; rise of the illustrated journal, the popular magazine, and trade publications; multiplication of annual reports, college catalogs, and other special types; also periodicals in all fields of knowledge, but particularly the scientific and technical ("From now on the specialized research journal!" as Kirchner exclaimed)[3]
4. From 1890, the era of mass communications largely made possible by the linotype and similar inventions and by cheap paper;[4] application of photographic techniques; rise of processed publications; intense specialization in all fields of knowledge; great increase in government documents at all levels, including the international

It was awareness of what was happening in the twentieth century that led Esdaile to protest that "the periodical has added a new terror to research."[5] When a bibliographer who has mastered the intricacies of cancels, points, states, typography, etc., is led to such an assertion, it is clear that a major change has taken place in the publishing world. Esdaile continued his observations about periodicals by saying:

A century ago there were few, and all but a handful of those that existed were insignificant, though the most worthless literature, if it be popular, is

---

[2] C. T. Hagberg Wright in the *Encyclopædia Britannica* (Chicago, [1952]), v.17, p.512, divides the history of serials from a literary point of view into five periods, as follows: "It may be said, generally, that there have been five definite epochs in periodical literature: its birth in the 17th century; its jubilee in the 18th century, when Addison and Steele did their brilliant work; its rapid expansion in the first half of the 19th century; the revolt of the specialists in the latter half; and the vast output of the present, with popular approbation as its objective."

[3] Joachim Kirchner, in the *Lexikon des gesamten Buchwesens* (Leipzig: Hiersemann, 1937), v.3, p.613.

[4] Gerhard Menz in his *Die Zeitschrift, ihre Entwicklung und ihre Lebensbedingungen; eine wirtschaftsgeschichtliche Studie* (Stuttgart: Poeschel, 1928), p.114-20, links paper production and costs to the rise of the twentieth-century serial. Then to give a graphic idea of the amount of paper consumed by a modern periodical in a single year, he analyzed the requirements of *Jugend* which in 1913 had a circulation of 85,000. Six thousand trees, each about fifty feet high, must be pulped in a factory where fifty men labored day and night for two months to produce the paper. A freight train would require 57 cars to transport the 8,700,000 sheets. Thereupon 18 presses and 63 men would be occupied throughout the year printing the magazine.

[5] Arundell Esdaile, *A Student's Manual of Bibliography*, rev. by Roy Stokes (3d ed.; London: Allen and Unwin, 1954. The Library Association Series of Library Manuals, 1), p.335.

in time of value as an index to social habits and ideas. Now the periodical contains a very large proportion of the first appearances of important literature of the imagination, criticism, essays, and the like, and practically the whole of the original work done in science. A bibliography which ignores articles in periodicals is a one-eyed leader of the blind.

Awareness of the twentieth-century situation is of fundamental importance to librarians who must adjust their collections and services to the new state of affairs. It would be unwise in the extreme to think that the trend will be reversed (even though there may be concern over the maintenance of adequate supplies of paper, as the Unesco and FAO surveys indicate). In other times people have been exercised over the number of serials, yet the number increases generation after generation. In 1716 apprehension was felt about the overproduction of periodicals whose remainders would have to be bundled up and sold like rotten old cheese; in 1739 the cry was: "Journals! Journals! They are the means whereby our present century distinguishes itself from all others."[6] In 1831 it was declared:

This is the golden age of periodicals. Nothing can be done without them. Sects and parties, benevolent societies, and ingenious individuals, all have their periodicals. Science and literature, religion and law, agriculture and the arts, resort alike to this mode of enlightening the public mind. Every man, and every party, that seeks to establish a new theory, or to break down an old one, commences operations, like a board of war, by founding a *magazine*. We have annuals, monthlys, and weeklys—reviews, orthodox and heterodox—journals of education and humanity, of law, divinity and physic—magazines for ladies and for gentlemen—publications commercial, mechanical, metaphysical, sentimental, musical, anti-fogmatical, and nonsensical . . .

Whether we travel, or stay at home, we are feasted with periodicals to a surfeit—they pervade the atmosphere of the country like an epidemic. Go to a tea-party, and you find souvenirs served up with the confectionary; dine with a friend, and you get reviews with your wine; walk in the street, and a fellow assails you with a prospectus; take refuge in a book-store, and your retreat is cut off by huge piles of periodicals.[7]

The theme was the same in 1845:

Whatever may be the merits or demerits, generally, of the Magazine literature of America, there can be no question as to its extent or its influence. The topic—Magazine literature—is therefore, an important one. In a few years its importance will be found to have increased in geometrical ratio. The whole tendency of the age is Magazine-ward.[8]

---

[6] Ernst H. Lehmann, *Einführung in die Zeitschriftenkunde* (Leipzig: Hiersemann, 1936), p.6.

[7] "Periodicals," *Illinois Monthly Magazine* 1:302-3, 1831.

[8] "Graham's Magazine," *The Broadway Journal* 1:139, 1845. Cf. Frank Luther Mott, "A Period of Expansion in Periodicals," in his *A History of American Magazines* (Cambridge, Mass.: Harvard Univ. Pr., 1939), v.1, p.340-42. Mott points out that "in most of the estimates and tables given throughout this period the newspapers form about nine-tenths of the total periodicals."

Thus each of the last three centuries has been impressed with the number of serial titles it has produced. With this reading of history, the only wise conclusion to draw is that the serial production of the next century will dwarf the accomplishments of the past hundred years, stupendous though they have been.

The Library of Congress has reacted vigorously to meet the challenge of increasing serial production. At the end of 1953 it had just over two hundred serial specialists on its staff, people who spend the major part of their time handling serial publications. The reason for such a concentration of manpower is not hard to find. No less than three fourths of the publications that find their way into this, the nation's largest library, are serial in character. One explanation for the high proportion of serials at the Library of Congress is that one third of all monographs are published in series. All told, the Library of Congress has in its serial catalogs entries for a third of a million serial titles, new and old. American and Canadian libraries together probably acquire from a quarter to a third of a million different serial titles each year, figures they could surely double through systematic and thorough coverage of the field.

The number of periodical articles printed every twelve months is prodigious. In 1949 the International Federation for Documentation found that some four hundred indexing and abstracting agencies—roughly a third of those in existence at the time, but those the major ones—list about 1,200,000 contributions annually (many of the items being listed twice or more), yet a good guess is that no more than half the useful articles are so recorded. Bernard Fry's figures are still more breathtaking. He estimated that in the middle of the twentieth century there were 50,000 scientific periodicals producing 1,850,000 articles a year.[9]

In addition to the problems created by sheer numbers, library acquisition is complicated by the brief life span of the typical serial. Kuhlman found that the defunct titles in the first edition of the *Union List of Serials,* which was published in 1927, had existed for an average of 9.9 years, while the continuing titles averaged 25.1 years.[10] The Library of Congress has compiled comparable data for the second edition of the *Union List of Serials,* published in 1943. By then the average life of defunct titles had increased to 11.4 years and of con-

[9] Bernard M. Fry, *Library Organization and Management of Technical Reports Literature* (Washington: Catholic Univ. of America Pr., 1953. Catholic University of America Studies in Library Science, 1), p.4.

[10] A. F. Kuhlman, "Administration of Serial and Document Acquisition and Preparation," in *The Acquisition and Cataloging of Books,* ed. by William M. Randall (Chicago: Univ. of Chicago Pr., 1940), p.96-97.

tinuing titles to 27.2 years.[11] Since the items in the *Union List of Serials* constitute a select group, it is extremely improbable that these statistics would stand for serials of all types. In 1943, and certainly in 1927, the life of the average serial would probably be closer to five than to ten years. However that may be, it can be seen from evidence presented by Brigham and Mott that the life expectancy for serials has steadily increased. Brigham said: "The mortality in newspapers before 1821 was notable. Over half of the total of 2120 papers in this period, to be exact, 1118 papers, expired before they had reached two years of existence."[12] Mott, whose figures do not include newspapers, said: "Sixty per cent of the magazines of 1741-94 did not outlast the first year, and only four reached the ripe age of three and a half years. Four died a-borning at one month."[13] In these circumstances it is not surprising to find Noah Webster saying pessimistically in connection with his *American Magazine:* "The expectation of *failure* is connected with the very name of a Magazine."[14] As late as 1828 a journal in its sixth year stated that "the average age of new periodicals in this country is found to be six months—some have reached nine—and a few dragged on a lingering existence to the mature age of twelve";[15] but Mott was inclined to set the average age of periodicals from 1825 to 1850 at nearer two years. For 1850 to 1885 he calculates the average life generously at four years.

Oddly enough, while the eighteenth and nineteenth century publications had to struggle for existence, three serials founded in 1665 are still current. They are the *Journal des savants,* the *London Gazette,* and the *Philosophical Transactions* of the Royal Society of London.

The present situation is that hundreds of thousands of different

[11] C. Sumner Spalding, *Certain Proposals of Numerical Systems for the Control of Serials Evaluated for Their Application at the Library of Congress* ([Washington], 1954), p.21.

[12] Clarence S. Brigham, *History and Bibliography of American Newspapers, 1690-1820* (Worcester, Mass.: American Antiquarian Soc., 1947), v.1, p.xii. Lawrence C. Wroth in *The Colonial Printer* (Portland, Me.: Southworth-Anthoesen Press, 1938), p.233, comments: "This high mortality among the newspapers can be best accounted for by the lack of capital of their promoters, an ever-present factor in lost causes, and by the difficulty experienced at various times and places of securing a steady supply of reasonably cheap paper." In Hellmut Lehmann-Haupt's *The Book in America, a History of the Making and Selling of Books in the United States* (2d ed.; New York: Bowker, 1951), p.38, Wroth adds: "This was indeed a high mortality rate, but a more interesting reflection upon the figures is that the rate was not higher, even, than here shown in view of the difficulties under which periodical journals must be published in an undeveloped country."

[13] Mott, *op. cit.,* p.21.

[14] *American Magazine* 1:130, 1788.

[15] "American Periodicals," *The New-York Mirror and Ladies' Literary Gazette* 6:151, 1828.

serials are published each year, conceivably somewhere between half a million and a million titles. Since these publications have a relatively short life—perhaps an average of ten years—continual alertness is necessary if libraries are to maintain complete files and to acquire new titles as they appear. The names of these publications change frequently, and it is estimated that the corporate bodies with which many of the serials are connected change their names an average of once every fifteen to twenty years. Miss Pierson has reported a work which experienced forty-one changes in corporate name or title in fourteen years. Strange things happen to the collation and numbering of the publications, and they have been known to come to life again after being thought dead for a century: witness the *Memorias* of the Academia de Buenas Letras de Barcelona, volume 1 of which was published in 1756, volume 2 in 1868; also the *Memoirs* of the Connecticut Academy of Arts and Sciences, volume 1 of which appeared from 1810 to 1816, volume 2 in 1910. Moreover, new types of serials keep rising to the fore. The most recent form to assume major proportions is the technical report. The demand for greater speed than even the periodical can afford has led to this development, as Lieutenant General Kuter has indicated:

> The era in which we live is one of incredible speed. Many, many years ago, it was already apparent to writers and teachers that the production of books as a means of recording current knowledge was far too slow. That was the time when journals were established and came to take the place in our lives that they now have. It was and still is possible for new and valuable facts to be publicized rather swiftly through journals. However, more recently the journal has proved to be too slow, and a new form of literature, the near-print document or ephemeral paper, has come to take its place in our working lives. Recorded information can be made available in this special form much more simply and rapidly.[16]

Forewarned is forearmed. Realizing the complexities of the situation as well as the sharply defined trend towards publication in serial form, libraries should make whatever adjustments may be necessary in the second half of the century. As Miss Ditmas has said, "the literary, scientific or technical periodical has come to stay—more, it has won such an honoured place amongst the tools of research that it has attained the right to be treated *sui generis,* and not as a poor relation of the book."[17] This is perhaps the sternest lesson to be learned by the general library, a lesson which, as Miss Ditmas observes, the special library learned at its inception.

---

[16] Laurence S. Kuter, "What Makes a Special Library Special in an Academic Institution," *Special Libraries* 45:159, 1954.

[17] David Grenfell, *Periodicals and Serials, Their Treatment in Special Libraries;* foreword by E. M. R. Ditmas (London: Aslib, 1953), p.v.

Problems of selection, acquisition, cataloging, indexing, preservation, and cooperative use must be faced squarely by libraries. At the same time certain attitudes must be changed: the idea of a serial as a poor relation of the book, for instance, and the all-or-nothing theory of serial treatment which is widely prevalent in cataloging, classification, and binding. The dominant idea must be to get serial publications under control; but staff, quarters, and funds must be forthcoming if this objective is to be achieved. In this connection, note that serials can and should be brought under control without monumental methods. It is wise to aim at a compromise between elaborate treatment and comparative neglect, which seem to go hand in hand in so many libraries, where a minor periodical or annual report is cataloged in detail, but a major government publication is neither cataloged nor classified; or upwards of a dollar is spent for the lettering on the spine of an approved serial, but nothing for the lettering on other serials.

There has been heightened interest in serial publications of late. The literature on the subject has grown rapidly in extent and importance, and significant developments have been taking place in numerous institutions, the Library of Congress and the New York Public Library for instance. One can almost say that the turn of events in the Department of Agriculture Library, where the effectiveness of the visible index has been questioned, has elements of dramatic interest —even though in the same breath one must add that a good visible index is still the best equipment for the checking records in the typical general or special library.

Perhaps the small public library has most to learn about exploiting periodicals.[18] In his home the average reader may be less familiar with books than he is with newspapers and magazines, so a public library might conceivably succeed in broadening reading tastes through devoting more attention to these mediums. The idea is not new. John Cotton Dana said:

Many a small library could do more to stimulate its community, broaden its views and sympathies, encourage it to study, if it diverted a larger part of its income than it now does from inferior books, and especially inferior novels, to weekly journals and popular and standard magazines. What a community needs is not a "library"—it may have a street lined with "libraries" and still

[18] In the field of special libraries the law library has apparently lagged in exploiting periodicals (although of course it leans heavily on other types of serial publications, notably law reports). William R. Roalfe, in his *The Libraries of the Legal Profession* (St. Paul, Minn.: West, 1953), p.51-52, reports that 40 of the 184 law libraries he surveyed do not receive any legal periodicals currently, while another 60 receive only from one to ten titles. Further, no more than 108 of the 184 subscribe to the *Index to Legal Periodicals.*

dwell in outer darkness—but contact with the printed page. Get this contact, then, by means of attractive rooms and clean, wholesome, interesting books and periodicals.[19]

Clearly serials have their part to play in the smallest public library as in the greatest research library.

---

[19] John Cotton Dana, *A Library Primer* (Boston: Library Bureau, [1920]), p.68-69.

CHAPTER 1

The Library Approach to Serials

THE FIGURE OF SPEECH which special and general libraries alike have repeatedly applied to serials is that they constitute the backbone of the research collection. Serials are basic to organized reference work in almost any kind of library. They comprise much of the librarian's stock in trade, just as they are indispensable to the scholar and the research worker. As Margaret Hutchins remarked:

> It is no longer necessary to argue for the importance of periodicals and newspapers in reference work. From childhood up the present generation has read them and used them for information more than books. In view of the innumerable enthusiastic testimonials of reference librarians as to the supremacy of periodicals as reference materials it may become necessary to write an apologetic for books, lest the periodicals elbow them entirely out of libraries, and serials departments monopolize reference work.[1]

Some testimonials follow.

Charles H. Brown says: "Studies have shown that over 95% of the references cited by scientists are to scientific periodicals and society publications."[2] The *Handbook of Medical Library Practice* stated:

> A well-rounded medical library must consist in major part of periodical material, including journals and serials of many types. . . They contain the first recorded reports of scientific discoveries and additional ever mounting comments, criticisms and supplements on these reports. After periodical literature, monographs and textbooks on special subjects are a necessary part of the library.[3]

The Science-Technology Division of the Special Libraries Association believes that "periodicals constitute the most important part of a science library's resources since they publish the immediate results of experimental research and announcements of technical developments."

---

[1] Margaret Hutchins, *Introduction to Reference Work* (Chicago: American Library Assn., 1944), p.103.

[2] Charles H. Brown, *Library Resources in Selected Scientific Subjects at Louisiana State University* (Baton Rouge: Louisiana State Univ. Library, 1950), p.2.

[3] Medical Library Association, *A Handbook of Medical Library Practice,* ed. by Janet Doe (Chicago: American Library Assn., 1943), p.65.

The Division goes on to say that "the periodical files available in a science-technology library may well be a true indication of the worth of the whole collection."[4] The Public Business Librarians Group of the Association states that "rapid changes in the business and economic world today have caused emphasis to be placed on periodicals rather than books."[5]

An obvious reason for the constant accumulation and consultation of serial files is that they contain facts and figures necessary for both general information and research work: bibliographical references, contributions by authorities, news, popular presentations of knowledge, up-to-the-minute data, and so on. The closest analog to a serial is a pamphlet. Out of the serials and pamphlets of the day will come many of the monographs of the future.

The historian Sir Charles Oman, writing in 1921, gave an illustration of the way in which contributions in periodicals may outrun monographs. He said:

> No general manual or authoritative work on Early British Coins, before the Roman Conquest, has appeared since Sir John Evans published his monograph on them more than a generation ago. But in the last forty years an immense amount of information concerning these primitive but interesting coins has cropped up. The discoveries of numerous hoards of issues unknown in 1860 have enlarged the facts at the disposal of the archaeologist, and have even enabled the historian to add some undoubted deductions to the annals of Early Britain. But all these new facts and deductions are preserved only in the numbers of the *Numismatic Chronicle,* and certain other journals of learned societies. If these journals did not exist, the knowledge would never have got into print, but would have remained in the brains of the researcher, and have perished with his death—to be discovered perhaps again by another researcher in another generation, with much waste of duplicated labour.[6]

This was to Sir Charles an evidence of the way in which a great part of historical, literary, and scientific research "first takes shape in papers or monographs, which appear in periodicals of the more specialised sort." It led him to conclude: "I regard therefore the Proceedings and Journals of learned societies as one of the most important sections of every library."

But the full impact of the ascendancy of serials is not felt until it

---

[4] Special Libraries Association, Science-Technology Division, *Technical Libraries, Their Organization and Management,* ed. by Lucille Jackson (New York: Special Libraries Assn., [1951]), p.56.

[5] Special Libraries Association, Public Business Librarians Group, *Business and the Public Library; Steps in Successful Cooperation,* ed. by Marian C. Manley (New York: Special Libraries Assn., 1940), p.41.

[6] Sir Charles Oman, "Note on the Present Hindrance to Research Caused by the Enhanced Price of Printing," *Library Association Record* 23:326-27, 1921.

is realized that three fourths of the ten million publications in the Library of Congress are serial in character in one way or another. In an epoch-making statement the Library of Congress said:

> Serial publications (including newspapers, periodicals, bulletins, reports, most Government documents, and books in series) constitute perhaps 75 percent of all publications, an indispensable part from the viewpoint of research. It is in serial publications that advance information and discussion are found; in them are found also the detailed records which support most scientific, legal, and historical study. Attention to the acquisition and recording of serial publications is, therefore, of first importance to every large research library. Because the separate issues of serials cannot be treated individually as are books, but must be considered in conjunction with other issues, they represent the form of publication which is most difficult to control at all stages—acquisition, accessioning, processing, and service.[7]

Note that this statement refers to books in series in addition to the vast mass of newspapers, periodicals, government serials, etc. In themselves the component parts of monograph series are so numerous that in Schneider's estimation "more than a third of all books nowadays appear in this form."[8] Another indication of the extent of books in series is the Card Division's statement that "about one-tenth of the cards in stock at the Library of Congress are for publications in series."[9]

Probably the most picturesque account of the library approach to serials was provided by Dr. Bishop in an address to library-school students in 1922:

> Periodical publication is now truly *the* fashion of the day in all lines the world over. This form came into vogue in the seventeenth century with the *Journal des Savants* and other similar learned publications. For seventy-five years now it has been increasingly *the* mode for the publication of the results of study in any and all fields. Thousands of journals keep hundreds of thousands of specialists abreast of the growth of knowledge in their several lines of investigation. Yea, more, thousands of other journals inform the banker, the merchant, the artisan, the tradesman, the professor, the teacher, even the librarian, what is going on in his field. The journals are usually about five years ahead of the books in every subject. They form the record of progress in the sciences and the arts, in the crafts and trades and occupations. They wax more numerous with every month and in every clime, despite rising costs of paper and presswork, and in the face of a severe mortality in journalistic circles. Well may the perplexed and devout librarian say with the Psalmist—*"Lord, how are they increased that trouble me!"* How to get,

[7] *Annual Report* of the Librarian of Congress, 1946 (Washington, 1947), p.400.

[8] Georg Schneider, *Handbuch der Bibliographie* (4th ed.; Leipzig: Hiersemann, 1930), p.370.

[9] Library of Congress, Card Division, *List of Series of Publications for Which Cards Are in Stock* (4th ed.; Washington, 1932), p.1; see also its *Handbook of Card Distribution* (8th ed.; Washington, 1954), p.50.

how to keep, how to index this mass of periodical and serial printed matter! We must have it—we never have enough journals—we never have enough indexes to the mass of original materials concealed beneath their multitudinous and multiform varieties of publication. Woe to the librarian who fails to get and to bind and to use these journals. They are the present-day mode of retailing (and frequently rehashing) thought and discovery. "Fractions drive me mad" was a favorite tag in my boyhood. How true of these days! It is not the sound and single volumes which come from the publisher which trouble us and bring our grey hairs in sorrow to the grave. Rather it is these *lieferungen, heften, livraisons,* parts, fascicles, special numbers and supplements which do drive the poor librarian frantic. And how solid the satisfaction, how firm the reward which attends the completion and binding of any fractious and long-broken set! Journals—and still more journals—all printed on wood-pulp paper destined doubtless to disintegrate in the lifetime of these students of library economy—here you have the chief problem of the careful librarian of any research library. Will the fashion change? How long *can* it last? Will the whole literary output of the world soon be in periodicals? Shall we always be paying subscriptions, writing postcards for title pages and indexes, preparing for binding, paying for binding, buying older sets, renewing our worn-out *Poole's Index* and *Index Medicus?* These questions I leave with you to ponder. I and my generation shall never get away from journals; perhaps the journals will get away from you younger folk—by the simple process of chemical decomposition.[10]

Definition of a serial

The general notion of a serial is that of a work whose parts are issued serially or periodically, that is, with either numbers or dates whereby the parts may normally be arranged and recorded. From the idea of parts issued serially (numbered seriatim) there arises the concept of a serial in the literal sense of the term, namely a work whose parts may be, and usually are, arranged by the serial numbering on the fascicules, issues, volumes, etc.; and from the idea of parts issued periodically there arises the concept of a periodical in the literal sense, namely a work whose parts may be arranged by the day, week, month, etc., specified on the successive issues. In practice the two types often overlap. Although the resultant logical order is identical, many publications exhibit both a numerical and a chronological sequence, a concomitance which in the United States is required for second class mail.

Schneider added two characteristics to help in distinguishing serials from non-serials issued in parts or sets. The first difference he found in the publication program for serials:

By nature they are unlimited. They may be suspended, but they do not conclude. External circumstances, but scarcely ever exhaustion of the subject,

---

[10] William W. Bishop, *The Backs of Books, and Other Essays in Librarianship* (Baltimore: Williams & Wilkins, 1926), p.324-26.

bring about their end. A second difference lies in the number of their authors. Apart from collections and composite works, books possess more than one author only by way of exception. With periodicals it is the reverse.[11]

The American Library Association definition of a serial is "a publication issued in successive parts, usually at regular intervals, and, as a rule, intended to be continued indefinitely."[12] The definition goes on to specify that "serials include periodicals, newspapers, annuals (reports, yearbooks, etc.) and memoirs, proceedings, and transactions of societies, and may include monographic series and publishers' series." In the introduction to its *Serial Titles Newly Received* the Library of Congress defined serials as "publications of indefinite duration appearing in sequence under a common title, the order of which can be determined from numbers or dates appearing in each issue." The Department of Agriculture Library also reflects the current tendency towards liberalizing the idea of a serial. In that library "the term serial is interpreted broadly to include any title issued in parts which is incomplete in the library collection, thus periodicals, annuals, biennials, and even incomplete works-in-parts are considered serials."[13]

The term "serial" is growing in importance and extent of use in the United States. Publications like *New Serial Titles* and *Serial Slants* by their very name disclose this trend; and since 1942, when the Central Serial Record of the Library of Congress was first mentioned, the *Annual Report* of the Librarian of Congress has made frequent and important reference to serials, whereas it paid scant attention to them earlier. British practice, however, is apparently moving away from the term. Grenfell, at least, prefers "periodical" as the generic word. He says:

> The term 'serial' is becoming unpopular and a more comprehensive interpretation is being given to the term 'periodical.' The latter term finds almost universal favour in other European countries, added to which it is one which is more easily interpreted by the layman. Whether a distinction is necessary is a highly debatable point and warrants the closest examination by those responsible for the various aspects of international standardization in library work.[14]

Nonetheless, there is a certain advantage to the word "serial." It may

---

[11] Georg Schneider, *op. cit.*, p.369.

[12] *A. L. A. Cataloging Rules for Author and Title Entries* (Chicago: American Library Assn., 1949), p.233.

[13] Bella E. Shachtman, "Current Serial Records—an Experiment," *College and Research Libraries* 14:240, 1953. In her earlier article, "Simplification of Serial Records Work," *Serial Slants* 3:6, 1952, Miss Shachtman says simply: "Our definition of a serial is: Any title issued in parts, which is incomplete in the library collection."

[14] David Grenfell, *Periodicals and Serials, Their Treatment in Special Libraries* (London: Aslib, 1953), p.143.

be vague in some respects, but it is not ambiguous. "Periodical," on the other hand, is ambiguous: it may mean serial in general or magazine in particular, and in the latter sense it may also have to be distinguished from society publications (for example in the subject heading Mathematics—Periodicals which the Library of Congress employs in addition to the heading Mathematics—Societies).

A sound definition of a serial (periodical, newspaper, etc.) has been sought for a long time, especially in legal and trade circles and by German scholars. The futility of the quest can be seen from a study of the attempts made by Du Prel,[15] Kienningers,[16] and Lehmann.[17] The last named, for instance, is at pains to list nine characteristics of periodicals: timeliness, periodicity, continuity, the publication program, popularization, universality, collectiveness, association with an editorial office, and mechanical reproduction. After 36 pages of elaboration (in the course of which he pointed out that libraries adopt a very wide interpretation), Lehmann arrived at the following definition:

> A periodical is a regularly appearing printed work, founded with the expectation of unlimited duration, which is not predominantly concerned with events of the day or else regards only the latest developments in a special field. Its issues are manifold both in their contents and in their layout, yet they exhibit—the whole continuing series of them—an internal and external unity brought about by established editorial policy. Periodicals for the most part serve limited fields; the extent of their audience is therefore varied. In their form they correspond to the needs of a circle of readers who are often widely scattered and who are therefore only loosely connected with the place of publication.[18]

Legal definitions are equally wide of the mark regardless of whether they stem from cases in court or from statutory law relating to second class mail, which consists of newspapers and periodicals. The following, while not a good definition, is still good law:

> A periodical, as ordinarily understood, is a publication appearing at stated intervals, each number of which contains a variety of original articles by different authors, devoted either to general literature or some special branch of learning or to a special class of subjects. Ordinarily each number is incomplete in itself, and indicates a relation with prior or subsequent numbers of the same series. It implies a continuity of literary character, a connection between the different numbers of the series in the nature of the articles

---

[15] Maximilian Du Prel, *Der Zeitungsbeitrag im Urheberrecht unter besonderer Berücksichtigung der Unterscheidung zwischen Zeitung und Zeitschrift und die Autorrechte* (München, 1931. Zeitung und Leben, 5).

[16] Werner Kienningers, *Die Einteilung der periodischen Pressschriften* (Straubing, 1932).

[17] Ernst H. Lehmann, *Einführung in die Zeitschriftenkunde* (Leipzig: Hiersemann, 1936).

[18] *Ibid.*, p.81.

appearing in them, whether they be successive chapters of the same story or novel or essays upon subjects pertaining to general literature.[19]

In his *History of American Magazines* Frank Luther Mott purposely avoided a definition. He pointed out that the terms periodical, journal, magazine, newspaper, etc., "are all more or less indistinct and confused in common usage, and the more so when one looks back over the last two hundred years. It would be pedantry to insist upon erecting . . . arbitrary distinctions which do not actually exist in usage, and it would be bad philology and bad history as well."[20] He is on safe ground, too, when he says that format is the decisive characteristic of a newspaper. "Any other interpretation is untenable and leads to inextricable difficulties."

A number of writers have pointed out that the connotation of the various terms has changed from century to century. Thus Kirchner has defined an eighteenth-century periodical,[21] but his definition is not valid for later publications. Likewise the close connection between periodicals and the postal service has been brought out.[22] This is a late development; the first periodicals were sold issue by issue like books, so much so that in 1716 it was suggested that the word "bookstore" should be supplanted by "periodical store."[23] In the United States, as a consequence of the connection between periodicals and the postal service, current numbers may not be bound by the publisher if they are to qualify as second class mail, the basic requirements for which are:

1. The periodical or newspaper must regularly be issued at stated intervals, as frequently as four times a year, bear a date of issue, and be numbered consecutively.
2. It must be issued from a known office of publication.
3. It must be formed of printed paper sheets, without board, cloth, leather, or other substantial binding, such as distinguish printed books for preservation from periodical publications.
4. It must be originated and published for the dissemination of information of a public character, or it must be devoted to literature, the sciences, arts, or some special industry; and it must have a legitimate list of subscribers.[24]

---

[19] *Houghton v. Payne* (1904) 194 U. S. 88, 24 S. Ct. 590, 48 L. Ed. 888, affirming (1903) 22 App. D.C. 234.

[20] Frank Luther Mott, *A History of American Magazines* (Cambridge, Mass.: Harvard Univ. Pr., 1939), v.1, p.8-9.

[21] Joachim Kirchner, *Die Grundlagen des deutschen Zeitschriftenwesens* (Leipzig: Hiersemann, 1928), v.1, p.32-33.

[22] Gerhard Menz, *Die Zeitschrift, ihre Entwicklung und ihre Lebensbedingungen; eine wirtschaftsgeschichtliche Studie* (Stuttgart: Poeschel, 1928), p.121 ff.

[23] Lehmann, *op. cit.*, p.4.

[24] *United States Code,* Chapter 39, Section 226. College announcements, bulletins, catalogs, etc., qualify as periodicals under these requirements.

It is clear that a truly precise definition, if it is ever achieved, will entail a large amount of elaboration, all the more so since the essential characteristic of a serial—namely, its formation by volume, year, etc.—is not always present. On the one hand, there is a whole category of publications known to librarians as unnumbered series; there are numbered series whose first volumes lack numbering; there are serials republished in simple monographic form; and there are serials whose numerical or chronological arrangement is taken from the edition statement or the date of publication as given in the imprint—even from the sales number in the case of some League of Nations and United Nations documents. On the other hand, there are the so-called author series (that is, a succession of works by a single author, held together by serial numbering) which most libraries do not regard as serials; and there are non-serials (for example, the Pauly-Wissowa *Real-encyclopädie der classischen Altertumswissenschaft*) which have all the earmarks of a serial: their volumes are numbered, they never seem to exhaust their subject, they have a plurality of authors, and so on.

One other factor must be borne in mind. Experienced serial librarians cannot always tell whether an item is a serial or a non-serial when it first appears, and on occasion counsel treatment as a monograph until such time as it may be necessary to reopen the case, i.e., on receipt of other issues. It is all very well to say that periodicity and seriality are the infallible signs of a serial; difficulties arise because the intent of the publisher is not always known or ascertainable. It is not at all uncommon for a library to decide on the evidence of the first issue that a title is not a serial, only to reverse the decision when the publication's true character has at length been discerned. The editor of the *Union List of Serials* repeatedly met with titles which some libraries treated as monographs whereas others had taken them for serials.

On all counts, therefore, it seems wiser to adopt a working definition than to confuse both theory and practice with endless exceptions and borderline cases. Fortunately the choice of terms and the definition of a serial or a periodical are among the least consequential of their library aspects. Some librarians like to make hard and fast distinctions—particularly between periodicals, society publications, and government documents—but, as the working definitions at the Library of Congress and the Department of Agriculture suggest, the practical issues are far more significant than the theoretical.[25] Thus on practical

[25] The Enoch Pratt Free Library is practical in its treatment of serials, but its terminology is unusual. "The term 'serials' has been used in this Library to designate free or inexpensive serial publications, put out by institutions or governments

grounds a serial can be defined as any item which lends itself to serial treatment in a library; that is, to listing in visible indexes and other specialized serial records.

In accepting as a serial any item to which a library chooses to apply serial techniques of one kind or another, it is well to distinguish three special borderline types: continuations, provisional serials, and pseudo-serials.

Continuations

When a library acquires part of a non-serial set which it desires to complete as soon as the rest is published, it commonly lists the title in a special order record for follow-up purposes. These sets are generally referred to, in library parlance, as continuations. Many libraries do not class such continuations as serials in any way. Most would not accord them serial treatment when there are only one or two volumes still to come, when the set will be completed without much delay, or when the numbering is in no wise complicated. But in some libraries, the Department of Agriculture Library, for instance, continuations of all kinds are recorded in the serial check list. Hence they become, for the time being, subject to the serial techniques of listing and follow-up. At the Library of Congress in 1953, when the Serial Record Section was detached from the Order Division to become the Serial Record Division, the pendulum swung the other way, and a natural effort was made to eliminate entries which could not be considered true serials. Thus the Order Division was persuaded to place orders for monograph continuations on an "until completion" basis rather than on a "continuation" basis. Titles ordered on an until completion basis are no longer entered in the visible index in the Serial Record Division; instead they are the responsibility of the Order Division.

Provisional serials

When they are to run for some time or have complicated numbering, extensive non-serial sets should generally be listed in the visible

(except the U. S.), which are not accessioned or completely cataloged. The distinction between such publications and periodicals is necessary only as a designation for shelving in order to keep the less used and less important publications apart from the magazines." By contrast, "the term 'periodicals' has been used to cover not only magazines, but proceedings, journals, and bulletins of societies or institutions providing that the publication is cataloged as a magazine—i.e. without a call number. Most annuals are handled by the Order Department with the book subscriptions and standing orders because annuals are generally classified and cataloged like books, according to subject matter; department heads sometimes prefer to have certain annuals treated as periodicals, in which case they are handled by the Periodicals Assistant."—Enoch Pratt Free Library, *Staff Instruction Book* (Baltimore, 1936), ¶1014, 1066.

index until they are complete. For example, the British Museum *General Catalogue of Printed Books,* which has been in course of publication for many years, and which will not be completed for some years to come, may to advantage be recorded in the visible index and be checked in as a serial as the successive volumes are received. Upon completion, or eventually when it may be acquired as a completed set in the original or in reprint form, it should be considered a non-serial. Retrospectively, Dickens' *Pickwick Papers* appeared originally in serial form, but there is now no practical reason for regarding it as a serial. As with the British Museum *General Catalogue,* such a work may be thought of as a serial while current, and as a non-serial when complete.

Pseudoserials

A pseudoserial is a frequently reissued and revised publication which quite properly may be, and on first publication generally is, considered to be a monograph. After it has been reissued several times, however, it may conveniently be regarded as a serial, no matter whether the library keeps merely the latest issue or a back file as well. Commonly the serial numbering for pseudoserials must be taken from the edition statement or the date of publication.

The *Guide to Reference Books* and *Periodicals for Small and Medium-Sized Libraries* are examples of potential or actual pseudoserials. The former has gone through seven editions, the latter eight. Most libraries have entered the successive editions of the *Guide to Reference Books,* as well as the supplements, under three discrete headings—first Kroeger; then Mudge, perhaps with an added entry for Kroeger; and, with the seventh edition, Winchell, with an added entry for Mudge—whereas a single serial entry would serve (see Figure 1). The Library of Congress cataloged the first seven editions of *Periodicals for Small and Medium-Sized Libraries* as independent monographs under the name of the compiler, Frank K. Walter. On receipt of the eighth edition, prepared by a subcommittee of the American Library Association's Editorial Committee, the work was recataloged as a serial under its title.

It took much longer for the Library of Congress to convert the records for Burke's *Peerage* to serial form. In volume 22 of its *Catalog of Books Represented by Library of Congress Printed Cards* there are no fewer than sixty-four separate catalog entries under Sir John Bernard Burke for editions of this work; but in volume 6 of the 1942-47 supplement a serial entry under *Burke's Genealogical and Heraldic History of the Peerage* replaced the monographic entries. The serial entry is easier to locate in a catalog, for it is no longer necessary to remember Burke's forenames to find the title. Moreover, the serial entry avoids the filing problems which arise through changes in the wording of the title from edition to edition, and at the same time it simplifies determination of the call number for the latest issue, the one usually wanted.

The titles under "United States. Laws, statutes, etc." in volume 153 of the Library of Congress Catalog (which covers cards printed through July, 1942) furnish a series of case studies along similar lines. The following examples of frequently reissued publications are drawn from that source; each might preferably be given serial treatment in most libraries.

Title	*Years Published*
Laws relating to agriculture	1929, 1931, 1933, 1934, 1935, 1936, 1937, 1938, 1941
Liquor laws	1923, 1925, 1927, 1929, 1930, 1932, 1934, 1935, 1936, 1937, 1938
Naturalization laws[26]	1926, 1929, 1931, 1934, 1935, 1936, 1937, 1938, 1939, 1940, 1941
Pension laws	1919, 1923, 1927, 1928, 1930, 1933, 1934, 1935, 1936, 1937, 1938, 1940, 1941
Radio laws	1929, 1930, 1931, 1933, 1934, 1936, 1937, 1938, 1941

Especially when the years from 1942 on are added to this tabulation, it is natural to ask what value there is in making new entries for such titles year after year, filling up the catalog with repetitious main and secondary entries. In itself each of the editions may quite properly be regarded as a non-serial, but unless a library can justify non-serial treatment, it is wiser to process the successive issues as serials, with the date of publication supplying the serial element. Note the gains that follow from serial handling:

Serial follow-up methods are applicable once the titles are on the visible index.
There are fewer titles to catalog each year.
Processing costs are reduced.
Entries are more readily located in the catalog, both because the mass of

[26] On the other hand, the Library of Congress has accorded serial treatment to the *Naturalization Laws and Regulations* issued by the Bureau of Naturalization. In connection with pseudoserials issued by the United States government, note that the Superintendent of Documents' regulations permit the disposal of "any publication which is revised after the revised edition is received." Among depository libraries, all but a relatively small number of historical research libraries should avail themselves of this provision. When a library decides to keep the latest edition only of any work, serial techniques facilitate the procedure; they provide a medium for recording the necessary instructions, just as they save on cataloging and decataloging.

cards is reduced and because the filing arrangement is not affected by the vagaries of wording in the titles of the successive issues.

The latest edition, which is the one most commonly sought, can be called for in a simple way. If it is located in the reference collection, this fact can be brought out clearly.

A simple program for the discarding of superseded issues can be set up, if desired.

Latest = RR 1.6
Ref 600.4. Also Lamont
Earlier = KSF 544
Guide to reference books. Chicago, American Library Association

For a full record of the Library's holdings apply to the Reference Desk or the Serial Division.

FIGURE 1. Serial entry, as used in the Harvard College Library, for Winchell's *Guide to Reference Books.*

Local custom and a readiness to take advantage of favorable circumstances are more important than theoretical considerations in the determination of what shall be treated by serial methods in any given library; hence serial practice may and does vary in some respects from one institution to another. Obviously what is needed in the treatment of serials, as in other library operations, is a large measure of agreement in principle, together with great latitude in practice.

CHAPTER 2

Over-all Organization of Serial Work

IN LIBRARIES which are large enough to require specialization of function there are three principal areas of serial activity, each of which may have one or more staff members who work exclusively with serials: the acquisition department, with its visible index; the catalog department, where there is commonly a serial division; and the periodical room, which is sometimes supplemented by a newspaper or a document room.[1] Naturally other parts of a library are concerned with serials, notably the circulation and reference desks; but their concern is as a rule incidental to their general duties, as can be seen from the fact that only rarely is one of their assistants a serial specialist. As such, serial librarians are almost invariably drawn from the ranks of the three departments named.

It is possible for any one of the three departments to assume the major responsibility for serials and to be called the serial section, serial division, etc. In recent years there has been a tendency in some quarters to centralize serial activities to the extent that a full-fledged serials department is called for, coordinate with the acquisition, catalog, and other departments. In point of theory it is difficult to lay down

[1] The upper limits for specialized serial staff are set by the Library of Congress. In December, 1953, it had 129 serial specialists, distributed as follows:

Processing Department	
Order Division	3
Serial Record Division	53
Descriptive Cataloging Division	9
Subject Cataloging Division	4
Binding Division	2
Reference Department	
Serials Division	43
Slavic Room	4
Orientalia Division	7
Music Division	1
Law Library	2
Legislative Reference Service	1

In addition to these full-time specialists, it had another 73 posts whose incumbents devoted about seven eighths of their time to serial publications.

hard and fast rules for the location of serial functions. A good case can be made for each of the three departments already mentioned—and for none of them. The orthodox arrangement is to divide the work among the three. The Library of Congress followed that plan until 1953, when it established the Serial Record Division as a separate unit. The change was brought about because of the highly specialized nature of the function of recording serials, the considerable size of the operation and of the staff necessary to perform the work, the development of *New Serial Titles,* and the prospective development of a comprehensive union list. In the Harvard College Library, where the visible index is in the Catalog Department, the focus of serial activity is that department's Serial Division. At the University of California Library in Berkeley the Serials Department comprises the periodical room and the checking records, the latter being some fifteen feet behind the public Periodical Desk. In the Washington Square Library of New York University a separate Serials Division was established to care for all phases of work with serials. In some recent realignments the major center of serial activity is in a processing department, a hybrid type of organization brought about in no small measure by the existence of overlapping serial functions in the traditional acquisition and catalog departments. Still other arrangements are possible: the principal serial activities may be divided between any combination of departments or may be duplicated in some of them.

The acquisition department

An acquisition department is concerned with books and pamphlets for the most part only until they have been absorbed in the library's collections. With serial titles, however, it has a continuing interest, because year after year renewals must be cared for, bills paid, and so on.

In the acquisition stages there is a fairly strong affiliation between books and serials. Dealers frequently combine books and serials in a bundle or on an invoice, and items ordered as simple monographs may on receipt prove to be parts of monograph series which must be checked off as serials. Hence there is something to be said in favor of receiving and checking both books and serials in the one department where mixed bundles can be processed and cleared for payment readily.

The unwrapping of serials, as of books, is an untidy operation that should be performed in as inconspicuous a spot as possible. For preference it should not be done in a public area such as a periodical room. This is another argument in favor of receiving and checking serials in the acquisition department, which is essentially a workroom.

In some library buildings it is possible to plan for a workroom adjoining the periodical room. However, when the current periodicals are received and checked in a periodical room, the over-all serial acquisition program may be weakened. Current periodicals may receive special attention, but other serials may be relatively neglected. There is much to gain from having one strong unit care for all incoming serials impartially. A greater degree of specialization is then practicable, with more informed and capable supervision. Lastly, the fact that visible indexes are quite generally located in acquisition departments suggests that there are good practical reasons for such disposition.

The catalog department

Most if not all of the serial staff in an acquisition department are clerical assistants. The claim of a catalog department to be the principal center of serial activity is based primarily on the presence there of serial librarians who are professional in grade. These are the people who become fully conversant with the intricacies of serials. Their work is basic to serial operations throughout the library—for instance, the visible index cards in most libraries use entries supplied by the serial catalogers. Their knowledge, skill, and enthusiasm are essential to the building of sound serial collections.

When all serial processing is concentrated in a single section of the catalog department there is opportunity for superior direction through the experienced serial catalogers. There is, however, one danger in this type of organization. Processing of current issues is the most demanding phase of serial activities; the staff at the visible index must be maintained so that the work will not fall behind. Catalogers may have to interrupt their regular duties to serve as interim checkers; but an even greater claim on their time comes from resolving problems for the checkers, answering the telephone, and otherwise performing activities connected with the visible index. Accordingly, if the catalogers are to give undivided attention to their regular work, there is something to be said for keeping the visible index out of the catalog department. The same comment can be made about combining the operations in a processing department.

The periodical room

The desire to give prompt service to readers may justify the checking in of magazines in a periodical room. Otherwise a reader may have to wait while a telephone call to the acquisition department discloses whether the latest issue of a given title has arrived or whether an issue not on the shelves was ever received. An outstanding example of this type of organization is to be found in the General Library of the University of California at Berkeley. There the Serials File is restricted to non-government serials and is a record of receipt, holdings, claims, and binding. After posting in the Serials Department (i.e. the Periodical Room), some titles are shelved in the stacks and some go to branches and other services. The Serials File is not directly accessible to readers, but is consulted extensively by assistants in the Order Department, the Gifts and Exchange Department, and elsewhere.

Administratively it may be expedient, especially in a college or university library, to combine visible index and public service duties in order to justify the manpower necessary to staff a periodical room at all times. The disadvantage is that the clerical function of checking may devolve on professional personnel; or, if the periodical room staff is clerical or subprofessional, the checking process, follow-up work, and preparation of volumes for binding may lack proper supervision. In research libraries the partial conversion of a periodical room into a processing unit may result in an unfortunate division of serial functions. The opportunity to develop a strong serial processing section may thereby be lost. As a consequence many serials may have to be handled in the acquisition department without benefit of expert serial supervision.

The self-contained serials department

In some libraries the idea of specialization has been carried so far that a separate serials department has been set up with responsibility for all phases of work with serials: acquisition, cataloging, servicing, housing, etc. The Washington Square Library of New York University moved in this direction in 1939. It expressed its philosophy as follows:

> The major place of serial publications in the modern university collection is . . . given recognition by the organization of a separate serials department within the Washington Square library. Virtually all phases of collecting, binding, shelving, and servicing are handled here, ensuring proper attention to the whole field. The Commerce library has taken a similar step by establishing a serials division, which includes among its other functions the acquisition and administration of Government publications.[2]

A year later it added:

> Work with serials was organized and carried on under a separate department for the first time in 1939-1940. This type of organization is in line with a general trend in the library field, a recognition of the importance of serials and the special problems connected with their administration. . . Under the

[2] New York University, *Report of the Director of the Libraries, 1938-39* (New York, 1939), p.6-7.

new setup, all serials, except in law, were shifted to the serials stacks in order to coördinate all work with serial publications.[3]

It was the considered opinion of Rothman (who established the Serials Division at New York University) and Ditzion that the self-contained serials department is the best type of organization. Their conclusion, based on a survey of methods in 126 college, university, and public libraries, was that "complete centralization of functions relating to serials offers the best solution of vexing problems."[4] Beatrice Simon has likewise stated her preference for a consolidated serials department:

> The amount of time wasted on cross consultation; the number of costly mistakes made because each assistant knows only part of the tale at any one time, is fantastic. Time costs money and money buys more periodicals, or hires more staff, so I am very jealous of time. That is the reason why I believe so whole-heartedly in the separate serials division. If you can delegate all operations concerning serials to one person, or one group of persons, and you have the courage to set up a separate serials division, where periodicals are received, processed and serviced as a continuous operation, you will find that great economies will ensue and you will have, in addition, an unusually competent group of people ready to give reference service of a very high quality.[5]

Complete centralization is, of course, not possible. So many library tools are serials, reference books in particular, that they will naturally be located where they are of most use. Rothman and Ditzion themselves made an exception to the centralization of serial collections in favor of subject departments:

> In virtually every instance where there is a serials division in a library, there are also subject departments. The only difference is that the serials division handles these serial publications up to the point where they go to the shelves; only at that time are they sent to the subject department. In other words, serials falling within the scope of a departmental collection are separated from serials in the main collection for purposes of shelving and circulation.[6]

Certainly a self-contained serials department solves many problems, just as it gives due recognition to the importance of the publications it services. At the same time, though, it gives rise to problems of another kind, and in the area of cataloging it can easily lead to serious trouble. Serials and non-serials overlap in significant respects in

---

[3] New York University, *Report of the Director of the Libraries, 1939-40* (New York, 1940), p.16.

[4] Fred B. Rothman and Sidney Ditzion, "Prevailing Practices in Handling Serials," *College and Research Libraries* 1:169, 1940. See also Rothman's "Pooh-bah of the Serials Division," *Library Journal* 62:457-59, 1937.

[5] Beatrice V. Simon, "Cataloguing of Periodicals," *Ontario Library Review* 33:239-40, 1949.

[6] Rothman and Ditzion, *op. cit.*, p.168.

cataloging, just as they may do on the classified shelves. Many of them are intimately connected through the corporate entry, which is common to both types of publication. Others are connected through the series entry. In general it must be realized that classification, subject heading, the shelf list, and above all the card catalog itself, are in themselves sufficiently unitary concepts that they should come under a single jurisdiction. It is true that responsibility for cataloging serials and non-serials has been divided in a number of libraries, but unless extremely favorable circumstances exist difficulties are bound to arise. One difficulty is that the catalogers in a self-contained serials department may be forced to work at a distance from their principal tool, the card catalog, or, to avoid this, the catalog may have to be divided at the risk of splitting corporate entries and duplicating history cards and references.

Organization of the document collection

By means of their document collections Ethelyn Markley has divided libraries into three types: the non-depository, the selected, and the complete depository.[7] In the non-depository type the documents acquired are specially wanted. Upon acquisition items of real value are incorporated in the general collection, and the rest go in vertical files or pamphlet boxes as self-cataloging material. In the selected depository type, Miss Markley favors segregation of most of the documents in a self-cataloging collection exploited through printed indexes. So that people will learn about the indexes and the collections, she advocates generous use of references in the card catalog, particularly from subjects and from names of government agencies. In the complete depository she again favors segregating most documents, cataloging items not covered by the printed indexes as use demands and the budget permits.

The critical element in this schematization is the amount of material to be detached from the document collection for integration in the regular bookstock. On this point Miss Markley said:

> Certain titles or series may be more useful in the ready reference collection or in the general collection or with the periodicals, than in the documents collection. There should be no hesitation in placing such titles in the collection best suited to their use, but these cases should be regarded as exceptions made for cause and they should be kept at a minimum. Some libraries select such titles by artificial means, choosing all documents not members of a series or all entered by L. C. under personal name rather than corporate name, but this seems to be evading the issue. There is general

[7] A. Ethelyn Markley, *Library Records for Government Publications* (Berkeley: Univ. of California Pr., 1951), p.7-16.

agreement that the Congressional set should be arranged separately by serial number, but in all other cases permanence and convenience in use should determine the policy. The advantages of placing a document with the book collection should be so obvious that there can be no question of keeping it with the separate collection. Repeated and frequent evidence that patrons look for it in the book stacks or expect to find it entered in the card catalog are useful criteria.[8]

This statement can be interpreted in two ways. It can easily be taken as a defense of past practice in libraries which have been content to write off documents as frugally as may be, or it can be taken as a statement of enlightened policy such as the Library of Congress follows. The former would be unfortunate. Many libraries have skimped on the processing of their document collections, which contain extremely valuable informational and research materials which should be dispersed throughout the classified shelves and be represented in the card catalog by a serial entry. There is no doubt, for example, that the political science shelves are robbed when the publications of the Department of State are not in their normal place together with works about the agency. It is true, of course, that there is a core of general documents that ought to be held together, as the Library of Congress recognizes in its J classification; but there is also much that should be scattered by subject.

Ellen Jackson, unlike Miss Markley, is completely in favor of separate and frugal treatment for documents as a distinct species of serials:

The library must give its government documents separate and special consideration, for the origin, the method of publication, the format, and the methods of indexing of publications of government agencies set them apart from publications of the commercial press and even from those of nongovernmental research agencies, learned societies, and other privately sponsored organizations . . .

Unity of intent and effort is basic to the efficiently operating research library, but as must be clear from the nature of government publications, their origin, their form, their indexing, their methods of distribution, they can be handled most efficiently as a separate and cohesive unit by a specially trained and experienced staff.[9]

The distinction Miss Jackson draws might have been truer in earlier times, but today it is difficult to distinguish many items and types. For example, one has to look very carefully to discover who issued a Latin American tourist magazine which is so like an ordinary periodical that it comes as something of a surprise to learn that it is a government

[8] *Ibid.*, p.9-10.

[9] Ellen P. Jackson, "Administration of the Government Documents Collection," *ACRL Monographs* 5:1, 9, 1953.

publication, and the new technical reports literature may originate either in a government or a non-government source. But apart from this consideration, the distinction between government and non-government serials is false and unwise when it results in uneven treatment. An all-or-nothing policy for serials is bad. Serials are serials, no matter what their issuing body may be. This is fundamental in the general library just as it is in the special library. Serials in an uncataloged or self-cataloging collection have been given substandard treatment.

While many libraries have followed the Library of Congress pattern for documents in their main collections, few have followed it in providing current reading room facilities for documents. The traditional periodical room has held to a rather narrow interpretation of the term "periodical." One of the major challenges to library administrators is to provide serial reading rooms which care for all high-frequency serials.

Whatever the over-all organization of serial work may be, then, no library should rest content until document serials are acquired, checked in, cataloged, and made available to readers in the same way as other serials. Self-cataloging methods are not good enough for the Department of State *Bulletin,* the *Farmers' Bulletin,* the *Monthly Labor Review,* the *Report* of the Atomic Energy Commission, *School Life,* the *Statistical Abstract of the United States,* the *Yearbook of Agriculture,* and a host of other government serials. If a research library wishes to economize on the processing of its government documents it can do so by refraining from analyzing them. But it is false economy to conceal the serials themselves, just as it is a mistake to exclude them from the general visible index. The substitute, which may be a combination shelf list and checking record,[10] is at best a makeshift, and as such is to be deprecated. On all counts it is desirable to treat documents like other serials. Substandard treatment is a counsel of expediency.

Organization of the newspaper collection

There is considerable justification for according newspapers special treatment because of their bulk and because check-listing is better for them than cataloging. Nevertheless, some libraries record newspapers on their regular visible index and house them in the periodical room. In libraries where the newspapers are expendable, checking is frequently dispensed with. In public libraries a separate newspaper reading room is often provided.

---

[10] Cf. Markley, *op. cit.,* p.22-27, 59-62.

Organization of a technical reports collection

World War II brought about a tremendous increase in technical reports and in technical report libraries. Bernard Fry, whose handbook is invaluable for such collections, said:

> A new and important body of scientific and technical report literature has arisen in recent years which presents new and highly specialized problems of library administration. At the present time, more than 75,000 unpublished technical reports are issued annually in this country by research projects supported by the Federal Government. These reports, the majority of which are security-classified, are prepared by numerous industrial and university contractors and by Government laboratories throughout the country.[11]

In 1953 the Air University Library had no fewer than 400,000 of these reports, 80 per cent of which were security classified. Its rate of acquisition is 40,000 a year. In 1950, 194 colleges and universities were engaged in contract research for the United States government. Naturally these institutions have copies of the locally produced reports, many of which are security classified.

Because the technical reports collections comprise both classified and unclassified documents, the latter accessible to uncleared as well as to security-cleared personnel, they cannot fit into the ordinary organization of a general library. Fry says of the university security-classified library: "Although such projects are under university contract, they tend to become separate organizations for operational purposes, with separate library service distinct from the university library system."[12]

Technical reports libraries are of two types: one where all the documents are integrated, the other where security-classified documents are separated from the unclassified or declassified ones. The latter practice, Fry said:

> permits access of uncleared personnel to the unclassified collection, and also is more economical of filing equipment in that open shelves or unlocked cabinets can be used to house unclassified documents, as contrasted to expensive combination-lock safes required for classified storage. The principal disadvantage of this method is that it frequently breaks up the group of reports issued by an organization and separates them without regard to program or project unity.

He went on to point out that some libraries which segregate the two types of report

> file their unclassified reports with the book and periodical literature. This

[11] Bernard M. Fry, *Library Organization and Management of Technical Reports Literature* (Washington: Catholic Univ. of America Pr., 1953. Catholic University of America Studies in Library Science, 1), p.1.

[12] *Ibid.,* p.35.

appears to reflect a recent tendency among technical libraries holding collections of both types of literature to integrate as far as possible the unclassified reports with the large body of traditional scientific literature. This practice makes good sense because many, perhaps one-third, of the unclassified reports eventually will be published as journal articles. Thus, it is possible to have a Secret report moving successively to the declassified (unclassified) collection and later to the periodical shelves.[13]

Here, then, is a rapidly expanding area of serial activity which is closer to documentation in some respects than it is to regular library techniques. Because of the security aspect, technical reports will continue to call for a special type of organization.

A separate serial catalog

Whenever there is talk of a self-contained serials department, separation of the official catalog into serials and non-serials should be considered. A few libraries have divided their catalogs in some such way. In the Reference Department of the New York Public Library, for instance, the official catalog has been divided by putting personal-name entries in one file and serials and corporate-entry non-serials in another. This division is of interest because it demonstrates the strong affinity between serials and corporate entries. Most libraries prefer to maintain their catalogs as a unit. In a divided catalog, author and subject entries are usually separated. As catalogs continue to grow and as serials become still more numerous there may be greater reason for establishing a serial catalog, but so far there is no trend in that direction. In fact, in 1948 the Yale University Library moved in the opposite direction by interfiling its public serial catalog with its main catalog. Simpkins has reported an interesting development at the Linda Hall Library in Kansas City. There a one-record serial catalog was established. The Kardex serves as checking record, public catalog for serials, and shelf list. Simpkins said:

> Patron use of the Kardex has been light compared to patron use of serials. Most patrons seem to appreciate being able to present a citation directly to a page or librarian without being required to look up a call number beforehand. Other patrons, with more general problems in mind, have free access to the catalog at all times, but this has not seemed to interfere measurably with its workings.[14]

A problem in organization

The preceding sections have indicated some of the complex problems to be considered in organizing extensive serial collections. The

---

[13] *Ibid.*, p.29.

[14] Edgar G. Simpkins, "A Study of Serials Processing," *Serial Slants* v.2, Jan. 1952, p.16.

idea of a separate serials department offers no simple solution to the problems. Nevertheless, it performs a useful service by highlighting the fact that serials have grown so enormously in number and consequentiality in the twentieth century. This trend is likely to continue indefinitely, possibly even at an accelerated pace, so there is good reason for libraries to debate where they want the principal center of serial activity to be and whether they want a separate serials department. If outright centralization is not the answer, at least much can and should be done in many a library to coordinate functions better, to provide more adequate staff and quarters for serial work, and to conserve serial files properly.

In larger institutions serials do admittedly present a problem in organization, but it is a problem that ought to be related to a larger one. At a time when library departmentalization so often amounts to compartmentalization, it is of more than academic interest to ask whether the creation of a serials department would mitigate the evils of departmentalization. Because so many parts of a library are concerned with serials, this particular problem of organization affords an excellent approach to the wider issue of departmentalization in libraries. In the long run, then, the theoretical justification or rejection of a self-contained serials department must stand or fall with a clarification of the aims of library specialization and departmentalization.

Actually, it is not necessary to set up a self-contained serials department to achieve the correlation of interests that its proponents are seeking. The traditional pattern can be highly successful with the requisite direction and support, leading to coordination of serial processes in the acquisition and cataloging departments and in the periodical room. Quite evidently, there is room for development of consolidated records in some libraries and for cooperation between the units concerned with serials in others. In many libraries the scope of the periodical room should be enlarged so that it can care for most high-frequency serials. So, with thoughtful consideration for the developing role of serial publications in libraries, the traditional pattern of divided responsibility for the different functions can be continued satisfactorily in most institutions.

CHAPTER 3

Principles of Serial Selection

TWO MAJOR DIFFICULTIES have hitherto had to be faced by those concerned with recommending the procurement of new serials. One of these has been the lack of complete and prompt tools for serial selection. Fortunately this is an area in which notable progress has been made and more can be expected, thanks in no small measure to *New Serial Titles,* which the Library of Congress started publishing in January, 1953, as a successor to its *Serial Titles Newly Received.* In it can be found a listing of serial publications from all over the world whose first issue appeared on or after January 1, 1950. The extensive coverage comes about because numerous American and Canadian libraries rich in serials, including the Library of Congress itself, report their current acquisitions for inclusion in *New Serial Titles.*

The other difficulty relates to the theory and practice of book selection. The very name of this branch of librarianship shows that the theory of serial selection has been subordinated to the selection of non-serials, and thereby has been neglected to a considerable extent. Examination of textbooks on book selection shows how far this subordination and neglect have gone. Bonny[1] includes only two or three pages on the selection of magazines, plus about twelve more of suggested titles. Drury's textbook[2] contains a dozen pages which are very good as far as they go. Helen Haines in her classic *Living with Books*[3] has merely incidental serial references, mainly relating to reviewing journals. Ranganathan[4] has several short though rather unusual passages. Wellard[5] disregards serial selection, and there is no paper on

[1] Harold V. Bonny, *A Manual of Practical Book Selection for Public Libraries* (London: Grafton, 1939).

[2] Francis K. W. Drury, *Book Selection* (Chicago: American Library Assn., 1930).

[3] Helen E. Haines, *Living with Books; the Art of Book Selection* (2d ed.; New York: Columbia Univ. Pr., 1950).

[4] S. R. Ranganathan, *Library Book Selection* (Delhi: Indian Library Assn., 1952).

[5] James H. Wellard, *Book Selection, Its Principles and Practice* (London: Grafton, 1937).

serials in the University of Chicago Library Institute which dealt with book selection.[6] In short, the manuals have for the most part contented themselves with either a popular or else a narrow approach to the theory and practice of building up library collections.[7]

In extenuation of this situation it is not sufficient to say that serial selection follows exactly the same principles that apply to books. In both theory and practice the selection of serials is much harder than the selection of monographs. True, there are fewer titles to choose from, but these titles involve more deliberation, perhaps by a number of library officers, unless they belong in an area in which intensive collecting is being undertaken. As examples of the decisions that must be made, the following are the titles that came up for serial selection during a single day's activity in the Harvard College Library. Note that practically none of these is a trade publication. Serials, unlike non-serials, are predominantly non-trade publications and must be sought through special channels.

Board of Commissioners of the Port of New Orleans. 56th Annual Report, 1952.
Boletín oficial de la zona de protectorado español en Marruecos, ano 41, num. 15, Abril 1953.
Citizens and Their Schools, vol. 3, no. 8, May 1953.
Costa Rica. Direccion General de Estadistica y Censos. Boletin informativo, ano 3, no. 34-5, Nov.-Dic. 1952.
Diplomatic Information Office, Madrid. Facts about Spain, 1-20, 1952.
Erziehung; Bildungswege und Probleme der Gegenwart, 6. Jahrgang, Heft 1, Jänner 1953.
The Fortnightly Review of French Letters, no. 4, December 15, 1952.
Guatemala. Secretaria de Propaganda y Divulgacion. Noticias de Guatemala; boletin informativo, no. 8, 8 de Abril, 1953.
Indian Council of Agricultural Research, New Delhi. Statistical Newsletter, vol. 2, no. 3, October 1952.
Israel Office of Information. RP 24-44, April 1953.
Meddelelser fra Københavns Universitet, nummer 4-8, 1953.
Moroccan Office of Information and Documentation. Free Morocco, no. 1, April 20, 1953.
New Zealand. Census and Statistics Department. Report on the Agricultural and Pastoral Statistics of New Zealand, 1950-51.
Puerto Rico. Auditor. Informe, 30 de Junio 1952.
Sveriges officiella statistik. Levnadskostnaderna i tätortshushåll år 1948 av Kungl. Socialstyrelsen, 1953.
Thailand. National Economic Council. Monthly Bulletin of Statistics, vol. 1, no. 4-5, Sept.-Oct. 1952.

---

[6] *The Practice of Book Selection,* ed. with an introduction by Louis R. Wilson (Chicago: Univ. of Chicago Pr., [1940]).

[7] As an exception to the general practice, it is rather refreshing to find serial selection accorded priority over book selection in the *Handbook of Medical Library Practice,* edited by Janet Doe (Chicago: American Library Assn., 1943).

Specimen numbers miscellaneous in character as these constantly find their way into libraries. For the most part they merit careful consideration. Some questions to be answered are: Should they be acquired by purchase, gift, or exchange? Should a complete file from the beginning be sought? Should the sample numbers be passed on to another library in the vicinity because they fall into its special field of collecting activity? The help and advice of a professor or other specialist may be necessary before a decision to purchase is given. If an item is to be sought on exchange the *quid pro quo* may have to be determined so it can be mentioned in the letter requesting the exchange.

In a library with an active serial program much time must be allowed for correspondence and incidental record work. The whole operation is time consuming; it involves an exacting routine when carried out promptly as it should be; and all too often it leaves the selection officer with a sense of doubt about what he is doing, both for the amount of material acquired and for the amount rejected.

While a certain amount of deliberation takes place before a monograph is acquired, a decision to acquire a serial publication (whether by gift, exchange, or purchase) should be checked and double-checked. One cause for concern is the fact that a serial once started may continue to come year after year as the successive issues appear, even though the title may eventually outlive its usefulness, if indeed it was of real value in the first instance. The sorcerer must be on guard to see that his apprentice does not unloose a perfect torrent of serials. If, on the other hand, the initial opportunity to obtain a serial is not accepted, much effort and expense may one day be entailed to repair the omission, certainly if a complete set is then desired.

Another cause for concern lies in the fact that serial subscriptions represent fixed charges which are a first lien on the annual book budget. How large a proportion of the budget may go for serials can be gauged from the situation in the Harvard Law Library where in 1953/54 $59,799.22 was spent for serials as against $19,254.02 for nonserials. When the outlay for serials is at all big, the ratio between book and serial expenditures should be watched closely. In this connection, a weather eye needs to be kept open for the occasional periods of financial stringency which may affect the book budget. At such times it is difficult to cut the fixed charges without serious, and possibly irreparable, harm to the serial files. More than one library looks back with regret to an across-the-board decision to curtail serial subscriptions so that the level of book purchases might be maintained. In the Harvard College Library, for instance, it has been regretted on a number of occasions that in 1920 subscriptions were terminated for many French local history periodicals, an area in which the library has notable holdings. The alternative to cutting serial subscriptions is to cut the purchase of non-serials particularly drastically. This is a wiser procedure in the research library, for the majority of non-serials can be acquired at a later date, whereas it is difficult, if not impossible, to fill serial files.

Another factor to be kept in mind in serial selection is that the cost of binding serials may be a major item in each year's budget, and just as the typical serial costs more than the typical non-serial to bind, it also costs more to shelve because of its bulk. The cataloging and recataloging of serials is also expensive—their recataloging in particular, which, when done in the traditional manner, is the costliest form of library cataloging, yet must be faced in some way when changes of name, scope, etc., occur.[8] Furthermore, serials may give rise to space problems, especially in smaller libraries, because of their bulk and steady growth.

Serial selection, like book selection, is an art, not a science. Its skilled performance depends primarily on the exercise of trained, informed judgment. There are, however, certain principles and procedures that are relied upon by the experienced librarian in determining whether or not to add a new serial title to the collection, among which the following should be emphasized.

Acquire the tools that open up the literature of a subject or country.

Acquire titles that are analyzed in standard indexing services.

Give special attention to the acquisition of the basic journal or journals in any field of interest.

Whenever possible and desirable, obtain sample copies to make the selection process more judicious.

In order to maintain a systematic program of serial selection, check *New Serial Titles* each month. In many libraries certain supplementary lists should be checked regularly too.

Enrich the resources of a locality, region, or group of libraries by carrying out, just as far as possible, a program of cooperative acquisition.

In each area develop a coordinated program for the preservation of local publications.

Build up serial files on the basis of long runs, not broken files. In the case of annuals and other low-frequency serials, however, rather than do without a worthwhile title altogether, consider subscribing to every second or third issue.

---

[8] In his "Some Persistent Problems of Serials in Technical Processes" *(Serial Slants* v.1, Jan. 1951, p.8), Arnold Trotier says: "I have been particularly concerned over the effect on these costs of certain rules of entry affecting serials. I have in mind the rules whereby serials entered under title must always be entered under the latest title and publications entered under a corporate heading must always be entered under the latest form of that corporate heading. No one who has had extensive experience in the cataloging of serials can fail to be impressed with the costs involved in the recataloging made necessary by the application of these rules."

In research libraries, allocate a sum of money each year for the purchase of sets and back files to round out the collection. When originals cannot be procured, acquire microreproductions.

Control duplicate subscriptions on the basis of relative values. Which will further the library's program to best advantage: extra copies or additional titles?

Always think of the possibilities of acquiring a title by gift or exchange. These methods of acquisition are extensively employed in serial procurement. They help immeasurably in enriching a collection.

Review each entry on the visible index every three years or so to see whether the title or the extra copies are still worth while.

Professional tools

The first principle of serial selection is to acquire the tools of serial selection, the reference works that are serial in nature, and in general the serials that the librarian requires for successful work performance.

The librarian—just as much as the craftsman, engineer, or surgeon—should have these tools, even though they are expensive, to discharge his daily activities skillfully and effectively. First in line are the publications which open up the literature of a subject or country. Many of these are recorded in the *Index Bibliographicus; Directory of Current Periodical Abstracts and Bibliographies* which is issued by Unesco and lists serials that abstract, index, record, or review the literature of various fields. Close on their heels come works of a reference character, which are disclosed by Winchell's *Guide to Reference Books.*

Indexed periodicals

The periodicals of greatest potential value in a library are those that are indexed in standard indexing services.[9] Some periodical dealers take cognizance of this fact by indicating in their catalogs the relevant indexing mediums. *Indexed Periodicals,* issued by the F. W. Faxon Company, is a good illustration of the practice. The indexing

[9] Occasionally libraries signify the importance they attach to indexed periodicals by designating the indexing medium on the entries in their visible indexes. So, for example, in the Los Angeles Public Library "abbreviations in red, such as R.G., A.I., I.A.I., I.I., Arts I., Ed. I., Chem. Abs., Eng. I., indicate the indexes including the serial. When a new title is added to the checklist it must be looked up in the various indexes taken by the library, and this information added to the checklist." Los Angeles Public Library, Serials Division, *Workbook of Serials Procedure* (Los Angeles, 1932), p.10. At the Linda Hall Library it was decided to bind only indexed serials; hence the checking records show whether and where each title is indexed. See Edgar G. Simpkins, "A Study of Serials Processing," *Serial Slants* v.2, Jan. 1952, p.8.

medium is also specified in selection tools such as *Ulrich's Periodicals Directory* and Lyle and Trumper's *Classified List of Periodicals for the College Library.*

Thus a basic principle of selection is to acquire titles that are covered by the *Readers' Guide to Periodical Literature,* the *International Index to Periodicals,* and other standard indexes. At the Montclair Free Public Library the ruling was adopted that

> when a magazine title is considered for inclusion in the library's subscription, it must meet a test similar to that applied to books. It must either serve an obvious local need, or its contents must be indexed regularly in one of the standard periodical indexes.[10]

This principle applies to the acquisition of back files and older titles just as it does to current subscriptions. For example, many libraries consider that a title indexed in *Poole's Index to Periodical Literature* is especially worth acquiring because the reference staff and readers have at hand a detailed listing of its contents. In some libraries so much value is placed on titles covered by Poole that they are shelved together for convenience of consultation. The general library is better served by this principle than the special library. The specialized index may be so inclusive that it is not particularly helpful as a selection aid in a library that must be selective.

Basic journals

When a library does not aim at inclusive collecting in a field that it wishes to cover, its primary endeavor should be to acquire the basic journal or journals. There are several ways of determining whether a journal is basic. One is to check standard lists such as the following:

For small public libraries

Abridged Readers' Guide to Periodical Literature, July 1935- New York: Wilson.

Periodicals for Small and Medium-Sized Libraries. 8th ed. Chicago: American Library Assn., 1948.

For medium-sized public libraries

International Index to Periodicals, 1907- New York: Wilson.

Periodicals for Small and Medium-Sized Libraries. 8th ed. Chicago: American Library Assn., 1948.

Readers' Guide to Periodical Literature, 1900- New York: Wilson.

For large public libraries

Ulrich's Periodicals Directory; a Classified Guide to a Selected List of Current Periodicals, Foreign and Domestic. 7th ed. N.Y.: Bowker, 1953.

---

[10] Margery C. Quigley and William E. Marcus, *Portrait of a Library* (New York: Appleton-Century, [1936]), p.29.

For school libraries

Abridged Readers' Guide to Periodical Literature, July 1935- New York: Wilson.

Madison, Wis., Public Schools. Magazine Committee. *Magazines for Elementary Grades.* Rev. ed. Madison, 1949.

Laura K. Martin. *Magazines for School Libraries.* Rev. ed. New York: Wilson, 1950.

For junior college libraries

Frank J. Bertalan. *Books for Junior Colleges.* Chicago: American Library Assn., 1954.

Southern Association of Colleges and Secondary Schools. Commission on Institutions of Higher Education. *The Classified List of Reference Books and Periodicals for College Libraries;* ed. by W. Stanley Hoole. Rev. ed. Birmingham, Ala.: The Association, 1947.

For college libraries

Guy R. Lyle and Virginia M. Trumper. *Classified List of Periodicals for the College Library.* 3d ed. Boston: Faxon, 1948.[11]

Charles B. Shaw. *A List of Books for College Libraries.* Chicago: American Library Assn., 1931-40. 2v.

Southern Association of Colleges and Secondary Schools. Commission on Institutions of Higher Education. *The Classified List of Reference Books and Periodicals for College Libraries;* ed. by W. Stanley Hoole. Rev. ed. Birmingham, Ala.: The Association, 1947.

For special libraries[12]

Index Bibliographicus; Directory of Current Periodical Abstracts and Bibliographies. Paris: Unesco, 1952- .

Special Libraries Association. Public Business Librarians Group. *Business and the Public Library; Steps in Successful Cooperation;* ed. by Marian C. Manley. New York: The Association, 1940.

Special Libraries Association. Science-Technology Division. *Technical Libraries, Their Organization and Management;* ed. by Lucille Jackson. New York: The Association, 1951.

When lists such as these are not sufficiently inclusive to serve precise needs, recourse may be had to specialists (a department head or a faculty member, for instance), or else librarians must make their own tests. For example, if a library wanted to acquire one and only one magazine devoted to Asiatic studies, a list of possible titles could

---

[11] Public libraries should note that the Enoch Pratt Free Library considered most of the periodicals in this bibliography of value for adult education, so it checked the list carefully. Its comment was that "substantial reference material of this sort is considered 'on the main line' in this library." See Enoch Pratt Free Library, *The Reorganization of a Large Public Library; Ten Year Report of the Enoch Pratt Free Library 1926-1935* (Baltimore, 1937), p.16-18.

[12] Selected lists for special libraries of various kinds can be found recorded in *Library Literature* under the headings "Periodicals, Aeronautical," "Periodicals, Agricultural," etc.

be compiled from *Ulrich's Periodicals Directory* and other sources, sample numbers could be solicited, and a choice made by comparing the publications themselves.

A comparatively simple technique for determining the basic journals in a scholarly field is to check footnote references in periodicals on a given subject to see which titles are referred to most frequently. Duly weighted (for example, to allow for new but highly significant titles), the most cited titles can be considered the basic publications. In 1927 Gross and Gross applied this method to chemical journals.[13] In the 1940's tabulations in a number of scientific disciplines were prepared for the Association of Research Libraries. Unfortunately they have not been published, although they have been utilized by the Association of Research Libraries as a criterion for membership and by Charles H. Brown in his listing of lacunae in the Louisiana State University Library. The titles cited by Brown bear notation which tells how high the items ranked in the lists for agronomy, biology, botany, chemistry, general science, geology, mathematics and statistics, physics, physiology, and soil research. Numerous lists of most cited journals have also been published. Brown has cautioned against their indiscriminate application:

> Complaint has been made that some libraries ordered periodicals on such lists without any consideration of the needs of their communities. Any list, whether of books or periodicals, must be considered from the viewpoint of the community to be served. In most universities some periodicals not on the list may be of more value than those listed. For example, in Louisiana, some periodicals covering the chemistry of sugar would be much more valuable than other periodicals high on the "Most Cited Lists."[14]

Estelle Brodman applied the Gross and Gross technique to physiology and came to the conclusion that the underlying assumptions are not true:

> The Gross and Gross method has been extremely valuable in helping administrators to build up periodical collections in many diverse fields about which they would not themselves have expert subject knowledge. For this reason it has probably been accepted more or less uncritically, with the feeling that any method was better than no method. Yet it appears to be a somewhat unscientific and unscholarly method as well as one which gives untrustworthy results. In spite of these extremely grave drawbacks, the method will probably continue to be employed by librarians until the library profession is presented with a better one. Individuals using the method, however, should be aware of the small dependence which can scientifically be placed on its results.[15]

---

[13] P. L. K. Gross and E. M. Gross, "College Libraries and Chemical Education," *Science* n.s. 66:385-89, 1927.

[14] Quoted in *Serial Slants* v.1, Jan. 1951, p.25.

[15] Estelle Brodman, "Choosing Physiology Journals," *Medical Library Associa-*

An interesting and significant application of the reference-counting method is to be found in the document entitled *Is American Attention to Foreign Research Results Declining? A Tentative Attempt at Measurement for Selected Data from Seven Fields of Pure and Applied Science, 1889-1954,* by Karl W. Deutsch, George E. Klein, James J. Baker, and associates, submitted for the Committee on International Relations of the American Academy of Arts and Sciences, June 9, 1954. This study arrived at the conclusion, supported by 23 graphs, that American scientists are becoming far more nationally self-preoccupied in absolute terms, but are becoming slightly more international in their reading if the shift in their sources of relevant information is taken into account. For librarians there is much food for thought in this study. To what extent have selection policies influenced the domestic/foreign ratio of what scientists are reading?

Sample numbers

Just as the book selection process is facilitated when books can be obtained on approval, so too the procurement of specimen copies of periodicals and some other serials may be an aid in selection. Sample numbers of journals can generally be obtained on request, and should be got unless there is a clear case for subscribing. Farmington Plan dealers have been instructed to supply sample copies whenever possible.

Systematic checking

Every library throughout the world interested in developing its serial resources should check the monthly issues of *New Serial Titles.* The listing it contains is, of course, limited to the titles supplied by the cooperating libraries. Because of this limitation many libraries must still check a variety of supplementary bibliographies: notably reviewing journals in specialized fields and national lists like *British National Bibliography* (which records the first issue of new serials published in

---

tion Bulletin 32:482, 1944. On page 483 she lists 22 items compiled on the basis of the Gross and Gross method. These are in such diverse fields as agriculture, chemistry, child guidance, dentistry, education, electrical engineering, geology, and mathematics. Miss Brodman's findings are given in full in her Columbia University Library School thesis entitled *Methods of Choosing Physiology Journals.* William D. Postell has presented additional evidence "to bolster the conclusions of Miss Brodman that the Gross and Gross method for evaluating journals cannot always be relied upon as a valid criterion of the selection of the outstanding journals in any particular field." See his "Further Comments on the Mathematical Analysis of Evaluating Scientific Journals," *Medical Library Association Bulletin* 34:109, 1946. In a systematic review, Rolland Stevens concluded that, despite Miss Brodman's basic criticisms, the reference-counting method has proved its usefulness in a number of ways. See his "Characteristics of Subject Literature," *ACRL Monographs* 6, 1953.

Great Britain) and the *Annual Catalogue of Australian Publications* (which has special sections devoted to government publications and to non-government serials).[16] To increase the coverage of *New Serial Titles,* as many libraries as possible, especially research and special libraries, should report their relevant acquisitions.

Before *New Serial Titles* appeared, many libraries were in the habit of checking several far less inclusive aids which still have their value. These include: "Births and Deaths," a feature in the *Bulletin of Bibliography;* the annual review of new periodicals which appears in *College and Research Libraries;* and the list of outstanding United States government publications which appears annually in the *Wilson Library Bulletin.* These and other lists, taken in conjunction with *New Serial Titles,* provide excellent, though still far from complete, coverage of the world's output of new serials.

It is important to add, in view of the importance of serials as materials for research and information, that the checking of *New Serial Titles* and other serial selection aids should be given a high priority in the press of library work. Many serials are extremely elusive. Some of them go out of print or cease publication before they can be acquired. Systematic checking and eternal vigilance are the price of a fine serial collection.

Cooperative acquisition

The total number of serial titles published each year, both domestic and foreign, is so great[17] that libraries have become increasingly aware of the need for dividing between themselves the fields of collecting activity. On a national scale the Farmington Plan has had some influence in this direction, though its principal concern has been with non-serials. Apart from the Farmington Plan, most cooperation has been at the local level. Two or more libraries in a locality may

---

[16] For a list of supplementary sources, see Carl Björkbom, "Bibliographical Tools for Control of Current Periodicals," *Review of Documentation* 20:19-24, 1953, and for an illuminating study of the diligence and enterprise required for thoroughly systematic checking, see the section "How to Find out about the Existence of Government Publications" in Rose L. Vormelker's "Government Publications—Availability and Use from the Special Librarian's Point of View," *Special Libraries* 34:213, 1943.

[17] The periodical *Le droit d'auteur* attempts to give annual statistics for the production of periodicals in various countries. These figures are far from complete. Evidence afforded by the visible index at the Library of Congress, which in 1954 was estimated to have 160,000 titles, suggests that the libraries of the United States and Canada are currently acquiring between a quarter and a third of a million different serial titles, and that they are adding to the number each year. World production must be vastly in excess of this estimate, especially when local publications, mimeographed serials, and technical reports literature are taken into account.

develop a plan whereby they confer among themselves to determine which library will subscribe to a new title when it is not necessary for more than one of them to acquire it. Perhaps the most notable achievements along these lines have been those of several small groups of colleges; for example, those comprising the Hampshire Inter-Library Center in Massachusetts. The first annual report of the Center showed the benefits that derive from cooperative serial acquisition:

> The branch of activity first begun . . . concerned periodical subscriptions, 119 of which have now been placed by the Center in the interest of its members. During the year the faculties of the three member colleges [Amherst, Mount Holyoke, and Smith] examined their own current subscription lists and recommended journals which might be foregone on the local campus if the Center would take responsibility for them. While a large number of the suggestions are still under review and discussion, agreement in these 119 instances represents a remarkable accomplishment when viewed against the background of local self sufficiency and autonomy which had previously prevailed. They fall into two broad categories: (a) journals previously maintained by one, two, or three of the members (a total of 98), (b) journals new to the area (a total of 21). The former represent economies effected by reducing what had been 180 subscriptions to 98 journals nearly by half. The latter exemplify the Center's constructive potentialities.
>
> A third purpose has also been served in at least two instances where substantial journals threatened by cancellation for reasons of economy have been taken over by the Center. Thus, in this area of current subscriptions alone, three types of service have been rendered: reduction of expenditures, increase of resources, conservation of resources.
>
> Current issues of these journals are circulated to the three member libraries, in each of which they are on separate display for a period of a month. A routing order has been set up for each journal to allow priority for particular local needs and interests. As volumes are completed they are . . . bound and stored by the Center.[18]

Local agreements of this kind should be supplemented by inserting entries for the serial titles concerned in the catalog of each participating library, provided there is no local union list of serials to serve as a substitute. In the case of the Hampshire Inter-Library Center "cataloguing has been done by the Mount Holyoke College Library, which has supplied cards for the Center and for the members. The latter have filed these cards in their public catalogues."

While agreements of this kind are all too few and should be multiplied a thousandfold, it has been quite common practice, when the purchase of a serial set is being considered, to check the *Union List of Serials* to see whether there is already a copy in a neighboring library or in the region. A library on the West Coast may well buy an

---

[18] Hampshire Inter-Library Center, *First Annual Report, 1951-1952* (South Hadley, Mass., 1952), p.1-2.

item if the only holdings known to the *Union List of Serials* are in the East or the Middle West. On the other hand, this same institution might put its money into another title if it saw that the work in question was in another West Coast library. The object of both the consultation and the checking is to reduce the duplication of highly specialized titles, foreign language material, and little-used publications generally, at the same time conserving the means of enriching the collections in a given area. Beatrice Simon, in speaking of "the utter impossibility of any of us being able to acquire and house every serial we might like to have, even if we had the money," said:

It doesn't really matter much if six libraries in the same city buy the same book, but is it sensible, even sane, for six neighboring libraries to buy, bind and store complete sets of the *Commercial and Financial Chronicle*. . . Yet that is exactly what is happening all over the country to a greater or lesser degree and, at the same time, other valuable contemporary records are not being bought, bound or stored at all. . .

Whether we like it or not, this is the age of co-operation, and only through co-operation are we going to survive and have libraries. Co-operation extends all the way from nations to such seemingly small matters as whether two libraries in the same city will preserve the same periodical. Certain titles will be duplicated currently in nearly all libraries of the same type; others need not be. But complete sets, dealing with all phases of our own culture, and foreign titles should be preserved somewhere on this continent. Those universally useful should be dotted about . . . at strategic spots. Nor should this be considered impossible in this day of microfilm. Some kind of co-operative, regional planning for the acquisition, preservation and use of serials should be substituted for the haphazard and "isolationist" policies now in operation in so many of our libraries.

Furthermore, it is perfectly feasible and possible to carry out such a program with all types of libraries participating: public, university and even the private libraries of societies, research institutions, industry and business, to say nothing of the government libraries. On a modest scale, and in select groups of libraries, co-operative buying and storing has already been put into successful operation.[19]

This statement goes to the heart of the matter. Some titles are so significant that complete sets must be acquired, bound, and stored, regardless of cost or duplication. Some titles should be acquired currently, but do not need to be bound or preserved permanently except in the institution that undertakes the responsibility on behalf of others. For other titles one library can accept full responsibility so that nearby institutions do not have to acquire even the current issues.

Cooperation should apply most definitely to less-used and marginal materials. Classes that deserve special attention are: foreign language

[19] Beatrice V. Simon, "Let's Consider Serials Realistically," *Library Journal* 71:1297, 1946.

publications (particularly those in the less-known languages), learned society journals and reports, local items, government documents (notably at the state and local level), press releases and other mimeographed matter, directories, and annual reports. In applying this principle the Midwest Inter-Library Corporation listed among the initial classes of material collected: American newspapers (especially the foreign-language press), college catalogs, federal processed documents, foreign newspapers, foreign parliamentary proceedings, house organs and trade journals, and state documents.

Local publications

The number of serial publications which a large library can handle effectively is limited. The Library of Congress has about 330,000 serial titles, almost half of them on its visible index. The other research libraries of the United States and Canada can probably contribute another 330,000 titles. Impressive as these figures are, the number of serials not collected by libraries, especially at the level of local material, is so great that quite evidently much spade work remains to be done if they are to be collected. Consequently some library in every locality or region should take the responsibility for collecting serials issued in its area, partly to relieve the larger libraries and partly because it may be able to collect local material more easily and surely. Local publications are issued by churches, colleges and schools, firms, local government bodies, local societies, newspapers, and student bodies, among other groups. If such collecting is done adequately at the local level, the larger research libraries can avoid the acquisition of much ephemeral material, and can devote their energies and resources to systematic collecting on a world-wide basis. As with cooperative serial acquisition in general, some kind of a serial council seems desirable to see that full coverage is obtained and that needless duplication is avoided.

Limited selection

Funds do not always permit the purchase of a back file when a subscription is initiated some years after the first volume of a given title was published. Commonly, when a subscription to an established journal is placed, the file is started with the preceding or following January, or at all events with the beginning of a new volume. If the title is only two or three years old, the subscription generally should cover everything from volume 1, number 1 on, but for older titles acquisition of a complete file may have to be weighed carefully.

For some titles, mostly annuals, it may be necessary, in order to conserve funds, to subscribe every second or third year, but not each year. Out-of-town city directories, for example, may often be acquired in this fashion without unduly reducing service. Such an expedient may be acceptable if it adds to the resources of a library in a desirable but limited way, without imposing too much on the fixed charges for serials.

Back files

If possible, an appropriate sum should be set aside each year for the purchase of serial sets as well as parts of sets that will complete runs already in the library. The Science-Technology Division of the Special Libraries Association suggests that two to five hundred dollars a year should be budgeted by the small scientific library for the purchase of back files, and adds: "Back files are not always available for purchase so that it may be necessary to wait for opportunities to procure them, in which case money should be accessible whenever needed sets are offered."[20] When desiderata lists have been compiled, such as the one Charles H. Brown prepared for Louisiana State University Library, the money can be spent on a sound basis. Otherwise careful consideration must be given to items in dealers' lists or to the purchase of microreproductions.

For the most part, libraries should avoid the piecemeal filling in of sets. There is a temptation to add odd pieces by gift or exchange, sometimes from large-lot purchases, simply because they are available. Unless a title is particularly important and scarce, or unless a crucial gap can be filled, it is better to restrict the filling in of sets to the addition of at least a whole volume. Brown has offered the following comment on the filling in of back sets:

> Almost all the scientific publications used and cited by research workers are classified as "serials." Back sets of these publications are referred to constantly. Thirty years ago complete sets of scientific publications could be purchased without too much difficulty and even odd volumes could be picked up at reasonable prices with the probability that missing volumes could be obtained later. Conditions changed very rapidly after 1930 and especially after 1940. Volumes lacking in a set are, in most cases, now extremely difficult to obtain. If odd volumes of a periodical are purchased, it is frequently found that the volumes obtained are the less important and that the volumes still missing are both the more important and more difficult to obtain.[21]

---

[20] Special Libraries Association, Science-Technology Division, *Technical Libraries, Their Organization and Management,* ed. by Lucille Jackson (New York: Special Libraries Assn., 1951,) p.20. On the problem of acquiring back files, see Robert A. Miller, "The Purchasing of Books and Journals in Europe," *University of Illinois Library School Occasional Papers* 36:8-9, 1953.

[21] Charles H. Brown, *Library Resources in Selected Scientific Subjects at Louisiana State University* (Baton Rouge: Louisiana State Univ. Library, 1950), p.3.

Duplicate holdings

When demand arises for extra copies of a purchased serial, it must be decided whether the ends of the library are best served by duplication or by spending an equivalent amount of money on another title, thereby increasing the institution's resources. The answer is not difficult in popular and special libraries that emphasize service and the wide dissemination of selected titles, but elsewhere, particularly in university libraries, duplicate subscriptions should be rigorously controlled.

The pressure for duplicate subscriptions is to provide service copies for current consultation and in library systems to accommodate both the main and branch or departmental collections. In special libraries it is frequently desirable, and may be necessary, to enter duplicate subscriptions for the current issues of journals that are routed to a considerable number of people. In the United Nations Library the norm was set at one copy for each eight names on the routing slip. Service copies are rarely bound, though they may be utilized to round out a volume for binding. In some cases they may be held for a number of years to satisfy circulation needs or to provide reserve copies.

To a limited extent some libraries find it desirable to duplicate subscriptions so that perfect copies will be available for binding or microfilming. This practice applies principally to newspapers and a few hard-used periodicals.

In large library systems duplicate subscriptions do or should give rise to administrative concern over the cost of acquiring, binding, and preserving multiple sets, each volume of which may easily cost ten dollars or more to purchase and bind. The Bailey report at Harvard University should stand as a warning against uncontrolled duplication. Concentrating in the field of botany, Professor Bailey found that in 750 instances there was duplication in complete sets or long runs of periodicals; in another 412 cases there was miscellaneous duplication. Altogether he found that there were at Harvard approximately 30,000 excess duplicate volumes of botanical serials. He estimated these to be worth $130,000.[22]

Gift and exchange

Since the budget for subscriptions is seldom adequate to serve all demands, thought must be given, as part of the serial selection process, to the possibilities of obtaining an item by gift or exchange instead of

---

[22] Irving W. Bailey, *Botany and Its Applications at Harvard* ([Cambridge, Mass.: Harvard University], 1945), p.84-93.

by purchase. Collections can be enriched tremendously by judicious attention to these methods.

Periodic review

At regular intervals, possibly once every three years, all titles on the visible index should be scrutinized to see whether, in the light of the serial program as a whole, they should continue to be acquired. Doubtful cases should be reviewed not merely from the records themselves, but with a specimen copy in hand; and it may even be desirable for the head librarian to pass on them. To facilitate a general reexamination and to allow for a number of subject specialists and staff members to participate, the Acquisition Unit at the United Nations Library has on several occasions compiled a *List of Periodicals and Newspapers Currently Received.* This list tells how many copies are received, where they are located in the library, and the mode of acquisition—by gift, exchange, or purchase.

By means of a periodic checkup it is possible to eliminate titles that are no longer worth acquiring, duplicate subscriptions can be reduced or justified afresh, and, as the Hampshire Inter-Library Center has demonstrated, cooperative aspects of serial collecting can be developed.

CHAPTER 4

The Acquisition Process

SERIALS LEND THEMSELVES to efficient, businesslike methods. All aspects of their acquisition should therefore be simple and straightforward. The principal acquisition record is the visible index, which is discussed in Chapter 6. Other records should be as few in number as possible.

Decision slips

Many libraries employ printed or mimeographed form slips, which can be attached to sample numbers, to formalize the various courses of action that should be recommended in the process of serial selection. The decision slip used by the Library of Congress is shown in Figure 2. Some libraries maintain a record of the decisions given on such forms. This record may show, among other things: who recommended the acquisition or non-acquisition of a title; whether a sample copy is to be procured before the final selection decision is made; where the current file is to be located, and on occasion the period for which the file is to be current; whether the file is to be bound; whether a back file is to be acquired; whether earlier or superseded issues are to be discarded; and whether an annual is to be bought every second or third year instead of every year. Since information about items that are acquired is usually transferred to the current records, the decision file is more useful as a record of negative decisions than of positive ones. The negative values come about because, when a decision not to acquire an item is reviewed, it has been found advantageous in some libraries to be able to document the previous action.

If the decision slips are of catalog-card size, the file may be composed of the actual forms initialed by department heads and others; if not, the information on these slips may be transferred to standard size cards which are more manageable in the file. The cards sometimes go in a separate file and sometimes are incorporated in the serial catalog that supplements the visible index.

While many libraries—small, medium, and large—maintain deci-

NEW SERIAL TITLE

☐ Series ☐ Subseries

Routing **Cleared**

.... Selection Officer ....

.... For recommendation ....

.... **Wanted for the Library** .... **Not wanted for the Library**

Keep .... **sets** .... **Review before binding**

.... **Retain current issues only** .... **Retain this issue only**

Acquire .... **Back numbers** .... **Bound vols. only** .... **Continuation**

.... **By purchase** .... **By exchange or gift**

.... Recommendation review shelf, Ser. Rec. Div.

.... Subject Cataloging decision shelf ....

.... **Sets collected** .... **Sets monograph**

Analyzed .... **In full** .... **In part** { .... **This part** / .... **Not this part** }

Not analyzed ....

.... Descriptive Cataloging decision shelf ....

.... Serials Section, Descr. Cat. Div. ....

.... Slavic Languages Section, Descr. Cat. Div.

.... Cataloging Sect., Ser. Rec. Div.

.... New Serial Titles Section, Ser. Rec. Div.

.... Monthly Checklist of State Publications, E & G Div.

.... East European Accessions List, E & G Div.

.... Monthly List of Russian Accessions

....

.... Exchange and Gift Division ....

.... Order Division ....

.... Copyright Office—for claiming ....

.... Card Division

.... Preliminary Cataloging Section, Descr. Cat. Div.

.... Serials Section, Descr. Cat. Div.

.... Slavic Languages Sect., Descr. Cat. Div.

Custody

.... Serials Div. Sample File .... Slavic Room

.... Periodicals Reading Room .... Orientalia Div.

.... Government Publications RR .... Armed Forces Med. Lib.

.... Law Library .... Dept. Agriculture Lib.

....

SERIAL RECORD DIVISION
LIBRARY OF CONGRESS

(Form 0174—No. 4—9/18/53) U. S. GOVERNMENT PRINTING OFFICE

FIGURE 2. Library of Congress decision slip.

sion files, many of all sizes find that they can operate as well without them. A decision file is one more record to maintain; it does serve some purposes, though most of these are slight and negative. With something to be said on both sides, it is natural to expect that some acquisition departments will continue to have a decision file, while others will manage without them. As a compromise, a library could decide to make decision records only for doubtful cases, not for titles obviously unwanted or for all the sample and odd numbers received.

Files of sample periodicals

Instead of throwing away the sample numbers for titles not to be acquired, acquisition departments often preserve them in a special file arranged alphabetically. The decision slip is generally attached to them or the pertinent information is written on them. The sample periodical file can substitute for a decision file, but sometimes both are maintained: the sample file for possible bibliographical value, since the issues are commonly volume 1, number 1; the decision file as a convenient work record. When the sample periodical file is old and extensive, as is the case at the Library of Congress,[1] it is of real value to the bibliographer.

Order records

It is advisable to keep the records for purchased serials entirely distinct from those for purchased books and pamphlets. In particular, serials and non-serials should not be on the same order sheet, and serial order cards should not go in the regular outstanding order file. It may even be desirable to adopt distinctive order cards for serials, as the Los Angeles Public Library did when it chose white cards for serials and yellow for non-serials. Sometimes the separation of records occurs naturally; for instance, when the orders go to an agent who deals exclusively with serials. It is with foreign orders especially that care must be taken to differentiate between serials and non-serials.

Records are separated partly for accounting and statistical purposes, but still more to demarcate the ordering and receipt of serials as an operation to which specialized staff should be assigned if the work load warrants. It has also been found expedient to employ two different mailing addresses, one for books, the other for serials. The

[1] In 1950 the Library of Congress collection of sample numbers contained about 28,000 items. In 1949 the Harvard College Library presented its accumulation of sample numbers to the Library of Congress. Although the Harvard collection had been in existence for over a hundred years, it seemed wiser to add to the fine file at Washington instead of continuing a separate one that would thereby be of less value.

former may simply be "Acquisition Department," while the latter may be "Serial Section, Acquisition Department," the periodical room, or a department library. The distinctive address for serials is more apt to be passed on to the consignor when serials are ordered separately. Attention to this detail can often save extra handling and expedite the checking process.

Apart from the decision file already mentioned, the principal order records for serials are the serial outstanding order file, possibly supplemented by sheet records; the visible index; and in some libraries a card record of older titles not on the visible index. There may be others, for instance a separate file for annuals, but separate files should

TITLE	Order No	Vendor or agency	No. Copies	Address
Phillips research reports...Elsevier Bk Co, NY	4445Y	Science Subsc. Inc. NY	1	OD
Phillips statistical reports(incl. indexes, binders)	5519Y	Subscriptions Inc NY	2	OD
Phillips statistical reports(Incl. indexes, binders)	5520Y	Subscriptions Inc NY	1	LRS
Physical society. London. Proceedings: Sections A & B	1245X	Brit. Periodicals Ltd	1	OD
Progress of theoretical physics. Tokyo (Irregular)	7890Z	Nippon subcr. agency	1	OD
Public Health (monthly) Soc.Med. Officers of Health, London. Received as gift—ORDER CANCELLED 7/9/49	6678Y	Brit. Periodicals Ltd	1	OD
Public Ledger Daily. Honolulu, TH	4522Y	Subscriptions Inc. NY	1	SD
Quarto: the bibliophiles' journal. New Haven CEASED CANCELLED 9/6/57	9787Z	University Subsc. Co.	1	OD
Que. London CANCELLED 7/28/57	3342X	Que Publ. Ltd	1	OD
Quebec Evening Mail. Literary magazine(wkly)	4775X	Subscriptions Inc. NY	1	OD
Quebec Press SEE Quebec Public Press				
Quebec Press-Times Sunday magazine	1989Y	Canabooks	1	OD
Quebec Public Press	2234X	Public Press Ltd	1	SD
Research reports, Phillips. SEE Phillips research..				
Revista bancária brasileira. Rio de Janero(Airmail)	6282X	Livros Cpe.	1	LRS
Revue d'Alsace(Inst. des Hautes Études Alsaciennes)	7111Y	Import Books Co. NY	1	OD
Rutgers university library. Journal.	1871X	Rutgers Library	3	OD

FIGURE 3. Library of Congress flexoline entries.

be avoided as far as possible unless they are built around a special feature of the library like the corporation reports in Standard and Poor's Corporation Library. In fact, in a library with sufficient visible index trays few additional records are desirable. The Library of Congress, for example, operates with three principal records: a file of orders placed, a visible index with about 160,000 entries, and a supplementary card file of live and dead serials which brings the total number of entries in the serial record to more than 330,000. The Library of Congress also has a special record of some note, namely a flexoline visible reference index to outstanding serial orders which contains approximately 15,000 entries and is a distinct aid to rapid checking. Author, title, order number, agent, number of copies ordered, and the abbreviation for the division in which the current issues will be housed are entered in the index (see Figure 3).

The catalog of older titles is maintained in probably only a small number of libraries. In the Department of Agriculture Library it is called the Alphabetical Serial File; in the Harvard College Library it is known as the S-Card (that is, Serial Card) File; in the Library of Congress it is referred to as the Old Serial Record,[2] and contains—

1. Entries, holdings, location, and treatment of bound and unbound serials not included in the visible index; that is, serials which have ceased publication or of which no issues have been received since 1948
2. Entries for all serials which have been cataloged and classified
3. Holdings of all fully cataloged serials through 1942
4. Additional bibliographical information not on the visible index entries.

The record of older serials is invaluable for reference work, and economical searching is made possible by catalogs of this kind, particu-

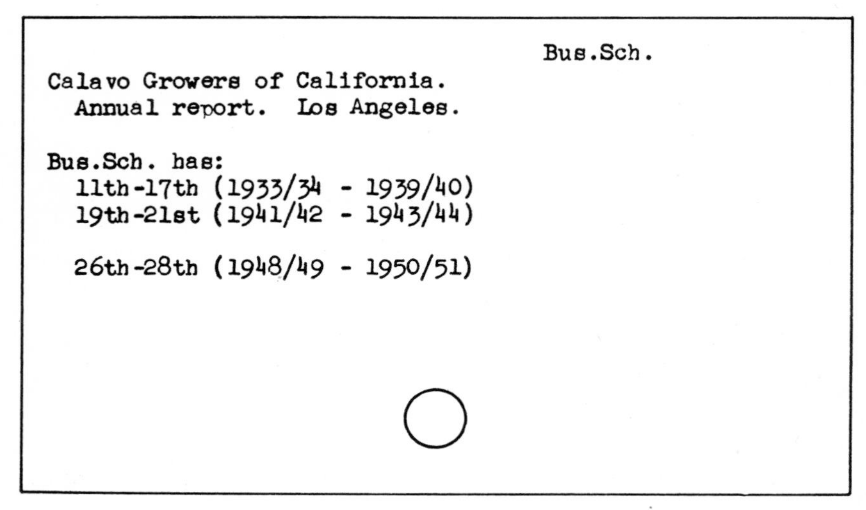

Bus.Sch.

Calavo Growers of California.
Annual report. Los Angeles.

Bus.Sch. has:
11th-17th (1933/34 - 1939/40)
19th-21st (1941/42 - 1943/44)

26th-28th (1948/49 - 1950/51)

FIGURE 4. S-Card from the Harvard College Library.

larly for the serials that come in large lots received by purchase, gift, or transfer. Unfortunately, however, these catalogs are rarely complete, so that titles must also be searched occasionally in the public or official catalog when the work records fail to disclose them. A card from the S-Card File at Harvard is reproduced as Figure 4, and one from the Old Serial Record at the Library of Congress as Figure 5.

Agents

Except when other reasons make it desirable or necessary to deal directly with the publishers, it is best to utilize the services of a good

---

[2] For some years the Library of Congress has been engaged in an editorial project which, among other objectives, aims at the closer correlation of the visible index and the Old Serial Record.

agent.[3] One good reason for operating through an agent is that thereby the paper work is reduced. If hundreds of publishers had to be paid small amounts each year, the advantages that derive in some instances from dealing with them directly might be offset. Paper work in an acquisition department is always heavy; more should not be added if it can be avoided. Usually, though not always, when a publisher allows a discount or a special rate for multiple-year subscriptions, the agents pass the benefits on to libraries.[4]

Service is by far the most important factor to be sought in choosing an agent. Prompt, regular, and reliable service is imperative if serial

SB 379 .C3C3 Calavo growers of California. Annual report.

	3d-6th		1926-1929					4 v.					
	8th-20th		1930/31-1942/43					13 v.					
In progress													

FIGURE 5. Card from the Library of Congress Old Serial Record.

files are to be maintained without gaps. It is not difficult to secure good service in Canada, Great Britain, and the United States,[5] but in many countries good service is rare.

[3] Cf. Jerrold Orne, "A Serials Information Clearing House," *Serial Slants* v.1, April 1951, p.10-17, where a number of cases in which it is better to place subscriptions directly with the publishers are described. The entire article is worthy of careful study by acquisition librarians.

[4] On the relations between libraries and dealers, see Edwin B. Colburn, "Mutual Problems of Serial Agents and Librarians," *Serial Slants* v.1, Oct. 1950, p.20-26; Albert H. Davis, "The Subscription Agency and the Library; Responsibilities and Problems from the Dealer's Viewpoint," *Serial Slants* v.1, Oct. 1950, p.14-19; and Ralph Lessing, "Subscription Problems as Seen by an Agent," *Serial Slants* 4:5-7, 1953.

[5] For a selected list of agents, see *Periodicals for Small and Medium-Sized Libraries* (Chicago: American Library Assn., 1948), p.17-20; for a list of British agents, see David Grenfell, *Periodicals and Serials* (London: Aslib, 1953), p.157-58.

When they purchase books, libraries expect to get standard discount rates as well as proper service. Discount for serials is not standardized. It is forthcoming on popular titles and on some multiple-year subscriptions. Two other types of discount are described by Orne:

Another class of serials information concerns publishers equipped and able to handle orders on a "till forbid" basis, with liberal discounts. Many institutions, like Washington University, subscribe to a considerable number of journals produced by a major source. We receive twenty or more journals published by the University of Chicago Press. We now have all subscriptions to their journals on a "till forbid" basis, and receive an annual bill of 10 percent discount. A comparably large group of publications is placed direct with the McGraw-Hill Publishing Co. They are locally represented and prefer to deal directly with large purchasers, offering considerable financial advantages to obtain your order directly. Here again billing is automatic; the discount is better than any jobber can offer. Some organizations and publishers are not only equipped but eager to take a standing order for all or specific publications, giving excellent service and good discounts. Thus *American Industries,* published in series at prices varying from $1.00 to $2.00, can be had at three for $2.50 on standing order. The American Council on Education in return for a stand-order assures a 20 percent discount on its publications. In some cases a membership is combined with a standing order, as in the case of the Modern Language Association of America. Our standing order for their *Monograph Series* comes at a 30 percent discount when placed direct.

The field of library memberships deserves to be thoroughly reexamined from various points of view. Certain library memberships are very advantageous. Thus the Business Historical Society (Boston, Mass.) has a $10.00 membership fee which brings its *Bulletin* plus the *Harvard Studies in Business History*. By our count the *Studies* alone last year cost at list $14.00. An associate membership in the National Bureau of Economic Research at $5.00 brings three series, the Annual Reports, Occasional Papers, and Technical Papers, as well as a guaranteed one third off on any other publications. A membership in the British School at Athens costs less than $6.00, and yields its *Annual* and a 50 percent discount on back volumes. The *Annual* alone if purchased through an agent costs $10.00. The *Transactions* of the American Philological Association sells for $5.00 through an agent. A membership including the *Transactions* costs $5.00 the first year, but $4.00 each year thereafter and allows special rates on any other publications.[6]

Bids

Service that leads to complete files is the major concern in choosing an agent. It follows, then, that government regulations are a hindrance when they require libraries subject to their control to secure bids before orders can be placed. It has been necessary for the United Nations Library, various federal agencies, and others to win free of this restriction; but there are still many municipal, state, and federal

[6] Orne, *op. cit.,* p.12-13.

libraries that are hampered by the system of bids. The routine involved in the procurement of serials by means of bids is considerable. Practice in the Los Angeles Public Library illustrates this point:

Periodicals are ordered by contract with an agent chosen by bid. All regular periodicals, which are not to be ordered from the publisher in club rates, or for other reasons, are listed, ten copies being made. One copy goes to the Order Department, one is kept in Serials Division, and the remaining eight copies are sent to agents so that they may submit bids.[7]

In this instance there is, first, the labor of compiling the lists; second, the paper work of sending out eight communications; and third, the labor of assembling and comparing the bids, after an appropriate interval to permit replies to be received (during which period follow-up action may be necessary). Such a system becomes almost impossible to follow through if the bids must relate to each item on a list instead of to the list as a whole; for commonly there is no lowest bidder on a particular item, and at times there may be no bid at all on a title since there is no margin of profit for the dealer. The net result of any bidding system is that a library suffers delays because it cannot order new titles promptly through an established agent or with a publisher; the cost of the operation may far outweigh any financial gain from the low bid; and emphasis is placed on discount rather than service. In comparison with the results obtained by alert acquisition librarians the system of bids is penny wise and pound foolish.

The dealer's attitude towards bids is expressed by the following statement:

A certain number of libraries—either due to regulations or by choice—ask for quotations before placing or renewing periodical subscriptions. This practice imposes additional work on libraries and dealers alike, and its merits are open to serious question.

Periodical prices change constantly. For the last ten years there has been a steadily upward trend. Thus to protect himself against losses from possible price changes, a dealer will insert in his bid an "escalator clause" allowing him to make certain additional charges should the publishers raise the subscription rates. This clause is indispensable; for if a firm bid is requested, the bidder must raise his prices sufficiently to insure against losses which he cannot pass on to the subscriber. And such higher bids, of course, defeat the purpose of the entire procedure and are costly to the library.

Concluding, therefore, that the "escalator clause" is beneficial to both parties, the library as well as the bidder, we encounter still another pitfall: the constantly rising prices of periodical subscriptions actually serve to penalize the best-informed bidder. Since he knows the latest (and hence the highest) prices, he will find himself *ipso facto* the highest bidder and will not be awarded the order. On the other hand, the most ignorant bidder may

---

[7] Los Angeles Public Library, Serials Division, *Workbook of Serials Procedure* (Los Angeles, 1932), p.10.

receive the order simply because his outdated prices are lower. Needless to say, this low bidder must eventually make a greater number of additional charges when he finds out the actual subscription rates than his better-informed competitor. . .

We have, therefore, come to the conclusion that in evaluating bids two points must be constantly borne in mind:

1) Asking for firm bids, without an "escalator clause," forces bidders to increase the prices quoted.
2) The lowest bidder on a quotation may well prove to be the one whose prices are most obsolete, and the most expensive one after all additional charges are in.[8]

Some serials are simply not obtainable on any system of bids. The publications of the H. W. Wilson Company, for example, which are sold to libraries on a service basis,[9] must be obtained directly from the publisher. And for some items personal or institutional membership is required.[10]

The system of bids is less objectionable when the successful bidder keeps the subscriptions indefinitely. It is completely unacceptable when the subscription list must be submitted for new bids every year, or whenever there is the risk that a title may be transferred back and forth from one agent to another, so jeopardizing both adequacy and continuity of service.

Few libraries have unlimited funds for the purchase of serials. The guarantee that funds will be husbanded and expended wisely lies not in a system of bids, but in the natural controls that come with good library administration: the desire and determination of librarians to make their dollars go further so they can give their community as much and as fine service as possible.

Exchanges

When a library has significant publications of its own to offer, or when it can readily draw on other publications (for example, government documents or publications of university presses), it is in a strategic position to acquire many worth-while serials and monographs on an exchange basis. In fact, the dollar situation throughout the world is

---

[8] *Stechert-Hafner Book News* 7:20, 1952.

[9] This is not the place to discuss the merits of the service-basis charge for serials. The American Library Association and the Association of Research Libraries have debated the matter repeatedly. The Harvard Business School, among others, has investigated and justified the service charge. For a detailed study of the problem see John L. Lawler, *The H. W. Wilson Company; Half a Century of Bibliographic Publishing* (Minneapolis: Univ. of Minnesota Pr., [1950]), p.115-35.

[10] When personal membership in a society is required, it is necessary to figure some way of reimbursing a staff member or, in an academic community, a faculty member who joins a society in the interests of procuring its publications for the library. On the question of memberships see Orne, *op. cit.*, p.12-14.

such that some items may be procured more easily by exchange than by purchase.

Both the Library of Congress and the Department of Agriculture Library have noteworthy exchange programs. In 1950 the Department of Agriculture Library reported that 90 per cent of its serials received during the year were acquired by exchange.[11]

The most fruitful sources of exchanges are colleges and universities, government bodies, learned societies, libraries, and other societies and non-profit-making institutions. Since its inception in 1947, the *Unesco Bulletin for Libraries* has been the informational medium for exchange possibilities. It should be supplemented by the more systematic *Handbook on the International Exchange of Publications* published by Unesco in 1950.

Periodicals and monograph series are valuable items to be able to offer on exchange. Once the exchange of a periodical has been established the record work in maintaining it is comparatively slight. For example, for foreign exchange the Harvard College Library has some 75 subscriptions to the *Quarterly Journal of Economics.* Once a year a bill is rendered and paid for these multiple subscriptions. In the meantime the journal itself goes to the exchange outlets without further complication, and the 75 or so publications which the Harvard College Library receives in return, year after year, call for no individual invoices or annual payment of bills.

There are two levels at which an exchange program needs to operate. On the policy level an officer of the library must be responsible for determining and initiating desirable action, as well as for approving or disapproving exchange requests that come to the library. Thereafter the exchanges should function in a routine way, being referred to the officer only when a change occurs or when he asks for a periodic checkup.

Exchange correspondence should be held together as a unit instead of being interfiled with other acquisition correspondence. It should be arranged by country, then by locality, and should be supplemented by a card file similarly arranged. In this card file is kept a digest record of the number of items received from and dispatched to each institution. Names of serials should be given, whereas monographs are commonly merely tallied. If the exchange is on a priced basis it is necessary to record the price of each shipment received or sent. Since payments for the various exchanges are usually made through the ordinary acquisition routines, the exchange assistant must work closely with the order librarian.

---

[11] Department of Agriculture Library, *Report, 1950* (Washington, 1950), p.5.

Periodicals, monograph series, and other serials received on exchange should not be recorded in detail by the exchange assistant. That would constitute needless duplication of effort. Instead, once the exchange has been set up, the items are checked on the visible index in the regular way, the only qualification being that the visible index entry specifies that the item is received on exchange, or signifies this by entering exchange items on cards of a distinctive color. Colored cards enable the whole exchange program to be reviewed at will and facilitate the count of titles received on exchange.[12]

The Smithsonian Institution does not play a particularly active role in the general exchange of serials unless these are part of bulk shipments,[13] but the United States Book Exchange emphasizes serial exchanges. Its director, Alice Ball, has said:

> Most important of the unique characteristics of USBE as an exchange organization is the fact that member libraries can *order periodicals directly*, without waiting for their appearance on an exchange list. The direct-order and back-order system of USBE is made possible by the agency's pooling operation. Because of the number of periodicals in stock and in the daily receipts of USBE, this service offers one of the surest, as well as one of the most inexpensive, ways for a library to locate back issues of serials.[14]

Domestic exchange, unlike foreign, is largely preoccupied with duplicate issues and volumes. The problems in the exchange of duplicate serials are the cost of compiling lists of offerings and the labor of checking and searching the lists received. The exchange of duplicates can be profitable when bound volumes or good runs are involved, but scrappy holdings are expensive to list, check, search, and add to a collection.

A number of clearing houses have been organized to promote and facilitate the exchange of serials between libraries. The outstanding success in this field belongs to the Medical Library Association ex-

---

[12] The literature on exchanges is extensive, as can be seen from the entries in *Library Literature* under the caption "Exchange of books, periodicals, etc." For a general study, with special reference to Latin America see Laurence J. Kipp, *The International Exchange of Publications: a Report of Programs within the United States Government for Exchange with Latin America, Based upon a Survey Made for the Interdepartmental Committee on Scientific and Cultural Cooperation, under Direction of the Library of Congress* (Wakefield, Mass., 1950). Among the more significant general articles on serial exchanges are: Alfred H. Lane, "Exchange Materials Used in College and University Libraries," *College and Research Libraries* 8:44-49, 1947; and Ivander MacIver, "The Exchange of Publications as a Medium for the Development of the Book Collection," *Library Quarterly* 8:491-502, 1938.

[13] For an account of its program see "Smithsonian International Exchange Service," *Unesco Bulletin for Libraries* 3:166, 168, 1949.

[14] Alice D. Ball, "Exchange Supermarket," *Library Journal* 78:2059, 1953. See also her "Serials Acquisition through the U. S. Book Exchange," *Serial Slants* v.2, July 1951, p.7-19; and "Costs of Serial Acquisition through USBE," *Serial Slants* v.2, April 1952, p.11-15.

change. Both the American Association of Law Libraries and the Association of College and Reference Libraries have sponsored duplicate exchange unions, and for many years the H. W. Wilson Company has maintained a Periodicals Clearing House.[15]

There are two reasons for maintaining domestic exchanges of duplicate serials. First, the system usually operates on a nominal piece-by-piece basis. Second, it is a transaction that would cost libraries dearly if all duplicates were turned over to dealers and had to be purchased from them at an enhanced price. Because of the expense of conducting an exchange program, however, it is generally better to confine direct domestic exchanges to bound volumes and fairly good runs, except when an organization such as the Medical Library Association is ready to provide the financial backing for more extensive work.[16]

Gifts

The routines for handling gifts have so much in common with exchanges that the two functions are commonly the responsibility of a single individual or unit. When items are being considered for acquisition, a decision must be made as to their means of procurement. Items for purchase are turned over to the order section; but items that may be sought by gift or exchange are generally referred to the gift and exchange assistant or unit.

John Shaw Billings, first director of the New York Public Library, believed that the library should grow as much by gift as by purchase. Consequently an active gift section has always been a feature of that library, and it is not surprising to find that approximately 50 per cent of its current periodicals are received from the publishers as gifts. Few libraries can approach that record; nevertheless, each acquisition department should weigh the possibilities of a gift subscription before setting out to purchase an item.

In most libraries government documents at all levels—federal,

---

[15] On the Medical Library Association exchange see "The Exchange and the Policies Underlying Its Administration," *Medical Library Association Bulletin* 33:357-59, 1945, and Mildred V. Naylor, "Exchange," *Medical Library Association Bulletin* 34:167-75, 1946. On its British counterpart, see F. N. L. Poynter, "A Duplicate Exchange Service for Medical Libraries," *Library Association Record* 52:41-43, 1950. On the American Association of Law Libraries exchange union see the article by Arie Poldervaart, *Law Library Journal* 37:97-98, 1944. On the Association of College and Reference Libraries exchange union see Donald E. Thompson, "Duplicate Exchange Union," *College and Research Libraries* 6:158-60, 1945. On the H. W. Wilson Periodicals Clearing House see Lawler, *op. cit.*, p.78-80.

[16] For a study of the cost of an exchange program see Alfred H. Lane, "The Economics of Exchange," *Serial Slants* 3:19-22, 1952.

state, and local—should to a large extent be requested as gifts. Since the Second World War the percentage of government documents in all countries which must be purchased has increased sharply, yet there is still a large quantity of free material that may be obtained directly from the issuing body, through a congressman, or otherwise.

Some libraries are designated as depositories to receive federal and other documents in part or in full. In the case of United Nations documents many of the depository sets are exchanges rather than gifts. One notable advantage inherent in blanket schemes of this kind is that in the acquisition department the record work for these documents is sharply reduced or, on occasion, eliminated.

In smaller institutions, notably in small public libraries, there may be an administrative problem in connection with periodicals published and supplied gratis by sects, propaganda agencies, and pressure groups. These items may bulk too large in the periodical collection and do more harm than good to the library. It may therefore be better to decline them, on the score that a public library must be as impartial as possible in religious and political affairs. A famous French author said that a word once written has a tendency to defend itself; unfortunately gifts also have a tendency to defend themselves, and are accepted into a collection where they would certainly not have been chosen had they gone through the normal process of serial selection.[17]

As with exchanges, gift correspondence and records should be kept separate, and gifts may to advantage be recorded in the visible index on cards of a distinctive color.

The serials that some institutions and individuals constantly present to libraries, sometimes in small quantities and sometimes in large lots, usually need careful screening. The same is true of transfers from another agency. When mixed collections—partly non-serials, partly serials—are received by gift, transfer, or otherwise, the serials should be segregated and dealt with independently. In a preliminary sorting many items can be rejected forthwith: either they are obviously unwanted duplicates or they have little or no value to the library.[18] Often in the preliminary sorting it is well to have a copy of the *Union List of Serials* at hand so that still other items can be rejected in a simple, economical way. The items that survive this screening must be checked against the official records, when many more will prove to be duplicates. Titles new to the library and scrappy additions

---

[17] Cf. L. Dimmitt, "Complimentary Publications," *Wilson Library Bulletin* 14:240, 1939.

[18] Formerly libraries accepted broken sets and scrappy additions more uncritically than now. Higher operating costs have forced librarians to review this policy, for incomplete and broken files are disproportionately expensive to process, maintain, and service.

to sets should then be passed on by a responsible officer, who should determine whether they are worth incorporating into the collections or whether they should be discarded.

Gap records

Whenever Harry Miller Lydenberg was complimented because the New York Public Library had a much-needed but scarce item, he was inclined to temper his satisfaction by recalling items that the library lacked. More than once he commented that it is more important for the librarian to know what his library lacks than what it has. Such is the philosophy, the natural reaction, of the acquisitive librarian; and those concerned with serials should be acquisitive librarians par excellence. In line with this philosophy, a few libraries have attempted to compile lists of their serial gaps. Not only is this a major undertaking, but it may be something of a losing battle too—for one thing, a gap record constitutes one more place to be checked when gaps are filled—but Marjorie Plant of the British Library of Political and Economic Science has spoken with enthusiasm of the gap record of her library:

> In the course of cataloging a loose-leaf register of gaps is compiled. From time to time sections of this list of wanted parts are stenciled and issued to likely donors, newsagents, and second-hand booksellers, sometimes with the happy result that the words "with gaps" can be deleted from the catalog and the entry in the register of gaps withdrawn.[19]

Compilation of special lists of gaps can be undertaken whenever time and staff are available. Periodic drives of this kind are effective means of keeping serial files reasonably intact. The lists are usually sent out to the libraries with which exchange relations have been established, and may in fact accompany a list of duplicates offered on exchange.

Renewals

Once a library is on the mailing list for a gift or an exchange serial the item can be expected to come for an indefinite time without

---

[19] Marjorie Plant, "Periodicals Procedure in a University Library," *College and Research Libraries* 3:63, 1941. The fact that this library can carry out the program Miss Plant describes demonstrates one of the advantages the special library has—or ought to have—over the general library. There is a spirit of enterprise about the special library that leads to undertakings like this. An example of general library use of the method is furnished by the Enoch Pratt Free Library, which reported conspicuous success in filling gaps in its holdings of United States documents. Mimeographed copies of its list were sent to 231 state, university, and other libraries, with the result that thousands of items were supplied, practically all as gifts. (See its *The Reorganization of a Large Public Library* (Baltimore, 1937), p.19.

requiring any further communication, but periodicals which are acquired by subscription must generally be renewed at stated intervals unless dealers or publishers are ready to accept orders on a till-forbid basis. Some serials, such as yearbooks, are treated by dealers as standing orders and are billed as each issue is supplied.

Subscriptions are usually paid in advance. When a subscription is to be renewed, the individual notice from a society or publisher, or the list as supplied by a dealer, must be checked against the visible index to see that the renewal is in order, the number of copies is correct, and that all issues were supplied on the previous payment. If the check of a dealer's list is to be thorough, it should be made with his previous list in hand. Otherwise there may be no opportunity to catch up on titles omitted on the new list or to make an effective comparison of prices.

Billing information

Invoices for serial subscriptions must be checked against the visible index entries before renewals are in order. In the course of this check it is a relatively simple matter to record the amount of the subscription on the visible index card.[20] Most libraries do this as a matter of course. Why? There is little justification in libraries that secure bids, because fluctuations in the price of any one title are not a determining factor in awarding a contract that covers a whole list; and there is small reason for recording billing information for titles ordered through dealers who specialize in serials, as long as the library retains its invoices indefinitely. On the rare occasions when anyone wants to trace the cost of a periodical received through a firm like Faxon or Moore-Cottrell, it is not too much to ask him to go through the file of invoices for that firm. Whenever possible, therefore, billing information on serials should be restricted to the bills and vouchers.

In unsettled periods the tabulated record of payments on the visible index card may have more value than in normal times. It may serve, for example, to point up inflationary trends such as those disclosed by Charles H. Brown.[21] It may be useful for items which come direct from the publishers, and in some cases it may be desirable to

[20] In older libraries the record of payments may not be on the visible index but in a separate file arranged by dealers' names. Maintenance of a separate file is difficult indeed to justify. Every entry made in it represents an additional step, whereas the excuse for entering payments in the visible index is that when invoices are checked against it little extra time and labor are involved in adding the price.

[21] See, for example, his "Serial Costs in Relation to Other Library Expenditures and to Inflation," *Serial Slants* v.2, July 1951, p.20-24. The *Minutes* of the Association of Research Libraries have a number of references to postwar inflationary costs of serials.

show that the subscription has been paid, though a simple symbol on the checking record could serve that purpose. Is any of these a sufficient ground for engaging in the mass operation of duplicating information about subscriptions? Quite evidently the record is thought to have real value in libraries which have turned to punched cards for their serials.

The Yale Medical Library has cast doubt not only on the value of recording billing information but on the routine of renewals generally. It made arrangements with both Faxon and Stechert-Hafner, effective January, 1955, whereby non-itemized bills are submitted for the Yale medical subscriptions they carry. Both firms could just as easily supply itemized bills, but the Yale Medical Library feels that the mere presence of such bills invites the checking and recording it wishes to avoid. Most libraries, however, would probably prefer to receive an itemized bill for their order files. Thereafter, by steeling themselves, they could free the staff from an annual burden, as the Yale Medical Library has done. They would rely on the visible index, first to lead to the bills if and when necessary, and second to provide a sound follow-up program so that bills could be paid without careful checking.

Disposal of duplicates

The amount of time and space which a library can devote to the disposal of duplicates will in large measure determine its policy. The preparation of lists of duplicates for exchange purposes is a time-consuming process, for the listing of serials involves much detail and the detailed statements need to be accurate. Sufficient duplicates must be allowed to accumulate before a list is made and the items must be held while the lists are circulating, tying up valuable work space for considerable periods.

Duplicates and other unwanted serials fall into four main classes for disposal:

1. Many items should be held in the periodical room or elsewhere as possible replacements for missing or mutilated copies or as extra copies for circulation or assigned reading.[22] Most of these duplicates can be disposed of once the current volume has been bound.
2. Much material of slight consequence should immediately be classed as

[22] Some duplicates are, of course, worth adding to the regular collection, especially when they come in good runs. The Harvard College Library has attempted to build up extra sets of some titles (the *Atlantic Monthly,* for example) with copies in their original wrappers. At the Enoch Pratt Free Library "since 1926 duplicate unbound files of many important magazines used for reference work, sometimes with triplicate or more copies, have been built up (largely by gifts). These are carefully arranged for the convenience of the many readers who request them for home reference use, leaving the bound files intact for reference use in the library building."—*The Reorganization of a Large Public Library,* 1937, p.15.

waste paper and disposed of. Government documents often fall into this class, especially federal documents that are received on deposit and may not be sold. Other items are college catalogs, mimeographed publications, newspapers, and unsolicited gifts.

3. Certain items that the *Union List of Serials* indicates may be of value to another library should be offered to that library. Likewise, items in specified subject fields may by agreement be regularly forwarded to special libraries in the area: legal serials, whether duplicate or not, might go to a law library; medical publications to a medical library; and so on.
4. Selected items of some importance or extent may be segregated and listed for possible exchange.

Other material may be offered to the United States Book Exchange, one of the clearing houses, or a dealer who specializes in serials. Items that none of these will take should therefore be classified as waste paper.

In private institutions, such as college and university libraries, proceeds from the sale of duplicates and waste paper may generally be added to the book funds. In public institutions the money must as a rule be paid into the municipal, state, or federal treasury. Accordingly public institutions have good reason to promote an exchange of their duplicates, since publications received in return benefit the library directly, whereas funds paid into the treasury generally result in little if any gain to the library.

Statistics

The budget and the accounting system should be set up, if at all possible, in such a way that they will provide controls over serial costs for (1) current publications, (2) sets, and (3) binding. Commonly the head librarian takes special interest in the figures for these three classes of expense and wants to see periodic reports on them. In particular he needs to watch closely the amount spent for serial sets, so that the research collection may be developed advantageously year by year, and so that funds may be on hand at the proper time.

The non-financial statistics may originate in various parts of the library. While this generalization holds for the United Nations Library, as for other institutions, it was decided in that library to rationalize the reports by incorporating in the general circulation statistics the figures for items routed to readers directly from the visible index. The figures for serial pieces acquired by the Reference Section (chiefly United Nations and Specialized Agency documents) are therefore incorporated in the acquisition statistics. By such a device the story of acquisition and circulation is simply told, whereas otherwise it would have to be pieced together from several sources.

The most useful figures for control are those that take the form of an annual summary of serials by country, frequency, and type, as well as by gift, purchase, and exchange. The annual report of the New York Public Library featured such a table for many years. Much time is required to compile statistics of this kind, but the result is a record that is of first importance in developing an acquisition program. The United Nations *List of Periodicals and Newspapers Currently Received* is of still greater value, for reference and circulation purposes as well as for acquisition. It is this type of control record that may one day become fairly common through the application of punched card techniques to the records for serial publications. At present comparatively few libraries attempt any such control. Instead they rely on the annual count of pieces added to their collections. This count serves as a rough index of the work load at the visible index, as the following quotation from the annual report of the Library of Congress shows:

> Expectations aroused last year by the reorganization of procedures for handling this type of material have been fully justified. It was estimated that the reorganized Serial Record Section of the Order Division would be able to process 1,500,000 serial issues during fiscal year 1950 as compared with approximately 1,000,000 issues processed in fiscal 1949. The total for the year just ended was actually 1,599,432.[23]

The real value of a tally of pieces added is a moot question. A "piece" may be a bound volume, a single issue received either singly or in multiple copies, or even a title page and index. The same volume that counts as only one when it comes to the library bound might count as twelve or more pieces if it comes unbound; accordingly the count of pieces is far from being a precise index of work performance. It always seems a sad waste of effort when an assistant sets about the task of counting the number of pieces in a large unbound set, the sole aim of the operation being to add to the count of pieces received. Since the count by pieces is at best only a rough yardstick, the number of pieces in any large lot should merely be estimated rapidly. Unless a librarian feels that the count by pieces serves some useful purpose in his institution, he should consider dropping it.

---

[23] *Annual Report* of the Librarian of Congress, 1950 (Washington, 1951), p.106.

CHAPTER 5

The Theory and Practice of Serial Checking

THE ORGANIZED LIBRARY cannot do without a classification system for its books; it should choose the system most suited to its needs and develop appropriate policies for local application. It is much the same with a checking system for the serials it receives. There must be a checking system, and each library needs to determine the policies and practices that will suit it best.

On the surface it may seem superfluous to engage in a mass checking operation when the majority of serial titles reach libraries regularly without complication. Suppose, for example, a library discovers that its copy of the *Atlantic Monthly* has come like clockwork ever since the first issue appeared in 1857; should it go to the trouble of recording the successive issues month after month, year after year? Can it look back on a century of superfluous routine? Should it face another century of wasted, though trivial, effort? Reflection on cases like this might lead to a system of checking that applied only to delinquent titles; and a title would be presumed to be innocent until it was proved guilty.

This approach is unacceptable to libraries, especially to research libraries which preserve their serials more or less permanently. Experience and expedience point to the general need for detailed checking records. Nevertheless there is some practical value in debating the point. A library ought to know what ends its checking records serve and what titles can safely bypass the established routines, for in specific instances it is permissible to dispense with the checking operation for certain titles or certain classes of material, particularly newspapers and other items that are not preserved and mimeographed publications such as press releases. There are possibilities here even in research libraries where the completeness and preservation of files are of great importance.

The following are some cases for study. In considering them, due allowance should be made for the fact that both reader demand and alertness on the part of the public service staff may provide a measure of follow-up in instances of non-receipt.

A library receives the *New York Times* daily. It also subscribes to the microfilm edition. Is there any reason then for checking in the expendable daily issues?

Each day, immediately on receipt, a local newspaper is put out for public use. Should the paper be checked in first, at the risk of delaying its availability to readers? If it were checked in, special handling might be necessary to get it to its destination promptly, thereby increasing the cost of the operation.

Libraries are frequently on the mailing list to receive marginal material (propaganda, press releases, etc.). Rightly or wrongly some libraries decide to add such titles to their permanent collections. Should these libraries increase the cost of processing marginal material by checking it in regularly? Note, in this connection, that many items in this category lack serial control elements by which the completeness of a set can be determined, so that the checking may amount to a mere listing of issues in the library.

Should a library check in a popular title such as the *New Yorker* when it acquires and sets aside a second copy for binding?

Should a library check in the expendable issues of journals acquired on either the University Microfilms or the microcard plan whereby current issues are not bound and preserved after a volume has been completed because a microreproduction is eventually substituted for them?

Do library tools, like the *Publishers' Weekly* and the cumulative H. W. Wilson publications, need to be posted? The staff would quickly be aware of their non-arrival, especially when multiple subscriptions come in one shipment. In the case of cumulative publications, why post issues that will soon be superseded?

When there is little if any difficulty in securing a complete file for binding, should libraries post their own serial publications or those of the institution to which they may be attached?

Obviously there are individual items and classes of material whose titles can merely be listed in the visible index but which do not have to be posted each time the issues are received. New York Public Library practice for these titles is to mark the records with the instruction "Stamp and shoot"; that is, once the instruction has been noted, the piece is stamped and forwarded to its destination without further ceremony. In 1951/52 the Department of Agriculture Library eliminated the recording of issues of periodicals wanted for circulation only.

It is expedient, however, to post the great majority of items, especially those that are to be preserved. A basic reason for the maintenance of detailed checking records is summed up by the word "control." The Library of Congress says: "The control of acquisitions in serial form has been one of the principal problems of the Library of Congress and, indeed, of all large research libraries, during the past 10 years."[1] Serials by their very nature lend themselves to control measures. Although there are types, such as press releases, that have no fixed periodicity or seriality whereby the completeness of a file may be determined, in general the integration of a serial publication received seriatim can be controlled by checking each issue in by volume, number, etc. By means of its checking records, then, a library can see almost at a glance whether its files are complete or whether follow-up action should be taken. If the checking records were dispensed with altogether, it would be much more troublesome to reconstruct the story from the pieces themselves whenever this became necessary, for some of them might be in circulation, at the bindery, or missing.

Pressure of reference demands may be another major reason why detailed checking records must be kept. Each working day in the Library of Congress, for instance, the staff answers an average of 150 telephone inquiries about the receipt of material or about the library's holdings of a given title; and the corresponding figure for the Department of Agriculture Library is approximately a hundred. This amount of reference use is heavy; it is not typical.

In so far as an item lacks convenient notation for checking purposes (as is clearly the case with unnumbered monograph series), it constitutes a poor serial from the point of view of control. It may be recorded on the checking records, but only to the extent of providing limited information.[2] For example, it may specify whether the cataloger is to call for series cards or not.

Other reasons for setting up a detailed checking system relate to the multiple copies that may be received either by design or by accident. It sometimes happens that two or more copies come from different sources; they may be destined for two different parts of the library. With a standard checking system, copy one can be checked off and sent to its destination without let or hindrance. When copy two comes, it also follows its appointed course; because the records show clearly what should happen to it it is neither missent nor discarded as a duplicate. Likewise, when unneeded duplicates are received, they may safely be discarded on the evidence of the records, and finally, checking

---

[1] *Annual Report* of the Librarian of Congress, 1951 (Washington, 1952), p.80. Elsewhere in the same report (p.16) the following comment is made: "Serial publications (*i.e.,* periodicals and other repetitive publications) present a special problem because they are by far the most numerous publications the Library receives, and they are also the type of publication most used in defense-related research."

[2] Some libraries go to the trouble of recording by author and title the items in unnumbered series. The visible index record so compiled is a mere accessions list, and may become cumbersome because it is not as a rule arranged systematically. The record has no validity as a control unless it can be checked periodically against a printed list of contents for the series.

records represent the most businesslike way of verifying serial bills for payment. If the serial checking records did not exist, some other device would have to be employed to tell how an issue is to be treated once it arrives in the library: to whom it is to be routed; what its current location or call number is; whether it is to be analyzed; whether superseded issues are to be discarded; and a whole series of other operational details.

Centralization of serial checking

In each library system it must be determined whether economy and efficiency result from centralizing or scattering the checking records, or in some cases from duplicating them. In public libraries there is room for much latitude, since branch subscriptions are usually expendable duplicates. It may be better for multiple subscriptions to come to the main library from which the order originates. There they can be checked off and prepared for use as simply and economically as multiple copies of books. On the other hand, time and routine can be saved when newspapers and other expendable items go directly to the branches. As a rule the branches of a public library—certainly the smaller ones—do not require checking records. When necessary they can telephone to the main library for information about their subscriptions, and their serial files are usually small enough so that branch records are not essential. Whenever circumstances warrant, however, the records may be decentralized or duplicated; some public libraries prefer to have the checking records in the branch which has the publications. Note that decentralization of serial receipts may call for processing routines in the branch library: checking, stamping, covering, adding book pockets, etc.

At Enoch Pratt Free Library magazines for the branches are checked off centrally, marked with the branch number,[3] and sent to the Stations Department in time to go out by the morning delivery. A card check list is kept at each branch to register the issues of all titles received, as well as to record other data, such as price. After a periodical has been posted in the branch check list, the branch stamp is put on the cover, title page, and first page of text. When an imperfect copy is received it is returned to the Central Library, which arranges for a replacement.

In the Reference Department of the New York Public Library it

[3] When a public library has more than a few branches, it may be more convenient and accurate to use a number as the branch symbol. While the number is not as meaningful as an abbreviation based on the branch name, it takes up less space as a checking symbol, particularly when there are two or more branches whose names begin with the same initial.

was decided in 1931 that duplicate records should be installed in the Periodicals Division because of pressure of demand there and the varying intervals of time that elapsed between recording in the Acquisition Division and receipt in the Periodicals Division. The New York Public Library indexes many of its current periodicals after they have been posted on the visible index. The indexing process can delay for some days, even for a week or more, the transmission of an item to the Periodicals Division. When an investigation of the situation disclosed the desirability of checking periodicals in the Periodicals Division as well as in the Acquisition Division, a visible index was somewhat reluctantly installed in the Periodicals Division, despite the cost. Some years later a duplicate visible index was installed in the Economics Division for government serials.

Some university libraries centralize all their processing functions, but there is a much better argument for the decentralization of checking records in a university library system than there is in a public library. Multiple copies are not as common; files are intended for preservation, as a rule; and a large quantity of gift and exchange material comes directly to a departmental library. Moreover, the processing of current numbers tends to be simpler, because comparatively few university libraries use cellophane covers or require book cards for their current periodicals, since current numbers generally are not permitted to circulate enough to require such public library apparatus. The most compelling reason for decentralization, though, is that the department libraries are thereby left free to adopt progressive special library methods.

Form of entry

Just as libraries started out with the international-size card for their checking records, once they turned to cards for checking purposes, so too they tended naturally to make the entries on these cards in standard cataloging form. There is a certain advantage in utilizing the catalog entry, for it is common to the work of practically all parts of a library. One can go from the card catalog to the visible index and vice versa without complication when the headings agree. For these obvious reasons the vast majority of checking systems in use in libraries—or at any rate in general libraries—are based on the catalog entry.

From the point of view of the checker, however, there are three significant disadvantages in the use of catalog entries on the visible index.

1. Visible index cards must be typed before the serials can be cataloged. Temporary records involve extra expense and additional work for a

staff that usually has all too much to do,[4] so much so that the checkers are commonly hard pressed if they find the requisite time for follow-up work on the scale on which it ought to be done. The temporary records may have to be changed when the catalog entry comes through eventually. At the Library of Congress it is estimated that "such adjustments . . . do not occur in more than about ten per cent of the entries set up."[5]

2. Even though the entries are the same at the beginning, it does not take long for differences to creep in. Changes of heading or title occur faster than most serial catalogers can keep up with them; and at times the catalogers purposely wait before changing an entry to see if the new title is really stable. Yet the visible index should be maintained under the latest form of entry. The tempo of work at the visible index is such that changes must be made immediately, not months or years later when the catalog may eventually be changed.
3. The catalog entry is frequently too technical for efficient and rapid checking. The checkers are generally clerical assistants, not library school graduates versed in the intricacies of the catalog code; and their language equipment may not be of the best. Supervisors may fret over wasted time when they see their assistants fumbling for a technical heading, particularly one in a foreign language; and on rare occasions they themselves may have trouble in locating a heading.

Take the case of a checker who does not know German, yet in the normal course of a day's work must check in a periodical whose title, as the piece in hand clearly shows, is *Berichte der Deutschen chemischen Gesellschaft.* When the entry is under the corporate name, the checker may look under "Berichte," "Deutschen," "Deutscher," or "Deutsches" before he finds the listing under "Deutsche." To the trained librarian the form "Deutsche chemische Gesellschaft. Berichte" is perfectly clear and obvious, though a corporate name in a less-known language might present difficulties. But to the checker the corporate name in any language may be far from clear, and the presence of technical entries in the visible index may repeatedly interrupt the steady progress of his work as he goes through the alphabet or his part of the alphabet. Moreover, these technical entries undoubtedly nullify some of the advantages of the preliminary arrangement of serials

[4] The visible index at the Library of Congress is by far the largest installation in any American library. The situation in that library is therefore not typical. Nevertheless, the following statement, when prorated, would strike a sympathetic chord in many another library: "About two and a half million pieces come in each year, and our Serial Record Section is staffed to handle about a million less than that."—*Annual Report* of the Librarian of Congress, 1951 (Washington, 1952), p.16. In these circumstances, the workload for the checking staffs is clearly heavy enough that nothing should be added to it which can be avoided, and use of the catalog entry does add a complication.

[5] Paul L. Berry, "Library of Congress Serial Record Techniques," *Serial Slants* 3:15, 1952. Since the Library of Congress receives nearly 15,000 new serial titles a year, the adjustments affect roughly 1500 entries annually or about six a working day.

undertaken to prepare them for checking. For instance, when each checker's responsibility is for part of the alphabet only, items may have to be passed from one to another, and there may be interruptions to the work of other staff members as colleagues are called on to determine the correct heading.

Accordingly some libraries—particularly special libraries, which are more sensitive to direct methods than general libraries often are—deviate from the catalog entry whenever a more convenient or natural form will help the checkers at the visible index. Practice in the Harvard College Library illustrates this device. There the form of entry for the visible index is adapted to the wording on the piece itself. Thus a typical entry reads "Bulletin of the New York Public Library," simply because that is the way the title reads on the pieces the checkers handle. But the *Bulletin* of the Association of Former Russian Naval Officers in America, Inc., is listed under the corporate name, not the title, because on the pieces themselves the name comes first, followed by the title. Accordingly, the checker no longer has to struggle with grammatical constructions in foreign languages, but quite readily finds the entry under forms like "Berichte der Deutschen chemischen Gesellschaft." The Harvard College Library makes two exceptions to this general practice. Federal documents are for the sake of convenience listed under "U. S." followed by their title; and annual (but not monthly or quarterly) reports go under the word "Report." The catalog entry is on the back of the visible index card when there is a

STANDARD & POOR'S CORPORATION — MONTHLY

YEAR	JAN	FEB	MAR.	APR	MAY	JUNE	JUL.	AUG.	SEPT	OCT.	NOV.	DEC.
1951												
1952												
1953	3/11	4/2	4/28	5/1	7/3	8/3	9/2	10/2	10/29	12/3		
1954												
1955												
1956												
1957												
1958												
1959												
1960												
1961												
1962												
1963												
1964												
1965												
1966												

PUBLISHER: U.S. Census Bureau
ADDRESS: Washington, D. C.
PRICE: EXPIRES:
SOURCE: Stafford (Washington Expediter)
BIND: Catalog at end of year 666.1 U
FILE: CONTAINERS - Glass - Facts for Industry
ROUTING: Research
Collins

FORM 763

NO. OF COPIES: 1 | TITLE: GLASS CONTAINERS - Facts for Industry M77C | FREQUENCY Mo | T. P. & INDEX.

FIGURE 6. Use of title entry instead of corporate name in Standard and Poor's Corporation Library.

difference between the catalog entry and the one used, and correspondingly the S-cards (see page 52) give variant visible index entries, making it possible to pass from one type of record to the other with little inconvenience.

Note that under this system the serial assistants need not concern themselves with punctuation, capitalization, or other details that may weigh heavily with the cataloger. The whole approach to the entry is a practical one: here is a heading in a work record which should be made as naturally, clearly, and concisely as possible for efficient and

Standard & Poor's Corp. WEEKLY

YEAR	JAN.	FEB.	MAR.	APR.	MAY	JUNE	JULY	AUG.	SEPT.	OCT.	NOV.	DEC.
1951												
1952												
1953	[illegible]	7/20	1/16	4/16	31/12	6/18	4/17	1/14	5/17	3/10	7/20	
	10/26	14/2	7/23	11/24		13/29	11/27	8/20	12/28	10/22	14/1	
	17/30	21/5	14/27	18/1	9/25	20/6	18/31	15/25	14/5	17/28	21/9	
	24/5	28/16	21/1	25/8	16/29	27/10	25/10	22/8	20/13	24/6		
	31/16		28/13		23/4			29/14		31/16		
					30/15							
1954												

PUBLISHER: Association of American Railroads
ADDRESS: 330 Transportation Bldg. Washington 6, D. C.
PRICE: EXPIRES:
SOURCE: Miss Dunn- Washington expediter
BIND: Catalog end of year - 385 A
FILE: Railroads- Revenue Freight Loaded & Received - W. CS 54 A
ROUTING:
1. Research
2. Hoffman

Form 3119

NO. OF COPIES	TITLE:	VOL. YR.	FREQUENCY	T. P. & INDEX
2	RAILROADS - Revenue Freight Loaded & Received	CS 54A	W	

FIGURE 7. Use of a catchword followed by a title in Standard and Poor's Corporation Library.

effective checking. This is the philosophy that applies, or should apply, in a library whose visible index is essentially a checking tool. In the Harvard College Library, which is probably typical in this respect, roughly 95 per cent of visible index use is for checking purposes. Hence it is natural to establish the records with checking rather than reference in mind, except in the relatively small number of institutions where reference questions relating to serials are unusually numerous. Even in these institutions it may be desirable at times to compromise between the form natural to a visible index and the form natural to a catalog.

Special library practice is always worth studying; it tends to be quite forthright since it can be tailored to the exigencies of the local situation. The following noteworthy practices at Standard and Poor's Corporation Library in New York show how the entry is based, not on the catalog record, but on the form most convenient for work in that particular institution.

A title entry may be preferred, as in Figure 6 where "Glass Containers" is the heading, supplemented by the name of the main series, instead of the cataloging form "U. S. Bureau of the Census. Glass Containers."

A catchword, e.g. "Railroads," may be employed to group all the publications of a given type. So in Figure 7 the entry becomes "Railroads—Revenue Freight Loaded & Received," not a title entry or the cataloging form "Association of American Railroads. Car Service Division. Revenue Freight Loaded and Received from Connections."

In the separate check list for corporation reports, which is a feature of the Standard and Poor's Library, various titles may be entered on a single card. Figure 8 has entries for advance reports, annual reports, press releases, and income accounts, instead of requiring separate entries for each title.

RES I

FISCAL

NAME

GULF OIL CORPORATION J.R.Moorhead, Jr., Treas

Dec. 31

STREET CITY STATE

ANNUAL

Gulf Building Pittsburgh 30 Pennsylvania

4th Tues April

WRITE TO:

YEAR	DATE RECEIVED	DESC.	NO. COPIES	JAN.	FEB.	MAR.	APRIL	MAY	JUNE	JULY	AUG.	SEPT.	OCT.	NOV.	DEC.
1948															
1949 over	Adv 4-5-50	5-5	2			Nsps Rel 5-11			I.A. 9-6 (3			Nsp Rel 10-27 (2			
1950	Adv 3-21-51	4-25	2			Nsp Rel 5-29			I.A. 8-7 (2			Nsp Rel 10-27			
1951	3-24-52	5-1	3			Nsp Rel 4-25			I.A. 8-6 (3						
1952	Adv. 3-23-53	5-1	2						I.A. 8-4			Nsp Rel 11-5 (2			
1953						Nsp Rel 4-25			I.A. 8-10 (3			Nsp Rel 10-28			
1954															
1955															

DIEBOLD CARDINEER FORM 30788 (301P25)

STANDARD & POOR'S CORPORATION

FIGURE 8. Example of multiple entries on a single card in Standard and Poor's Corporation Library. "Adv 3-23-53" means that an advance copy of the 1952 report was received on March 23, 1953. The column headed "Desc." has local significance; it denotes that a description of Gulf Oil, as carried on Standard and Poor's corporation records, was sent to the company for corrections and additions, and was returned on the date specified. The tally under "No. copies" indicates that two copies of the 1952 report were received. "Nsp Rel 4-25" when translated says that the March interim report, received on the 25th of April, was in the form of a press release. The notations under June mean that three copies of the income account for the period ending June 30, 1953, were received on the date given.

Obviously there is much for general libraries to learn from special library practice. There is much to be said for direct methods at the visible index, which represents a mass operation, especially when it is recalled that ways need to be found for checkers to do highly desirable follow-up work which is often neglected for lack of time. It is a matter of regret, therefore, that the Library of Congress, which started to experiment with direct headings in its visible index (as well as in *Serial Titles Newly Received),* reverted to the cataloging form of entry without making a contribution to the question of visible index headings.[6] However, experience gained from the checking records in the Science and Technology Project at the Library of Congress did lead Mortimer Taube to suggest modifications in the treatment of corporate entries.[7]

Part of the problem is, of course, the inordinate length of some corporate headings. A checker is inevitably delayed in his work if he must read through a two- to four-line heading when a few words would suffice; in addition, there is always the danger of recording an item on the wrong card when complex or verbose headings must be read through carefully to distinguish one title from another. The problem has a wider ramification. If a non-technical entry is natural in a visible index, may it not be the natural form in the card catalog as well? If, for example, citations are generally made in the form *Annals of the American Academy of Political and Social Science* and *Berichte der Deutschen chemischen Gesellschaft,* might not the catalog benefit from having its main entry under the same form? An added entry under the name of the corporate body would generally follow, whereas an added entry under title for non-distinctive titles does not necessarily follow in present cataloging practice. This is demonstrated by the fact that the Library of Congress card calls for a title entry under

---

[6] In a memorandum on the editorial project in the Serial Record Division, dated November 20, 1953, the situation at the Library of Congress is described as follows: "Policy as to cataloging rules to be followed in setting up entries in the Serial Record has varied widely since the setting up of the Serial Record. This variation has resulted in inefficiency of recording information in the record and in getting information from the record. In some cases, information as to bound holdings on 3 by 5 cards is under one heading and information as to unbound holdings is under other headings in the visible file. One of the primary objectives of the project is to bring all the Serial Record into conformity with the A. L. A. rules of entry and thus into conformity with the other catalog controls of the Library." Some of the changes in Serial Record practices are set forth in *Serial Slants* v.2, Jan. 1952, p.22-24; see also the Library of Congress *Departmental & Divisional Manuals* 20:55-58, 1952. For the change in *Serial Titles Newly Received,* compare the introduction to the issue for December, 1951, with that for January, 1952.

[7] Mortimer Taube, "The Cataloging of Publications of Corporate Authors," *Library Quarterly* 20:1-20, 1950. The Science and Technology Project handled reports from numerous laboratories and found it expedient to list them under their distinctive form of name; for example, the Cruft Laboratory at Harvard was listed under "Cruft" and not under the synthetic cataloging form dictated by the A. L. A. catalog code.

"Berichte" but not under "Annals." Amongst the publications of corporate bodies the case for entry under title is strongest for periodicals, and especially for those periodicals which are commonly referred to by initialisms. The matter has been discussed by medical librarians on a number of occasions. In a medical library the reader who speaks of the JAMA is likely to look for the catalog entry under *Journal of the American Medical Association* rather than under the corporate entry, and many medical libraries list their periodicals in this way. A somewhat similar plan has been followed by the British Library of Political and Economic Science, where

> title entry is adopted for all periodicals other than government publications (which are entered under the name of the country in alphabetical order of issuing departments). The *Journal of the Institute of Bankers,* for example, is so entered, with a reference from the name of the institute. As the only exceptions to this rule, "Report" and "Annual Report" are avoided as entry-words; the library contains several hundreds of bank reports alone, so that to concentrate *all* reports in one section of the catalog would probably cause the reader to turn away in despair.[8]

It is obvious from the foregoing that much experimentation and study remain to be done to determine the best form of entry for publications of corporate bodies, both in the visible index and in the card catalog, and that general libraries can learn from experience gained in special libraries. Until such studies are made each library must settle for itself the question of catalog entry versus checking entry in its visible index. On the one hand, standardization has much to say for itself; on the other, there is good reason for preferring the type of entry that facilitates the checking of tens of thousands of serials each year.

Enumerative statements of holdings

There are two ways of characterizing serial holdings. One is the enumerative statement common to visible indexes and other checking mediums where the individual issues are registered as received: daily, weekly, monthly, etc. The other takes the form of a summarized statement.[9] On a catalog card, for example, the library's holdings may be summarized as "vol. 1-285," which lets the staff and readers assume the completeness of every volume, completeness which the corresponding checking records could substantiate by virtue of their enumeration of the parts.

---

[8] Marjorie Plant, "Periodicals Procedure in a University Library," *College and Research Libraries* 3:63, 1941.

[9] Enumerative and summarized statements take on a special form for shelf-listing purposes. See Chapter 8.

The checking records for the first four volumes of *Serial Slants* demonstrate the nicety of enumerative records; at the same time they show how much easier the summarized statement is for ordinary comprehension.

v.1,	1950.	1/July	2/October
	1951.	3/January	4/April
v.2,	1951.	1/July	2/October
	1952.	3/January	4/April
v.3,	1952.	1/July	2/October
v.4,	1953.	1/January	2/April
		3/July	4/October

In the enumerative statement it is clear that volume 3 was complete in two numbers, whereas the summarized statement, "vol. 1-4," takes that fact for granted. In this instance the enumerative statement employs a twofold element of control, for both numbering and date are specified for each issue. There are numerous similar cases of irregularities of publication for which the detailed checking records afford the only means of establishing the number of issues comprised in a complete volume. There are also cases in which the original serial numbering or date was printed on the spine only and was lost when the volumes were bound, leaving the checking records as the sole source of evidence.

An axiom of serial checking is that the records should be so compiled currently that they can be relied upon implicitly in later years. The time to determine that volume one is complete in seven issues, volume two in ten, and volume three in eleven is when the crucial issues are first handled. The later history of the library file of a serial is built on these primary checking records.

Data on visible index cards

In many libraries it is customary to type the heading and other key information in the visible margin on both the face and the back of the checking card. Thereby the details are visible at a glance, regardless of whether the cards are lying in their normal position or are turned back. This duplication of effort is particularly desirable when postings of any kind must be made on the back of the card. Duplication of the heading can be avoided when no information goes on the back of a card. Herein lies one of the advantages that accrue from the use of overriding slips (see pages 107-10). Only rarely when they are employed must information go on the back of the permanent card—the basic entry card, as the Library of Congress calls it—so there is little or no occasion for typing the heading on the back of the card.

Since the number of characters that can go in the visible margin is relatively small, abbreviations may be freely adopted in transcribing the entry, as long as they are perfectly clear and do not affect the filing. It is proper to contract some words and to omit unnecessary words and marks of punctuation.

The information given on visible index cards in the Library of Congress represents the full range of data usually recorded (see Figure 9). It includes the following items, not all of which will be needed by most libraries:

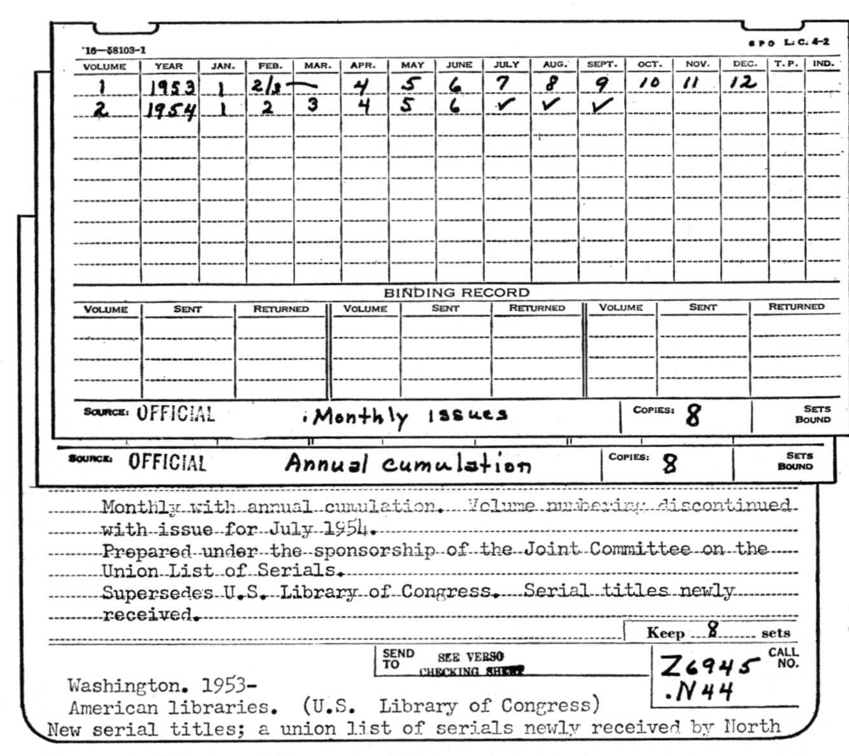

'16—58103-1 GPO L.C. 4-2

VOLUME	YEAR	JAN.	FEB.	MAR.	APR.	MAY	JUNE	JULY	AUG.	SEPT.	OCT.	NOV.	DEC.	T.P.	IND.
1	1953	1	2/3	—	4	5	6	7	8	9	10	11	12		
2	1954	1	2	3	4	5	6	✓	✓	✓					

BINDING RECORD

VOLUME	SENT	RETURNED	VOLUME	SENT	RETURNED	VOLUME	SENT	RETURNED

SOURCE: OFFICIAL Monthly issues COPIES: 8 SETS BOUND

SOURCE: OFFICIAL Annual cumulation COPIES: 8 SETS BOUND

Monthly with annual cumulation. Volume numbering discontinued with issue for July 1954.

Prepared under the sponsorship of the Joint Committee on the Union List of Serials.

Supersedes U.S. Library of Congress. Serial titles newly received.

Keep 8 sets

SEND TO SEE VERSO CHECKING SHEET

CALL NO. Z6945 .N44

Washington. 1953-

American libraries. (U.S. Library of Congress)

New serial titles; a union list of serials newly received by North

FIGURE 9. Library of Congress visible index card and overriding sheets.

1. The basic entry cards give:
   a. The title or entry by which the publication is identified in the Serial Record Division or the Library, with an indication of any difference between the Serial Record entry and the official cataloging form
   b. The record of serial titles not retained by the Library, with an indication of disposition[10]

[10] When a library continues to be on the mailing list for a serial it does not wish to keep, for example the publication of a propaganda agency, it is well to have an entry on the visible index so that the issues may be discarded in a simple way. Otherwise the decision record, wherever it is located, would have to be consulted frequently or a fresh decision might have to be given repeatedly.

c. Sufficient bibliographical information to distinguish similar titles, usually restricted to the place of publication
d. Essential bibliographical history of the item
e. The number of sets retained in the permanent collections
f. The location of the permanent sets (i.e., their call numbers) and of the service sets in reference assignment
g. The custodial division which services unbound issues or volumes
h. The next routing station for processing (e.g., the Binding Division, Labeling Unit, or Preliminary Cataloging Section) and intermediate stations for entry in accessions lists
i. Treatment decisions for monograph series

2. Bound holdings that are permanently retained are recorded on special overriding slips.
3. The checking overriders show:
   a. The posting of issues or volumes currently received, whether bound or unbound
   b. The sources from which copies are received
   c. A record of binding progress

As the checking overriders are completed, and when all material recorded on them has been bound, the statement of holdings is consolidated on the special overriding slip and the checking sheets are then destroyed.[11]

Checking practices

The second class mail should be opened on a long counter or table when it is at all extensive. The job is done in the Reference Department of the New York Public Library on a hinged counter in the corridor by the Acquisition Division, the counter being lowered after the operation has been completed. In the United Nations Library pigeonholes help to sort the mail. For preference the checkers should open the wrappers, possibly with the aid of other acquisition assistants. For many years these two groups have collaborated in the New York Public Library, arriving an hour before the rest of the staff to open and sort the mail. In most libraries, however, the second class mail is not delivered until later in the day.

Mail for individuals and special destinations should be sorted out for redelivery. Letters, renewals, etc. should be set aside for later action. Any rush items as well as bundles from periodical dealers should be separately grouped for priority checking. If desirable a list of titles that should be processed on a rush basis can be compiled and posted for ready consultation. Wrappers should be inserted in the pieces and should not be discarded until the pieces have been checked off. Diffi-

[11] For Library of Congress checking practices in general, see its *Departmental & Divisional Manuals* 20:44-63, 1952. Note, however, that this manual was compiled before the Library of Congress reverted to the cataloging entry for its visible index and before the editorial project in the Serial Record Division was begun.

culties may be encountered in the checking process if the wrappers are not with the pieces to make their source clear. As the mail is opened it can be roughly alphabetized, either by each letter of the alphabet or by the part of the alphabet each checker is responsible for in the visible index. The more exact arrangement of the pieces should be left until they are about to be posted, whereupon they should be grouped in manageable piles either in working areas between the units of the visible index or on book trucks.

The posting of the rush items and the periodicals that come in dealers' bundles should precede the strict alphabeting of the non-rush material. Among the rush items may be current newspapers and titles such as the *Publishers' Weekly* which should go without delay to some member of the staff. The bundles should be given priority, either because they can be checked off rapidly in their own tray or because they should be checked off as a unit so that the source of none of them is left uncertain. Apart from bundles and rush items, checking should proceed in the normal alphabetical sequence without backtracking until the main job has been completed. In general it is better to defer items that are appreciably out of sequence, putting them in a separate pile, possibly with a notation of the correct entry.

The checkers usually stamp and mark each piece as it is posted. The stamping, however, can be done more economically as a separate operation after the checking has been completed on all items. Riders or routing slips must be prepared and inserted when necessary, and the checking directions on the visible index card must be carried out.

When the checker has been once through the alphabet, or his part of the alphabet, the serials may be in four groupings:

1. Pieces normally posted, stamped, and otherwise marked, ready to go to their destination
2. Pieces out of order that should now be checked off or passed on to another checker
3. Unwanted duplicates, some to be held in reserve, others to be discarded
4. Items not on the visible index which must be checked against the decision file, the old serial records, the official or public catalog, or which must be sent to the appropriate officer for a selection decision

When gaps are noted, the claim can be made out immediately or, in libraries where the claiming is done by a clerk-typist after the checker has completed his work, by noting the title or adding a warning slip to the visible index card. There are two advantages in having the checker make the claim immediately: first, the address can be taken from the piece itself (which is sometimes more accurate than an address on the visible index card); and second, there is no risk of postponing an operation that all too often suffers from neglect. Many libraries, however, want the checkers to press forward with their posting, leaving the follow-up work for the supplementary activities.

It is good to equip each checker with a large pad on which he can note matters to be cared for once the checking has been done. These may include gaps to be attended to, full cards to be retyped or full overriding slips to be replaced, changes of name or title which involve title inserts or other action, the conversion of temporary records to permanent records, the tally of pieces added, and other questions and problems that arise in the course of the checking. All such matters (with the possible exception of gap work) should be attended to after the orderly process of checking is ended. That orderly process should not be interrupted for details that can be cared for later, since the principal objective is to get the mass of new serials posted and off to their destination as rapidly as may be. Material that does not originate in the mail (bundles of gifts, transfers, etc.), since it does not have to be processed rapidly, can also be left for the clean-up period, as can letters, renewals, etc.

Methods of posting in the Library of Congress are as follows:

> When recording serials in the Visible File the accessioner normally enters the issue on the checking sheets rather than on the basic entry card. The method of recording used by the accessioner is largely determined by the checking pattern originally established by the Serial Record catalogers. Serials are recorded by the most important sequence indicia, which commonly are numbers or dates. It is at times advisable, however, to record material by both numbers and dates, e.g., official gazettes. The checking sheets are designed either for number or date checking, with several varieties for each . . . but these sheets may easily be adapted for checking by both number and date. In the method of checking by number *or* date, a check mark (√) is placed beside the number or in the date box; where checking is by *both* number and date, a date is placed beside the number or a number is placed in the date box. The checking pattern is planned to give sufficient information for proper identification in as economical a manner as possible.[12]

This practice is well conceived. The last sentence of the quotation should be the guiding principle for all checking systems. When a simple check can take the place of the issue number, the posting process is simplified and speeded up. It should be adopted whenever the serial controls are adequate without resorting to the issue number.[13] As another economy measure, the subseries should be recorded in detail, but generally not the main series. It is only in rare circumstances that both the series and the subseries need to be recorded. Further, when

[12] Library of Congress *Departmental & Divisional Manuals* 20:50, 1952.

[13] Although as a principle of sound economy serials should be checked in with regard to a single control element as far as possible, it is as a rule desirable to note both volume and year, because titles are sometimes cited in one way, sometimes the other.

two copies are received simultaneously, they can be checked off as one. However, should multiple copies be received at different times and from different sources, it is necessary to have a check for each. Two or three checks are clear enough, but for more than three copies numbers should be employed. Alternatively, extra overriding slips can be pressed into service, each copy being checked off on a different slip; but this practice is desirable only in unusual circumstances.

Because it is of the utmost importance in research libraries to see that files are complete, and because enumerative statements are often not easy to peruse, it is highly advisable when a volume is complete to add some symbol to the checking record. A red check by the volume number or the year, or a ring around either, can act as this quickly interpreted guarantee; or a special column can be provided in which a C (for complete) can be inserted. On complicated records this device can save much time whenever the slip or card is scanned for gaps. In itself it is an adjunct to follow-up work, just as it is an aid when the summarized statement is being brought up to date on the permanent records. Attention to this small detail in the course of the day's work will prove in the long run to be a valued labor saver.

Some libraries, particularly special libraries, like to record on the visible index the date of receipt for each issue, even though the pieces themselves are stamped with the date. When this practice is followed the day and the month are generally given (usually in the form 2/24), but not the year; they are written, not stamped, on the checking record. The reason for including this detail is that it can answer occasional requests for the approximate time when a new issue may be expected. A considerable amount of work is involved in adding the date of receipt to tens of thousands of postings annually. Since this information is recorded on the pieces themselves, the date can safely be omitted in most general libraries; it should not be recorded by any library that utilizes a progressive tab system (see page 114); and when it is recorded it should for preference be restricted to low-frequency serials—quarterlies, annuals, etc.—and possibly monthlies. The checking slips and cards are far clearer when they are not cluttered up with the date of receipt in each checking square. There is real gain in having clear and simple records, especially for scanning purposes and for follow-up. Figures 6, 7, and 9 should be compared in this connection.

Preparing checked serials for use

Once the pieces have been checked in they should be treated according to the special directions on the checking slips or according to a general plan. Some items should be end-processed in the way described in Chapter 8; for example, the bound volumes that need lettering, bookplating, shelf-listing, analyzing, etc. Others of the annual-report type that are to go into pamphlet boxes, manila rope bundles, vertical files, or other containers in the stacks must have the call number added; and on occasion a new container must be requested. It may not be necessary to add the call number to items that go to the periodical or other special reading room, but it is helpful to add the shelving symbol when current periodicals, etc., are arranged in broad subject groupings.

The library's stamp—usually combined with the date of receipt, sometimes with even the hour specified—is put on the cover of unbound serials or on the verso of the title page when there is one. All too often these stamps are unattractive, and their poor effect is heightened when the stamping is done hurriedly and carelessly. Monographs receive better treatment than serials in this respect. In the Harvard College Library a symbol is added to every piece as it is checked in to show catalogers and others that it has definitely been processed serially. The symbol used is a delta placed above the call number or mark of location. When multiple copies are received, some of which are to be preserved permanently and some to be used as service copies, it may be desirable to apply distinguishing marks so that service copies will not find their way into the permanent collections. A simple device is to add "copy 1," "copy 2," etc., to the permanent copies, and "copy A," "copy B," etc., to the service copies.

Riders may be inserted in the pieces to serve any of a variety of purposes. They may be mimeographed or printed, especially when they convey routing instructions; or they may be blank slips on which the checker writes or stamps the information. Their most common uses are to indicate that an item should circulate to an individual or a number of individuals and to convey cataloging instructions. A rider may also indicate that leaves should be cut. It is undesirable to circulate publications with uncut leaves, because readers are apt to damage the pages when they themselves cut the leaves, usually without the benefit of a paper knife. In some libraries unbound serials are sent to the bindery to have their edges trimmed by machine. More often the pages are cut by the periodical room attendants or by attendants in various parts of the library whose duties are light enough that they can undertake a certain amount of busywork of this kind.

CHAPTER 6

The Visible Index And Its Rivals

ALTHOUGH THE VISIBLE INDEX was developed with business offices in mind, libraries were quick to see its potentialities for work with serials. It was realized that the receipt of serials, like various business transactions, could be posted faster on cards whose fore edge disclosed the entry at a glance than was possible on cards in drawers or files. Because it was invented for business firms, no feature of the visible index has been specially designed for library purposes, but the checking forms are adapted to library needs, quite often to those of an individual library.

Several libraries installed visible indexes in 1913 soon after the equipment came on the market. Two types were exhibited at the American Library Association Conference in Washington in 1914. They gave rise to the following comment:

> It would be extremely hazardous to predict that the standard size card would ever be forced to give over to any other indexing device any of the ground it has gained as an essential feature of library equipment. There seem to be, however, very good possibilities that the visible indexing devices manufactured by the INDEX VISIBLE COMPANY and by the RAND COMPANY may come to fill an important place in library equipment, supplementing the card index. Many large business offices have recognized the importance of these devices, enabling them to index long lists of names in very small space in such a way that any name on the lists can be quickly and conveniently found. Both the INDEX VISIBLE and the RAND VISIBLE INDEX are made in many sizes and styles, adapted to so many purposes that they seem to give good promise of satisfactory adaptation to library purposes.[1]

[1] American Library Association, *Descriptive Catalog of the Exhibit of Labor-Saving Devices and Library Equipment* (Washington, 1914), p.26-27. The Committee on Library Administration, under the chairmanship of Arthur E. Bostwick, which sponsored the exhibit, added: "The committee will not undertake to say what the future possibilities of these indexes in library service may be, but it would seem as though the devices were of sufficient interest and offered sufficiently good possibilities for adaptation to library service at some time in the near future, if not at present, to justify their inclusion in the exhibit and to make it worth while for librarians to give them careful consideration." *A. L. A. Bulletin* 8:81, 1914.

Since 1913 a number of firms have manufactured visible indexes. The Index Visible Company, which was established in New Haven in 1912 by Professor Irving Fisher, merged with Remington Rand in 1925. The differences between the products of the various firms are not as great as might be anticipated, due in some measure to the fact that one firm may hold a patent which another makes use of. The basic difference is between the Kardex type, which sets the checking card into a pocket, and the Acme type, in which the card hangs independently from a wire or other attachment. Some manufacturers carry both models. Among the leading American makes are Acme, Globe Wernicke, Kardex, Postindex, Victor, and Yawman and Erbe. The corresponding British makes are Acme, Kardex, Roneodex, and Vistem.[2]

Libraries have adapted three varieties of visible index equipment to work with serials: the title-a-line form is used mostly for quick reference work; book units that hold the checking cards are often found in small libraries; but the type most generally employed by libraries has the checking cards lying flat in shallow trays in cabinets of varying sizes.

Visible reference indexes

Readers and staff members often wish to find the call number of a serial quickly. They are helped when a library's periodicals (or preferably its serials) are listed on a title-a-line visible reference index.[3] They can check that record rapidly without having to hunt through the card catalog.[4] Commonly the information on the visible reference index is limited to the title, call number, and an indication of the location of current numbers when they are not in the periodical room. The reasons for limiting the information are that this is not a posting record and that an attempt must be made to confine all the data for a given title to a single line six to eight inches long.

---

[2] Cf. David Grenfell, *Periodicals and Serials, Their Treatment in Special Libraries* (London: Aslib, 1953), p.26.

[3] When a library has both a visible index and a visible reference index there may be some difficulty in distinguishing between the two by name when generically they are both visible indexes. Since the visible reference index is more strictly an index, it is best to apply another term to the checking records. So the Library of Congress refers to the checking records as the "visible file," while the Harvard College Library employs the expression "visible record." For tracing purposes the latter uses VR for the checking records and VI for its rotary reference file. Throughout this book "visible index" refers to the checking records, "visible reference index" to the title-a-line reference type.

[4] Printed, mimeographed, and other check lists serve a similar purpose. In libraries which arrange their periodicals alphabetically, a simple plan is to check the library's holdings in the front of the periodical indexes.

Frequently the entries in the visible reference index have no protective covering. Since they may become soiled through constant fingering, or may be marked with pencil or ink, some libraries prefer to have the strips containing the entries enclosed in celluloid tubes. These tubes can accommodate either a single-line entry or a multiple entry that takes up two or more lines.

Multiple entries serve a number of purposes. When a library has two or more publications of a corporate body, space is saved by listing the name of the body only once, and hanging indention effectively sets off the titles of its publications. A similar scheme can be followed for the different parts of a serial; e.g., for the historico-philosophical and the mathematico-physical sections of a learned society publication. A segment of entries from the visible reference index in the Harvard College Library illustrates the practice.

Boston Association for the Relief & Control of Tuberculosis. Annual report	Med 1760.75
Boston Athenaeum. Report by the librarian	B 8411.3.21
Boston Browning Society. Papers	23444.29
Boston Center for Adult Education. Adult education program	Educ 7361.141.15
Boston. Children's Mission to the Children of the Destitute. Annual report	Soc 2735.4
Boston College alumni news (uncat)	EducU 3500.1275
Boston courier and hotel news	News
Boston directory	RR 2300.15 & Dir 203
Boston evening transcript	News
Boston herald	Lamont
Boston medical and surgical journal	Sci 3320.3
Boston monthly magazine	P 132.2
Boston. Museum of Fine Arts	
Annual report	FA 46.4.17
Bulletin	FA 46.4.19
Boston. Port & Seamen's Aid Society. Report	Soc 2735.17
Boston. Public Library	
Annual report	B 8411.2.20
Brief reading lists	Ref 71.1
More books	B 8411.2.72
Quarterly	B 8411.2.72.3
Boston quarterly review	P 132.3
Boston Real Estate Exchange. Bulletin	Sch. Pub. Adm.
Boston Society of Natural History	
Bulletin	Sci 1720.17
Occasional papers	Sci 1720.18
Proceedings	Sci 1720.15
Boston Symphony Orchestra. Programme	Mus 55.1
Boston University law review	Law Sch.

Attention has already been called to the fact that in the Order Division of the Library of Congress equipment of this type has been effectively utilized as an index to outstanding serial orders (see Figure 3).

Fusion of reference and checking functions

In a few libraries the visible reference index has been made to do double duty as a combined reference and checking record. This effect is achieved by replacing the title-a-line strips in the panels with regular checking forms. For the person who merely wants a call number, the information is available in the same way as on the regular visible reference index. There are proportionately more panels in the double-duty file, but what he sees at a glance is to all intents and purposes the same in both instances. If he should wish to see whether the library has the volume or issue he is interested in, he merely opens up the checking record and discovers what he wants to know. The checker, however, is not so well served. He cannot operate as conveniently as behind the scenes at a cabinet-type visible index. The checking must be done on the vertical panels—unless he wants to detach them each time—so there is no flat surface on which to make the postings. And he must compete with others for use of the file, since it is both a public and an official record. An example of this setup can be observed in the Science Reading Room at Massachusetts Institute of Technology.

An alternative procedure is to locate the regular visible index where it may be consulted by readers. In the Wellesley College Library, for instance, the visible index is adjacent to the public catalog. Despite this juxtaposition, the regular main and secondary cards for serials are maintained in the card catalog. At the Babson Institute, however, where the visible index is utilized as at Wellesley, there are no serial entries in the card catalog; and a somewhat similar scheme has been followed in the Linda Hall Library.

Practices of this kind are fairly common in special libraries where ready access to serial files is of paramount importance. In libraries where the periodicals are received and checked in the periodical room, the intention is to make the information on the records conveniently accessible to readers even though it must be obtained through the periodical room staff.

Visible versus blind files

In the early part of the twentieth century the standard equipment for serial checking records, as demonstrated by library supply catalogs, consisted of 7.5 by 12.5 centimeter cards which were housed in ordinary catalog drawers and cabinets. Cards housed in this way constitute a blind file because they present no visible margin or heading as the trays are opened, except for the guide cards. Many libraries still use standard catalog trays with specially printed checking cards to record the receipt of serial publications, but librarians who have converted from this style to the visible index have been uniformly happy with the results. After a visible index was put in operation at the British Library of Political and Economic Science, the verdict was: "The time saved by using a visible index has in itself fully justified the initial expenditure."[5] At Los Angeles in 1932 when a visible index was installed the reaction was: "It is difficult to restrain undue exuberance in contemplating the benefits of this visible system . . . It is believed that the expense is justified by efficiency in operation."[6] At Los Angeles, as in many other instances, the installation of a visible index provided the occasion for a consolidation of serial records which in itself was cause for congratulations:

> Periodicals and newspapers had been ordered and checked in the Periodical Department; documents in the Catalogue Department; continuations in the Order Department. In all of these departments chief interest was centered on their major tasks which were not concerned particularly with the keeping of these specialized records. Therefore, finding the various unions more and more incompatible, finally a complete separation has been achieved, and a more equable and decorous combination permitted, bringing into being the Serials Division of the Order Department.[7]

The situation at the Library of Congress as late as 1940 was more complicated than that at Los Angeles before 1932: "At that time, in order to check on Library of Congress serial holdings, it was necessary to consult records in 14 different locations and in some of these locations there was more than one catalog to be consulted—a total of some 32 separate files."[8]

It must be pointed out that the benefits of consolidation should be appraised apart from any question of the merits of a visible index. At Yale, for example, it was reported in 1948 that "seventeen separate card files have been eliminated or consolidated; others are under consideration,"[9] a task for the Serial Department completely dissociated from the installation of a visible index.

The change-over to a visible index was made in the Harvard College Library in 1939. Prior to that date a number of separate files

---

[5] Marjorie Plant, "Periodicals Procedure in a University Library," *College and Research Libraries* 3:60, 1941.

[6] Los Angeles Public Library, Serials Division, *Workbook of Serials Procedure* (Los Angeles, 1932), p.7-8.

[7] *Ibid.*, p.2.

[8] *Annual Report* of the Librarian of Congress, 1952 (Washington, 1952), p.84-85. Chapter 8 of this report tells the story of how the visible index was installed and developed at the Library of Congress.

[9] Yale University, *Report of the Librarian*, 1947-48 (New Haven, 1948), p.15.

had existed: for non-document serials, government publications, Slavic titles, Hispanic material, and for serials of all kinds in the field of education. Obviously there was much overlap between these records. The file for non-document serials contained approximately a hundred thousand cards. It consisted of two fifty-tray units, each drawer of which was uncomfortably full. The live titles, some three or four thousand in number, were not segregated, but were scattered throughout the catalog. In the daily checking process the serial assistants had to contend, in seeking each live title, with twenty-five or so inactive entries.

Some idea of the physical labor involved in a day's checking in the former Harvard file can be gathered from the fact that a full tray weighed about eight pounds. If a checker had an entry to make in each tray and lifted another 25 trays in backtracking, he would have lifted a ton in the course of a single day's operation, half a ton in setting the trays before him and half a ton in replacing them. With the expenditure of so much physical energy, it would not be surprising if fatigue set in to slow down the checking or to produce errors. Naturally a visible index was a welcome change since it involved so much less sheer labor. Moreover, the trays were not adequately guided, so there was much finger work in trying to locate an entry. Often, too, although printed form cards were used, data was not in a standard place because the standard-size cards filled up so rapidly. For many years a change to a visible index had been desired. In 1935, in a memorandum to the director of the library, T. Franklin Currier had said:

> So far as the advantage of a visible record system is concerned as against the present antiquated card system, there is no need to take time to debate, for it is already unquestionably recognized as a necessary feature in well-managed libraries, and it makes greatly for prompt service and economy. Moreover, the concentration of information about all current periodicals at one station in the Library will be a distinct addition to the service we now give and will notably help those who use the Library.

These details are recounted because it is important to point out that the change from a number of poor blind files to a consolidated visible index ought to lead to rejoicing, but the comparison is not a fair one. What ought to be compared is a good blind file and a good visible index. If the three or four thousand live entries in the main Harvard College checking record had been segregated and consolidated with the live entries in the other files there would have been less objection to the former system. In the typical visible index space cannot be afforded for completed or inactive serial records. Neither should it be allowed in any other form of current check list. Add to the reduced but consolidated file a really good system of guide cards;

space the cards generously in each drawer—perhaps in a tub tray—and the result would be something to compete with the visible index, as has been demonstrated in the Department of Agriculture Library, whose findings are described later in this Chapter.

One feature of the Harvard College system was excellent. For newspapers and for certain complicated serials (for instance, the *Mercure de France* that ran from 1672 to 1820) sheet records had been preferred, with appropriate references in the card file. These loose-leaf sheet records, on typewriting paper, provided in an admirable way for long and involved statements of holdings. Some serials do not lend themselves to listing on cards. In particular, newspaper holdings can be listed most satisfactorily and clearly on sheets by year, month, and day. The sheet records have served for many years at Harvard as a clear, straightforward, efficient tool, convenient to use and easy to handle. Put the same records on standard-size cards (or even 6 by 4 inch cards) and a complete contrast would be achieved. Needless to say, the sheet records were preserved and maintained when the visible index was installed.

Careful thought was given in the Harvard College Library in 1939 to the possible retention of the old blind file, rearranged and improved so that it would have a maximum of effectiveness. Retention would have meant that the majority of cards must be typed afresh. Many of the old ones had manuscript headings, and it is certainly better to have the entries typewritten. Reconstruction of the file could have been accomplished without concern since it would have cost far less than the sum in hand for the conversion of the records. But there were three major objections: (1) a 6 by 4 inch card is much superior to the standard-size card for checking purposes; (2) overriding slips to extend the life of the checking records could not have been adopted; and (3) the records would have been too concentrated for convenience. Accordingly a visible index was installed, a consolidated record sufficiently spread out that several people could consult it simultaneously.

The visible index was not settled upon, however, until experiments had been carried out with other types of equipment. The Electrofile and the Wheeldex were set up and studied under working conditions. In the Electrofile, by means of a keyboard and a system of coding, the appropriate card can be made to jump up in the file, and can be removed for posting and returned anywhere in the file without concern about refiling or alphabetical order. Despite its real potentialities, there were certain drawbacks. The coding presented some obstacles, but these might have been surmounted; the real trouble lay in the fact that the keyboard controlled only one tray at a time. Likewise the Wheeldex, a rotary file (see page 98), seemed to offer attractive possibilities, especially the model set in a desk at which a checker could work with several thousand records comfortably at hand and clear space in front of him. At that time, however, neither the Wheeldex nor the Cardineer had been electrified, a development which might have affected the result. But in all tests the visible index was first in speed and efficiency, just as its employment of overriding slips guaranteed economy in maintenance.

The findings in the Harvard College Library must be set beside the more recent contrary findings in the Department of Agriculture Library. There a change has been made from a visible index to a blind file: truly a "revolutionary" change, as Miss Shachtman observes; or, in Shakespeare's words, "and thus the whirligig of time brings in his revenges." The former Victor visible index in the Department of Agriculture Library had 3 by 5 inch cards, about three fourths of which were housed in trays intended for 6 by 4 inch cards. Other people besides the checkers consulted the files extensively. In Miss Shachtman's words:

> The current files are in constant use not only by the periodical checkers, but also by the permanent serial records assistants who answer all requests for information on holdings, by Acquisition Section assistants for searching purposes, and by Division of Bibliography assistants for information of value in the preparation of new bibliographies. The permanent serial records assistants alone account for about 2000 uses a month.[10]

Because of this heavy non-posting use the twenty visible index cabinets were put on swivels, two units to a swivel. Normally the files faced the checkers, but when someone else wanted to consult a file it was swung around to face the other side of the desk.

The checkers worked at the files all day long. "We wondered how much time was being used just to pull out and push back trays, thereby lessening the amount of time available for recording material. And how much was fatigue toward the end of the day lowering the output of the checkers?"[11] So as an experiment part of the alphabet was rearranged in a standard file, a relatively simple procedure in the Department of Agriculture Library because headings were already typed at the top of the 3 by 5 inch visible index cards.

> We asked the checker responsible for this part of the alphabet to separate her publications, so that she could record publications part of the day in what remained of her visible files and the other part of the day on the cards in the 3 by 5 tray. Four hours were spent working with the 3 by 5 tray and the checker averaged handling seventy pieces per hour; four hours were

[10] Bella E. Shachtman, "Current Serial Records—an Experiment," *College and Research Libraries* 14:241, 1953.

[11] Bella E. Shachtman, "Simplification of Serial Records Work," *Serial Slants* 3:10, 1952.

spent working with the visible files and the same checker averaged forty-one pieces per hour, showing an increase of twenty-nine pieces per hour in using the 3 by 5 tray.[12]

The experiment with 3 by 5 inch trays was so successful from a production point of view that a special twenty-tray cabinet was designed, four trays high. Thereupon all trays were within normal arm's reach, in contrast to the situation that prevailed before when some of the visible index units were twenty trays high. The new trays were designed with sixteen inches of filing space, and had pulls and label holders at each end to permit the checkers on one side and the consultants on the other to get at them readily. Soft wood was used for the front, sides, and back of each tray and composition board for the bottom, to hold the weight down and to reduce the risk of fatigue from handling many trays in the course of a day's work.

You can imagine what this meant to our checker. In the first place, the trays she now used were lighter than any trays she had previously used. Secondly, instead of pulling out and pushing back eighty-nine trays for her part of the alphabet, she now used only seventeen 3 by 5 trays. Lastly, with her file set up in front of her within easy reach, she had much more work space available on her desk, without using part of another desk as she had had to do with the visible files.[13]

Miss Shachtman kept production records for several months while the experiment was in progress. The figures recorded work at the visible index, at the blind file, and in two cases work at the visible index after a spell at the blind file. The following comparative average production figures were obtained for each worker over a period of several months' work with each kind of file.

Percentages of Work Effectiveness

	VISIBLE INDEX	BLIND FILE	RETURN TO VISIBLE INDEX
First checker	85	109	103
Second checker	95	98	99
Third checker	110	118	

The evidence shows that although there is a gain in production in each case

[12] *Ibid.* Pearl H. Clark in *The Problem Presented by Periodicals in College and University Libraries* (Chicago: Univ. of Chicago Pr., 1930), p.27-29, reported time studies for the posting of three hundred periodicals, two fifths of which were in foreign languages. Identical records were set up in a blind and a visible file. Two individuals checked the periodicals in groups of fifty titles at a time, first in one file and then in the other. For experimental purposes the periodicals were not arranged alphabetically. The average time was 17.4 minutes for the posting of fifty titles in the visible index, 23 minutes in the standard file. Mrs. Clark cautioned against taking these figures at their face value, since different results might have been obtained under ordinary library conditions. Because of the marked discrepancy between Mrs. Clark's figures and Miss Shachtman's, there is evidently room for an extensive time-and-motion study of blind and visible files.

[13] Shachtman, *op. cit.,* p.12.

when the 3 by 5 files were used, over the production in using the visible files, a comparable drop is not shown upon returning to use of the visible files, and in fact, production may continue to show an upward trend. The old management principle seems to be proven anew—motivation and training play the most important part in producing high worker efficiency regardless of the equipment used. The motivation in this experiment came from the enthusiasm of each checker in participating in the experiment and her interest in the results. Further motivation came from each checker's desire to stop working with visible files from which she had to pull out and return so many trays in comparison to the number worked with in the experimental file.[14]

As a result of this experiment the Department of Agriculture Library has given up its visible indexes and has reverted to a blind file. Ten double visible index units have been replaced by six specially designed cabinets,[15] and eight desks have been replaced by six. Apart from the gain in space, the following advantages were anticipated:

Handling of fewer trays by the checker, thereby lessening fatigue.
Accessibility of most of the file to the checker while part of the file is being consulted by another assistant.
Easy insertion of new titles with no need for shifting.
Use of guide cards at quarter to half inch intervals will avoid the necessity of preparing an insert for each title.
Informational letters may be interfiled with the cards temporarily.
Better morale by improvement in the appearance of the section.[16]

In weighing the evidence presented by Miss Shachtman a number of factors must be taken into account. Most visible indexes are devoted overwhelmingly—95 per cent or even more—to the daily routine of posting incoming serials; and the reference use is to a considerable extent through the checkers themselves. In the Department of Agriculture Library, on the other hand, the checking and non-checking functions are fairly evenly divided, so the files have been organized to serve the checkers and others equally. The general plan of the work is not typical either, since the checkers do not open and arrange the mail or give information from their files. In most libraries these incidental functions provide variety in an otherwise rather monotonous operation.

The fact that several different models of visible index equipment were in operation before the change-over also has some bearing on the

[14] Bella E. Shachtman, "Current Serial Records—an Experiment," *College and Research Libraries* 14:242, 1953. For an explanation of the percentages of work effectiveness, see her "Simplification of Serial Records Work," *Serial Slants* 3:11, 1952.

[15] In the permanent installation the cabinets were somewhat modified. The free filing space was reduced to fourteen inches, and the cabinets were designed for fifteen trays in three rows, so limiting the height of the cabinets to sixteen inches which, by coincidence, is the height of a thirteen-tray visible index unit.

[16] Shachtman, *op. cit.*, p.242.

matter. Whereas twelve or thirteen trays to each visible index unit is generally taken to be the norm, the Department of Agriculture Library had units twenty trays high. Constant stretching for the upper trays not unnaturally tired the arms.[17] Altogether the equipment and the layout left much to be desired.

The style of checking card in the Department of Agriculture Library is unusual in several respects. Whereas experience has shown that a 6 by 4 inch card is best for serial checking, a smaller card is favored by the Department of Agriculture Library because it is intended to last no more than three years. For publications issued

298.8
So82

CX S P
Exp D
Freq W

Southwestern miller.

860-69 Board of Trade Building
Kansas City, Mo.

	JAN	FEB	MAR	APR	MAY	JUN	JLY	AUG	SEP	OCT	NOV	DEC	
55													

FIGURE 10. *(See also page 95.)*

semimonthly or less often the checking card has a capacity of three years; for more frequent publications a new card is substituted each year. In effect the whole file is renewed every three years, and incidentally much desirable follow-up work is accomplished as a by-product of the transfer of information to the permanent holdings file.

The special design of the card gives it an ingenious application to follow-up work. The name and address of the publisher are typed in a strategic location so that the cards can be photographed when necessary to constitute a claim. The cards are also photographed to produce new checking records as well as bindery notifications (see Figure 10). The claims so created are simply inserted in an open-faced

[17] The problem of stretching has been solved in the Johns Hopkins University Library by rearranging the visible index trays so that the alphabetical sequence is lateral. Before working on a given part of the alphabet the checker pulls out all the trays in a row. The trays are returned to position before those in another row are pulled out.

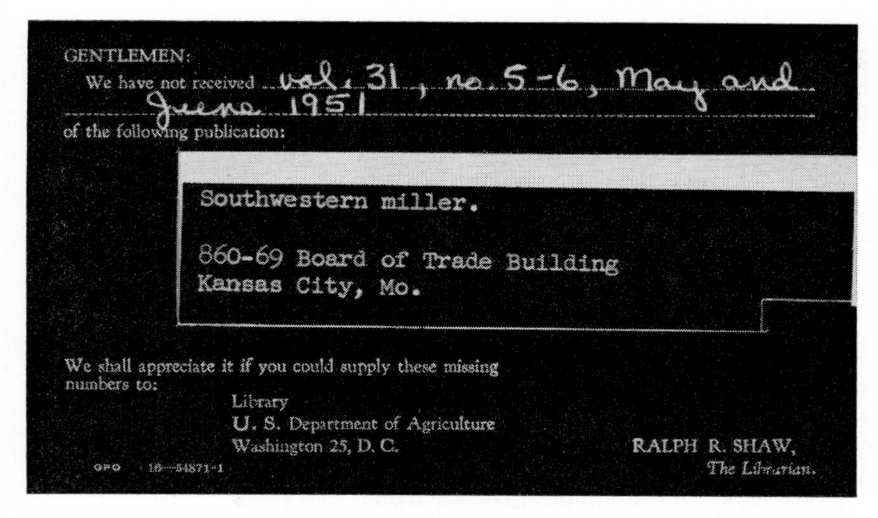

GENTLEMEN:
We have not received vol. 31, no. 5-6, May and June 1951
of the following publication:

Southwestern miller.

860-69 Board of Trade Building
Kansas City, Mo.

We shall appreciate it if you could supply these missing numbers to:

Library
U. S. Department of Agriculture
Washington 25, D. C.

RALPH R. SHAW,
The Librarian.

GPO 16—54871-1

298.8
So82

Southwestern miller.

860-69 Board of Trade Building
Kansas City, Mo.

BINDERY

CX S P
Exp D
Freq W

	JAN	FEB	MAR	APR	MAY	JUN	JLY	AUG	SEP	OCT	NOV	DEC
49	27/45	49	28/1	2 Aug 6	10	15	19	23	28	32	36	41
	46	50	2	7	11	16	20	24	29	33	37	42
	47	51	3	8	12	17	21	25	30	34	38	43
	48	52	4	9	13	18	22	26	31	35	39	44
			5		14			27			40	

BIND 1 COP JAN 28 1952 BIND 1 COP JAN 21 1953

FIGURE 10. Photographic applications of the checking card in the Department of Agriculture Library. A new checking card, claim for a monthly, and bindery notification, all photographically produced, are illustrated.

envelope and mailed to the dealer or other source. The success of the operation can be gauged by the fact that an annual workload of 19,000 claims can be carried, surely a consummation devoutly to be wished.[18]

[18] See Ralph R. Shaw, "Photoclerical Routines at USDA," *Library Journal* 78:2064-70, 1953. The routine of claiming is illustrated on page 2069. See also his *The Use of Photography for Clerical Routines* (Washington: American Council of Learned Societies, 1953), especially pages 14, 55, 57, 61-63, 68, and 70 where comparative figures are given for claiming and other serial operations.

In such ways, then, this library effectively utilizes a smaller card than most other libraries care to employ.

These circumstances are sufficiently atypical that no library should follow suit and abandon its visible index until it is sure that some or all of the factors that applied in the Department of Agriculture Library apply to it as well, or until it is sure that there is some other good reason for the change. This is another way of stating that libraries should acquire and develop the equipment that will serve their purposes best.

Punched cards versus the visible index

The statement by Frederick Luther to the effect that "the trend now seems to be away from visible indexing and toward coding,"[19] was made in an entirely different connection, and has no bearing on the adoption of punched cards by a small number of institutions. One of these is the John Crerar Library, which reported:

> Here plans were made to transfer 4 by 6 visible record cards to a tub file. When shipment of the tub was delayed, the trays were temporarily housed on a long table. This arrangement proved so satisfactory to those who used the files, that the order for the tub was cancelled, and trays are still lined up on the table, providing ample work space for the checkers, and easy accessibility to members of the technical processes department who need to consult the files. Plans are being made for a table built especially for these trays. Unlike the D. A. Library, we are transferring information from our old cards to new serial record cards which can be punched for title, frequency, classification, country and fund. However, by using the same size cards, old and new cards can be interfiled until the process of transferring is completed.[20]

The John Crerar Library was motivated by a desire to have supplementary information which can be obtained fairly readily from punched cards but only with difficulty from other types of record. Under the new plan it is relatively easy to draw off lists by dealers to facilitate renewals, just as it is to compile a list of all serials from a given country or on a given subject and thereby to review the adequacy of the acquisition program. Figure 11 shows two forms of punched cards used by the John Crerar Library.

McGaw lists a number of other libraries that have turned to punched cards of various kinds.[21] Some of them employ the punched

[19] "S.L.A. New York Chapter Looks at Mechanical Aids," *Library Journal* 75:723, 1950.

[20] Editor's note in *Serial Slants* 3:13-14, 1952.

[21] Howard F. McGaw, *Marginal Punched Cards in College and Research Libraries* (Washington: Scarecrow Pr., 1952), p.151-55. For IBM equipment as an adjunct to serial work, see Ralph H. Parker, *Library Applications of Punched Cards: a Description of Mechanical Systems* (Chicago: American Library Assn., 1952), p.14-16.

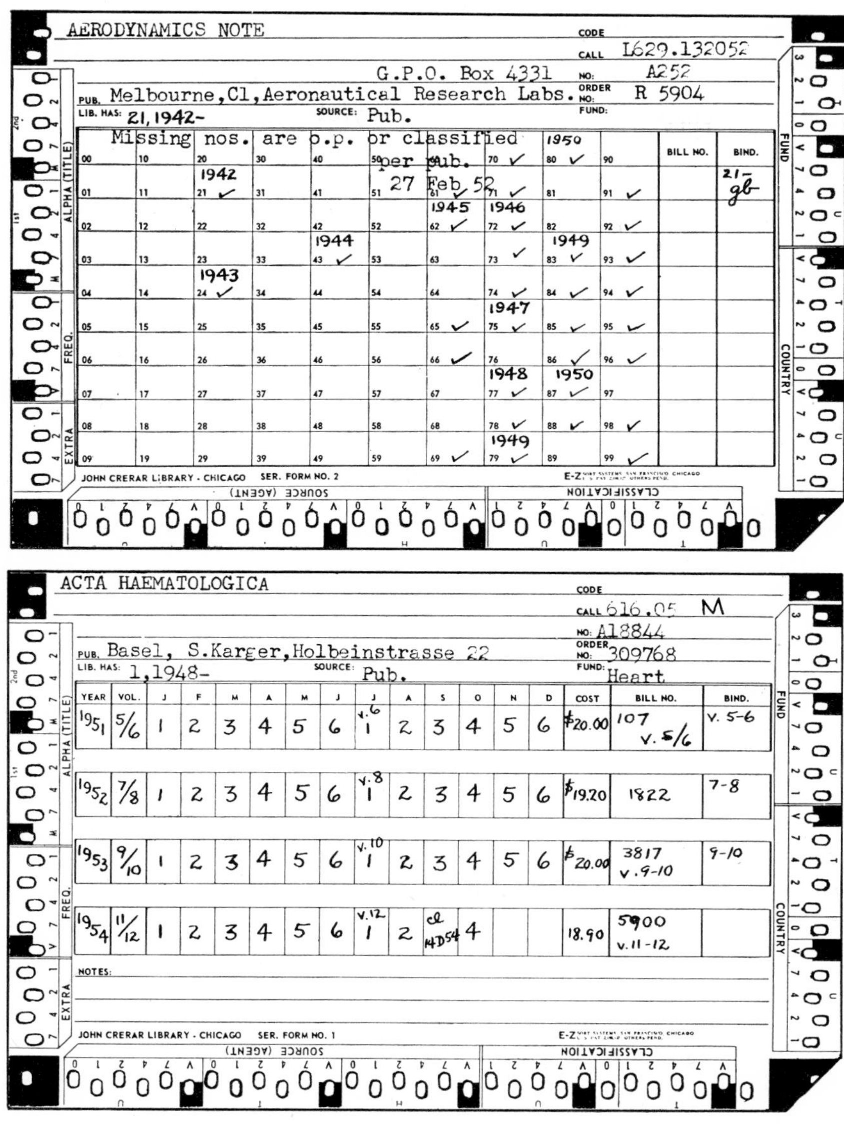

AERODYNAMICS NOTE

CODE

CALL L629.132052

G.P.O. Box 4331 NO: A252

PUB. Melbourne, Cl, Aeronautical Research Labs. ORDER NO: R 5904

LIB. HAS: 21, 1942- SOURCE: Pub. FUND:

Missing nos. are o.p. or classified per pub. 27 Feb 52

00	10	20	30	40	50	60	70 ✓	1950 80 ✓	90	BILL NO.	BIND.
01	11	1942 21 ✓	31	41	51	61 ✓	71 ✓	81	91 ✓		21- gb
02	12	22	32	42	52	1945 62 ✓	1946 72 ✓	82	92 ✓		
03	13	23	33	1944 43 ✓	53	63	73 ✓	1949 83 ✓	93 ✓		
04	14	1943 24 ✓	34	44	54	64	74 ✓	84 ✓	94 ✓		
05	15	25	35	45	55	65 ✓	1947 75 ✓	85 ✓	95 ✓		
06	16	26	36	46	56	66 ✓	76	86 ✓	96 ✓		
07	17	27	37	47	57	67	1948 77 ✓	1950 87 ✓	97		
08	18	28	38	48	58	68	78 ✓	88 ✓	98 ✓		
09	19	29	39	49	59	69 ✓	1949 79 ✓	89	99 ✓		

ALPHA (TITLE) FREQ. EXTRA FUND COUNTRY

JOHN CRERAR LIBRARY - CHICAGO SER. FORM NO. 2

SOURCE (AGENT) CLASSIFICATION

ACTA HAEMATOLOGICA

CODE

CALL 616.05 M

NO: A18844

PUB. Basel, S.Karger, Holbeinstrasse 22 ORDER NO: 309768

LIB. HAS: 1,1948- SOURCE: Pub. FUND: Heart

YEAR	VOL.	J	F	M	A	M	J	J	A	S	O	N	D	COST	BILL NO.	BIND.
1951	5/6	1	2	3	4	5	6	v.6 1	2	3	4	5	6	$20.00	107 v.5/6	v. 5-6
1952	7/8	1	2	3	4	5	6	v.8 1	2	3	4	5	6	$19.20	1822	7-8
1953	9/10	1	2	3	4	5	6	v.10 1	2	3	4	5	6	$20.00	3817 v.9-10	9-10
1954	11/12	1	2	3	4	5	6	v.12 1	2	cl 4D54	4			18.90	5900 v.11-12	

NOTES:

ALPHA (TITLE) FREQ. EXTRA FUND COUNTRY

JOHN CRERAR LIBRARY - CHICAGO SER. FORM NO. 1

SOURCE (AGENT) CLASSIFICATION

FIGURE 11. Marginal punched cards for numbered series and for periodicals as used in the John Crerar Library. On the series card the year of publication is shown whenever it is different from the year of the preceding number.

cards merely as an adjunct to the visible index. This may well be a wise compromise, since if they are used for checking, the record is necessarily restricted to a single card (overriding slips cannot be used);

the number of full cards to be replaced can become a burden; and eye-finding must be given up for finger-finding in the daily checking process. The IBM cards can likewise serve in an auxiliary capacity, as has been demonstrated by the University of Texas Library; but they should not be thought of for the daily posting of current serials. As Verner Clapp has pointed out, this is because of their "dependence on the machine, the insufficient capacity of the cards themselves, and the slowness of piece-by-piece sorting."[22]

TEMPLE UNIVERSITY
WHEELDEX FORM 701100

PRICE

FREQUENCY

VOL. OR NO	PRICE	INVOICE DATE	DATE RECEIVED	VOL. OR NO	PRICE	INVOICE DATE	DATE RECEIVED	VOL. OR NO	PRICE	INVOICE DATE	DATE RECEIVED

SOURCE

TITLE

FIGURE 12. Wheeldex form from the Temple University Library record of payments.

Rotary files

Other alternatives to the visible index are the various rotary files, among them the Diebold Cardineer and the Wheeldex, the Herring-Hall-Marvin Rotary Record File, and the Mosler Revo-file. The first two employ slotted cards that are held in place by a rod but can be detached quickly for posting. Three sides of the card are free for a signaling system. The other two take regular cards that are held in place, as the wheel rotates, either by flanges or by a belt. Only a portion of the top of the cards can carry signals.

[22] "S.L.A. New York Chapter Looks at Mechanical Aids," *Library Journal* 75:723, 1950. On the University of Texas system and for analysis of the benefits of punched cards in serial work, see Alexander Moffit, "Punched Card Records in Serials Acquisition," *College and Research Libraries* 7:10-13, 1946.

THE LIBRARY OF SWARTHMORE COLLEGE
WHEELDEX FORM 702547-A

VOL. & NO.	DATE RECEIVED	Vol. (~~PRICE~~)	~~INVOICE~~ DATE
v.40, no.1	10.14.53	v.40, no.7	11.24.53
v.40, no.2	10.19.53	v.40, no.8	12.2.53
v.40, no.3	10.28.53		
v.40, no.4	10.30.53		
v.40, no.5	11.10.53		
v.40, no.6	11.16.53		
To 11.30.54	Nov. 11.17.53 $100		
v.40, no.7	11.24.53		

CIRCULATE: ~~YES~~ NO
FUND: Library - Periodical
ANALYZED: ~~YES~~ NO
S.O. - L.C. CARDS: ~~YES~~ NO
FREQUENCY: Weekly
SOURCE: Public Affairs Information Service
PRICE: $100
TITLE: Bulletin
AUTHOR: Public Affairs Information Service

Reference
Z7163
+.P9
v.32

THE LIBRARY OF SWARTHMORE COLLEGE
WHEELDEX FORM 702547-A

VOL. & NO.	DATE RECEIVED	PRICE	INVOICE DATE
Painter Feudal Monarch	12.3.51	1.06	11.28.51
Starr Emergence of Rome	12.3.51	1.06	11.28.51
Baldwin Mediev. church	10.26.53	1.06	10.16.53

CIRCULATE: YES ~~NO~~.
FUND: History
ANALYZED: YES ~~NO~~
S.O. - L.C. CARDS: ~~YES~~ NO
FREQUENCY: Varies
SOURCE: Cornell Univ. Press
PRICE: $1.06
TITLE: The development of Western civilization
AUTHOR

Classed separately

FIGURE 13. Wheeldex checking records from the Swarthmore College Library. The address, claim record, binding instructions, and the standing-order number (but not the author and title) are on the verso.

In Standard and Poor's Corporation Library the electrically controlled Cardineer is the checking medium for the featured collection of corporation reports (see Figure 8). Great theoretical interest attaches to this installation, for side by side with the Cardineer is a visible index which cares for the remaining serials. Here is a library which is pleased with the performance of both types of checking record for their respective tasks.[23] At Temple University Library the Wheeldex is in operation as a record of serial payments (see Figure 12). In Swarthmore College Library it has been found to be a very satisfactory multi-purpose record for posting current issues, recording binding

THE LIBRARY OF SWARTHMORE COLLEGE
WHEELDEX FORM 702547-A

VOL. & NO.	DATE RECEIVED	PRICE	INVOICE DATE	VOL. & NO.	DATE RECEIVED	PRICE	INVOICE DATE	VOL. & NO.	DATE RECEIVED	PRICE	INVOICE DATE
v.32	4.20.53	5.00	4.20.53								
v.33	9.4.53	7.50	8.27.53								
v.34	1.7.54	3.00	12.21.53								
v.35	12.28.53	12.00	12.21.53								

CIRCULATE: YES ~~NO~~ | FUND Library - Contin. | ANALYZED YES ~~NO~~ | S.O. - L.C. CARDS YES ~~NO~~ | FREQUENCY Varies

Classed separately | SOURCE American Philosophical Society | PRICE Varies

TITLE Memoirs

AUTHOR American Philosophical Society ✱

Figure 14. Wheeldex checking record from the Swarthmore College Library, showing the signaling system. A blue clip on the right (shown in black in the illustration) indicates that correspondence relating to this title is in the regular file; an orange clip (shaded in the illustration) specifies a library continuation; a green clip a reference item; and a black clip that correspondence is in the follow-up file. Clips on the front are: red (claimed by date), green (pre-claim, volume not received), yellow (renew each year in the month indicated), dark blue (renew in even years), black (renew in odd years), light blue (not a standing order or definite yearly). Clips on the left side are: red (special attention), green (not yet sent to *New Serial Titles*). The star in the lower right, red in the original, indicates that previous full cards are in the dead file.

progress, etc. (see Figures 13-14). The Herring-Hall-Marvin Rotary Record File is very much liked at the University of California Library at Berkeley (see Figure 15); the Mosler Revo-file has been adopted at the Midwest Inter-Library Center. Both types take existing cards without adjustment when desired, a decisive factor at Berkeley where the

[23] For a further account of the Cardineer, see George N. Hartje, "Centralized Serial Records in University Libraries," *Serial Slants* v.1, Jan. 1951, p.15-16.

staff did not want to convert its 38,000 cards. It is usually found, however, that one of the real gains comes from setting up the file completely afresh, so money should generally be provided for conversion of the records.

Any library that commits itself to a rotary file must forego the advantages of overriding slips, and in so doing it condemns itself to the never-ceasing task of making new records to replace filled cards. Unless the file is limited to low-frequency serials, the rate of replace-

Unbound: LIB. SCH.
No. 2 — 14 13 12 11 10 9 8 7 6 5 4 3 2 1 — Card 7 — C X S
Entry: American library association, Chicago. Bulletin.
Gift | Exch. | Sm.
Mem. Ord. No. D6172
Date 6-8-28
Fund Current Serials
Call No: Z673 A5
Bound: 1(1907)-41, 43-46 (1952)
To Receive 1928+
Binding: √1/1/54 V.47

Year	Ser. Vol.	Jan.	Feb.	Mar.	Apr.	May	June	July	Aug.	Sept.	Oct.	Nov.	Dec.	TP-I-Sup.	Unbound Back File
1954	48	1 1/8/54	2 2/10/54											BD. IN LAST NO. OR COMES LOOSE IN NO. 1 OF NEXT VOL.	V.47(1953)I

University of California—General Library—Serials 11-5m-4,'52 (A325s) 4231

FIGURE 15. Herring-Hall-Marvin card (5 by 8 inches) from the University of California Library.

ment is upwards of a fifth of the file each year. Folding cards can, of course, be employed to reduce the incidence of retyping, and these, when judiciously planned, provide a certain amount of build-up to facilitate finger-finding. Evidently the University of California was not perturbed by the constant burden of retyping thousands of filled cards every year, for although its checking cards are 5 by 8 inches in size it designed its records for monthlies to last only six years (see Figure 15). By contrast, overriding slips eliminate the retyping of cards, and a 6 by 4 inch monthly slip lasts twenty years.

Another disadvantage of the rotary file is that checking cards are removed for every posting. In such circumstances the checker must be trained as a filer as well; otherwise cards may easily be misfiled, especially when the records are concurrently consulted for reference purposes. Some serial librarians welcome the visible index because staff members from various departments are deterred from removing cards and taking them away from the checking area. The University of California, however, purposely sought a system whereby checking cards could be withdrawn freely for periods of a few minutes to several days, sometimes for use in the room, sometimes elsewhere; it has even provided special "Card Out for 5 Minute Room Use" dummies.

One definite advantage the rotary file has over the visible index is the relative ease with which new cards can be intercalated. It is not uncommon for visible index trays to become crowded because of reluctance to redistribute the cards.

Rotary files are quite compact in comparison with visible indexes. At the University of California it has been found that the capacity of a wheel is 4200 cards of the stock that libraries require. This is the equivalent of three and one half thirteen-tray visible index cabinets with three-sixteenths inch visibility. The compactness is satisfactory when only one person works at the files or when the space is limited, as at California. It may be less satisfactory when various people need to consult the file constantly and simultaneously.

Libraries that elect rotary files should choose the electrical models. Although this feature offers little advantage in systematic checking, it does facilitate reference consultation; moreover, segments can be removed from the electrical models without throwing the wheel off balance, whereas removal of a segment from manually operated models impedes checking because the wheel is no longer in balance.

Rotary files, especially when motorized, are much pleasanter to operate than other non-visible files, cost somewhat less than visible indexes, take up less space than visible files, and, in the case of the Cardineer and Wheeldex, lend themselves to efficient follow-up work; but they are based on the principle of finger-finding rather than eye-finding, and they incur a heavy burden of retyping because of their inability to take overriding slips. They serve large installations better than small ones; in fact, libraries are advised not to consider the purchase of rotary files unless there are at least 2000 entries in their checking file.

In some libraries annual reports are not put on the visible index because the expensive equipment cannot be justified for relatively inactive entries. In the British Library of Political and Economic Science they were excluded because they do not require a progressive signaling system. Thus it may be that annual reports and other low-frequency serials are best served by rotary files. Experience in Standard and Poor's Corporation Library might tend to confirm this observation. The great concentration of entries on a wheel could hardly be a handicap for low-frequency serials as it may be for high-frequency ones, particularly periodicals. There may, however, be serious objection to the additional alphabet.

Motorized visible indexes

The Ferris Rotary File has a model which houses visible index units, thus combining the advantages of the motorized wheel and the visible index. It also has a model which houses Magnadex trays: tub trays with V-visibility induced magnetically when a guide card is touched.

Remington Rand has developed a visible index, the Robot-Kardex, which eliminates the pulling out and pushing in of drawers. Two counterbalanced banks of thirty trays each are housed in a unit that has a maximum capacity of 4020 entries. A tray is selected or returned at the touch of a key. Approximately three seconds are required for a tray to be in checking position after the index key has been activated. As is true of the wheel types, the motorized visible indexes would not be desirable in any library where posting, searching, and reference are carried on extensively and simultaneously. Trays can be removed for consultation elsewhere, as in other systems; but in general only one person at a time has access to the trays.

Hartje has written with enthusiasm about the potentialities of the Robot-Kardex, whose principal drawback is its cost.[24] As of 1954 no library had installed a motorized visible index.

Predominance of the visible index

Clearly much experimentation on types of indexes is necessary and new equipment must be exploited or developed before serial librarians can rest content. In the meantime the visible index is likely to remain as standard and reasonably satisfactory equipment for the great majority of libraries. This much is obvious at any rate: eye-finding is faster than finger-finding—otherwise there would be no occasion for guide cards in a catalog tray—so the visible index, which is based on the principle of eye-finding, has a head start on any non-visible file, whether it be a standard card catalog, a tub tray, a marginal punched card record, or a wheel type.

Unless experimental evidence can prove the contrary, libraries should utilize the visible index for their current serial checking. They may put low-frequency serials on a wheel type if they will accept two alphabets, otherwise they should use equipment based on the principle of eye-finding until or unless compelling reasons justify the adoption of finger-finding methods.

---

[24] Hartje, *op. cit.,* p.17-19.

Specifications for a visible index

When a collection is quite small, or when for any reason the records should be portable, the check list may be in book form. A book unit can hold up to 128 entries in the Kardex 6 by 4 inch style. In the Acme style the maximum is 168 entries for 6 by 4 inch cards with $\frac{3}{16}$-inch visible margin or 126 entries with $\frac{1}{4}$-inch visible margin. Usually, however, cabinets with trays are the norm for larger installations. Metal cabinets are preferable to wood, and for the most part duplex units, in which two rows of cards are visible at a glance, are preferable to single ones. Although all manufacturers do not build duplex trays, they offer real advantages to most libraries. It is possible to have 188 6 by 4 inch cards in a duplex tray with $\frac{3}{16}$-inch visibility or 142 with $\frac{1}{4}$-inch visibility; consequently fewer trays are opened and closed in the course of a day's work. The Library of Congress prefers single units to duplex, primarily because work in the latter ties up more of the file at any given moment. It also feels that duplex trays may be a little harder to pull out and push back.

If possible it is better to limit the height of the cabinets to twelve or thirteen trays. When the height is so limited, the checker does not have to reach far for any tray. Obviously with this height limitation the cabinets will be spread out rather widely in an installation that must provide for from five to twenty-five thousand entries or more. But this spread may have its advantages, since a checker can operate in close proximity to his records without blocking them for others who need to consult them. Furthermore, it allows for working space at regular intervals where serials may be piled up before and after checking.

In general, visible index cabinets should not be placed on desks, at least in larger installations. Except when the visible index is almost exclusively the province of one person it should be looked on as a utility record. As an aid in placing it at the disposal of others than the checkers, desk or other work space should be provided for the checkers elsewhere in the vicinity where they may perform a variety of ancillary tasks. Further, it is better as a rule to place the cabinets on work tables than on stands. The latter may have the benefit of movability, since they can be mounted on wheels, but they restrict the checker's work area and almost surely require the presence of a book truck to accommodate the serials that are being checked. When stands are preferred, they should be equipped with sliding work shelves; otherwise the bottom tray in each cabinet must be replaced by a slide, thus reducing the capacity of the unit. The advantage of work tables is that they allow for superior working conditions. They should therefore be favored whenever the records are used preponderantly for checking. At least one extra table should be provided for the receipt and sorting of the day's mail, for mail baskets, and for the *Union List of Serials*. If there is much material to be dispatched to different parts of the library, adequate shelf space should also be available.

In rare instances swivels may be provided so that the cabinets may be rotated. Their former application in the Department of Agriculture Library has already been noted.

Most manufacturers allow for a visible margin of a quarter of an inch at the bottom of the checking card. In some models it is possible to get an exposure of three-sixteenths of an inch. The smaller margin is acceptable for serial records, especially since it increases the capacity of each tray substantially, and should be considered favorably when available.

For Acme-type cards a bottom-line card holder should be acquired as an aid in typing the information that goes in the visible margin. No such aid is needed for Kardex-type cards which have perforated stubs that can be torn off after the card has been typed.

Some trays have small pulls that are hard on the fingers. Larger pulls are desirable, and these can be covered with rubber to advantage.

It is possible to buy cabinets that can be locked, but for ordinary library purposes locks are not required, nor are firedoors.

Cards and slips

The checking records themselves may consist of cards (either single or double), folded forms, or cards together with overriding slips. Most of the earlier library installations relied on single cards exclusively, and it is one of the disadvantages of the non-visible types of check list that they cannot utilize the multiple card forms. Both double cards and folded forms are employed to give greater capacity, and thereby to reduce the frequency of substitution of new records for old. Overriding slips in conjunction with basic entry cards, such as are used in the Library of Congress, are a still more effective device for prolonging the life of checking records. They too can be single or double, though a number of single slips will be found to be more effective than one double slip.

Cards and slips can be bought from the firms that supply visible indexes. Satisfactory standard forms can generally be secured, or individualized forms may be printed to accommodate a variety of local circumstances. The common experience in libraries has been that it is more economical to get the forms printed locally, at least after the initial installation. This is especially true in universities and other institutions which have their own printing plants.

The number of kinds of forms should be restricted to approximately four to six. Except in unusual circumstances there is no point in having more, since a form may be able to serve two or more types of serials equally well. The most common forms are for weeklies, monthlies, irregular publications, and annuals or numbered series. If newspapers are checked in, there must be a form for dailies.

Blank or ruled cards can fill a number of utility roles. They may be used for irregular publications, unnumbered series, outstanding

Vol.	No.	Date	t.p.i.	Vol.	No.	Date	t.p.i.
1	1	Winter 1947		6	1	Winter 1952	
	2	Spring 1947			2	Spring 1952	
	3	Autumn 1947	✓✓		3	Autumn 1952	✓✓
2	1	Winter 1948					
	2	Spring 1948					
	3	Autumn 1948	✓✓				
3	1	Winter 1949					
	2	Spring 1949					
	3	Autumn 1949	✓✓				
4	1	Winter 1950					
	2	Spring 1950					
	3	Autumn 1950	✓✓				
5	1	Winter 1951					
	2	Spring 1951					
	3	Autumn 1951	✓✓				

Harvard Library bulletin B 8416.73

FIGURE 16. Overriding slip and basic entry card from Harvard College Library: the ruled slip is adaptable to any frequency.

orders, and references. They may also serve as dummies on the occasions when it is necessary to remove a card from the file, e.g. to change the heading in some way. Colored stock may be desirable for outstanding orders, references, and dummies. The color tells at a glance that there is no point in opening up the file to look for checking information.

The typical single card for weeklies lasts four years, for monthlies ten. At the expiration of that time the card must be replaced by a fresh one onto which has been copied all the essential data from the superseded card. When the checking is done on single cards the serial staff must plan for a large conversion job at the end of every four and every ten years, with a certain amount of conversion going on continuously. This process would be almost prohibitive in larger libraries where periodicals for the branches are checked in centrally, because the cards would expire much too rapidly. For these libraries double cards or folded forms provide four times the normal checking space. The folded forms fill out the tray to some extent, but unless they create too much build-up this is not serious, and a moderate amount of build-up makes it easier to turn up the cards at a desired spot.

By far the most successful device for overcoming the necessity for periodic replacement of entries due to full records is the overriding

ACME 27390-6

Vol.			JAN.	FEB.	MAR.	APR.	MAY	JUNE	JULY	AUG.	SEP.	OCT.	NOV.	DEC.	T. P.	IND.
42		1949	✓✓ 1			✓✓ 2			✓✓ 3			✓✓ 4			✓	✓
43		1950	✓✓ 1			✓✓ 2			✓✓ 3			✓✓ 4			✓	✓
44		1951	✓✓ 1			✓✓ 2			✓✓ 3			✓✓ 4			✓	✓
45		1952	✓✓ 1			✓✓ 2			✓✓ 3							

Cop 2 = HU 136.14

Harvard theological review CF 58.4

FIGURE 17. Overriding slip and basic entry card from Harvard College Library: two checks indicate two copies.

slip in conjunction with a basic entry card. Figures 16-21 show the overriding forms used in the Harvard College Library. As many as five or six of these auxiliary slips can be attached to an entry. The Library of Congress has at times added as many as ten, but that number seems to result in excessive build-up. Under the system of basic entry cards and overriding slips the cards bear the permanent information: details of entry, call number, checking directions, summarized statement of holdings, billing data, etc. The whole of the card, both front and back, is free for these notations, though usually only the front is required. Ruled cards may suffice for all these purposes, or special forms may be preferable. The overriding slips are the printed checking forms, for weeklies, monthlies, etc. They are expendable and can be used on both sides, thus doubling the life of the checking

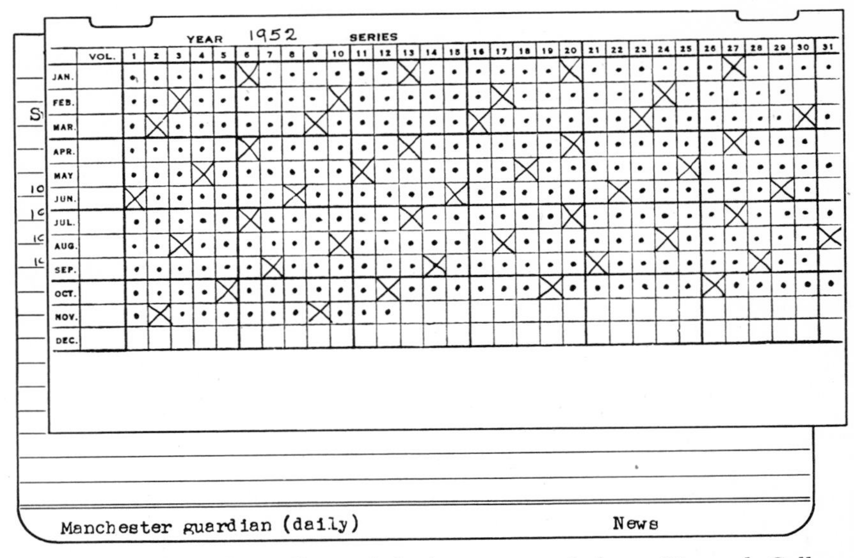

YEAR 1952 SERIES

	VOL.	1	2	3	4	5	6	7	8	9	10	11	12	13	14	15	16	17	18	19	20	21	22	23	24	25	26	27	28	29	30	31
JAN.		•	•	•	•	•	X	•	•	•	•	•	•	X	•	•	•	•	•	•	X	•	•	•	•	•	•	X	•	•	•	•
FEB.		•	•	X	•	•	•	•	•	•	X	•	•	•	•	•	•	X	•	•	•	•	•	•	X	•	•	•	•	•		
MAR.		•	X	•	•	•	•	•	•	X	•	•	•	•	•	•	X	•	•	•	•	•	•	X	•	•	•	•	•	•	X	•
APR.		•	•	•	•	•	X	•	•	•	•	•	•	X	•	•	•	•	•	•	X	•	•	•	•	•	•	X	•	•	•	
MAY		•	•	•	X	•	•	•	•	•	•	X	•	•	•	•	•	•	X	•	•	•	•	•	•	X	•	•	•	•	•	•
JUN.		X	•	•	•	•	•	•	X	•	•	•	•	•	•	X	•	•	•	•	•	•	X	•	•	•	•	•	•	X	•	
JUL.		•	•	•	•	•	X	•	•	•	•	•	•	X	•	•	•	•	•	•	X	•	•	•	•	•	•	X	•	•	•	•
AUG.		•	•	X	•	•	•	•	•	•	X	•	•	•	•	•	•	X	•	•	•	•	•	•	X	•	•	•	•	•	•	X
SEP.		•	•	•	•	•	•	X	•	•	•	•	•	•	X	•	•	•	•	•	•	X	•	•	•	•	•	•	X	•	•	
OCT.		•	•	•	•	X	•	•	•	•	•	•	X	•	•	•	•	•	•	X	•	•	•	•	•	•	X	•	•	•	•	•
NOV.		•	X	•	•	•	•	•	•	X	•	•	•																			
DEC.																																

Manchester guardian (daily) — News

FIGURE 18. Overriding slip and basic entry card from Harvard College Library: method of checking a newspaper. Billing information is on the card underneath.

ACME 27391-6

1953	✓ 1	11	21	31	41	51	61	71	81	91
1953	✓ 2	12	22	32	42	52	62	72	82	92
	3	13	23	33	43	53	63	73	83	93
	4	14	24	34	44	54	64	74	84	94
1953	✓ 5	15	25	35	45	55	65	75	85	95
	6	16	26	36	46	56	66	76	86	96
1953	✓ 7	17	27	37	47	57	67	77	87	97
	8	18	28	38	48	58	68	78	88	98
	9	19	29	39	49	59	69	79	89	99
	10	20	30	40	50	60	70	80	90	00

Vol. I General characteristics | Vol. 2 Non-farm housing | Vol. 3 Farm housing | Vol. 4 Residential financing | Vol. 5 Block statistics

United States census of housing: 1950 — Econ 8219.50.10

FIGURE 19. Overriding slips and basic entry card from Harvard College Library: five overriding slips for a work treated as a serial.

ACME 27390-6

Vol.		JAN	FEB	MAR	APR	MAY	JUNE	JULY	AUG	SEP	OCT	NOV.	DEC	T. P.	IND
1	1948			1			2			3			4	✓	✓
2	1949			1			2			3			4	✓	✓
3	1950			1			2			3			4	✓	✓
4	1951			1			2			3			4	✓	✓
5	1952			1			2			3			4	✓	✓
6	1953			1			2			3					

Cop. 1 - Sci 890.45

Cop. 2 - Engin. Lib.

cop. 2 - Engin. Lib.

Quarterly journal of mechanics and applied mathematics Sci 890.45

FIGURE 20. Overriding slips and basic entry card from Harvard College Library: multiple slips for two copies.

ACME 27390-6

			JAN.	FEB	MAR.	APR.	MAY	JUNE	JULY	AUG.	SEP.	OCT.	NOV.	DEC.	~~T. P.~~	~~IND.~~
1953			1	6	10	14	18	23	27	31	36	40	45	49	Register 1-13 ✓	
			2	7	11	15	19	24	28	32	37	41	46		14-26 ✓	
			3	8	12	16	20	25	29	33	38	42	47		27-39 ✓	
			4	9	13	17	21	26	30	34	39	43	48			
			5				22			35		44				

Reihe A. Neuerscheinungen des Buchhandels Ref 622.13

Reihe B. Neuerscheinungen ausserhalb des Buchhandels Ref 622.13.3

Deutsche Nationalbibliographie

FIGURE 21. Overriding slips and basic entry card from Harvard College Library: multiple slips for two series.

records. Eventually, when both sides are full, the slip can be removed and a substitute added with a minimum of effort. When the substitution is made the summarized statement on the permanent card should be adjusted—a routine which must be carried out much more frequently under other systems—and there may be other data as well to add to the new overriding slip.

Multiple overriding slips may be pressed into service when there is more than one publication under a given heading, for example the name of a corporate body, or they may facilitate the checking of copies that come from different sources or that go to different destinations. In these circumstances the checking directions should go on the overriding slips, not on the basic entry card. At times it is helpful to cut away part of the bottom margin of multiple overriding slips so that the headings on the covered slips may be partly or wholly visible (see Figures 19-21).

The Library of Congress destroys its superseded checking records. On the other hand, some libraries like to preserve them; but there is no real reason for so doing once the summarized statement of holdings has been added to the basic entry card or the permanent serial records. There is a better case for preserving superseded checking records when the visible index is itself the permanent serial catalog. In this situation a compromise between discarding old checking records and keeping them indefinitely may be made by keeping one old card for each title, discarding it in turn as it becomes superseded, since it is unlikely that earlier records will need to be consulted.

Optimum size of visible index card

Early card checking records for serials generally adopted the international size, 7.5 by 12.5 centimeters (sometimes 3 by 5 inches). These cards could easily be housed in regular catalog cases, with a varying number of trays in each case.[25] Experience soon taught, however, that these cards were too small for efficient work. Larger cards up to 5 by 8 inches were therefore adopted. The most common size was 6 by 4 inches, and these are the dimensions that are now recognized as standard for serial checking records.[26] The 6 by 4 inch card provides a reasonably large visible margin, even with 3/16-inch visibility, in

[25] Some libraries still manage with equipment of this kind, others with 3 by 5 inch cards in visible index trays. The equipment itself has no bearing on the size of card; similar sizes are available for both a regular catalog tray, a tub file, a wheel, and a visible index.

[26] Hartje, *op. cit.*, p.22, gives the card dimensions for eight university libraries and the Library of Congress. Three of them use 3 by 5 cards, four 6 by 4 cards, and two 5 by 8 cards.

which to record the name of a serial plus certain standard details. The checking squares are big enough to carry several types of information, among them the issue number, checks for multiple copies, the date of receipt if that is required, and checks for Library of Congress cards for analyzed series; and elsewhere on the front or back of the card there is space for checking directions, billing records, cataloging information, statements about issues not published, summarized holdings, etc. Cards larger than 6 by 4 inches preclude the utilization

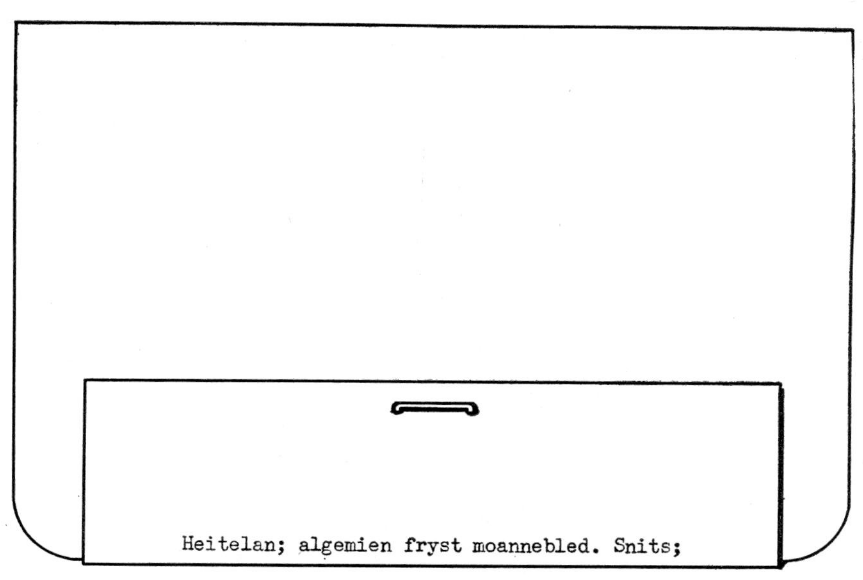

FIGURE 22. Temporary entry in the Library of Congress visible index.

of duplex trays, make the file more extensive and costly, and yield far less checking space than overriding slips on 6 by 4 inch cards. Smaller cards may result in cramped and crowded statements, thereby either sacrificing legibility and accuracy or requiring some data to be maintained on supplementary files.[27]

Title inserts

When an entry in a Kardex-type index requires a new heading it can be typed on a thin strip called a title insert which can then be

[27] Fleming Bennett implemented his idea of a multi-purpose serial record by installing 6 by 4 inch cards in duplex trays; see his "A Multi-Purpose Serials Record," *College and Research Libraries* 9:231-37, 1948. The more librarians think of centralized serial records, the more they must incline towards multi-purpose records.

inserted in the celluloid covering that protects the visible margin in Kardex files. Just as overriding slips can reduce the amount of retyping due to full checking cards, so title inserts can save retyping due to change of title or corporate name. The celluloid covering itself, which keeps the cards clean, may be a useful feature in hard-worked systems, although it should be noted that in the Department of Agriculture Library glare from the celluloid strips in its former visible index was considered objectionable. Manufacturers of non-Kardex type cards supply plastic sprays to protect the visible margin just as the celluloid covering does. In most installations, however, neither the plastic spray nor the celluloid covering is really required.

Even though the cards do not have celluloid strips to cover the visible margin it is still not necessary to retype the whole entry because of a change in heading. Slip-on sheaths, also known as visible margin protectors, are on the market and can be attached to any card to permit the addition of a title insert. A simpler method is to type the new information on plain paper which is then pasted or stapled to the card. The Library of Congress makes temporary entries by stapling onto a blank card an aniline reproduction of the purchase requisition in such a way that only the heading shows on the face of the card (see Figure 22).

Arrangement of entries

Since the visible index is a work record, its entries should be arranged or filed in the way that will most effectively serve the requirements of the people who work with it. The more simple and natural this arrangement can be, the better. Most libraries do as the Library of Congress does, arranging the visible index entries according to the filing rules for the card catalog. Those rules may, however, be more technical than is desirable in a work record and may need to be adjusted in a variety of ways if the mass operation of checking is to be expedited.

Several special breakdowns may be desirable.[28] If, for example, serials are received both individually and in bundles, a supplementary arrangement for the titles that come in bundles may prove to be a real convenience. Some overseas agents, in Great Britain and Germany, for instance, accumulate current periodicals for an individual library and forward them in weekly packages. It saves time to segregate the entries

[28] In the Harvard College Library the main alphabet is supplemented by the following breakdowns: Allen (Great Britain), Harrassowitz and Koehler (Germany), Harvard University publications, the Organization of American States, Slavic material, Stechert, United Nations documents, and United States serial documents.

for the titles so received and to group them in a special tray or trays under the name of the dealer. Both the items and the bills can then be checked off rapidly, and it is easy to compile renewal lists. When such a plan is followed, references for each such title should be inserted in a title-a-line supplementary record or in the main alphabet.

In a university with an extensive publication program it may save time to group the entries for all serials issued by the university, regardless of whether they would normally go under the name of the institution or under their title. Frequently there are multiple copies of and multiple locations for these publications, and it may be desirable for a single staff member to be responsible for them because of the personal contacts and special arrangements sometimes associated with them.

Slavic titles, particularly those in the Cyrillic alphabet, are often grouped, partly because they may have to be checked off by a language specialist and partly because they may call for more watchful attention than publications that can be obtained more readily. It is extremely difficult to fill gaps in Slavic titles, especially when an interval after normal receipt is allowed to elapse. The follow-up work for them must therefore be much more strict and rapid. In other countries it is customary for gift and exchange serials to continue year after year until countermanded, and publishers and dealers frequently accept till-forbid subscriptions, but the subscribing library must generally undertake the responsibility for renewal of Slavic titles if it is to ensure the continuity of its files. Obviously renewal procedures are facilitated when the entries are held together. For special language breakdowns like Slavic it is not necessary to put references in the main part of the alphabet. There is an even stronger argument for segregating titles in Oriental languages, because specialists must work with them. It may even be desirable to locate the Oriental language records near the staff that handles Oriental material.

The biggest question of arrangement is whether it is better to interfile document and non-document serials or to keep them independent of each other with document specialists in charge of the document file. It will generally be found that there is much to gain by consolidating the checking records and putting them in the hands of a single group of checkers, even though specialized staff may be desirable in the largest libraries to procure or service government serials. If the checking records are not interfiled, one of the files may receive preferred treatment while others suffer neglect because of sickness, vacations, etc. A common staff that must keep all the work on a current basis, regardless of type, and where one person can step in when another is absent, will maintain the checking operation more satisfactorily in every respect.

References

Since space in expensive equipment is at a premium, references in visible indexes are commonly held to a bare minimum. They may be made somewhat more freely in non-visible indexes, but even there they should be held to a minimum lest the file become too large. References are made principally to artificial cataloging entries and special filing arrangements. References from former titles should be omitted unless the checking records constitute the library's serial catalog, as in the Linda Hall Library. In the Harvard College Library references were for a time inserted in the visible index. When it was realized that more than a fourth of the entries were references, they were removed and recorded on title-a-line "Insite Indexes," one unit for each two duplex visible index cabinets.

Follow-up systems

The two fundamentals of a good checking system are completely reliable records and a vigorous and enlightened follow-up program. Libraries frequently experience great difficulty in training the checkers to institute prompt and systematic follow-up. Sometimes this is caused by overelaborate acquisition routines that hamper claiming and replacement work, sometimes simply by pressure of work. Sometimes it is caused by neglect, and supervisors must constantly remind their staffs that incomplete files are a burden to a library at every turn. They inconvenience reference and circulation service, prevent volumes from being bound on schedule (and may result in damage or further loss to the unbound parts), increase the cost of acquisition work because of the correspondence incidental to the completion of files, and increase the cost of cataloging because of broken records and extra processes, such as bundling.

Follow-up work can be based on a system of tabs or can be relatively informal. Tabs come in two basic styles: those that clip on and those that slide along the visible margin. The clip-on tab is made chiefly for non-visible records. It acts as a signal to show that a missing number has been written for and that further action may be called for if the gap is not filled in a reasonable time. These tabs are generally made of metal for longer life. For visible indexes, however, transparent signals are preferable so that the data in the visible margin which they may cover will not be obscured. Sliding tabs may specify either the date of the last issue received or the date when the next one is due.

The real motive for installing a visible index in the British Library of Political and Economic Science was to be able to tell at a glance when follow-up action should be taken.

> This has been achieved by a simple system of tabbing; not, of course, by the old-style tab which took the clumsy a minute or more to fix in place, but by one held in a transparent groove and flicked to its new position in a matter of two seconds. The bottom edges of the marking-off cards have a blank space at each end but are otherwise divided into twelve monthly divisions and five weekly divisions (as there may be five Tuesdays, say, in any one month). In one of the monthly and one of the weekly divisions of each card a green tab has been fixed. In the space at the extreme right a tab of another color signifies a particular year. Taken together these three tabs show, correct to the nearest week, *not the date of issue* of the periodical part last received nor of the next one due, *but the date when the next part is due to reach the library*. A black and white striped tab at the extreme left of the card signifies that, owing to irregularity of publication, this date may be uncertain, while the insertion of an orange one shows that, the periodical in question having become overdue, action has been taken.[29]

The signaling systems for visible indexes have been greatly improved in recent years. The different possibilities need to be studied carefully before one is adopted. Special libraries generally favor the use of tabs on their visible indexes while general libraries are more inclined to do without them. The general library is apt to consider them an expensive device to operate, despite Marjorie Plant's "two seconds." When the New York Public Library installed its visible index in 1919 it decided against a signaling system because it estimated that the equivalent of one full-time checker would be required to manipulate the tabs.

In any library which finds the manipulation of tabs time-consuming, the system should be changed to informal but productive follow-up. The informal approach is a scheme whereby the checkers or special follow-up assistants go through the entire visible index at stated intervals looking for overdue items. The file should be completely checked every quarter, if at all possible. More frequent systematic checks should not be necessary in most cases, since the current checking procedures should disclose most gaps; for instance, if in recording the receipt of the June issue it is noticed that the May number has not been checked in, follow-up action should be started.[30]

---

[29] Plant, *op. cit.*, p.60. Miss Plant goes on to give several examples of how her signaling system operates. For a special study of signaling systems, see R. M. Jacobs, "Focal Point: a Composite Record for the Control of Periodicals Using a Visible Signalling Device," *Journal of Documentation* 6:213-28, 1950.

[30] Each library must determine for itself the time interval that is to elapse before action should be started on publications of various frequencies. The interval for overseas publications should be somewhat longer than for domestic ones, as a rule.

A combination of these two procedures gives most libraries all the coverage they need. The heart of the task is to see that the checkers really do take steps to procure missing issues, whether on evidence derived from their daily work or from a quarterly review of their files. The advantage of a signaling system is that the checker is kept constantly aware of the need for prompt follow-up action. As a compromise—to take advantage of the system without accepting all its detail—a library could employ a signaling system for low-frequency serials but not for dailies and weeklies.

In libraries where the checkers are responsible for follow-up action they should have on hand a supply of postal cards that can be filled out simply and quickly on the basis of information on the checking records. The postal cards should be filled out and dispatched with as little formality as possible, preferably with none, for follow-up activity should be as automatic as possible.

A related activity that should proceed as automatically as claims for missing issues is the requisitioning of replacement copies for items that are lost or mutilated during their stay in the periodical room or elsewhere. Order department routines should be adjusted to permit essential ordering of this kind to be carried on in a routine fashion. The periodical room staff commonly starts action by filling out a postal card. If the visible index is not in the periodical room, the card should be routed through the checkers so that the replacement request can be noted and the replacement copy sent to its proper destination when received—otherwise it may be discarded as a duplicate.

A symbol in the appropriate checking square, denoting that the delinquent copy or the replacement has been requested, can serve most purposes. The symbol should preferably be in a distinctive color. An alternative is to clip or otherwise attach a three by five slip or other memorandum to the checking record, recording the action taken and informing the checker of the destination of the item when received. Clip-on tabs may also be employed to call attention to the need for further follow-up procedures if the first request is not successful; but such delinquencies will be noted in any library that checks through its files periodically in a ceaseless quest for missing numbers.

So important is it for a research library to have a trustworthy follow-up system that in the larger institutions thought should be given to the possibility of having a part-time or full-time assistant whose primary responsibility is to read the files continuously, in much the same way that shelves have to be read in order to keep the book collection in proper condition.

Under pressure of work, any function is bound to suffer if it is not recognized as a primary one. In too many instances follow-up work has been considered a secondary function of serial librarians who, if the truth is known, are so fully occupied with their primary tasks that talk of secondary functions is academic. A possible remedy is to say to the checkers that follow-up activities are one of their primary responsibilities, as is the case when fully developed signaling systems are in operation, and to organize their work so that they have time and opportunity to maintain their files thoroughly. The checkers must then understand that it is not sufficient to check off each day's mail, even though there is a feeling of accomplishment and satisfaction in leaving the work area clean at the end of the day. It is of fundamental importance that all the time necessary be allowed and taken to note gaps and to request missing numbers;[31] and in addition to go through the files systematically, a certain amount every week. Thereafter if some serials are left over at the end of a day's work, the supervisor can tell that more manpower is needed. It is worth noting, too, that when the checkers take on follow-up work as one of their primary responsibilities, they are thereby introducing an element of variety into what can become a very routine operation.

There are very few libraries which like the Department of Agriculture Library have an enviable record for follow-up work or which can say with Marjorie Plant of the British Library of Political and Economic Science: "The checking for overdues is carried out weekly; the whole process occupies only a few minutes."[32] There is no doubt that special libraries give more attention to follow-up work than general libraries. Typical of the general library is the situation at the Library of Congress where an automatic system has been sought for some years, and at Yale which in 1951 reported: "For the first time since we moved into this building, records for serial purchases were checked through completely from A to Z to find out which ones were not coming currently, and the same process was begun for serials received on exchange."[33] It is good to see the general library coming to grips with this trying but most insistent problem.

Binding records

The date when volumes are sent to and returned from the bindery may or may not be added to the visible index cards, depending on

[31] The Serials Division at the Library of Congress follows an alert practice which is worthy of mention: "By examination of each issue of the *Bulletin of Bibliography* for 'death' notices we are promptly informed when a title ceases, and can secure missing issues, if any, before they become collectors' items." Library of Congress *Departmental & Divisional Manuals* 9:16 (Washington, 1950).

[32] Plant, *op. cit.*, p.61.

[33] Yale University, *Report of the Librarian*, 1950-51 (New Haven, 1951), p.13.

local circumstances. If the best interests of a library are served by centralizing serial record work, then the visible index can readily be called into play for binding records and instructions. If, on the other hand, it is better to consolidate all binding records, those for non-serials and serials alike, then the visible index should dispense with current binding information. In that event it may be found that a considerable amount of routine is involved in recording the location of serials that have not yet reached the stacks, and that a certain amount of duplicate effort is expended on newly acquired items that go directly from the visible index to the bindery. At the Library of Congress

> the Binding Assistant records in the Serial Record the progress of the binding of serial issues, working from binding slips prepared by the binding units of the custodial divisions. This Assistant is also responsible for verifying the accuracy of the processing information on the binding slips and their conformance with selection decisions.[34]

In the Harvard College Library, where the binding information is not on the visible index, a considerable amount of work is entailed in making out and filing a charge card in the circulation file for each serial sent to the bindery, and eventually in canceling the charge. In the New York Public Library a special file is maintained at the Information Desk to show when volumes are sent to and returned from the bindery so that readers can be sent to the Periodicals Division only if the issues are there. Additional routines and files like these are expensive. They point up a problem which may perhaps best be met, if service demands permit, by utilizing the visible index for the record of binding action.

Whether or not they carry current binding information, the checking records must carry special instructions relating to binding. Through the title page and index the checking function is intimately connected with preparation of files for binding.

In many libraries the binding costs for serials are a charge against the book funds, the same as the purchase price. It is best to attempt no detailed breakdown or recording of costs. Likewise it is best, when a number of book funds must be drawn on for binding, to arrive at an across-the-boards figure for all funds instead of calculating precisely so much from this one and so much from that. Periodicals bought from specially restricted funds may necessarily be an exception to this practice, and the binding records can show that their binding cost is to be charged to a specified fund.

---

[34] Library of Congress *Departmental & Divisional Manuals* 20:58 (Washington, 1952).

Notes from dealers and publishers

The following represent some of the notes that libraries consider worth preserving as part of the bibliographic history of a set:

V. 1, no. 3 never published.
V. 6 complete in five numbers.
The issue for June 1953 completely o. p.
No. 273 misnumbered 278.

Brief notes like these, taken from reports made by dealers, publishers, and others, are added to the permanent checking records when occasion arises. The notes are usually documented by the name of the dealer or other source, as well as the date of the communication, so that reference may be made to the original source when necessary. Not infrequently the information comes in response to a follow-up inquiry—another indication of the importance of trying to fill gaps systematically.

CHAPTER 7

The Theory of Descriptive Cataloging

ONE SCHOOL OF CATALOGERS holds that serials should be cataloged according to the general principles laid down for monographs. The *Rules for Descriptive Cataloging in the Library of Congress* take this point of view. They assert that "the general principles for cataloging serials are the same as those for cataloging monographic publications; wherever suitable, the rules for the cataloging of monographs are to be applied to serials."[1] But this is an oversimplified approach to a difficult and technical field, just as it is in sharp contrast to the dictum expressed by Miss Ditmas that the serial has attained the right to be treated *sui generis* and not as a poor relation of the book. The only really important point of connection between monograph and serial cataloging is the corporate entry which is common to both. Beatrice Simon has been outspoken on the difference between the two types of cataloging:

> No one can seriously maintain that a serial is like a book in any but the most superficial aspect, and yet we have never ceased to try to force serials into the techniques and routines evolved for books. Look, for instance, at the absurd way in which some of us try to get the statement of a badly broken set onto the card form designed for the bibliographical notation of a book. The resulting confusion presented to the user of the catalog is enough to send him away in disgust at our inefficiency. Look, too, at the way in which many libraries scatter periodicals throughout a classification by the reckless addition of .05 at any given point in the scheme. Surely it is time to admit frankly that, excellent as were the principles laid down by our illustrious predecessors for the acquisition, arrangement and cataloging of books, the rules are not adequate for the reality of a library bulging with serials. It is no reflection on these people to acknowledge that they were not gifted with second sight and so did not provide for this contingency. It *is* a reflection on our own intelligence if we continue to make use of their inadequate methods and do nothing constructive to improve them.[2]

---

[1] Library of Congress, Descriptive Cataloging Division, *Rules for Descriptive Cataloging in the Library of Congress* (Washington, 1949), p.51.

[2] Beatrice V. Simon, "Let's Consider Serials Realistically," *Library Journal* 71:1296, 1946.

Whereas monograph cataloging is for the most part static, since the typical book or pamphlet is a unit complete in itself, serial cataloging must to a large extent be dynamic to provide for publications which may persist for centuries before they are complete and may undergo major or minor changes during their lifetime. The cataloging of monographs is comparatively straightforward; serials run the gamut from the straightforward to the wayward, if not the downright perverse. Many of them lie squarely across another problem area, that of the corporate entry. Accordingly the serial cataloger must be versatile and patient enough to wrestle with a combination of two of the toughest problems in cataloging. Miss Goss says of the vast field of serials, "The Pilgrim who enters this field must be prepared to flounder through the Slough of Despond, to struggle up the hill Difficulty, and, with Hopeful to cheer him on, make his progress toward the Celestial City of Truth."[3]

The Library of Congress has specified the following as the ways in which serial cataloging differs from book cataloging:

a. A serial publication in several volumes with varying bibliographical details is described from the latest volume, with the variations from that volume noted, whereas a monographic work in several volumes is cataloged from the first volume, with variations noted.
b. The editor statement is given as a supplementary note instead of in the body of the entry, because the more prominent position following the title is devoted to the statement of "holdings" and because, when editors change, the adding of that information is more convenient and economical if the editor statement has been given in a note.
c. The catalog entry for a serial publication should show the record of the volumes published and indicate which ones are in the Library's collections or should refer to a listing of such volumes.
d. An important feature for the characterization of a serial, and occasionally for its identification, is the frequency of its publication.
e. If the statement of holdings does not show the duration of publication, supplementary notes are essential to show it. This includes the facts of suspension and resumption of publication.
f. The fact that a serial is the organ of a society or other body must be stated.
g. Serial publications frequently have special numbers that must be described.[4]

This statement fails to note, except perhaps incidentally, the most significant difference between serial and monograph cataloging: whereas there are complementary records for serials, the catalog entries for monographs must stand entirely on their own for the most part. No approach to serial cataloging is satisfactory that does not make due

---

[3] Edna L. Goss, "The Cataloging of Serials," *Catalogers' and Classifiers' Yearbook* 2:73, 1930.

[4] Library of Congress, Descriptive Cataloging Division, *op. cit.*, p.51-52.

allowance for the role played by the visible index, the *Union List of Serials,* and other serial records. The accident that these records may not be located in the catalog department or with the public catalog—that they may be in the acquisition department or the periodical room—makes no difference. As has been said, serial records, wherever they may be located, must not be looked on as one of the victims of departmentalization. They must at all times be considered as joint records, serving all parts of a library fully and freely.

There are, of course, serials which require few if any supporting records: those which have ceased publication and of which the library has a complete file. The catalog entries for "complete and dead" serials do have much in common with the entries for monographs, but for the active files, the incomplete and continuing runs of serials, the complete account can to advantage be divided between the card catalog, the visible index, and other serial records. The two types of record should not duplicate each other beyond a bare minimum; to justify their existence they must be complementary, otherwise the cost of serial cataloging is bound to be excessive.

A simple illustration of the duplication of effort that may ensue if this principle of complementary records is ignored is afforded by the statement of frequency, which the Library of Congress specifies as "an important feature for the characterization of a serial."[5] The visible index is vitally concerned with frequency of issue; its records are detailed check lists. Is it necessary, then, to repeat frequency statements on the catalog cards, especially when it is realized that these statements often are not as simple as they may seem, but must be adjusted as changes take place? Some of the detail that may be involved is disclosed by the following statement of practice in the Library of Congress:

If the frequency of publication can be described by a single adjective or brief phrase, it is given immediately after the collation, unless it is obvious from the title of the publication; e.g., *Quarterly journal of current acquisitions.*

v. illus. 21 cm. annual.
v. illus. 21 cm. 3 no. a year.
v. illus. 21 cm. monthly (except July and Aug.)
v. illus. 21 cm. semimonthly (during the school year)

This conventional form of note is not used if a more extended statement is necessary. For example:

Issued several times a week.
Monthly, accompanied by a midmonthly supplement.

[5] Library of Congress, Descriptive Cataloging Division, *op. cit.,* p.52. Beatrice Simon in her "Cataloguing of Periodicals," *Ontario Library Review* 33:242, 1949, says: "We are only interested in the periodicity of the *current* issues, and that information is readily available on the checking-in record."

Four no. a year, 1931; 5 no. a year, 1932-34.
Monthly, 1901-June 1904; quarterly, Sept. 1904.

If there are numerous changes in frequency of publication, the information is omitted or represented by the general note, "Frequency varies."[6]

The practice in the Yale University Library is added in order to bring out some of the technicalities that may not be apparent from a simple statement of the rule.

A. If frequency is obvious from the title, the information is not repeated later on the card; *e.g.,*

Andean quarterly. (No frequency note necessary)

If frequency appears in subtitle, it is omitted in transcribing the title without marks of omission and given following collation or in note; *e.g.,*

Title reads:

Soviet studies; a quarterly review of the social and economic institutions of the U.S.S.R.

Catalog entry reads:

Soviet studies; a review of the social and economic institutions of the U.S.S.R.

B. If frequency is not obvious from title and has not changed, it is given 2 spaces after size in the collation; *e.g.,*

illus., maps. 24 cm. monthly.

C. If there has been one change in frequency, give in first note; *e.g.,*

Weekly, 1925-1929; semimonthly, 1930-

D. If there has been more than one change in frequency, do not list them but use note:

Frequency varies.

E. List of terms commonly used to express frequency.

daily
weekly
monthly
semimonthly
bimonthly
quarterly
annual
semiannual
biennial
triennial
irregular [use sparingly]
3 no. a year
monthly (except July and Aug.)
monthly during the school year
monthly (irregular)[7]

---

[6] Library of Congress, Descriptive Cataloging Division, *op. cit.,* p.56.

[7] Yale University Library, *Cataloging of Serials in the Yale University Library* (New Haven, 1951), p.13-14.

In speaking of the visible index the statement was made that it is the foundation on which other serial records are built. If the current records are sound and adequate, all later work can rely on them. They are official records. Even though they may not be under the control of the serial catalogers, and even though they may be compiled and maintained by clerical assistants, they have as much validity as the catalog entries themselves. Comparatively few libraries have taken full advantage of the principle of complementary serial records. Much economy can result from its full realization,[8] for it is true that the cataloging of serials does not need to be as technical as it has been made.

Why serials are cataloged

The reasons for cataloging serials are brought out by an analysis of the conditions that prevailed in the United Nations Library until 1949. In the formative years of the library the catalogers could not keep pace with the intake of publications, particularly of serial publications. These serials were numerous; they contained a large admixture of government documents; they were in many instances of fundamental importance to the delegations and the Secretariat of the United Nations.

All library functions were adversely affected by the shortcomings in serial cataloging. The Acquisition Unit, instead of devoting full time to its normal activities, had to take up much of the slack. It had to maintain a file that listed all items received in the library. It had to assign class marks to numerous serial titles in order to know where to send successive issues as they arrived. In other words, it had to do a considerable amount of temporary cataloging. The Catalogue Unit and the reference staff wasted much time trying to locate items requested by readers. The Circulation Desk had to struggle with a

---

[8] Arnold H. Trotier analyzed the situation in the University of Illinois Library from this point of view. He pointed out that "the record of holdings of serials in the Acquisition Department files is largely duplicated in the official shelf list, the public shelf list and the general card catalog maintained by the Catalog Department; and the record of bound serial volumes found in the Binding Department is duplicated, for the most part, in the two shelf lists as well as in the card catalog." After proposing a central serial record, he went on to say: "Fundamental to the program I have in mind is the acceptance of two propositions, namely, that the visible files of the central serials record should be the basic record for current serials, whereas, in the case of serials which have ceased publication, the standard entries in the card catalog should form the complete and authoritative record. For current serials the record in the catalog can then be kept down to the bare essentials. Beyond the most important subject entries only those secondary entries will need to be made as will enable the user to establish that the library has the publication he wants."—"Some Persistent Problems of Serials in Technical Processes," *Serial Slants* v.1, Jan. 1951, p.7, 9.

charging system arranged by author and title, since arrangement by call number was out of the question when so many items lacked one. A given serial title might be recorded in the charge file in a variety of ways because complicated titles and a wide range of foreign languages often made it difficult to bring charges for the same item together; discharging was therefore particularly troublesome. Care of the stacks suffered because of the extensive assortment of uncataloged and unbound material on the shelves; also because service copies regularly found their way to the stacks, along with permanent copies, the shortcoming here being that the shelf list did not control the flow of publications to the stacks. Clearly it was necessary to get the serials cataloged, and cataloged promptly, to allow all parts of the library to function normally.[9] Thus it can be seen that serials are cataloged for the following basic reasons:

To provide essential data for the visible index, e.g., the call number
To produce a uniform medium for the arrangement of the charging system
To control the shelving of material in the stacks
To allow serials to be bound systematically
To permit various departments of a library to concentrate on their normal activities without let or hindrance because of unrecorded serials
To promote a maximum of self-service on the part of readers who consult the card catalog

Another reason for cataloging is that it facilitates cooperative undertakings such as *New Serial Titles* and the *Union List of Serials*. All these functions are evident and practical. There is nothing esoteric about them. In so far as any of them do not apply—for instance, in a public library branch that does not preserve its periodicals in bound form—the cataloging can be simplified or even dispensed with entirely. Moreover, substitute methods, such as are found in the Linda Hall Library, may be embarked on safely as long as the basic functions are taken properly into account. On the other hand, in so far as other functions can be developed and justified for a library, the cataloging may become more detailed.

The want of a sharp definition of serial cataloging functions can be seen from the fact that repeatedly two similar libraries are found to follow widely different programs. One college or university library may, for instance, do much more detailed serial cataloging than another, when there is no apparent difference in their service requirements. Presumably, therefore, the variations are for subjective rather

---

[9] The principles and practices developed for the United Nations Library in 1949 are given in detail in its *Manual of the Cataloguing Unit* (Lake Success, N.Y., 1950), p.36-42.

than objective reasons. The need for sharper definition can also be seen from the changes that have taken place in the Library of Congress since 1949 when its practice was redefined. The serial elements in *Rules for Descriptive Cataloging in the Library of Congress* represent a marked change from "the gay science" to which Harriet Wheeler Pierson[10] and Mary Wilson MacNair[11] made such sterling contributions, and an even greater change was introduced in 1951 when simplified rules were adopted for less important publications.[12]

History cards

The authority cards for serials are chiefly the history cards made for corporate bodies, which are sometimes important enough to be developed into information cards for the public as well as the official catalog. The Library of Congress has printed a number of these information cards. Frequently libraries find them worth acquiring for their own catalogs. A few libraries make history cards for periodicals.

Harriet Wheeler Pierson has recorded some of the story of history cards at the Library of Congress.[13] She gives an idea of the massive effort that once went into the making of history cards for society publications. Library administrators who are concerned over the cost of cataloging should read her article and reflect on it. So much time can be expended on the making of history cards (for example, the New York Public Library formerly had several catalogers in its Serial Section whose sole duty was the making and revising of history cards) that libraries should determine whether they really need such records. Many libraries of all sizes operate satisfactorily without history cards, except for an occasional information card; so their value is open to question.

A development of note is the application of the principle of "no conflict" cataloging to history cards, which has led to the idea of "limited search" in making the cards. The rules for history cards adopted by the New York Public Library in 1952 illustrate the application of this development.

1. *Purpose*. All corporate names used as authors or subjects are "established" in order to insure consistency of entry in the catalog and to

[10] Harriet W. Pierson, *Guide to the Cataloguing of the Serial Publications of Societies and Institutions* (2d ed.; Washington, 1931).

[11] Mary W. MacNair, *Guide to the Cataloguing of Periodicals* (3d ed.; Washington, 1925).

[12] Library of Congress, Descriptive Cataloging Division, *Rules for Descriptive Cataloging in the Library of Congress: Supplement 1949-51* (Washington, 1952), p.16-19.

[13] Harriet W. Pierson, "The Forest of Pencils, Adventures in Corporate Entry," *Library Quarterly* 4:306-13, 1934.

relate the various forms of such names appearing in the catalog.

2. *Information recorded on authority cards.* Information regarding corporate bodies is generally not made available in the public catalogs. Information recorded on authority cards is restricted, therefore, to data which can be used for purposes of cataloging to distinguish one body from another and as a basis for cross references. The following data are considered to be useful:
    1) name
    2) date of founding, establishment, incorporation, etc.
    3) changes of name
    4) affiliation or union with other bodies
    5) date of dissolution
    6) headquarters

   The inclusion of additional data on authority cards is not authorized.

3. *"Limited search" principles used in establishing corporate names.*
    a. In establishing corporate names, the principle of "Limited search" is to be applied. This principle is used for corporate names in much the same way as the "no-conflict" principle is used for personal names, the idea being that it is unnecessary to search for, find, and record information which does not have *direct* bearing on the form of entry.
    b. Whenever possible, corporate names will be established using the material at hand for both form of entry and information about the entry; in other words, *it is unnecessary to verify such information in other sources.* In cases where the material at hand does not answer such questions as are enumerated above, outside sources should not be consulted unless the information sought is essential in making a decision as to the *form of the entry proper.* It is not necessary to consult outside sources in order *merely* to discover the date of founding, headquarters, etc.
    c. It is recognized that there are times when consultation of a familiar reference work offers a quicker means of finding facts of the kind which may be required for entry establishment than does extensive reading of the text of the material at hand.[14]

Title-page cataloging

One of the accomplishments of *Studies of Descriptive Cataloging*[15] was the freeing of the catalog entry from the tyranny of the title page. In serial cataloging the title page never held sway as it did in monograph cataloging: for one reason, some serials lack title pages; for another, the successive title pages for a serial may pass through numerous transformations. Yet undesirable elements of title-page cataloging persist with serials. The Library of Congress rule reads:

---

[14] New York Public Library, Preparation Division, *Technical Order* 52-49, 1952.

[15] Library of Congress, Processing Department, *Studies of Descriptive Cataloging* (Washington, 1946).

The data given in the body of the entry, with the exception of the record of holdings, are taken from a single source as far as possible. If the publication has no title page, the title is taken from the cover, caption, masthead, editorial pages or other place, the order of preference being that of this listing. The source of the data is specified if it is not the title page, cover, caption or masthead. However, if there is no title page and the cover, caption or other titles differ, the source of the title used is specified and the other titles noted.[16]

Instead of this stiffness, great latitude is needed to make the most of individual circumstances, especially if the transposition and "integration" advocated in *Studies of Descriptive Cataloging* are to be meaningful in serial cataloging.

The most important practical consequence of the title-page approach to serials is that descriptive and subject catalogers alike are reluctant to catalog a serial until the first volume at least is complete, preferably with a title page. Catalogers may, of course, make temporary cards on the basis of the first number or numbers, but when a volume has been completed they replace the temporary records by definitive entries compiled on the basis of more substantial evidence. Naturally these procedures increase the cost of serial cataloging; they also interrupt the otherwise orderly progression of a volume from the periodical room to the bindery to the stacks. If, on the other hand, relatively permanent records can be made as soon as the first issue is received in a library, the load on the serial catalogers is appreciably decreased and the incidence of delays in serial cataloging is reduced.

Of less significance are the technical details which sometimes pay scant attention to the title page and sometimes cling to it. A short title may be adopted when by this device minor variations in the wording on various issues can be disregarded. Subtitles are omitted unless they are necessary for identification or to specify the scope of a publication. Adjectives that denote frequency are omitted from the titles of reports; e.g., "Report," not "Annual report" or "Biennial report"; and "Financial statement" instead of "Monthly financial statement." Serial numbering that is included in the title is omitted; e.g., "Report of the annual meeting," not "Report of the first annual meeting."[17] On the other hand, expressions on the title page which accompany the serial numbering are retained, regardless of whether retention of such wording facilitates or retards comprehension of the entry. Thus, "Aviation equipment red book. 1944- ed." is the approved Library of Congress form, in which the word "edition" is retained merely because it occurs

[16] Library of Congress, Descriptive Cataloging Division, *Rules for Descriptive Cataloging in the Library of Congress* (Washington, 1949), p.52.

[17] *Ibid.*, p.52-53. Note that a number of these details do not represent former Library of Congress practice, nor are they followed in all libraries. The new Library of Congress forms are cited throughout this chapter.

on the title page, not because it has any value on the catalog card. A simpler entry that satisfies all serial demands would be: "Aviation equipment red book, 1944- ."

The use of brackets shows a further confusion in theory. The Library of Congress practice for the statement of holdings is:

> The data . . . are not enclosed in brackets when ascertainable from the issue being cataloged even though they do not appear on the title page or title page substitute which forms the basis of the catalog entry. Brackets are not used to enclose the "v." or comparable designation if it appears in a later volume of the publication.[18]

Thus the interpretation of v. [1]-4 is that volume 1 was not designated as such anywhere in the volume. The other volumes are numbered somewhere, but not necessarily on their title pages. Note that this practice is dissimilar to the practice in monograph cataloging, where brackets indicate data taken from another place than the title page. While the serial practice here set forth is distinctive, it does not coincide with the use of brackets in the *Union List of Serials* or in *New Serial Titles,* in both of which brackets signify an incomplete volume. Another application of brackets that is difficult to reconcile in theory is illustrated by the following:

National Book League, London.
Book list[s].

No rule covers this conversion of a singular to a plural. Yet the practice, which the Library of Congress has not followed for many years, suggests deference to the title page, despite the lack of regard already instanced.

Description of an incomplete set

The normal supposition would be that a library with an incomplete set would catalog exactly what it has and nothing more, but oddly enough some libraries prefer to catalog not what they have but a complete set. Having cataloged a complete set, they then make a note specifying the gaps in their file, hoping that readers and staff will read through the whole entry to discover that after all the library does not have what it started out to say it had. The Library of Congress rule reads:

> The collation statement is prepared as far as possible to describe the completed set. If the Library of Congress does not have a complete set and if the information is easily ascertained, the total number of volumes is indicated. Illustrative matter is described for the set as a whole.[19]

[18] *Ibid.,* p.54.

[19] *Ibid.,* p.55. At the Library of Congress there may be more justification for the practice than elsewhere. The Card Division naturally wants a complete entry to sell to subscribing libraries.

Practice in the Yale University Library brings out in greater detail the procedures that may be followed in attempting to describe a complete set when an incomplete file is on hand.

If Yale lacks first issue but information as to date of publication can be ascertained easily, this information is included but crossed off lightly in pencil; *e.g.,*

~~v.1- May 1949-~~

If Yale lacks first issue and information found as to date of publication of that issue is questionable, leave space for statement of holdings blank and give information in a note instead of in the place for statement of holdings; *e.g.,*

Began publication in 1944? – *cf.* Ulrich's Periodicals directory, 1947.

If available evidence indicates that Yale has a complete set but there is no definite proof of this, add note to history card:

No more published?[20]

If Yale's set lacks only one or two volumes, catalog as a closed entry and indicate in pencil under call number on history card which volumes are wanting; *e.g.,*

Wanting
v.9, 12

If Yale's set is scattered or quite incomplete and LC has a closed entry for the set, card may be used by marking in pencil under call number *Incomplete* and making statement card.

If first and/or final issues are not available or if Yale has only a scattered file, catalog as an open entry and make note on the statement card *only* of final date of publication. This note goes on the line following that of last volume published.

Ceased publication with v.6, no. 7, Jan.1922.
Ceased publication with 1943.

a. If statement card does not allow for all volumes in set, add ceased publication note in pencil at bottom of last card used so that it can be erased and moved to another card if necessary; *e.g.,* if set closed with v.66 and last volume in Yale was v.46, which would be on statement card 3, add ceased publication note in pencil at bottom of statement card 3.

If the date of the final issue is uncertain, such a note is followed by a question mark; *e.g.,*

Ceased publication with v.5, 1942?[21]

Although both Yale University Library and the Library of Congress specify that the details of the complete set must be easily ascer-

[20] Harriet Wheeler Pierson wistfully observes: "It may take hours of research to establish the truth of the distilled statement 'No more published' (it takes 150 pounds of rose-leaves to yield less than an ounce of attar of rose!)."—*Library Quarterly* 4:308, 1934.

[21] Yale University Library, *op. cit.,* p.9-10.

tainable, it is clear that much routine is involved in attempting to catalog what is not on hand. Nor can the results be at all satisfactory, for bibliographies of serials are noted for their practical value rather than their real soundness. The *Union List of Serials*, for example, is a tool of inestimable worth; but its bibliographical details are constantly open to question. The serial cataloger who relies on inadequate aids may be guilty of poor bibliography. Moreover, readers can easily be misled by descriptions of complete sets which are not locally available. This is all the more possible because the statement of holdings is prominent by comparison with the note which records gaps, especially when a printed card is used. And the practice of lightly lining out a statement such as "v.1-" may lead to similar misunderstanding.

The only sound practice for a library is to describe what it has. It should be axiomatic that serial librarians catalog what they have in hand, not what they lack. This is a principle of economy. It does not result in questionable bibliography, and it does not confuse readers.

Entry under latest form of name

The serial cataloger is constantly confronted with two troublesome variables: the title or subtitle may change, or the corporate entry or its subdivision may change. The rule that requires entry under the latest name or title implies that the catalog records will be revised whenever significant changes in title or heading occur, but only a few libraries can keep pace with the necessary revisions. Even though it is a losing battle,[22] serial catalogers wage a spirited struggle, as Harriet Wheeler Pierson has indicated:

> As societies multiply and the number of books increases, we sometimes ask ourselves, where will it end? This mass of human experience, discovery, achievement, must be preserved, the records must be kept clear, the tangled threads of changing titles must be patiently straightened out; but to the thoughtful person it is an inspiring task, for enfolded in those pages which, perchance, few but the cataloguer will ever see in their unbroken sequence, is the history of modern civilization, the written result of organized human effort, the panorama of life itself. The cataloguing of it is not, after all, a science, but an art—a plastic art, if you will—and *art is long*; is there not proof of this in the memoirs of a well known academy whose first volume appeared in 1756 and whose second volume followed one hundred and twelve years later, in 1868?[23]

---

[22] In 1940 the author asked Miss Pierson how many changes of name her staff could revise each year at the Library of Congress. The answer was approximately thirty. At about the same time Miss Hinchey of the New York Public Library estimated that that library was about thirty thousand changes of name behind.

[23] Harriet W. Pierson, "The Gay Science—the Cataloguing of the Publications of Learned Societies," *Proceedings* of the Catalog Section, American Library Association (Chicago, 1929), p. 144. The memoirs mentioned by Miss Pierson are those of the Academia de Buenas Letras de Barcelona.

British and American librarians have adopted different practices for the treatment of serials that involve changes of name. The British prefer to make the main entry under the earliest name; the Americans under the latest. There is much to be said on both sides, for the British avoid the expense of constant recataloging, and the Americans emphasize the entries that readers are most likely to seek. But when all is said and done, the serial catalogers of both countries are seen to be on the horns of a dilemma. One consequence of both plans is that in many instances either the entry tells the full story of the serial or else it is a mere reference.[24] Too much information may be provided in the full entry; too little in the reference, especially for those who are seeking call numbers after checking periodical indexes. A middle ground is possible in libraries which do not record serial holdings in their card catalogs except for items that are complete and dead. Such a plan (which is in operation in the Harvard College Library) envisages form cards for open-entry serials. These cards simply refer to the Serial Division where full information is accessible (see Figure 1). In addition to the statement of holdings, the records in the Serial Division list changes of name and title, as well as the tracing. On this basis it is a relatively simple procedure to add an entry under a changed title whenever desirable. This scheme takes care of changes of title satisfactorily. It does not contribute to a solution of the problem of change of corporate name which affects serial entries as well as monograph. That problem remains an extremely vexing one.

It has frequently been proposed—and the Library of Congress is now putting the proposal into operation in some cases—that titles be cataloged under the form of name a corporate body had when they were published. If this plan were followed, recent publications of the Armed Forces Medical Library would go under "U. S. Armed Forces Medical Library," earlier publications would go under "U. S. Army Medical Library," and still earlier ones under "U. S. Surgeon General's Office. Library." *See also* references would be the links in the chain of these headings. The big stumbling block in the way of successful realization of this plan is the serial title which persists through two or more changes of corporate name. Duplication of serial titles under all necessary headings is an expensive procedure; failure to duplicate reduces the effectiveness of the plan.

---

[24] Examples of the all-or-nothing type of entry are given in Mary W. MacNair, *Guide to the Cataloguing of Periodicals* (3d ed.; Washington, 1925), p.20-22. Note, for instance, on page 22 that full information is given for *The Journal of Industrial Education and Manual Training* and for *The American Journal of Manual Training;* but *The Journal of Industrial Training* merits a mere reference. Arnold H. Trotier reported that most of the libraries in his study inclined to cross references rather than added entries for the earlier titles of serials that have changed their names *(Catalogers' and Classifiers' Yearbook* 4:32, 1934).

Entry under title?

Since the serial cataloger is constantly confronted with two elements subject to change, the title and the corporate name, it is natural to ask whether the two should not be reduced to one. This could be accomplished by cataloging serials under their title, with an added entry, when necessary, for the corporate body. At least one library, the British Library of Political and Economic Science, follows this practice for the majority of its serials. Note in this connection that added entries under variant forms of corporate name could be multiplied freely, without occasioning recataloging. Here, then, is a possible solution to a vexing problem, a solution that is rendered all the more plausible because some corporate-body publications with non-distinctive titles are already cataloged under title main entries. When the name of the corporate body precedes the title in such a way that it can quite properly be construed as an integral part of the title, the practice is to prefer a title entry. This practice is an extension of the rule which relates to entry under a distinctive title. Thus the Library of Congress has made title main entries for the *Aberdeen University Library Bulletin,* the *Harvard Library Bulletin,* the *Huntington Library Quarterly,* and the *United Nations Bulletin.* On the other hand, corporate entries were preferred for the *Bulletin* of the Grosvenor Library in Buffalo, the *Bulletin* of the New York Public Library, and the *Library Bulletin* of Dartmouth College Library, to name only a few parallel cases. The present system is halting and leads to incongruities. Thus the *Library Association Record* was accorded a title entry by the Library of Congress, whereas the *Library Association Year Book* was cataloged under the corporate name.

In their early enthusiasm for the corporate entry, catalogers shunned title main entries for serials to a considerable extent.[25] A title had to be really distinctive before it was preferred to a corporate entry. Practice has become more liberal as the interpretation of "distinctive title" became less strict. Enlightened visible index practice is to employ title entries still more liberally, but no sooner is an entry like *Bulletin of the New York Public Library* found satisfactory for a visible index than the question of its applicability in the card catalog arises.

The statement of holdings

Common library practice in the first part of the twentieth century was to maintain the statement of holdings on the main, added entry,

---

[25] As late as 1928, when the author joined the staff of the New York Public Library, title main entries for government documents were strictly avoided by the document serial catalogers there. Even when a government periodical had a truly distinctive title, entry under the name of the issuing body was preferred.

and subject cards in all catalogs, public, official, and departmental. As an annual report or a bound volume of a periodical was added, the statements on the cards were revised and brought up to date. A reader or staff member could tell from the catalog records which was the latest volume on the classified shelves, just as he could tell whether any given volume was held by the library. So great was the burden of catalog maintenance entailed by the incidental add-to-cards work that in the course of time some libraries decided to limit the statement of holdings for open entries to the main cards. The secondary cards were thereupon stamped with a reference to the main entry. This is a possible compromise, tenable as long as a library can afford even this degree of catalog maintenance. In still other libraries, however, it was decided that the statement of holdings could be eliminated from the main entry cards as well. When this practice is followed the cards read "1902- ," "v.1–date," etc.; or else all cards of a set refer to the serial check list where the statement of holdings may be found when desired (see Figure 1). Many libraries do not add to a "one-plus" entry in their catalogs, or indeed to any "——date" entry unless it becomes necessary to specify an earlier year or volume than was originally given. A terminal volume or date may be added when the serial ceases publication, though commonly the title is recataloged with a closed entry at that time. The weakness of the simple one-plus system is that readers and staff may be misled as to library holdings when files have not been kept up to date.[26]

Open entries which do not specify holdings are possible in institutions in which readers and staff tend to take it for granted that the library has reasonably complete files, especially of the more recent volumes. They are clearly indicated in any type of library for reference works such as *Who's Who in America,* the latest volume of which will be placed on the reference shelves as rapidly as possible after receipt, and more rapidly than the holdings in the card catalog are likely to be changed. Beyond that, however, is it necessary for a library to show in its card catalog the latest bound volume on the classified shelves of the *Atlantic Monthly,* the *Library Journal,* or the *New York Times?* And if a one-plus entry is satisfactory in the *Union List of Serials,* should it not be considered equally satisfactory in the card catalog? These questions are raised because the answers have a direct bearing

---

[26] For this reason Dorothy Litchfield in her "Paleolithic Practices in the Checking and Cataloging of Periodicals," *Library Journal* 60:60, 1935, spoke of "the exasperating and often misleading 'v. 1-date.' " At the Enoch Pratt Free Library "a stamp reading 'to date' is used on all catalog cards for current periodicals currently received. A list of such titles is checked annually to insure the correctness of the information."—Enoch Pratt Free Library, *Catalog Department Manual,* prepared by Lucile M. Morsch, Baltimore, 1940, p.58.

on the whole theory of serial cataloging. When statements of holdings do not need to be maintained in the card catalog, except for titles that are complete and dead, then the main entry loses its significance. Thereupon all cards in a set have equal importance in providing the call number—by contrast with the all-or-nothing theory—and all imply a one-plus set kept up to date or else refer to a serial check list for the detailed story of holdings. Libraries are increasingly, if reluctantly, coming to recognize the wisdom of the philosophy expressed by Beatrice Simon, who has said of statements of holdings:

> My experience is that the public does not use the information. It is the staff who find it helpful, and as long as the people who answer the questions have easy access to the record that is all that matters. It is an expensive and time-consuming routine to keep the public catalogue up-to-date. It involves the filing of temporary cards when the original is out having the entry corrected. Large libraries have worked out elaborate systems of triplicate travelling cards for this purpose so that there is always a full record in the catalogue and not just a title saying "Card temporarily removed." These are complicated and expensive to install and administer. Unless you place the burden on your library user of determining, through the cataloguer, that the library has the volume or issue which his reference calls for, then I think it unnecessary to have more than the title represented with a note telling the user to consult the Serials Record for detailed holdings.[27]

Considerations of this kind indicate the importance of avoiding gaps in serial holdings as far as possible. The expensive records to maintain and service are those for incomplete files.

Hanging indention

One of the numerous technicalities in serial cataloging is the employment of hanging indention for main entries under title. Susan Gray Akers has justified hanging indention as follows:

> This arrangement makes the first word of the title stand out clearly on the card and is the form to be followed whenever there is no author, editor, compiler, or the like, to be used as author. "Capitalize the word following an initial article in any entry having a hanging indention (collections, serials, series, etc.)." . . . With anonymous books, however, since it is expected that the author will be found at any time, the title of the book begins on the fifth line at the second indention.[28]

---

[27] Beatrice V. Simon, "Cataloguing of Periodicals," *Ontario Library Review* 33:241, 1949.

[28] Susan G. Akers, *Simple Library Cataloging* (3d ed.; Chicago: American Library Assn., 1944), p.86. This statement is omitted from the fourth edition, published in 1954, although hanging indention is still recommended for serial title main entries. The distinction for anonymous works is hardly valid, for libraries almost invariably recatalog books whose authorship has been discovered. Note too that whenever the first word of the title is an article, there is little gain in having it stand out prominently.

Until 1949 hanging indention was also applied by the Library of Congress to the editor, imprint-varies, and title-varies notes on serial entries. Other notes followed regular paragraph indention. Since 1949, however, paragraph indention has been the rule for all notes. A practical inconvenience that results on occasion from the use of hanging indention is that the preparation of copy for printing or mimeographing may necessitate a change from one style to the other. When the cataloger chooses a corporate body for the heading which the

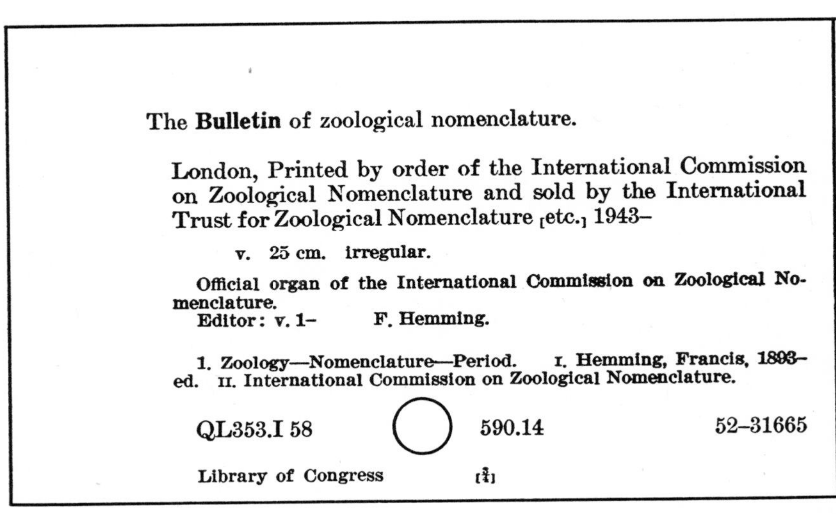

The **Bulletin** of zoological nomenclature.

London, Printed by order of the International Commission on Zoological Nomenclature and sold by the International Trust for Zoological Nomenclature [etc.] 1943–

v. 25 cm. irregular.

Official organ of the International Commission on Zoological Nomenclature.
Editor: v. 1– F. Hemming.

1. Zoology—Nomenclature—Period. I. Hemming, Francis, 1893– ed. II. International Commission on Zoological Nomenclature.

QL353.I 58 590.14 52-31665

Library of Congress [½]

FIGURE 23. Example of hanging indention.

reviser alters to a title entry, or vice versa, the change in heading must likewise be accompanied by a change in form.

Simplified rules

Some libraries (for instance, the Library of Congress, Harvard College Library, and Yale University Library) have simplified rules for the cataloging of serials of less anticipated use. The Yale rules are given in detail in the *Cataloging of Serials in the Yale University Library*. At the Library of Congress and at Harvard selection of titles for simplified cataloging is based on judgment; but at Yale certain categories have been specified, as follows:

A. Includes incomplete or scattered files of non-current serials which seem unimportant in the Yale Library or which are of interest almost entirely because of the organization which issues them (main entry, therefore, sufficient; subject coverage and arrangement of them not essential).

B. Includes volumes in poor condition.

C. Includes very minor monograph series if we have several and subjects are not worth classifying individually.[29]

Yale and Harvard have set up special classes for these minor serials, so that there is no subject approach to them on the shelves. The Library of Congress, however, classifies them normally.

These developments are of great importance, because research libraries do preserve and catalog numerous titles of slight consequence. Since serial cataloging at best is expensive, it is highly desirable that some economical mode of handling the less significant serials be employed.

Need for revision of cataloging rules

The weakest sections of the *A. L. A. Cataloging Rules for Author and Title Entries* and of *Rules for Descriptive Cataloging in the Library of Congress* are those relating to serial cataloging. Though the amount of descriptive detail has been greatly reduced by the Library of Congress since 1949, the rules are very technical. Some technicalities cannot be avoided, in view of the complex materials that must be recorded, but all rules should be scrutinized closely to see whether they are necessary. One obvious complication is that when additional information is given (in the body of the entry, the imprint, collation, or notes), it tends to snowball. Changes are likely to occur in all parts of the catalog entry, and if changes occur the natural tendency is to list them. Notes in particular are likely to prove troublesome and expensive. The Library of Congress lists nineteen types of notes, all of them subject to some measure of change.

1. Frequency of publication, which for numerous changes is designated by the phrase "Frequency varies"; otherwise by a specific statement (if terse, in the collation; if longer, in note form).

   Annual, 1949-50; semiannual 1951-
   Issued several times a week.
   Semimonthly (during the school year).

2. Report year, when the period covered by an annual report is not the calendar year.

   Report year ends June 30.
   Report year for 1928-30 ends June 30; for 1931-34, Dec. 31.
   Report year irregular.

3. Duration of publication when not specified in the statement of holdings.

[29] Yale University Library, *op. cit.,* p.48. Rolland E. Stevens in his "Characteristics of Subject Literature," *ACRL Monographs* 6:20, 1953, lists first among his suggestions for storage "serials which are rarely referred to (e.g., house organs, annual reports of railroads, state agencies and commissions, etc.)."

Began publication with Apr. 1943 issue. Cf. Willing's press guide.

Ceased publication with v.4, no. 4 (Aug. 1935?) Cf. Union list of serials.

Published 1820-64. Cf. Union list of serials.

"Published . . . since 1909."

4. Suspension of publication.

Publication suspended during 1919.
Publication suspended 1923-31.
Publication suspended with Dec. 1942.
Publication suspended with v.11.

5. Irregularities and peculiarities of numbering, unless they occur within a volume number: double numbering, confusion in the use of series numbering or whole numbers, preliminary editions not regularly numbered, etc.[30]

An introductory number was issued Nov. 30, 1935, called v.1, no. 0.

Issues for 1892-1902 called v.2-12; 1903-April 1906 called v.1-4, no. 4; May 1906-July 1910 called v.1-5, no. 3.

Issues for Feb.-Mar. 1939 have no vol. numbering but constitute v.1, no. 1-2.

Vol. numbers irregular: v.15-18 omitted; v.20-21 repeated.

6. Connection with other publications.

Began publication in May 1935, superseding the federation's Bulletin.

Published during the suspension of Bookplate booklet.

Supersedes an earlier publication with the same title, issued 1919-36.

7. Statement that the publication is the organ of a body, unless the fact is evident from the heading.

---

[30] In connection with irregularities of numbering, Sarah Dickinson tells of some of the "strange twists and combinations" with which serial librarians must contend. "A minor, but a bothersome, trick, is to skip numbers when the issues are not published. The *Proletarian* of Chicago is one illustration. Dozens of numbers have been omitted, but hope springs eternal in that man's breast, and he is always thinking he may fill the gaps. So when I receive no. 5, May, and then no. 9, September and claim, he answers, 'We skipped 6 to 8.' Why under the sun not call the next issue 6, even if it was published in September? . . .

"The most remarkable example of this kind of a thing was the *Altruist* of St. Louis. We started out with it bravely in 1903, paid our agent, but though it was a monthly, numbers 1 to 6, and 12, were not published. The next year 4 out of the 12 came; the next 3 out of the 12; but always numbered as though the others had come out. And when I claimed and claimed, the same answer would come: 'I called it no. 10, because it would have been, if numbers 1 to 9 *had* been issued; I still hope to catch up.'

"But alas, a record of 14 years showed that out of 204 due, only 89 arrived. But who can blame that publisher? The price was first 10 cents a year, then 25 cents—postage from St. Louis included."—"Idiosyncrasies of Periodicals," *Catalogers' and Classifiers' Yearbook* 2:94-95, 1931.

Journal of the Minnesota State Medical Association and of other medical societies in Minnesota.

Official medium of the International Association of Liberal Physicians (formerly National Association of Drugless Physicians) Dec. 1939-

Official organ of the Interne Council of America, 1938-41; journal of the Association of Internes and Medical Students, 1942-

8. Variations in title, for minor changes designated by "Title varies slightly" or "Subtitle varies"; otherwise by statements such as:

   Title varies: 1891, New Zealand post and telegraph gazette.—1892-1902, The Katipo; a journal of events in connection with and circulated only in the New Zealand post office and telegraph service (subtitle varies slightly)—1903-Apr. 1906, The New Zealand post and telegraph officers' advocate.

   Title varies: Feb. 1903-Jan. 1905, The Lamp.

   Title varies: Sept. 1934-Dec. 1936, The American Welding Society journal (running title: The Welding journal)—Jan. 1937- The Welding journal; the journal of the American Welding Society (caption title: The American Welding Society journal)

9. Variations in the corporate name and changes in authorship.

   Issued 1920-June 1933 by Babson's Statistical Organization, inc. Report for 1845 issued by the society under its earlier name: Foreningen for norske fortidsmindesmaerkers bevaring.

10. Issuing bodies.

   Issued 1925-Jan. 1933 under the auspices of the New Mexico State Highway Dept. (with the Dept. of Game and Fish, July 1931-Jan. 1933)

   Published by the Westinghouse Club (formerly the Electric Club)

   Vol. 1 published by the students of the Claremont Colleges and La Verne College; v.2- by the students of Pomona College.

11. Editors for whom added entries are made.[31]

   Editor: 1939- H. L. Mencken.

   Editors: 1894-1926, A. Sauer (with J. Nadler, 1914-26, G. Stefansky, 1926)—1927-31, J. Nadler, G. Stefansky and others.—1932-33, G. Stefansky and others.—1934- H. Pongs (with J. Petersen, 1934-38)

[31] With statements like this in mind, Beatrice Simon (*op. cit.*, p.242) observes: "Elaborate notes concerning editors and changes in commercial publishers are, in my opinion, a complete waste of time. The rare person who needs this information finds it by going to the journal itself. Furthermore, his need of the information is usually in connection with some serious piece of work and, believe me, he will not take *your* note as his authority. He will verify at the source. Anyone who is interested in knowing that a library has a copy of the Tatler, knows who the editor was. If he is discovering this fact for the first time, he will discover it in a much more pleasant way than by plowing through the added entries in a library catalogue."

12. Variations in imprint.

    Imprint varies: 1922-Oct. 1937, Chicago, Trade Union Educational League [etc.]—Nov. 1937-Mar. 1945, New York, Communist Party of the United States of America.

    Published in Rotterdam by Nijgh & Van Ditman, 1916-40.

    Vol. 3, no. 2, published by J. Debrett.

13. Titles absorbed.

    Absorbed the Philadelphia medical journal, June 20, 1903; Medical news, Jan. 6, 1906; Medical record, May 3, 1922; Medical herald, Feb. 7, 1934; Medical mentor, Mar. 7, 1934.

    Absorbed the Proceedings of the Pacific Northwest Library Association in Oct. 1937 and became the association's official organ.

    "Incorporating the Journeymen bakers' magazine."

14. Mergers, unions, etc., qualified by a date when the library's holdings are not complete or when the merger does not occur immediately after the publication of the last issue.

    Absorbed by Monumental news-review.

    Merged into New York medical journal (later Medical record)

    Superseded by Wille und Macht in Dec. 1936.

15. "No more published?" is used to express doubt about what is really the final issue. The expression is always placed last, or next to the last when contents are given.

16. A brief contents note may characterize a work as a whole, designate the parts of a set, or "justify" items brought out as added entries.

    Includes Federal regulation of exchanges, stock markets, corporation reports, margins, commodity exchanges, and cotton exchanges.

    Vols. 26- issued in 3 sections: Aufsatzteil, Referatenteil, and Wirtschaftlicher Teil und Vereinsnachrichten.

    "A preliminary investigation into the state of the native languages of South Africa, by C. M. Doke" (with bibliographical appendices): v.7, p.[1]-98.

17. Supplements which may be monographic or serial in character, and may be treated in several ways.

    Blätter für Volksbibliotheken und Lesehallen. 1.-
    Jahrg.; Jan./Feb. 1900-
    Leipzig, O. Harrassowitz.
    v. 24 cm. bimonthly.
    —— Ergänzungshefte. 1.-
    Leipzig, O. Harrassowitz, 1905-
    no. diagrs. 24 cm.
    Ceased publication with no. 5 (1915) Cf. Union list of serials.

    The Oregon state bar bulletin. v.1-
    Dec. 1935-
    Portland.
    v. 26 cm. bimonthly (except Aug. and Oct.)
    Vols. 1- issued as a suppl. to the Oregon law review.

18. Indexes to more than a single volume are displayed in tabular form.

INDEXES:
Vols. 1-9, 1881-90, *with* v.9.
Vols. 10-15, 1891-96, *with* v.15.
Vols. 1-20, 1881-1901, *with* v.20.
Vols. 21-40, 1902-21, *with* v.40.

INDEXES:
Author index.
Vols. 1-6, 1915-21, *with* v.6.
Subject index.
Vols. 1-6, 1915-21, *with* v.6.

19. The record that an item is bound with another.

Bound with v.2: Emmons, Nathanael. A sermon delivered before the Massachusetts Missionary Society, at their annual meeting in Boston, May 27, 1800. Charlestown, 1800.

The seeking out and recording of detailed information for these nineteen points and for additional serial technicalities can be nothing but a time-consuming and expensive process.[32] It may easily take a day or more to check up on all points in a long and involved set. And the data are sought not by clerical assistants, as a rule, but by the serial catalogers themselves. Harriet Wheeler Pierson and Mary Wilson MacNair really enjoyed the patient and thorough investigation of serials. Today the burden on catalog departments, in terms of budget, work load, and arrearages, is generally so great that the details of serial cataloging need a complete overhauling. All rules of serial cataloging should be reviewed, especially in the light of the complementary services that the visible index and the *Union List of Serials* and its counterparts can offer. Beatrice Simon has presented a similar point of view:

I have here the preliminary edition of the Library of Congress "Rules for Descriptive Cataloging." There is a very useful section on Serials which sets forth, in excellent detail, all the problems which beset the cataloguer who attempts to describe a serial in bibliographic terms. Anyone who is called upon to catalogue a large collection of research periodicals would do well to study this section for a general knowledge of the principles underlying bibliographic description. However, I really cannot advocate the use of such descriptive detail in the average library. It is suited only to a library of rare items, or to a printed bibliography. It is not the function of the average library catalogue to set forth the full bibliographic description of the library's holdings in scholarly detail. The simplicity of the entries in the Serials List has demonstrated to us that, for all essential purposes, connected with the *use* of the information *in* the periodicals, all we need to know is whether a given volume of a given title is in the library or not.

---

[32] For a more extensive listing of these and other technicalities, see Ruth Schley and Jane B. Davies, *Serials Notes Compiled from Library of Congress Cards Issued 1947-April 1951* ([New York:] Columbia University Libraries, 1952).

> Now that is not to say that I think the Library of Congress should not do this kind of descriptive work. L.C. has undertaken the bibliographic task and its printed catalogue forms a valuable and scholarly tool for those who need it, and which once and for all obviates the necessity of our duplicating its work. If you feel that you must have such detail in *your* catalogue, then, by all means, buy the printed cards. But if your purpose is to show what the library holds, then simplify your statement to the bare essentials, necessary for identification.[33]

It is possible to reduce the amount of detail, especially for an open-entry serial, and at the same time to produce a thoroughly reliable and satisfactory serial entry. Since the basis of all good serial work is accuracy and dependability, it is consistent to propose a review of the rules for serial cataloging in the interests of simpler work that is completely up to date, and yet not disagree with the spirit of Harriet Wheeler Pierson's statement:

> Catalogers are not only transcribers, they are seekers after truth. It is argued by many, perhaps by the majority, that all that is needed for a catalog entry is the author's name as it appears on the title-page, a brief title, synthetic collation, and size—in short, a mechanized process for quantity production. Experience has shown that such cataloging is the most expensive that can be devised, for it leads to endless confusion. It is actually cheaper in terms of money to take time to make a full and complete entry than to dispatch a hasty, ill-considered one, for there is an inevitable day of reckoning, when mistakes are discovered and the work has to be done over. Thousands and thousands of catalogs and bibliographies have been made, and the bulk of them soon thrown aside and forgotten because they were found wanting. But the few that are painstakingly accurate remain and are treasured, and successors do not make them over—they begin where earlier ones leave off.[34]

As Miss Pierson has indicated, serial records must be thoroughly reliable. They can at the same time be relatively simple if the visible index and the catalog card each plays its own part.

---

[33] Simon, *op. cit.*, p.240-41.

[34] Harriet W. Pierson, "The Forest of Pencils," *Library Quarterly* 4:313, 1934.

CHAPTER 8

Cataloging Procedures

THE DEGREE OF COMPLEXITY of serial cataloging procedures is directly related to the policies that each library determines for itself. At best a large amount of detail is involved; but if the rules are highly technical and strictly applied, the procedures will naturally be exacting. How far afield they can lead is suggested by Harriet Pierson's description of the way in which the corporate name for a minor association was established at the Library of Congress: "The pursuit of information concerning this association led through encyclopedic articles and substantial volumes, through involved sentences, false trails and wordy jungles, to emerge finally in the Congo Free State."[1] On the other hand, the procedures can be greatly simplified, especially when the serial entries are brief or are on form cards, and when division of labor leads to the acceptance of work done by other serial librarians, notably those at the serial check list and in the periodical room. These are policy matters that a library must determine for itself. It must determine how valuable each item of information and each procedure is to it in relation to the cataloging situation and the budget, as well as in relation to the program of the library as a whole.

Preliminary sorting

Serials acquired by gift, transfer, or large-lot purchase should be screened before they are searched or otherwise acted on. Numerous items can be discarded without further consideration in the process of preliminary sorting. Old college catalogs, who's whos, obviously unwanted unbound issues of periodicals, and much other material—particularly if it is scrappy—can be eliminated at this stage. No special competence with serials is required to make the preliminary discards; as a matter of fact, a non-serial librarian may even save a certain amount of work by being more ruthless in rejecting material than would a serial specialist who is aware of the possibilities of rounding

[1] Harriet W. Pierson, "The Forest of Pencils," *Library Quarterly* 4:308, 1934.

out extra sets. Moreover, much of the work of preliminary sorting is done in connection with mixed lots of monographs and serials. Each of these types must be segregated, and in the act of separating the two it is possible for a non-serial librarian to make desirable discards from each group.

When the serials under consideration are particularly numerous and bulky it is commonly wise to have a copy of the *Union List of Serials* on hand during the preliminary sorting, so that more significant runs can be discarded informally. However, should a duplicate set be in excellent condition it should be compared with the volumes on the shelves. The condition of the stack set might indicate that a second set should be developed or that some or all volumes should be replaced by the new ones. Such comparison of copies is of increasing importance in research libraries, because of the steady wear and tear on journals in particular.[2]

Searching

The items that survive the screening are searched against the official records to see whether they are duplicates or not. Before they are searched they commonly need to be arranged to bring together all the parts of a set. If the sets are bulky they can be rapidly listed and then searched from the list, otherwise it is best to search with the item itself in hand.

Three groupings result from the searching process: items that can be added to existing files, duplicates, and titles new to the library. For each of these the searcher makes appropriate notations. For add-to-cards material the main official card may be withdrawn by the searcher when it is an aid in the adding operation. When this is not done, a searching slip should be filled out with the call number of the set and a statement of holdings. Adding to serial files should not be an automatic process unless the addition is substantial. Unbound and scrappy items should be reviewed to determine whether they are worth adding to the collections. Duplicates can generally be discarded automatically, particularly if they are unbound. It is better for the searcher to mark a searching slip with a designation such as "dup." than to write this on the serial itself. One reason is that the designation can go once on a slip, whereas it might have to go on many pieces; another is that when the duplicates have resale value it is best to leave them free of library markings. The designation can also be written on the top piece of unbound material and all of it tied up in a bundle so that there is

[2] Since periodical sets are both expensive and scarce, the effects of steady use, particularly of basic titles, over a period of time is perhaps the most worrisome aspect of book stock conservation.

no risk of the slip being torn or mislaid. Titles new to the library should be carefully screened to see whether they should be added. As an aid to the librarian who must pass on the material, it is commonly desirable to have the searcher check the *Union List of Serials* and report on other sets in the region.

The searcher may be one of the serial checkers. Much of the unsolicited mass of serials, being more or less current, naturally passes through the hands of the checkers. If they are called on to handle the older serials as well, an element of variety is added to their work. Otherwise it is customary to have subprofessional assistants who specialize in serial searching check the non-current publications. These assistants can be made responsible for acquisition searching as well. In general, serial and monographic searching should not be combined because of the specialized nature of serials. In many libraries the catalogers must do their own searching. Unless the staff is too small to permit specialization of functions, this is an uneconomical plan.

Sorting

The new titles disclosed by the searching process fall into two classes: current titles to be considered for acquisition and older titles new to the library. These must be passed on by an officer of the library. When the current titles are at all numerous, the acquisition decisions take considerable time. If it is ruled that a title is not worth acquiring regularly, the issue in hand may be consigned to the file of sample numbers or may simply be rejected. If it is decided that an item is to be acquired, it should at the same time be specified whether it is to be sought by gift, purchase, or exchange. No current publications should be forwarded to the catalogers without word about their continuation. Only in exceptional cases should current items be added without provision for their continuing receipt.

Sorting of non-current serials is based on judgment of the value of a set to the library. A bound file is more apt to be retained than an unbound one, because it does not entail binding costs and because it is not likely to have missing numbers. A complete set or a long run may well be retained, whereas a broken file might be discarded, especially when it is unbound. Retention of a broken file needs to be doubly justified in most libraries because the recording, preservation, and servicing of sets riddled with gaps is always troublesome, and therefore unduly expensive.

Economy results from making a number of cataloging decisions during the course of the sorting. For monograph series it must be stated whether the monographs are to be analyzed in full or in part, and whether they are to be scattered by subject or kept together as a set. At times it may be decided to limit the analyzing to author or subject analyticals. When it is ruled that current publications are to be analyzed in part, arrangements must be made so that each item as it is received will be brought up for an individual decision. It must be specified, too, whether the material is to be shelved in a special location, perhaps a special or departmental library or even a storage library. Occasionally a decision will be made to keep a second set, or to substitute a new set for the one on the shelves. The binding or bundling of the set must also be indicated, occasionally with special instructions about the treatment of supplements or advertising. Since the sorting decisions may be of so many kinds, libraries commonly have form slips on which the information is checked or written (see Figure 2).

Collating

A further function that the searcher or another subprofessional assistant can and should perform is the collation of incoming serial sets. Collation is a matter that requires control in several ways, otherwise there may be much duplication of effort, as is shown in Chapter 12. Checking for the nineteen special points listed in the preceding chapter, as well as for other data, may occupy a major part of the serial cataloger's time. If his time is to be conserved, much of the checking and collating should be delegated to a subprofessional assistant who can be taught to watch for, check, and record the various technical details that need investigation. The cost of collation can be reduced in this way, and the cataloger's production increased at the same time. The difficulty in setting up such a program is that the conscientious serial cataloger feels it necessary to do the collation himself, otherwise some detail may be overlooked, some unusual feature passed by.

Dr. Harvey Cushing had occasion, in an address at the dedication of the Allen Memorial Medical Library in Cleveland, to speak of the problems of collation:

Few more arduous and difficult tasks confront a curator of books than that of collating and getting bound the heterogeneous medical periodicals which comprise, it is estimated, about two thirds of the volumes in such a library as this. They vary to an incredible degree, and with no seeming rhyme or reason other than the fancy of the publisher, in their form, in their make-up, in their pagination, in their dates of issuance. There are "new series" and "old series," with changes in volume number, with changes in name, with changes in format. What was once a quarto becomes an octavo; volumes may cover irregular periods of time and have no relation to the calendar year; some use Roman numerals, some Arabic; there may be several sets of paging in the same volume; there may be separately paged supplements, serially paged advertisements and text. Journals may suddenly go out of existence with no obituary notice, or without publishing the banns they may intermarry and reappear hyphenated, scarcely recognizable in their new alliance.

How librarians with any bibliographical conscience keep their sanity under these circumstances should be more a matter of surprise than that they should exhibit testiness when you or I, as privileged characters, walk off with an unbound issue and forget to return it. It will be a happy day for these long-suffering persons when Ostwald's *Weltformat*—the size of the *Index Medicus*—comes to be obligatory for all medical journals.[3]

Some of the specific situations experienced at the John Crerar Library bring out still further the problems encountered in collation:

So many of the foreign journals delight in wheels within wheels;—periodical after periodical, all inside of the one which bears on its cover a simple name like *British Journal of Photography, Chemiker-Zeitung, Elektrotechnischer Anzeiger, Deutsche landwirtschaftliche Presse, Journal of Botany, Revista de Archivos, Bibliotecas y Museos*—and dozens of others. This method of publishing half a dozen journals together, under one cover, and books within periodicals, is one of the heaviest taxes on our time, patience and accuracy. For at the Crerar, it must all start right from the periodical room, all the sections be separated, and sent in the right direction. The English *Journal of Botany*, for instance, has since 1902, issued twenty-two different booklets, as separate paginations in the *Journal*—a few pages at a time, a single book sometimes running for several years. You can easily comprehend the care needed to avoid mistakes.

Der praktische Maschinen-Konstrukteur of Leipzig had at one time five regular separate journals in its insides,—all cataloged with different call numbers. And as for the Spanish library journal *Revista de Archivos*—words fail me. I have already puzzled over twenty-seven different supplements, some of which have been running for sixteen years, and have neither beginning nor ending. Of course they did all *start* sometime, though owing to an unfortunate gap in our files, I can't tell *when;* and apparently some of them are never going to end.[4]

Some types of publication, newspapers and government gazettes, for example, are particularly troublesome to collate. How does one determine the completeness of a set when there is no bibliographical check list to specify errors in numbering, issues not published, supplements, editions, etc.? What constitutes a complete file of a newspaper in view of the fact that there may be a number of editions of the paper each day?[5] On occasion the problems may be so knotty that even

[3] Harvey W. Cushing, *Consecratio Medici, and Other Papers* (Boston: Little, Brown, 1928), p.258-59.

[4] Sarah S. Dickinson, "Idiosyncrasies of Periodicals," *Catalogers' and Classifiers' Yearbook* 2:95-96, 1931.

[5] This is one of the problems that must be faced before files of newspapers can be discarded in cooperative enterprises. In a deposit library, for instance, two libraries might have files of the same paper, one set of which could be discarded after collation proved them to be straight duplicates. But the comparison may be put off because it is so onerous.

FIGURE 24. Catalog planning sheet ($8\frac{1}{2}$ x 14 inches) devised by the New York Public Library.

Art	Print	JET	SUBS	EX	REPL	ADD COP	SP LOC	___ SET
O		CD OUT	NO RE-FILE	VOL AU	ANAL SLUG	CLASSMARK		
Cds						Per. Div.		
3-		ESTD	NO C	INV	REFS			

ON SHELF	COPY
Not ✓	K
Ed not	S
Ser not	SAD
Sep not	SID
Lack:	NSCM
OC	NASCM
OD	ASRM
OS	ORO
A	PI
AA	KT
C	SCAT
I	
Checker	
Searcher	RB
S catr	DS/THL
D catr	

The Nigerian field. v.18, no 2 -
date; Apr. 1953 - date

(see over___)

Pl. Publ. Date
Woodchester, Stroud, Glos

Matrix — (v.) — pt.
Pl. no. — l. — pam.
p. — no. — piece

(illus (part col.)) plates port. map facsim. music — 25 cm.

Series (

CURRENT IN PERIODICALS DIVISION
Quarterly.
Journal of the Nigerian field society.

PQA

(see over ___)

Collection	ESTD	NOC	INV	RF
1. Natural history -- Nigeria.				
2. Nigeria -- Per. and soc. publ.				
3.				
4.				
5.				
6.				
I. Nigerian field society.			✓	
II.				
III.				
IV.				
V.				

OC	B	(MUS) (MUW) (MUR)	(RP) (RS) (RX)
OD	E	N	(RZ)
ED	G	O	*R
✓ OS, I, Ib	J	✓P, (1), 1, 2, I	RC
OSA	MP MR	PR	S
OSD	MS	(PRB) (PRBI) (PRE)	SP
OI OCC	MU	(PRET) (PRI) (PRL)	(SR)
OA OAG		(PRP) (PRV) (PRW)	ST
✓ PC, 1, 2, I	MUP	R	T
SL	MUA	(RA) (RAP) (RAL)	(U 1) (UM)
A	(MUD) (MUC) (MUF)	(RB) (RBR) (RD)	8
AH	(MUG) (MUL) (MUI)	(RF) (RI) (RIB)	(LC 1) (X 1) (Z)

6 8 10 12 15 18 20	NN	*	**	R	Z	EX	[A]	[AA]	[C]	[I]	Bkplate
	[K]	[NASCM]	[ASRM]	[ORO]	[PI]	[SAD]	[SID]	[S]	[NSCM]		Paste pl

VOL. & NO., etc.	DATE	m/r., bd., etc.	VOL. & NO., etc.	DATE	m/r., bd., etc.	Acc Res
						Cover
						No ink
						Sl OK
			IMPRINT DATE (if needed)			Tab cd

Figure 25. Verso of the New York Public Library catalog planning sheet.

Acknowledge to: | Ack' d;

M. E. Established by EIS: Authority cd to be made. Entry Investigator: ah

☐ No conflict ☐ Record info on Authority cd.

SUBJ. 1 2 3 4 5 6 7 established by EIS: Authority cd (s) to be made.

☐ No conflict 1 2 3 4 5 6 7 ☐ Record info on authority cd for 1 2 3 4 5 6 7

A. E. (I) II III IV V established by EIS: Authority cd (s) to be made.

[ ] No conflict I II III IV V [✓] Record info on authority cd for (I) II III IV V

Bk, v.18, no.2, Apr. 1953*; p.3 of cover (Affiliated to the Royal horticultural society)

[ ] Add info to authority cd for M. E. 1 2 3 4 5 6 7 I II III IV V

TO: DIVISION CHIEF, ROOM ______ Date ______

DO YOU RECOMMEND THIS BOOK FOR CONTINUATION?

____ Yes [C] ____ No

IF ANSWER IS NO, DO YOU RECOMMEND THAT THIS PART BE

____ Kept [SID] ____ Discarded.

DO YOU RECOMMEND THIS SERIAL FOR CONTINUATION?

____ Beg, but do not purchase? [C]
____ Beg, but purchase if necessary? [C]
____ Purchase? [C]

Beginning with which volume? ______

IF CONTINUATION IS REQUESTED, DO YOU RECOMMEND THAT SERIAL BE:

____ Not indexed or analyzed?
____ Indexed? [I]
____ Analyzed by author and subject [A]
____ Analyzed by author only? [AA]
____ Submitted for individual decision as to analyzing? [SAD]

IF CONTINUATION IS NOT REQUESTED, DO YOU RECOMMEND

That monographs in the series be:

____ Not indexed or analyzed?
____ Cataloged as separates only? [S]
____ Discarded?
____ Submitted for individual decision as to cataloging or discarding? [SID]

That issues of this non-monographic serial publication be:

____ Kept and cataloged? [K]
____ Discarded?
____ Sent to N.C.?

(FOR CURRENT PERIODICALS AND OTHER CURRENT MATERIAL)

____ I recommend that this title be checked, sent to current shelves, and cataloged.

____ I recommend that this title be checked, and sent to current shelves, the cataloging decision to be deferred for one year.

____ I recommend that this title be sent to current shelves without checking; material will be discarded by this division and will not be sent for cataloging.

TO ACQUISITION BRANCH, PREPARATION DIVISION

PLEASE INVERT THIS SLIP TO RETURN MATERIAL TO ACQUISITION BRANCH, PREPARATION DIVISION

INITIALS OF DIVISION CHIEF ______

DATE

the expert bibliographer is hard pressed to provide an answer (as the quest for an original copy of the *Ulster County Gazette* for January 4, 1800, shows).[6] Consequently it is generally wise for libraries to aim at check lists of newspapers and other elaborate items. A sheet check list may be most serviceable for this purpose, since it allows a clear display for long and involved statements.

Cataloging operations

At one time serial catalogers made work slips for items that came under their jurisdiction—material in process as well as items set aside for cataloging at a future date.[7] They kept these at their desks as an aid in locating titles that might be requested by anyone. It is now generally recognized that individual records of this kind kept on or in a cataloger's desk are not satisfactory; it is more common to record current serials without delay on the visible index, to list non-current purchased sets in the outstanding order file, and to make no record of non-current material received by gift, exchange, or transfer unless it is deemed wise to add them to the in-process or outstanding order file. As far as possible these records should be limited to titles new to the library, in order to keep the record work down and to contribute towards a situation in which new acquisitions are processed on a current basis.

When the cataloger is ready to catalog a serial, his first step is to study the information provided by the searcher or, if the set has not been collated, to go through the publication carefully, making notes about points that will come up in the preparation of the catalog entry. Slips may be placed in the set wherever they will facilitate organization of the data which is to be recorded on the catalog card. After the investigations have been carried out, problems have been resolved, and names have been established, a draft catalog entry may be necessary to arrange all the manifold details in proper sequence. When brief entries or form cards take the place of the elaborate record prescribed by *Rules for Descriptive Cataloging in the Library of Congress,*

---

[6] See R. W. G. Vail, "The Ulster County Gazette and Its Illegitimate Offspring," *Bulletin* of the New York Public Library 34:207-38, 1930; and "The Ulster County Gazette Found at Last," *Bulletin* of the New York Public Library 35:207-11, 1931. The Library of Congress has a printed statement about the *Ulster County Gazette* of January 4, 1800. In 1949 it answered no fewer than a hundred and twenty inquiries about that issue. It also has seventeen information circulars to help in distinguishing reprints from originals in the case of unusual newspapers that have at times been reprinted in facsimile.

[7] A "cataloguer's finding list of entries" is briefly described by Mary W. MacNair in her *Guide to the Cataloguing of Periodicals* (3d ed.; Washington, 1925), p.19.

no drafts are necessary beyond the pencil notations which the searcher and the cataloger may make incidentally. In other cases a catalog planning sheet of the kind devised by the New York Public Library (see Figures 24-25) may obviate the necessity for a draft entry.

Since the subject cataloging of serials is comparatively simple, it is customary to have the serial catalogers classify and subject-head their own material. In those libraries where the subject catalogers, not the serial catalogers, are responsible for this phase of the work, routines must be set up for the serials to be transmitted and returned specially.

After the catalog entry has been prepared, the cataloger must pass on to other staff members the information they require. The visible index assistants should be apprised of the call number, correct entry, and any other details that go on their records. At the Library of Congress the shelf-listers supply this type of information to the Serial Record Division. When the end processes are not performed by serial assistants, the preparation-for-shelves staff must be given any special instructions about shelf-listing, binding, or otherwise preparing the material for use, and the periodical room assistants must receive the advice they need for current items.

There may also be other matters to attend to, such as the preparation of an entry to go on the library's visible reference index, or the cancellation of an entry in the outstanding order file. Special cards may have to be called for, statement cards written up, and traveling cards prepared as exact duplicates of the official main entry cards. Book cards may on occasion be made by the serial catalogers or under their direction; more commonly the preparation-for-shelves staff attends to them when they must be provided. Records for *New Serial Titles* must in many libraries be made and dispatched—not to mention the burden that falls on serial catalogers when union lists are being compiled.

Serial catalogers must initiate action on Library of Congress standing orders for monograph series so that analytical cards will be supplied as soon as they are printed. The record work for standing orders is best handled on the visible index. When the regular posting is done with black pencil or ink, a good convention is to post the Library of Congress cards with red pencil in the squares where the pieces themselves are entered. Should the cards come after the piece to which they relate, they can immediately be written up. Should they come before the piece, they can be filed in a special tray and activated when the piece arrives. It can be seen that this practice serves to a certain extent as an acquisition follow-up device, for the dealer may need prompting to supply an item that the Library of Congress has already received.

Volumes added to existing sets often pass through the hands of the serial catalogers instead of being processed exclusively by clerical assistants. The reason the catalogers like to see added volumes is that they want to watch for any of the variables they record on the catalog cards; otherwise they are dependent on reports from the serial checkers or periodical room attendants. Cresap, McCormick and Paget, in their 1951 survey of the New York Public Library, recommended that the serial catalogers forego handling added volumes because serial adding is largely a routine which need not be organizationally related to professional cataloging. In any event, the more the data on open entries is simplified in deference to the data on the visible index, the less occasion there is for routine additions to be handled by the catalogers.

Recataloging

In most libraries with large serial holdings recataloging is a major function of the serial catalogers. It originates more from changes of name and title than from discovery of faulty records. Hence recataloging in the ordinary sense is not a major problem with serials. Since serial titles are not nearly as numerous as monograph titles, the incidence of recataloging should be proportionately smaller. But when a research library attempts to keep pace with changes of name and title, the serial catalogers must perpetually spend much of their time making over the records.[8] New York Public Library statistics of serial cataloging over a ten-year period show that the ratio of new cataloging to recataloging in that library was not far from two to one. In these circumstances it is fortunate that, of the items recataloged, eleven out of twelve could be cared for by correcting existing records. The situation at the Library of Congress in 1953 was as follows:

> In fiscal 1953 the Descriptive Cataloging Division did original printed card cataloging for 5,383 titles and it recataloged 1,927 titles. When the figure of 1,927 titles recataloged in one year is related to the estimated 50,000 printed open entries for serials now in the catalogs the rate of recataloging may be expressed as 3.9 per 100 title-years. Thus it will be seen that the problem is not so much the result of the frequency of changes in serial entries as of the

[8] Miss Pierson says "there is record of one society which changed either its name or title 41 times in 14 years." ("The Gay Science—the Cataloguing of the Publications of Learned Societies," *Proceedings* of the Catalog Section, American Library Association, 1929, p.137.) This, of course, is an extreme case, but it does point up the futility of trying to keep the main entry under the latest title or form of name, just as it explains why serial catalogers often wait to see if a change is stable before adjusting the records. In their *Survey of Preparation Procedures, Reference Department, New York Public Library* ([New York, 1951], p.6-11), Cresap, McCormick and Paget say: "It is reported that the average corporate issuing body undergoes a change of name every 15 to 20 years, and that this frequency of change requires the vigilance now exercised in cataloging new material."

volume of changes that results when a large number of serials is active and subject to even infrequent change. It is estimated that it takes 50 percent longer to recatalog than to catalog originally and if this is so, then about 35 percent of the time spent in the descriptive cataloging of serials for printed cards was devoted to recataloging operations and 65 percent to original cataloging operations. The work of the subject catalogers in recataloging serials is usually slight but shelflisters require the same amount of time for work on recataloged entries as for original shelflisting if the call number is not changed, and twice as much time if the call number is changed. (At the present time the call number is changed only when there is a change in corporate entry and a long run of earlier volumes is not involved.)[9]

Clearly, if the amount of recataloging is lessened and temporary cataloging is eliminated the serial cataloger's load will be materially reduced. Another way of putting it is to say that thereby the cataloger can more nearly keep abreast of his work. Thus once again there is good reason for proposing a division of labor between the visible index and the catalog records.

A special type of recataloging that recurs from time to time is the conversion to serial form of what was originally taken to be a monograph. Sometimes these publications were first called editions—though the word "edition" applies to serials as well as monographs, witness the annual *Handbook of Private Schools* whose 1953 volume was called the "thirty-fourth edition"—sometimes they are pseudoserials which are at last being accorded serial treatment. Miss Goss has provided some effective illustrations of the borderline area between monographs and serials:

When is a periodical not a periodical, but an individual author's work? No rule can solve these problems and I should like to mention here several examples which have come to our attention recently. The *Female spectator,* by Mrs. Eliza Haywood, was evidently considered a periodical by the Library of Congress, and included in the *Union list.* In 1928 the card was revised and the entry changed to Haywood, with a note "Originally issued in monthly parts, April, 1744-May, 1746, ostensibly by a club of four women."

Mykologische hefte . . . Hrsg. von Gustav Kunze und Johann Carl Schmidt, 1-[2] heft, Leipzig, 1817-23, is in the *Union list,* credited to one library only, and in Bolton's *Catalogue of scientific periodicals* (v.1 only), but the preface to the second number which appeared six years after the first states that it has lost the character of a periodical, although it was started as such.

Another example is *Nordische miscellaneen,* 1-28, 1781-91 and the following *Neue nordische miscellaneen,* 1-18, 1792-98, entered by the Library of Congress under the name of the author, August Wilhelm Hupel. Both are in the *Union list* under title and yet this was not recognized at first as a

[9] C. Sumner Spalding, *Certain Proposals of Numerical Systems for the Control of Serials Evaluated for Their Application at the Library of Congress* (Washington, 1954), p.2-3. He explains the term "title-years" as follows: "100 title-years means 100 titles for one year, 1 title for 100 years, 10 titles for 10 years, etc."

serial by catalogers at Minnesota and was almost overlooked for the *Union list* supplement.[10]

Temporary cataloging

A special cataloging problem arises in connection with serials that are accumulated in a periodical room or elsewhere until a volume has been completed for binding or bundling. These consist chiefly of government documents of various kinds and periodicals. Should they be cataloged when the first issue is received, or should they be covered by temporary records until at least the first volume has been completed, in the hope of having a title page to work with at that time? Descriptive catalogers generally choose to face the extra labor necessitated by making both temporary and permanent entries, since they prefer to have a title page, if at all possible, as the basis of their catalog entry. A case described by Miss Dickinson shows the justification for this attitude: "I remember I cared for the *Army and Navy Journal,* of Washington, for a full year, all records under that name, to be much surprised to have the title page, when it arrived, read *American Army and Navy Journal;* and consistency obliged me to make a number of changes."[11] Likewise, subject catalogers prefer to operate with a completed volume in hand, for although their class marks and subject headings must of necessity be quite broad for the typical serial, it is commonly felt that the first issue does not define the scope of a work sufficiently for their purposes. Hence, in many libraries temporary catalog entries are made for new periodicals and periodical-like publications. Then, when a volume has been completed —or, if there are gaps, completed as far as can be—it is returned to the serial catalogers for regular cataloging. The temporary entries give the location of the current issues, in the periodical room or elsewhere, not the call number, which would be inapplicable for a year or more. As a choice of evils, however, permanent records made from the first issue giving the call number are no more objectionable than temporary records which are not changed until long after there is a volume in the bookstacks.

Procedures at the Library of Congress are as follows:

---

[10] Edna L. Goss, "The Cataloging of Serials," *Catalogers' and Classifiers' Yearbook* 2:82, 1930. Cross classifications were repeatedly encountered by librarians as they checked for the editions and supplements of the *Union List of Serials.* The problem is troublesome enough to suggest that author series might preferably be treated as serials when they take on serial form, an added entry being made for the "author."

[11] Dickinson, *op. cit.,* p.95. Note, however, that the New York Public Library has given up the practice of cataloging from a completed volume in favor of cataloging from the first issue of a periodical; also, *New Serial Titles* requests contributing libraries to supply copy based on the first issue.

> The descriptive cataloging treatment consists of form card cataloging only; *i.e.*, the title of the serial (chiefly periodicals) or the author and title (most other non-monographic serial publications) is typed on a fluid process "master" and duplicated by the Preliminary Cataloging Section on a printed form card reading "Until bound and cataloged, issues of the above will be found in the ——." The name of the service unit in the Reference Department is printed or typed at the end of this statement. Indispensable added entries are traced, to be prepared on the same kind of printed form cards. Both the catalog card and the publication are signed and dated as if regular cataloging had been done, and the book marked "Temp. cat." The material is sent to the service unit and the copy for the form card to the Preliminary Cataloging Section for duplication for the catalogs.[12]

Eventually, when the volume is bound, it is sent to the Serials Section for cataloging.

Some libraries do catalog their periodicals and periodical-like serials from the first issue received. They are ready to take the data from the cover or caption, without waiting for a title page (which may never appear and which in any case rarely alters the entry materially), and they are not greatly concerned about possible refinements in the subject treatment, because in any case serial subject headings are broad and periodical indexes must be relied on for the analytical approach. Each library must decide for itself whether to be content with catalog entries based on the first issue or whether it can afford the time and money to make a temporary entry which will be replaced a year or so later. In any library that accepts the theory of complementary serial records a catalog entry based on the first issue or issues will suffice, the time for a definitive entry being when the title has ceased publication.

Add-to-cards procedures

Catalog maintenance is not a great burden to serial librarians when the catalog cards refer to the serial check list for full details or when one-plus entries are made. Maintenance is much more burdensome, however, when the catalog cards must be kept up to date with changes of holdings as well as the nineteen or more matters subject to variation.

There are sundry ways of adding to existing records in the public and official catalogs, as well as in departmental catalogs.[13] The simplest procedure is to have the serial cataloger adjust the main official

---

[12] Library of Congress *Departmental & Divisional Manuals* 8:43, 1950.

[13] The Cresap, McCormick and Paget survey of 1951 disclosed that the New York Public Library had at least 102 catalogs to maintain in its Reference Department. The catalogs are located in twenty different divisions. Not all of them, by any means, have serial entries that are kept up to date; but the catalog maintenance load in that library, as in other libraries with subject departments, is heavy.

card; then a clerical assistant can copy the changes onto the appropriate cards in the different catalogs, taking the official card as a model. For the most part only main cards are changed, but sometimes full sets must be altered, especially when the changes affect more than holdings. The add-to-cards assistant can make the necessary changes at the catalogs for statements of holdings recorded in pencil; in this way dummies do not have to be written, and cards do not have to be refiled. Naturally, when there are changes that require typing the cards must be removed and dummies must be inserted for the main entries, and later the cards must be refiled.

The traveling card (sometimes called the return-duplicate card) represents an elaboration of this plan. Essentially it is a card which travels between any two catalogs, particularly the public and official catalogs. It is an extra card made whenever a new serial title is cataloged as an open entry. When not in operation, the traveling card is filed either immediately behind the official card to which it relates or in a special supplementary file. When additions are made to the official card, they are at the same time made to the traveling card; whereupon it is a relatively simple task to substitute the traveling card for the main card in the public catalog. To complete the process, the replaced public catalog card then returns to the catalog department, either to start a similar process or to remain filed away until a new addition has to be made.

The traveling card system has the advantage that the cataloger sees the changes made on the cards for both the public and official catalog; whereas under the previous plan he sees only the changes made on the official records, leaving the work of the clerical assistant in adjusting the public catalog card unsupervised. It should be noted in this connection that, with the lapse of time, occasional differences between the public and official entries do occur in most libraries which post holdings in both catalogs. This should not occur when traveling cards are employed (except, of course, in the interim between adapting the official card and filing the traveling card in the public catalog).

The traveling card system has a number of disadvantages. The traveling card is not always forthcoming when wanted. The issues of some serials follow so rapidly on the heels of one another that there is scarcely time to add one part before another is received, and it does happen once in a while that a serial addition is set aside with the traveling card in it, so that the catalogers may wait for months before the card comes to light again. The traveling card may also be misfiled, partly because the presence of numerous duplicate cards complicates filing in the official catalog. At times, then, substitute traveling cards

1 bind

Fd10 J827 Journal of Near Eastern studies.

Purchase

VOL. OR NO.	PERIOD COVERED			VOL. OR NO.	PERIOD COVERED		
1	1942			{11	1952		
2	1943			12}	1953		
3	1944						
4	1945						
{5	1946						
6}	1947						
{7	1948						
8}	1949						
{9	1950						
10}	1951						

HOW ISSUED: T.p.i. in last no. Ser. cat. Current numbers recorded in Periodical Reading Room

II.41 bind

Yale review.

Library has:

COPY 1 CALL No. A89.Y12				COPY 2	COPY 3	COPY 4	Gift contin.
VOL. OR n.s.	PERIOD COVERED	IMPRINT DATE		Ynt71 R3	Ynt71 R3	Za Zy55	
41	1951/52			✓	✓	✓	
42	1952/53			✓	✓		
43	1953/54			✓			

Directions for Distribution over. Index; no t.p. Ser. cat. Current numbers recorded In Periodical Reading Room 21-Remington Rand Inc., 11 115-35336—'44

FIGURE 26. Tabulated cards as used in the Yale University Library.

must be made to keep the process moving. Further, a few libraries have gone to the effort of making not only traveling cards—of which there were approximately 60,000 in the New York Public Library for serial documents—but a permanent file of typed dummies as well, one of which can be dropped into place when the traveling card is removed. These dummies serve to trace traveling cards which are being sought. But what can be more fatuous than to see a cataloger make a substitute dummy to go in the permanent file of dummies because the original one cannot be found? The necessary extra filing must also be reckoned on the debit side.

In 1952 the New York Public Library abandoned the traveling card system which it had formerly employed for its document serials. It adopted tabulated cards for all its open-entry serials and set up a routine for photostating the official cards after they have been changed. The photostated cards are substituted for the main card in the public, division, and shelf-list catalogs, whereupon the replaced cards are thrown away. The tabulated card, which many libraries favor, is a device for separating the catalog entry and the statement of holdings. Essentially it is a check-list card which is tied or otherwise attached to the catalog card so that the two in conjunction contain the full record without crowding everything together. The New York Public Library utilizes only one tabulated card per title which may have a summarized statement for the earlier holdings and a check list for the more recent issues. Several tabulated cards are reproduced in Figure 26. The Yale University Library practice relating to this type of card is in part as follows:

A. Yale uses the following types of statement cards:

annual 1-50
monthly 51-100
daily 1-100
monograph copy 1-4

No rules can be laid down as to which kind to use for various types of publications. Experience with them gradually develops in a cataloger a basis for judging.

B. In making statement cards the following points should be kept in mind:

1. Heading on statement card (author and title or title alone) must be the same as on history card—*not* shortened.
2. Whatever designation (volume, year, etc.) appears in the first left hand column on the statement card is the designation by which the volumes *must* be marked.

   If set has a volume numbering which you do not use for marking, it *must* go in the 3d or 4th column on the statement card, *not* the 1st.
3. The statement card must show how many physical pieces there are on the shelf if more than one.
   a. If the volume entered on a line is bound in 2 volumes, that must be indicated; *e.g.*,

Vol.	Period covered	
1	1945	2v.

   b. If volume is in several parts unbound on the shelf, the number of pieces must be indicated, *even though the volume is complete.*

1) If complete, indicate number of parts; *e.g.*, 12 no.
2) If incomplete, indicate what numbers Yale has, not what Yale lacks.

4. If the set has more than one kind of numbering, indicate on statement card, if possible, the various numberings that appear on the volumes; *e.g.*, set may have volume numbering and continuous, or whole, numbering for each issue throughout the set; the numbering by which volumes are marked is given in 1st column on statement card and the other numbering in the 3d or 4th column.[14]

Whatever plan of add-to-cards work for serials is adopted, the task of keeping serial open entries up to date is costly, all the more so if statements of holdings must be adjusted as changes occur. Most libraries that maintain a statement of holdings in their card catalogs now limit the information to the main cards, whereas formerly quite a number maintained the information on secondary cards as well. Libraries must reckon up the cost of the program they adopt in terms of service. Do the returns justify continuation of the practice? Is it necessary, for instance, to tell readers and staff through the medium of the card catalog what volumes of the *Journal of Near Eastern Studies* are on the shelves?[15] Would it be better to free the serial staff as far as possible from the burden of catalog maintenance so it could keep up more easily with essential activities?

The shelf list

In the typical library the shelf list is the control record for material added to the classified shelves, the occasional inventory of that material, and the assignment of Cutter numbers. The shelf list is less significant in libraries that prefer class marks to call numbers, take no inventory, arrange their periodicals alphabetically, or house their serials in vertical files. In a branch public library, for instance, the expendable periodicals acquired do not need shelf-listing, and a small special library may operate without a shelf list.

Correspondingly there are serial librarians who think that there is no need for a statement of holdings on the shelf-list card, provided the listing in the visible index or other serial records is accurate and sufficiently full. They consider the addition of serial holdings to the shelf list a time-consuming duplication of effort. As for inventory, the advocates of this policy feel that it is not necessary to take inventory

[14] Yale University Library, *Cataloging of Serials in the Yale University Library* (New Haven, 1951), p.17-18. See p.18-19 for further details.

[15] Note that none of the systems described helps in the troublesome interim period when a volume is in the transition stage between the periodical room, the bindery, the catalog department, and the stacks.

of the individual volumes in a serial set. When the shelf-list card shows that a given title should be on the shelves, the person taking inventory can check to see that all volumes are in order and that no extraneous material has crept in among the unbound issues. This kind of inventory will not disclose the fact that part of the set may be missing, but it is justified on the score that when anyone wants a missing volume its absence will be discovered.

Yale University Library has adopted this philosophy, and a similar position was taken by Fleming Bennett at West Virginia University Library, who wrote:

> The serials record was to be both checking record and shelflist record in alphabetical order. It was realized that a shelflist record arranged alphabetically by author and title was a new departure, and would not be universally sanctioned. However, its practical merits far outweighed those of a classified arrangement. The latter, it was felt, would be completely justified only at inventory times, the intervals between which at West Virginia University Library are so great as to present no serious objection to the alphabetical arrangement. It was believed that, for inventory purposes, the cards in a single tray could be removed, arranged in classified order, rearranged after checking against stack holdings and location file, and replaced within a day's time. . .
>
> To prevent duplications in assigning call numbers it was determined that referral cards bearing call number, author, and/or title, and stamped with the legend, "For Holdings See Serials Record," would be inserted in the shelflist.[16]

When the shelf list is bypassed or reduced to skeleton form, the visible index must be developed more carefully and fully. The work of the checkers must be of unusually high caliber. Binding information must be on the visible index, and the summarized statement of holdings should be in shelf-list form.

Here again is a problem for the library administrator to think through. In how many places is permanent serial information to be recorded? Naturally, the visible index and its supporting serial catalog must be maintained, but what about the public and official catalogs, and what about the shelf list? This much is clear: many serial staffs are overburdened. It is better to maintain a system that is prompt and thorough than one that attempts too much and does not leave time for essential activities such as follow-up work. It was in this spirit that the Department of Agriculture Library in 1952/53 decided on the "limitation of permanent serials-holdings records to the basic inventory record, which is the Alphabetical Serial File."[17] Nonetheless many libraries feel that the shelf list is the basic record of their holdings, so

---

[16] Fleming Bennett, "A Multi-Purpose Serials Record," *College and Research Libraries* 9:232-33, 1948.

[17] Department of Agriculture Library, *Report*, 1953 (Washington, 1953), p.3.

much so that in a few cases the shelf list is kept in a fireproof safe for insurance purposes. For many institutions, then, the shelf list ranks with the visible index, and hence with supplementary records such as the Old Serial Record at the Library of Congress. The one reflects the way the serials appear on the classified shelves; the other check-lists them as they are received. For these libraries both types of record must be maintained meticulously, since between them they carry the official record of a library's serial holdings. They complement and duplicate each other in important respects, the duplication being justified because the data may be given in a different way on each and serve different purposes. Moreover, the binding information must be added to the visible index if it is not given in the shelf list. The two processes entail approximately the same amount of work, though there may easily be variations because of physical layout.

In describing the visible index it was noted that on the checking sheets or cards the holdings are displayed enumeratively, and that elsewhere on the visible index entry a summarized statement of earlier holdings is given. Still another convention is employed for the shelf-list statement of holdings. This statement is made in terms of the physical units on the shelves: bound volumes, bundles, envelopes, or other types of container. In effect, the shelf-list entries take the form of an extended summarized statement. Thus v.1-4, 5-8, 9-12 means that the twelve volumes are bound in the three groupings indicated. A ligature is sometimes combined with the inclusive numbers to make the limits of the physical units still clearer. At times, too, the statement of holdings is spread out to allow the date of each inventory to be stamped under the volume statement to which it relates. The disadvantage of expanded statements is that they require numerous shelf-list cards per title. The New York Public Library gave them up in 1952.

At times a rubber stamp is added at the end of the holdings statement to indicate that current issues in the periodical room or elsewhere have not yet been shelf-listed. Some libraries carry the practice further and omit the record of all unbound parts. Sometimes the shelf-list card carries a statement of the source from which the publication was received. A warning should be sounded in this connection, for serial sets may be built up from multifarious sources. Unless a serial has come constantly from one or two sources, it is a counsel of wisdom to omit the statement of source, otherwise one or more cards can easily be filled up with a valueless statement. This stricture applies equally to the visible index itself, and there is no reason why the shelf list should specify the source of an item on the visible index.

The figures for items added to the shelf list or withdrawn from it constitute the official count of a library's growth. As each item is added or cancelled a tally is generally kept, usually by broad classes, of the number of volumes involved. The tally should be maintained strictly, especially in the largest libraries which are less and less likely to take inventory in the future because of the size of the undertaking, so that it will be increasingly difficult to correct errors in the count.

There has been much debate, especially in the Association of Research Libraries, about the proper way of counting the book stock. Should the count be based on the physical units on the shelves, or should it take bibliographical units into account? The latter method certainly gives a truer picture of the extent of a library, enlarging the count to allow for monographs bound up by series and reducing it for volumes split through binding exigencies. However, compilation of figures based on bibliographical units is more complicated than a count of physical units. An accurate net count of serials is hard to maintain in any circumstances, because bundles, envelopes, etc., are constantly being removed from the shelves for readjustment, sometimes for binding. With much traffic in both directions, errors are difficult to avoid. For this reason the New York Public Library found it expedient for a number of years to subtract an appreciable figure annually, 7500 in 1931. Thereby the decennial recount of the library came out more consistently with the annual count.

End processes

Material for the end processes is derived from three main sources: (1) newly cataloged titles from the catalogers, (2) freshly bound volumes returned from the bindery—in very considerable quantities in the bigger research libraries, and (3) serials in publishers' bindings forwarded from the checkers at the visible index. In addition, some items are received from the catalog department or a service unit when changes or corrections are to be made.

The final cataloging process before serials are sent to the shelves consists of most if not all of the following activities:

Bound volumes are marked with the library's stamp which commonly includes the date of accessioning or acquisition. When a title consists of a number of issues which are not to be bound immediately, the stamp and call number are usually added to each piece.

Title pages, and in many libraries certain designated pages, are perforated or embossed with the name of the library.

Bound volumes are bookplated, unless library-bound books have special endpapers with the library's seal woven in. Such endpapers obviate the need for regular bookplating, provided no book fund or gift requires a specific bookplate.

Book pockets or date-due slips are inserted in serials which circulate. Sometimes this process is omitted on the score that the publications will not circulate enough to justify the labor involved.

Leaves are cut when necessary in bound volumes as well as in unbound items not immediately destined for the bindery.

The call number is lettered on the spine, also commonly on the inside of the front or back cover. The volume number should be included in the lettering when it does not occur clearly elsewhere on the spine.

Unbound serials which, for the present at least, will not go to the bindery are inserted in manila rope bundles, envelopes, or other types of container, unless of course there is already a container on the shelves into which they can fit.

Manila rope is fairly expensive, especially when it is bought not in the roll, but precut to standard sizes. It must be lettered after it has been shaped, and then tied with tape or lawyers' pink pulls (preferably not with string). Occasionally it must be reinforced with boards to support an oversize volume.

Envelopes and manila rope bundles have been found more satisfactory than boxes and metal containers. They protect publications better from wear and dust. They may be supplemented by a variety of other devices.[18] Brown paper may be used for items which will virtually be stored. Portfolios afford the best type of protection for unbound newspapers. At times pamphlet binders may be put on thin serials (an annual report, for example) when there is little likelihood of other numbers coming along later.

Analyticals

Libraries frequently make analytical entries for the component parts of serials which are monographic in nature. They are always made when the volumes of a set are dispersed, and as freely as may be when the set is kept together. The Library of Congress has printed tens of thousands of analyticals for more than 7000 series which it has listed, plus many others for unlisted series. It is customary for libraries to place standing orders with the Card Division so that they can acquire the analytical entries they want as soon as the cards are printed.[19] Once the serial routines have been established and are in operation through the visible index or otherwise, the making of analyticals is mainly the responsibility of the monograph catalogers. Nevertheless the serial staff must generally—

Indicate the heading to go on the series added entry.

[18] Patent binders with spikes, staples, etc. which damage the serials should be employed only for expendable material.

[19] Consult the latest edition of the Library of Congress *Handbook of Card Distribution* or the *List of Series of Publications for Which Cards Are in Stock* for operational details relating to standing orders. Some of the Library of Congress cards represent what are known as "paged analyticals" rather than monographs that are bibliographical units; but paged analyticals are really more elaborate forms of the index cards made by various libraries and described in Chapter 9.

Record on the visible index or elsewhere the receipt of cards on Library of Congress standing orders.

Supply the call number for kept-together series.

Specify that a set is scattered and, on occasion, that no series entry is to be made.[20]

Question whether duplicates are to be kept, possibly for subject in the case of kept-together series for which no over-all decision has been given.

College and university libraries analyze comparatively few document serials; instead they tend to rely on printed indexes, as well as the analytical entries in the Library of Congress printed catalogs. Apart from documents, however, far more titles could profitably be analyzed than most libraries now attempt. Even the Library of Congress has not been able to analyze all the serials it would like. As the *Handbook of Card Distribution* says: "There are many other series that have not been covered, having been passed by in recataloging in order to deal with the general books more promptly or because they were of a composite character *(i.e.,* made up of numerous short papers)."[21]

Special mention should be made of the fact that analytical entries are commonly made for a *Festschrift* whenever one is discovered in a serial. If this practice is in effect, the checkers at the visible index must be alert to catch the commemorative issues. A few libraries analyze plays found in incoming serials. This questionable policy is followed because the printed indexes to plays are neither prompt nor inclusive. A more uncommon type of analytical is mentioned by Pierson,[22] namely a subject entry for a feature brought out on the serial catalog card.

Series entries

When volumes are analyzed, an additional catalog entry is commonly called for under the name of the series. Such entries are of most value for scattered sets. Nevertheless, they are frequently made for kept-together series, surely a work of supererogation, since the items on the shelves duplicate the record from a series point of view.

In former times a contents book was maintained in certain libraries to provide readers with a list of items in series. Entries were generally

---

[20] When it is deemed that series added entries are not worth making for the card catalog, the visible index should not serve as a substitute. There may be some justification for recording the author, title, and call number of a sample volume, but a complete tabulation should generally be avoided.

[21] Library of Congress, Card Division, *Handbook of Card Distribution* (8th ed.; Washington, 1954), p.9.

[22] Harriet W. Pierson, *Guide to the Cataloguing of the Serial Publications of Societies and Institutions* (2d ed.; Washington, 1931), p.62.

handwritten, though printed lists might be cut up and mounted instead. A card in the catalog under the name of the series referred to the location in the contents book where the particular series was recorded. In nineteenth-century printed catalogs special attention was often paid to listing the contents of monograph series. Some catalogs made a reputation for their series entries, for instance, the *Catalogue* of the Peabody Institute of Baltimore which was published from 1883 to 1905. The printed catalog of the Library of Congress is increasingly

575 c.b. 21

N10 Columbia University. Faculty of Political Science.
C7 Studies in history, economics and public law.

Purchase

No.	Date	Author and title
575	1952	Bauer,E.K. Commentaries on the constitution, 1790-1860.
576	1952	Bigelow,D.N. William Conant Church and the Army and navy journal.
577	1953	Elbow,M.E. French corporative theory, 1789-1948.

HOW ISSUED

LC-SO
Analyzed.

11-REMINGTON RAND INC -13 141-2074 5M 10-52 (533)

FIGURE 27. Consolidated series card as used in the Yale University Library.

valuable on this account, as can be seen from the entry for the *Bulletin* of the United States Geological Survey in the first supplement and for the *Technical Paper* of the United States Bureau of Mines in the second supplement.

Today most series entries are simply unit cards at the top of which is added the name of the series and the volume number, if any. Such cards are called series added entries. The principal alternative, the typewritten consolidated series card (see Figure 27), is steadily giving way to the unit card. For example, the New York Public Library in 1952 changed over from consolidated series entries to drop-in added entries because the unit card system was felt to be better. By contrast with the unit series card, which is largely the responsibility of the monograph cataloger, maintenance of the consolidated series card is usually the concern of the serial cataloger. When not responsible for the consolidated series entry, the monograph cataloger must provide the serial staff with the necessary details to add to the series card, in particular the call number and the correct heading. One advantage the consolidated statement has over the unit card is relative compactness. In the New York Public Library it was estimated that a complete change-over to unit cards would add about 3 per cent to the size of the public catalog.

The monographs in some series are so numerous (for example, the Teachers College *Contributions to Education* comprise 974 titles) that the product of either of these methods is both expensive and space-consuming. The two examples from the Library of Congress printed catalog cited above run to 114 and 107 cards respectively—quite expensive sets to buy. A whole tray of unit cards is required for some monograph series, or about a fifth of a tray of consolidated series cards, which is an awkward quantity to tie and hold together. The alternatives in such cases are to hold the set together so that no series added entries or consolidated series cards are necessary or to refer to a printed list of volumes in the series, wherever one may be found. An effective plan is to shelve a publisher's printed list with the kept-together set for the benefit of anyone who requires that additional approach to the work.

In front of the series added entries or the consolidated series cards some libraries place regular catalog entries for the set. Since other libraries function well without that additional record, it is obviously a matter of policy to determine whether the extra work can be justified or not. The loss, if any, that comes from failure to catalog a series for which series added entries or consolidated series cards are made is from the subject point of view. How serious that loss is can be judged by asking whether a subject entry is really required for the Teachers College *Contributions to Education,* the subject heading being "Education—Collections," "Education—Societies, etc.," or "Education—Periodicals and society publications." In most libraries it would seem sufficient to make the catalog entry for kept-together series, omitting the series cards; and to make series cards for scattered sets, omitting the catalog entry.

Since series cards are among the least used entries in the typical dictionary catalog they should not be made unless there is a reasonable chance of their contributing to more effective library service. They can safely be omitted for kept-together series, most publishers' series, a large proportion of the series which a library does not wish to acquire beyond an odd volume or two (which is frequently the case in departmental libraries), series for which an adequate record is available in a standard source such as a trade or national bibliography, and for many unnumbered series, particularly older ones.

The appearance of Eleanora Baer's *Titles in Series*[23] makes the value of series entries even more questionable. It is now possible for libraries of all types to give up making series added entries or consolidated series cards for titles listed in Baer. It is not even necessary to annotate the work with call numbers; moreover, space can be created in the card catalog by cancelling the existing series cards for these titles. Because of *Titles in Series* (plus the current listings in trade and national bibliographies) serious consideration should be given to the elimination of the series entry altogether.

Simplified treatment of deposit material

Just as simplified rules may be followed for the original cataloging of serials destined for a storage library, so too the routines may be held to bare essentials. At Yale and Harvard the call numbers consist of a mere size designation, followed by a running number. Neither gives holdings on its shelf-list entries. Unbound material can be bundled or placed in envelopes or other containers, saving the cost of binding.

---

[23] Eleanora A. Baer, *Titles in Series Published Prior to January 1953; a Handbook for Librarians and Students* (Washington: Scarecrow Pr., 1953).

CHAPTER 9

Subject Cataloging

TECHNICAL PROBLEMS in the subject cataloging of serials do not compare in difficulty or extent with those encountered in descriptive cataloging. There are perennial problems, to be sure, such as determining the best plan for assigning book numbers to serials whose name or title changes, but for the most part the subject cataloger looks at serials with a quick glance and a generous appraisal, while his colleague, the descriptive cataloger, scrutinizes them with a jaundiced eye.

The serial character of a publication is fairly generally brought out in subject headings by a form subheading. This is less often done for government documents, however, than for other types of serials. The principal subheadings for serials employed by the Library of Congress are:

- Abstracts
- Collected works
- Collections
- Congresses
- Directories
- Periodicals
- Societies
- Societies, etc.
- Societies, periodicals, etc.
- Society publications
- Yearbooks[1]

A major difficulty met in applying the subheadings derives from the distinctions that may be drawn between types of serials, particularly between government documents, periodicals, and society publications. Unfortunately there is no discussion of the problem in Haykin's account of Library of Congress subject heading practice.[2] Whatever the historical reasons may have been for the distinctions that were made at the Library of Congress about the year 1900 (when serials were neither so numerous nor so frequently atypical), it is clear today that much can and should be done to rationalize the subject heading of serials.

[1] Not all of these terms are limited to serial publications. In fact, "Collected works" and "Collections" are applied more to monographs; as serial subheadings they relate to series and also to government documents for which subheadings like "Periodicals" and "Societies, etc." are used sparingly.

[2] David J. Haykin, *Subject Headings, a Practical Manual* (Washington, 1951).

Subject headings for periodicals

Although the individual articles in a journal may be highly specialized, the periodicals themselves can generally be comprehended under quite simple terms. Thus an abstruse publication may be covered by the heading "Physics—Periodicals"—not at all a difficult procedure.

When a specific subject heading may not be subdivided, the Library of Congress calls for a second entry under a broader term that is divisible. For example, the *Journal of Experimental Medicine* obviously takes the heading "Medicine, Experimental"; but since that expression is not subdivided, a second entry is called for, namely "Medicine—Periodicals." On occasion the form subheadings may also serve as sub-subheadings. Thus the *Journal of Central European Affairs* takes the heading "Europe—History—Periodicals"; the *Journal of Neuropathology and Experimental Neurology* takes "Nervous system—Diseases—Periodicals"; while the *Journal of Jewish Bibliography* takes both "Jews—Bibliography—Periodicals" and "Hebrew literature—Bibliography—Periodicals." That Library of Congress practice is not always consistent is indicated by the three headings for the *Journal of Unified Science:* the general heading "Philosophy—Periodicals," the specific yet subdivided heading "Logical positivism—Periodicals," and the heading "Philosophy—Bibliography" which is not further subdivided by "Periodicals."

Regional subheadings are not subdivided by form headings. Duplicate entries are called for instead. So the *Journal de la marine marchand et de l'Empire français* takes both "Merchant marine—France" and "Merchant marine—Periodicals" as headings, but not "Merchant marine—France—Periodicals." Many libraries, however, do not hesitate to subdivide either specific headings or regional subheadings, preferring to use one subject entry instead of two.

The subheading "Periodicals" is sometimes applied to government documents and to the publications of societies and institutions. The following are examples of Library of Congress practice.[3]

Harvard Library bulletin.

International Institute of Agriculture.
  Bulletin of agricultural economics and sociology.

---

[3] Whenever an example lacks tracing, the Library of Congress has assigned no subject to the work. The examples cited throughout this chapter have been drawn from the supplements to the Library of Congress printed catalog, a work which affords excellent case studies for serials under terms like "Bulletin," "Journal," "Society," "United Nations," and "United States." Note that as subheadings the Library of Congress abbreviates "Directories" to "Direct." and "Periodicals" to "Period."

1. Agriculture—Economic aspects—Period.

International Monetary Fund.
International financial news survey.
1. Finance—Period. 2. Economic conditions—Period.

New York Public Library.
Bulletin.
1. Bibliography—Period.

Society for the Bibliography of Natural History, *London.*
Journal.
1. Natural history—Bibl.—Period.

Society of Tropical Agriculture.
Journal.
1. Agriculture—Period. 2. Agriculture—Tropics.

United Air Lines, Inc.
News.
1. Aeronautics—Period.

United Nations bulletin.
1. United Nations—Period.

U. S. Atomic Energy Commission.
Nuclear science abstracts.
1. Atomic energy—Abstracts. 2. Atomic energy—Period.

In connection with the Atomic Energy Commission, note that its *MDDC* (Manhattan District Declassification Document) was assigned "Atomic energy—Societies, etc." as a subject heading, while its *Report* was given merely "Atomic energy"—an instance of three different practices for the serial publications of a single body.

Subject headings for society publications

A technicality which libraries other than the Library of Congress often avoid is the distinction between society publications and periodicals. The Sears *List of Subject Headings*[4] dispenses with the form subheading "Societies" altogether. A common library convention is to combine the terms "Periodicals" and "Societies" in a form subheading "Periodicals and society publications"; for example, "Medicine—Periodicals and society publications." Many years ago the Harvard College Library adopted the subheading "Periodicals and other serial publications" on guide cards to cover all types of serials indiscriminately. The form used on the subject cards is simply "Period."

The Library of Congress makes much of the subheading "Societies." It has four variant forms:

[4] Minnie E. Sears, *List of Subject Headings; with Practical Suggestions for the Beginner in Subject Heading Work;* 7th ed. by Bertha M. Frick (New York: Wilson, 1954).

Societies.

For collections, memoirs, reports, transactions, etc. of societies under the name of the subject or subjects of which they treat; e.g., "Botany —Societies."

Societies, etc.

For publications of universities, museums, and other institutions, and of certain commissions which are not societies in the ordinary sense of the term.

Societies, periodicals, etc.

For publications relating to individuals; e.g., "Dickens, Charles—Societies, periodicals, etc." which is the heading assigned by the Library of Congress to *The Dickensian; a Magazine for Dickens Lovers.*

Society publications.

For works on subjects where the connotation of the expression "Societies" might be ambiguous; e.g., "Ants—Society publications"; "Fungi—Society publications"; and "Insects—Society publications."[5]

As might be expected, the distinction between a periodical and a society publication is often a nice one, and at times two headings may have to be assigned instead of one. Thus for the *Journal of Dental Research* the Library of Congress assigned the headings "Dentistry—Societies" as well as "Dentistry—Periodicals." The reason for the duplication in this instance is that since 1934 the journal has been the official organ of the International Association for Dental Research, and includes the proceedings of this and other organizations. Still another technicality in Library of Congress practice is the non-use of the form subheading "Societies" for certain types of society publications. Instead a reference is made from the appropriate subject heading to the names of individual bodies. Haykin has said of this device:

A reference from the subject heading for a particular kind of society or institution should be made to the names of individual societies of that kind as a guide to such of their publications as describe their purposes, activities, history, and proceedings. This obviates the necessity of using the subject heading designating the kind of society or institution for every entry of this character. It is exactly parallel with the use of the reference from the name of the occupation to the names of individuals who follow that occupation for the purpose of guiding the reader to autobiographical material. The following are cited as examples:

Medicine—Societies
see also
Academy of Medicine of Cincinnati
Colorado State Medical Society
Medical Women's International Association

---

[5] Cf. Haykin, *op. cit.,* p.109-10. Cf. also Harriet W. Pierson, *Guide to the Cataloguing of the Serial Publications of Societies and Institutions* (2d ed.; Washington, 1931), p.61-63.

Women as physicians
see also
Medical Women's International Association

Agricultural experiment stations—France
see also
Beauvais. Station agronomique

Prisons—U. S.
see also
U. S. *Federal Industrial Institution for Women, Alderson, W. Va.*
U. S. *Northeastern Penitentiary, Lewisburg, Pa.*
U. S. *Penitentiary, Atlanta*

As a corollary to this rule, publications of a society or institution which are not solely descriptive of it or an account of its activities, but which contain contributions to knowledge in the field of its interest, require a subject heading under the name of the field of interest with the subdivision *Societies, etc.* The subdivision in this case serves to separate publications of societies and institutions from general treatises on the subject, periodicals, etc.[6]

The varied Library of Congress treatment of the subject headings of society publications may be observed from the tracings for the following serials. When no tracing is given, the inference is that a specific reference has been made to the name of the society.

Society for Army Historical Research, *London.*
Journal.
1. Gt. Brit.—History, Military—Societies. 2. U. S.—Hist.—Revolution—British forces.

Society for British Entomology.
List of members.
1. Insects—Society publications.

Society for Experimental Stress Analysis.
Experimental stress analysis; proceedings of the Society for Experimental Stress Analysis.
1. Strains and stresses—Societies.

Society for Georgia Archaeology.
Proceedings.
1. Georgia—Antiq. 2. Indians of North America—Georgia. 3. Mounds—Georgia.

Society for Nautical Research, *London.*
Annual report.
1. Naval art and science—Societies. 2. Voyages and travels—Societies.

Society for Research in Child Development.
Proceedings.
1. Child studies—Societies. 2. Children—Care and hygiene.

Society for the Advancement of Management. Detroit Chapter.
Lecture series.

[6] Haykin, *op. cit.,* p.17. On pages 16-17 Haykin gives examples of references to names of individuals from headings that designate occupations.

1. Factory management.

Society for the Promotion of Roman Studies, *London.*
Report of the Council.

Society of American Military Engineers.
Bulletin.
1. Military engineering—Societies.

Society of Antiquaries of Newcastle-upon-Tyne.
List of members.

Society of Artists, *Sydney.*
Society of Artists book.
1. Art—Yearbooks. 2. Art—Australia.

Society of Chemical Industry, *London.*
Journal.
1. Chemistry, Technical—Societies. 2. Chemicals—Patents. 3. Chemicals—Manufacture and industry—Gt. Brit.

Society of Industrial Designers.
Education bulletin.
1. Design, Industrial—Collected works.

Society of Philatelic Americans.
S.P.A. journal; the official journal of the Society of Philatelic Americans.
1. Postage-stamps—Collectors and collecting—Period. 2. Postage-stamps—Collectors and collecting—Societies.

Society of the War of 1812. District of Columbia.
1812; bulletin of the Society of the War of 1812 in the District of Columbia.

Subject headings for government serials

Library of Congress practice for government serials is still more vague than that for society publications. Commonly no form subheading is employed to indicate that a publication is a serial. Sometimes the terms "Collections" and "Collected works" are pressed into service, and at times the subheadings "Periodicals" and "Societies, etc." are applied. The following are examples:

International Monetary Fund.
Annual report of the executive directors.

International Monetary Fund.
International finance statistics.
1. Finance—Stat.

International Monetary Fund.
Report of the executive directors.
1. Foreign exchange.

United Nations.
Yearbook.
1. United Nations—Yearbooks. 2. International agencies—Yearbooks.

United Nations. Secretariat. Dept. of Social Affairs.
Population studies.
1. Population—Collections.

United Nations. Secretariat. Statistical Office.
Monthly bulletin of statistics.
1. Economic conditions—1945- . 2. Social conditions—1945- .

United Nations. Secretariat. Statistical Office.
National income statistics of various countries.
1. Income.

United Nations. Secretariat. Statistical Office.
Sample surveys of current interest.
1. Statistics.

United Nations. Secretariat. Statistical Office.
Statistical papers.
1. Statistics—Collections.

United Nations. Secretariat. Statistical Office.
Statistical yearbook.
1. Statistics—Yearbooks.

United Nations. Secretariat. Statistical Office.
Yearbook of international trade statistics.
1. Commercial statistics.

U. S. Air Force.
Air Force register.

U. S. Air Force. Air Matériel Command.
AF technical report.
1. Aeronautics—Collected works.

U. S. Army. Chemical Corps.
Chemical warfare field service bulletin.
1. Chemical warfare.

U. S. Brookhaven National Laboratory, *Upton, N.Y.*
Progress report.
1. Science—Societies, etc. 2. Atomic energy—Societies, etc.

U. S. Brookhaven National Laboratory, *Upton, N.Y.*
Report.

U. S. Bureau of Indian Affairs.
Bulletin.
1. Indians of North America.

U. S. Library of Congress.
Information bulletin.

U. S. Library of Congress.
Cataloging service.
1. Cataloging. 2. Catalogs, Card.

U. S. Library of Congress. Processing Dept.
Monthly list of Russian accessions.
1. Russian literature—Bibl.—Period. 2. Russian literature—Bibl.—Union lists.

U. S. National Archives.
Report.
1. Archives—U. S.

U. S. Office of Education.
Bulletin.
1. Education—Collections. 2. Public schools—Collections.

Form headings

In most libraries entries are not made under forms like "Periodicals" or "American periodicals" for individual journals. As can be seen from MacNair[7] and Pierson,[8] the Library of Congress formerly made added entries under the headings "Periodicals"[9] and "Societies," as well as under the name of a place followed by the subheading "Learned institutions and societies."

The United Nations Library decided to adopt a form heading "Periodicals" subdivided by the name of the country from which the publication came. The heading covers serials of all kinds, and is intended to provide a record of all serials received, particularly from the smaller countries. Some periodical rooms, for example in the New York Public Library, keep a card file arranged by country of origin to show what publications are available from various places. In most libraries, when a request comes for a record of titles received from a particular country, the information would be gleaned from the visible index or agents' lists. One advantage of a punched card system for current serials or for a national union list is the possibility of securing lists by country.

Form headings are assigned to works about non-individual serial publications, and duplicate headings are made for works about the serial publications of ethnic groups. So, for a work about German newspapers published in Switzerland, the headings would be "1. Swiss newspapers (German). 2. German newspapers—Switzerland"; for a work about periodicals in the English language published in Ireland, they would be "1. Irish periodicals (English). 2. English periodicals—Irish." An exception to this practice is made for works about magazines and newspapers published in the United States in languages other

[7] Mary W. MacNair, *Guide to the Cataloguing of Periodicals* (3d ed.; Washington, 1925), p.13-14.

[8] Harriet W. Pierson, *Guide to the Cataloguing of the Serial Publications of Societies and Institutions* (2d ed.; Washington, 1931), p.62-63.

[9] Julia Pettee in her *Subject Headings* (New York: Wilson, 1947), p.91-92, says: "The general form heading Periodicals is quite uncalled for. Why should a library assemble in one list all of its periodicals when it keeps a serial file and we have the *Wilson Union list of serials?*" For periodicals in foreign languages the Enoch Pratt Free Library makes form headings like "Spanish works—Periodicals." See its *Catalog Department Manual* (Baltimore, 1940), p.58.

than English. An illustration of this type of heading is "Swedish-American periodicals," with references from "American periodicals, Swedish" and "Swedish periodicals."

Subject indexing of periodicals

In addition to the analytical entries described in the preceding chapter, some libraries make a feature of including in their catalogs index cards for significant periodical articles. When such a program is embarked upon, it should be with the intention of supplementing the published indexing services, not duplicating them. And when extensive subject indexing of this kind is undertaken, the list of subject headings must be expanded to provide for the minute topics with which periodical articles deal.

When periodicals are indexed in a library, the visible index is marked to indicate the titles that are to go on receipt to an officer who selects the items to be indexed. Most of these titles are indexed by subject only. Some, however, are indexed by author or by author and subject. The subject catalogers should supply the subject headings when the entries are to go into the regular card catalog, whereupon the cards can be typed by trained clerical assistants.

One problem that index cards sometimes give rise to stems from the fact that the indexers generally take the name of the periodicals from the pieces themselves; that is, they record periodicals under the latest form of their name, just as the Wilson indexes do. Readers and staff may experience some difficulty in locating an issue which is still covered in the catalog and shelf list by a former title. Stack attendants who do not readily find the desired volume on the shelves may report that there is no such title on the given number, and the call slip must be verified. This situation may develop in the interim period after a volume has left the periodical room but is not yet in the stacks, possibly because it is still at the bindery. Despite this problem it is well to employ the latest form of name instead of the prevailing catalog entry, which may not be revised for some time to come.

In the New York Public Library a special check list was set up by the indexers to make sure that all issues of the selected periodicals would pass through the indexing operation. Records of this kind should be avoided as far as possible.

Several libraries have established an excellent reputation for index entries. Notable among them are the Armed Forces Medical Library, the New York Public Library, and the Peabody Museum Library at Harvard University. At the first two of these institutions the program was inaugurated by Dr. Billings. The genesis of his thoughts on indexing has been described in these terms:

The *Index-Catalogue of the Surgeon-General's Library*, called by Dr. William H. Welch "America's greatest gift to medicine," was conceived out of the need of a young medical student, John Shaw Billings. Mindful of his toilsome search through the literature of medicine preparatory to his doctor's thesis, he determined years later, when in charge of the Surgeon General's Library, to gather the books and journals of medicine in adequate numbers, to catalog them, and to index their contents, so that future generations would neither have to go to Europe to see the books nor handle the thousands of volumes which had heretofore been required for any thorough review of a subject.[10]

In Washington Dr. Billings aimed at a printed bibliography. But in the New York Public Library he arranged for the index entries to be filed in the public catalog and in the various divisional catalogs. Now that these entries have been made decade after decade, the card catalogs in that library afford a truly splendid starting point for research, listing as they do the book and periodical literature on a tremendous variety of subjects.[11] The card catalog in the Peabody Museum Library at Harvard makes a similar contribution to knowledge, but in the specialized field of anthropology. Over the years the articles in anthropological journals have been indexed to provide research workers with comprehensive coverage of their subject.[12]

At the Jefferson School of Social Science Library, Henry Black has found that judicious indexing of journals increases the extent of their consultation:

We index 20 periodicals. The index which contains some 35,000 cards, grows at the rate of 5,000 cards a year. With three or four periodicals, indexing is selective, but moves towards completeness. Primarily a subject index, author entries are made for the signed contents of about half the magazines. . . With the exception of two, none is indexed elsewhere. . . Indexing probably averages two cards per article. . . A skilled indexer can cover 12 to 15 articles per hour. . .

The periodical index has greatly speeded up work at the reference desk, both because readers can do more of their own searching and because far less time is spent leafing through journals for an item that someone vaguely—and frequently wrongly—remembers. It has greatly increased the use of

---

[10] From the unpublished appendixes to *The National Medical Library; Report of a Survey of the Army Medical Library*, by Keyes D. Metcalf and others (Cambridge, Mass., 1944), p.66. The published part of the survey (Chicago: American Library Assn., 1944) contains two chapters on the *Index-Catalogue*.

[11] Julia Pettee describes Dr. Billings' contributions in Washington and New York, and adds (*op. cit.*, p.44): "The catalog of the New York Public Library deserves a place by itself not only because of its importance as the largest and most fingered card catalog in the country, but because in its history are combined the various elements that have gone into the development of our standard dictionary form."

[12] For a brief account of this undertaking and its value see Margaret Currier, "Anthropology Indexing," *Library of Congress Information Bulletin*, May 18, 1953, p.7-8.

bound periodicals; several titles are now used from 200 to 1000 times a year. After we started indexing such a specialized periodical as the *Bulletin of the Atomic Scientists,* reference calls jumped from three or four a year to six or eight a month. . .

Between subscription costs, binding, and storage costs, a periodical volume represents a very substantial investment. If indexing will increase its use by several times, the "returns" are correspondingly enhanced.[13]

The outstanding venture on a world-wide basis was undertaken by the International Federation for Documentation in Brussels. It enlisted the services of specialists in many countries to index on cards the current literature of their subject, principally in scientific and technical fields. For the arrangement of the resultant card catalog, and to overcome the barrier of language for entries made in one country and another, the Federation developed the Brussels Classification, now known as the Universal Decimal Classification. Class marks from this system permitted the formation of a classified catalog and allowed for the expression of nice distinctions not possible in the dictionary catalog.

So significant for scholarship and research are card catalogs that contain a record of basic articles in periodicals, in addition to the usual entries for books, that libraries should consider seriously whether devotion to the details of descriptive cataloging is all clear gain. Would it be better to put some of this time and effort into indexing the contents of important but unindexed serials?

Subject classification for serials

To classify or not to classify is the major theoretical problem in the shelf arrangement of serial publications. While the orthodox plan is to classify items in the regular collection—or on the "classified shelves"—under special circumstances classification may be dispensed with for serials, or more particularly for periodicals, government documents, and vertical file material.

In special libraries subject classification of serials may have slight value because the publications are acquired for the contribution they make to the library's central theme. Hence notation may be more important than classification: notation to simplify the shelving of items with complicated entries or in non-roman alphabets and to facilitate the operation of the charge file. A good illustration of this principle is afforded by the following statement about the classification of serials in the Armed Forces Medical Library:

Periodicals and transactions were originally arranged by country and language, then by title. Transactions and proceedings followed the periodicals

[13] Henry Black, "Indexing Selected Periodicals Proves Sound Investment," *Library Journal* 74:1296, 1312, 1949.

in each language group. These were followed by state associations, and then came county societies and city associations. Incomplete volumes of periodicals were not shelved with the bound set, but were bundled, numbered, and shelved in the Binding Section, where a record was kept of the contents of each bundle in numerical order.

After the transactions came hospital reports, medical-school catalogs and reports, institutional reports, and reports of associations, foundations, and funds. Administrative reports of hospitals were shelved with documents.

With the extensive growth of the Library this plan was given up, and whole sections were shifted to new locations as a result of overcrowding. Hence, serial files are to be found scattered throughout the Library. . . Currently, serials are being rearranged in two alphabets of open and closed files, and according to the entries in the *Union List of Serials*. They are being concentrated in Library Hall and on the floor below. This is surely a step in the right direction.[14]

The same question arises, though in a less complicated way, in school and public libraries. Should they have a central repository for the files of periodicals they preserve? Or is it better to distribute the material by subject? The answer may be simpler to arrive at for a public library that has no divisions. There are certain advantages in locating the files of periodicals in the departments to which they relate. But periodical sets grow to such an extent that a grouping of them in the bookstacks may result in more efficacious space utilization. Marie Prevost considered classification a waste of time in the Newark Public Library. There is much food for thought in her observations on the subject:

The vague class number on a periodical has never been of use. It is not needed when a library splits into departments. Walk along the line glancing at the last volume of each title. Chalkmark it E for Education, A for Art, the mind working automatically. Withhold decision on doubtful titles until departmental urge appears.

The only inlet to periodical use is through indexes to their articles. The remedy for an unindexed periodical is not classifying but getting it indexed. Even if classified, recourse must be had to its own index.

Moreover we have with us an all important situation produced by the fact that the people who have done the most intensive work on checklists and indexes, giving us our prime tools (witness Gregory and Wilson) both list and refer to a periodical by each of its successive titles during the period in which that title is in force. This knocks the bottom out of our long-cherished habit of forcing them together by a call number; but it works with the least possible friction. A tyro shelves them correctly; the public find them under the expected name; the reference staff send directly to the shelves for the title given in checklist or index without recourse to catalog for call number or ancient title.

May I outline what I, myself, consider the ideal way of recording periodicals?

[14] From the unpublished appendixes to *The National Medical Library; Report of a Survey of the Army Medical Library*, by Keyes D. Metcalf and others (Cambridge, Mass., 1944), p.59-60.

All periodicals, current and bound, the entire responsibility of the periodical division.

All periodicals to be shelved by title current at date of publication, without call or accession numbers.

All holdings for a given title to be shown only on a Kardex card in its "visible" file. A new card for each change of name. This means that all bound volumes, note of volumes in bindery, the receipt of unbound issues including today's,—will appear in this spot only. (Newark has a card printed in this form.)

A card to be placed in the book catalog under each name of each periodical, and under each subject desired, with note: "For holdings see entry in Kardex record." Where change of name has occurred, the note will read: "This periodical has appeared under the following titles: . . . For holdings see entries in Kardex record." The titles to be listed chronologically but without dates. These cards *never* to be out of the catalog, a new one to be written at name change and substituted as the old one is removed,—a full time service impossible when periodicals are accessioned and classified.

Compared with the classifying method the above means: great speeding up of service at all points; much reduction in labor; complete and exact information always available at a single location; no laboriously kept-up, eternally incomplete cards for bound volumes to mislead the unwary into believing the file stops a year or two back at best.[15]

The general libraries of colleges and universities usually prefer to classify most if not all of their serials by subject so that the faculty and students may find much of the material on any topic, both monograph and serial, in the same general vicinity. Fine distinctions are not necessary to achieve this end. For example, the publications *Ethics* and the *Journal of Symbolic Logic* may be shelved quite acceptably among the philosophy journals, instead of with the monographs on ethics and on logic. Further, some libraries keep most of their government documents as a unit, some have serial sets in storage libraries, while in general microreproductions are segregated. But as a rule this is as far as college and university libraries will tolerate breakdowns in subject classification in their main collections. The situation may be different in departmental collections, which naturally take the point of view

---

[15] Marie L. Prevost, "Why Classify Periodicals?" *Wilson Library Bulletin* 15:85, 1940. See also Hans Muller, "Why Classify Periodicals?" *Wilson Library Bulletin* 14:758-59, 1940. Muller summarizes the problem by saying: "Classification provides a rough but convenient arrangement, which is especially important and almost indispensable for non-indexed periodicals. It simplifies administrative procedure in case of future departmentalizations and expansions. It solves the vexing problems in connection with changed titles. Shelf-reading and reshelving become less complicated and, hence, more accurate. Do these various advantages outweigh the two disadvantages of added work for the staff and, as far as patrons of the library would be affected, a slightly more cumbersome procedure in obtaining bound periodicals? The answer will depend (1) on the size of the collection (2) on the type of material in the collection, i.e., whether largely non-indexed or mostly indexed periodicals, and (3) on the relative patience and perseverance of typical patrons of the library."

of the special library; but sometimes, when processing is centralized, they too must follow the policies and practices of the main library.

When space is at a premium in a library, ideas on the shelving of serials may undergo a change. Sets may have to be withdrawn from departmental reading rooms and retired to the general stacks, or from the stacks to a storage library. Sometimes whole sets are so transferred, sometimes the earlier volumes. The latter is the plan at the Enoch Pratt Free Library, where "the dividing date between stack and first floor periodicals is not to be changed until several departments become seriously overcrowded, when the date will be changed for all."[16] The space problem has been responsible for the development of regional storage libraries, where serials may be found in large numbers. Amongst the first material that the Harvard College Library sent to the New England Deposit Library were files of serials: long runs that could be transferred with comparatively little record-changing. In the Deposit Library the serials are arranged by size and by running numbers, not by subject. Thus it is seen that a library that starts out with a subject classification for its serials may in time be forced into a different arrangement, in part at any rate, in the interests of economy of shelving.

In the long run, the answer to the question whether to classify or not to classify serials may prove to be a practical issue rather than a theoretical one. And the crux of the matter may be as Marie Prevost suggests: "The remedy for an unindexed periodical is not classifying but getting it indexed."[17]

The most progressive thinking on the subject of classification for serials has been done by Beatrice Simon. She advocates neither a classified nor an alphabetical arrangement, but groupings by form, e.g., periodicals, government documents, society publications, and serials issued by corporations. Only in the general library of a university would she consider a classified arrangement; there she says the classification should be broad, and books and serials should be separated. She points out the difficulty of classifying a publication like the *Canadian Journal of Economics and Political Science* so that both the economists and the political scientists will be happy. She observes: "I have seen several librarians start out with the alphabetical arrangement, and then change—not to a subject arrangement but to the one which gathers forms together."[18]

---

[16] Enoch Pratt Free Library, *Staff Instruction Book* (Baltimore, 1936), ¶1018.

[17] Prevost, *op. cit.*, p.85.

[18] Beatrice V. Simon, "Cataloguing of Periodicals," *Ontario Library Review* 33:244, 1949. This article should be studied carefully for the light it sheds on the whole problem of the classification of serials. See also her earlier article, "Let's Consider Serials Realistically," *Library Journal* 71:1296-1301, 1946.

Subject classification for documents

The United States Government has a network of depository libraries which receive all or a selection of the federal documents distributed through the Superintendent of Documents. The list of these libraries is published annually in the *Monthly Catalog of United States Public Documents.* It includes college, public, state, teachers college, and university libraries, and several school libraries. Thus numerous institutions must decide whether to classify the material or not. The alternative to incorporating the publications in the classified bookstacks, as the Library of Congress does, is to set up a collection of documents as a unit in itself.[19] In Chapter 2 this practice was described as substandard when the material is likewise self-cataloging and when in general libraries shirk their responsibilities. Usually such a collection is not as well organized, located, or serviced as the collection of current periodicals, though in some instances considerable pains are taken with the material, as in the University of Colorado Library. Often the collection is located in one of the more remote parts of the bookstacks, and it may be the responsibility of a student assistant or some other nonprofessional staff member. The principal tasks of this attendant are to check the receipt of the current documents, shelve them, and help in finding them when necessary.

Government documents are at least on an equal footing with current periodicals in the Library of Congress and the New York Public Library: witness the important bibliographical work produced in each of them.[20] When current documents are accorded this status, document librarians are in a position to give reference assistance of a high order and to aid in a vigorous acquisition program.

The collection of federal documents that comes nearest to completeness is under the direction of the Superintendent of Documents and is known as the Public Documents Library. Its catalog is a shelf list arranged by issuing bodies. The classification—that is, the notation developed for the publications of the issuing bodies—is given in the

---

[19] The chief protagonist of this type of organization is Ellen P. Jackson. See in particular her "Administration of the Government Documents Collection," *ACRL Monographs* 5, 1953. See also Ruth M. Erlandson, "The Organization of Federal Government Publications in Depository Libraries," in Anne M. Boyd, *United States Government Publications* (3d ed.; New York: Wilson, 1949), p.569-79. An older study which is still of value is Thomas P. Fleming, "The Organization of Work with Public Documents in University Libraries," in *Public Documents* (Chicago: American Library Assn., 1936), p.101-27.

[20] Since 1910 the Library of Congress has issued the *Monthly Check-list of State Publications.* The editorial offices of Public Affairs Information Service have for long been in the Economics Division of the New York Public Library. For a discussion of document reading rooms, see Chapter 10.

Checklist of United States Public Documents, 1789-1909 and since July 1924 in the *Monthly Catalog of United States Public Documents.*[21] In 1947 a survey disclosed that 174 depository libraries had found it expedient to arrange their federal documents by this scheme, making the check lists to some extent a catalog of their own collection. On the classification of depository sets Eastin has said:

> Classification systems vary throughout the depository libraries. Sixty-eight do not use any classification system for depository publications. The greatest number make use of the Superintendent of Documents classification system, a total of 174 libraries preferring this system. Fifty-four others use the Superintendent of Documents system in combination with the Dewey decimal system. The Dewey system alone is employed by 111 depository libraries, while 8 others partly use the Dewey, and 15 more combine the Dewey system with department and bureau treatment. The last-mentioned department and bureau system is used exclusively by 32 libraries. Various other systems, such as Cutter, Library of Congress, subject treatment, and 23 individual or specialized classification systems are also used.[22]

Ethelyn Markley has criticized the Superintendent of Documents classification on six grounds:

1. There are often delays of months in assigning numbers to ephemeral or declassified items.
2. Since the classification is by issuing body, awkward situations develop when titles are transferred from one issuing body to another.
3. The works of agencies which publish in the same or closely related fields are not brought together on the shelves.
4. Numbers that were assigned from 1909 to 1924 are hard to obtain unless they are taken from the unofficial schedules compiled by Miss Poole.
5. The notation is often long; it is difficult to read because of inferior and superior numbers; and it results in a fixed rather than a relative location for the publications of a department.
6. Direct access to the shelves by subject is precluded; an intermediary aid is required, such as an alphabetical author file or the *Monthly Catalog of United States Public Documents.*[23]

Accordingly she prefers Ellen Jackson's notation, which is applicable to all types of government publications,[24] though she also speaks well of Raynard Swank's scheme for state and local documents which is

---

[21] For a loose-leaf edition of the schedules, see Mary E. Poole, *Documents Office Classification,* compiled in North Carolina State College Library, Duke University Library, Virginia Polytechnic Institute Library ([Ann Arbor, Mich.: Edwards Brothers, 1946]).

[22] Roy B. Eastin, "Let's Use Public Documents!" *Library Journal* 73:1556, 1948.

[23] A. Ethelyn Markley, *Library Records for Government Publications* (Berkeley: Univ. of California Pr., 1951), p.18-19.

[24] Ellen P. Jackson, *A Notation for a Public Documents Classification* ([Stillwater: Oklahoma Agricultural and Mechanical College, 1946.] Its Library Bulletin 8).

intended to complement the Superintendent of Documents system.[25]

Most special libraries and many university libraries, as well as the Library of Congress and the New York Public Library, have felt the need for the subject approach which a regular classified arrangement of government publications affords. They have therefore distributed their documents throughout the classification, cataloging and classifying them as they do other material. In other words, they make no distinction between a government publication and a non-document as far as the organization of their book stock is concerned. This policy is desirable in library systems where large quantities of documents may be required both centrally and in department libraries. The demand may be such that holdings are at times duplicated between the two. The duplication is natural, for few department libraries can operate without government publications, least of all those whose fields are business, law, public administration, science, and technology. In such library systems there is less occasion to employ the Superintendent of Documents classification or any other special scheme. Instead, the regular classification scheme in operation in the main or departmental library serves to arrange the documents by subject.

The general serials which the Library of Congress classifies in J 1-999 are an exception to any plan of scattering government publications by subject. These include the "congressional set" of federal documents which in the Library of Congress and elsewhere is arranged by arbitrary numbers assigned to the publications of the fifteenth and later Congresses.[26] The current numbers are obtained from the *Numerical Lists and Schedule of Volumes* issued by the Superintendent of Documents. Since there is an interval before the numbers are made public, a congressional set has an assortment of unnumbered volumes at the end waiting for the numbers to be assigned. Much valuable material is to be found in the congressional set. For instance, Commodore Perry's *Narrative of the Expedition of an American Squadron to the China Seas and Japan, Performed in the Years 1852, 1853 and 1854* was published as a House of Representatives document. Clearly it should be analyzed to make it readily available to the historian.

There are two over-all plans for government documents, then, the prototypes being the Library of Congress and the Superintendent of Documents classification systems. There is at the same time a middle ground, with room for compromise: the general documents collection

[25] Raynard Swank, "A Classification System for State, County, and Municipal Documents," *Special Libraries* 35:116-20, 1944.

[26] An explanation of the serial numbers is given in Laurence F. Schmeckebier, *Government Publications and Their Use* (2d ed.; Washington: Brookings Institution, 1939), especially p.139-44.

can be enlarged in libraries that favor subject classification, and the segregated collection can be reduced by classifying worthwhile material by subject. In the latter case, compromises should be made on a liberal basis; otherwise anomalies are bound to occur, such as the presence on the document shelves of the publications of the Freer Gallery of Art.

It must be observed too that quantities of minor government publications form excellent material for cooperative acquisition and storage. For instance, the Midwest Inter-Library Center has always made a feature of them. Whenever storage of documents is proposed or practiced, the value of subject classification is left out of account. Further, one disadvantage inherent in the self-cataloging documents collection is that minor serials are held in the main stacks when they might be transferred to cheaper storage.

In theory there is no objection to dispensing with subject arrangement for government serials which are not worthy of regular treatment, any more than there is for non-government serials. The objection comes when standard publications which should be readily accessible to readers and staff alike are buried in uncataloged and unclassified collections. The consequences of discriminating against government publications are apparent from the *List of the Serial Publications of Foreign Governments*. Its listings indicate that there are only two strong document collections in general libraries in the United States, those at the Library of Congress and the New York Public Library.

In view of its great resources in public documents, it is not surprising to find that the Library of Congress has specially developed its classification scheme to provide for government publications of all kinds. By contrast, the special document sections of the Dewey Decimal classification are among its weakest parts, so much so that libraries with extensive document holdings using this classification have been forced to make many adjustments.

The classification of publications of international governmental organizations is discussed in Chapter 15.

Form symbols in the notation for serials

Stack service in research libraries generally attests to the fact that a mnemonic device in the call number is decidedly useful to show that an item is a serial. A reader in copying onto a call slip the author and title of an item in a set may fail to mention the volume number or other details essential for the procurement of the particular item; the stack attendant will then be unable to locate the desired publication. But if there is a mnemonic device in the call number, the omission of the essential data may be caught at the time the call slip is handed in.

One of the good mnemonic features in the Dewey Decimal classification is the form number 05 for periodicals. Whenever that number in any of its applications is noted at the delivery desk or in the stacks it is clear that a serial is being requested, and the time spent in attempting to locate a work or in verifying incomplete call slips may be reduced. The class AP General periodicals in the Library of Congress scheme serves a similar purpose; not so, however, the class AS Academies and learned societies, which combines both monographs and serials. The Dewey form number 06 for societies includes monographs as well as serials. Hence the problem encountered in subject heading is to some extent repeated here: what is the difference between a periodical and a society publication? In subject heading practice it is possible to straddle the question and to use duplicate headings, but in classification the issue must be faced squarely. The decision in cases of doubt should be to favor the form number for periodicals. In any event a choice must be made between dividing the periodical and periodical-like publications on a subject, or at times dividing the publications of a society. On all counts the distinction between periodicals and society publications causes trouble. It may well prove to be a false distinction that should be abandoned, or if not abandoned altogether at least redefined more realistically. No consistent pattern is followed in the Library of Congress scheme. General periodicals and general society publications are segregated in AP and AS, but elsewhere the treatment varies, even within a class. Thus the following dispositions may be found in Z Bibliography:

Shorthand
- Z53P General periodicals
- English shorthand
  - 54 Periodicals
  - 54Y Yearbooks
  - 55 Societies

Paleography
- Z108 Periodicals. Societies. Congresses

Book industries and trade
- Z119 Periodicals
- 119.5 Yearbooks
- 120 Societies. Trade unions

Binding
- Z267 Periodicals
- 268 Societies

Bookselling and publishing
- Z284 Periodicals. Societies

Libraries
- Z671 Periodicals

673	Library associations
General bibliography	
Z1007	Periodicals
1008	Societies, Congresses, etc.

Relations between subject catalogers and descriptive catalogers

Although subject heading and classification for serials are comparatively simple, it is customary for them to be assigned by the subject catalogers, not the descriptive catalogers. General periodicals and society publications are exceptions. Since these take no subject heading as a rule, and since their classification is more a matter of notation, the serial catalogers usually take complete responsibility for their subject and descriptive cataloging. In these circumstances, the shelf list for the general serial classes may be located near the serial catalogers for the sake of convenience.

Serials in specific subject fields are usually forwarded to the subject catalogers for classification and subject heading. Relations between the two groups are informal, for the most part. They may, however, be formalized in the interests of keeping track of serials in process and of passing along to the subject catalogers information that may be of use to them. The routines at Yale University Library illustrate this procedure.

A. When the descriptive cataloging of a serial has been completed, it must be sent to a classifier in the Catalogue Department for call number and subjects. Fill out classifier's charge slip in triplicate, giving classifier's initials and location, brief title or author and title, list of volumes sent if not too complicated a statement, your own initials, indication as to whether continuation or not, and date sent.
   1. List of classifiers of various subjects, with their initials and location, is on bulletin board in Serial Department.
   2. First copy of charge slip goes with volumes to classifier, second is sent to the serial catalog to show that the set is being cataloged, third is retained by cataloger until set is returned so that he may know status of set.

B. If Yale has other publications of the same organization, tell the classifier where they are classed and what subjects were assigned.

C. If, in checking entries, cataloger finds any information that would be useful to the classifier, note should be sent with set giving that information.

D. If serial is in a difficult language and cataloger has to translate author and/or title or any part of the introduction in order to know what it is about, note should be included telling the classifier what was found so that he will not have to repeat the work.[27]

---

[27] Yale University Library, *Cataloging of Serials in the Yale University Library* (New Haven, 1951), p.29. The routines followed by the descriptive cataloger after the publications have been returned are given on p.30-33.

Assignment of book numbers

Several technicalities are encountered in the assignment of book numbers. The most difficult of them in theory is the correct way to treat serials that involve one or more changes of name or title. Much labor may be involved if the book number is altered for a set that is held together despite changes in name or title, since all call numbers inside the volumes and on the spine must be corrected, as well as a variety of serial records. If the book number is not altered, a publication that becomes well known under a later title will be shelved according to the less-known earlier title, and may cause inconvenience to the person who consults the shelves directly. The alternative, suggested by Miss Prevost and others, of reclassifying a serial every time a change of name occurs is not altogether a happy plan. After all, *Ethics* is still the same publication as the *International Journal of Ethics* despite the change of title. Miss Pierson's mention of a serial that underwent 41 changes of name in fourteen years is a warning about what could happen if a file were really broken up according to this scheme.

Whether they like it or not, most libraries retain the original book number through all the vicissitudes in the life of a serial. As a rule, only when the change is of such magnitude that a new work has in fact emerged is the number altered. So classification tends to be somewhat conservative in holding material together.

Libraries can always learn from Library of Congress treatment of book numbers, no matter what classification scheme they themselves follow. The extent of the holdings in the National Library is so great that it has something to offer on most situations encountered elsewhere. For example, it has found a solution to most of the difficulties met in assigning book numbers to serial titles which begin with the words "American," "art," "music," "national," etc. It spreads or otherwise skillfully manipulates the book numbers to provide an effective arrangement instead of "grafting"[28] them on to a narrow base. Some details of Library of Congress practice are given in the following statement:

Periodicals, Documents, etc., present certain problems which are best solved by keeping materials in these forms together in larger groups, either at the head of a given class or in special numbers at the beginning of a block of class numbers covering a broad subject. Typical of the latter is the following sequence under Anthropology:

---

[28] To use an expression of Anna C. Laws, *Author Notation in the Library of Congress* (Washington, 1930), p.12.

GN
1 Periodicals.
2 Societies. Institutions.
3 Congresses.
Collections.
4 Collections by several authors.
6 Collected works of individual authors.
8 Minor collections of papers, essays, etc.
11 Dictionaries and encyclopedias.

Where a form sequence is needed for a single class, variants of the following are used for subclass arrangement:

.A1 Periodicals and Societies.
.A2-4 Documents in series.
.A5 Documents in monographic form.
.A6-Z Monographs.

Yearbooks, congress reports, and society publications are treated analogously. In each instance, the Shelflist must be consulted carefully because of the great variation in treatment between different parts of the classification schedules. They are frequently arranged by content, that is, the publications are assigned book numbers on the basis of their logical sequence and importance rather than upon the vagaries of their titles.

The book number having been determined, the shelflister then writes the full call number on both cards, leaving the copy as a temporary card in the shelflist, later to be replaced by the printed cards. Returning to his desk, the shelflister inscribes the call number in the book, on the verso of the title page, and prepares other copies of the master card for various records, using the fluid-process cards wherever possible. . .

For all materials in those categories where the Serial Record Division has maintained the record of holdings since 1942, the shelflister must prepare for that division an extra copy of the completed card giving all essential information and pertinent instructions for the treatment of future issues received.

Permanent cards are prepared for the Monograph Record showing the classification and analytical decisions entered on the Series Decision card and indicating the material handled when the permanent cards were made.[29]

As a collection grows, the assignment of book numbers that keep publications in strict alphabetical order becomes an increasingly formidable task. The difficulties are not so great when the classification scheme originally allowed a broad base; if it did not, frequent complications occur in assigning numbers, at the charge file, and otherwise. How far strict alphabetical order needs to be retained is a matter that will demand more and more attention as the problems multiply. An older plan, still operative in some institutions, is to arrange serials by the first letter of the entry only. Thereafter the arrangement is in accession order. So *Psychological Abstracts* might succeed rather than

[29] Library of Congress *Departmental & Divisional Manuals* 3:35-37, 1950.

precede *Psychological Bulletin.* There is some merit in this system, although it complicates consultation of the shelves to some extent. Whether convenient or not, adoption of devices of this kind may be necessary in parts of a classification scheme that have become overly complicated. Occasionally an unnumbered series is classed together. Arbitrary numbering may then be resorted to, the numbers thereupon becoming part of the call number for the analyticals. Special schemes must be developed from time to time for the publications of complex bodies. The Organization of American States, with editions in several languages, is a case in point. Unless such problems are studied carefully at an early stage, complications are bound to ensue.

If it is at all possible, the shelf-list card should be made in advance of the assignment of the book number. In the United Nations Library it is made at the same time as the work slip. The statement of holdings is added by the descriptive cataloger when the publication is cataloged, and the card can be dropped into place in the shelf list as soon as the book number is determined. The more complicated the statement of holdings which goes on the shelf-list card, the more desirable it is to follow this practice, as otherwise the details must be copied onto the permanent card when it is forthcoming, and the copying and filing processes add to the serial work load. The practice is particularly recommended for libraries employing form cards for open-entry serials.

Monograph series

In the act of either sorting or classifying, decisions must be given about keeping monograph series together as sets or scattering them by subject. Often it is difficult to predetermine the best course of action; hence decisions have to be reviewed as trouble develops, whereupon it may even be decided to keep part of a set together and to scatter the rest. Should duplicate sets be available, the first copy may be held together while the second is scattered; for example, Hunt and Poole's *Political History of England* may be treated in both ways.

When a complete set is on hand or on order, the presumption may be in favor of keeping a series together in the following instances:

- Series whose parts are not bibliographical units, *e.g. The Cambridge History of the British Empire.*
- Series with continuous paging.
- Pamphlet series, especially when many of the items would otherwise go into pamphlet volumes.
- Series on a narrowly defined topic, *e.g.* Byzantine art.
- Series whose parts might prove difficult to classify.
- Well known sets which are likely to be asked for as such, *e.g. The Harvard Classics.*

Unanalyzed series, even when the analyzing is merely postponed.
Government documents.
Near print, *e.g.* technical reports.
Works for which a cumulated index is issued, *e.g.* the *Skrifter* of the Norsk folkeminnelag which has an index covering v.1-49.

In the following instances the presumption may be in favor of scattering a series:

Works whose component parts should obviously be on the classified shelves by author or subject.
Unnumbered series.
Broken sets.
Series for which duplicate holdings are not desired, yet individual monographs should be in various locations in a library or library system.
Series which include titles that are reference books in the narrow sense.
Works which are broad in their coverage, particularly general series like *Everyman's Library*.
Publishers' series.
Series whose component parts look like ordinary monographs and are generally regarded as such.
Series which contain items on poor paper.
In institutions connected with deposit libraries, series which have items that should go to storage instead of to the classified shelves.

Divided holdings

Oftentimes part of a serial is shelved in one place and part in another. The reference collection in particular is responsible for much splitting of sets. The latest volume of a serial—a who's who, a city directory, a college catalog, or a work like the *Statesman's Year-book*—may be on the reference shelves; the next-to-the-latest volume may go to the catalog or order department, to save an extra subscription; and the back file may be in the bookstacks. Periodical sets are also divided in institutions which like to have the bound file for the last ten years on the reference shelves, the theory being that the greatest demand is for the more recent volumes.

Lack of space is the motive for division of another kind. Relief from overcrowded shelves is often obtained by transferring the earlier volumes of serial sets from department libraries to the main stack collection or from the stacks to a storage library. In a large library system, the serial staff may spend a considerable amount of time each year handling transferred sets, both complete and partial.

Whenever division of any kind occurs, separate shelf-list cards should be made for each location. Except in those libraries that dispense with a shelf list or with the statement of holdings on the shelf-list card, the shelf list for the reference room should show the volumes of serials shelved there, even though the practice is to keep only the

Latest = RR 1011.12
Next to latest = Catal. Rm.
Earlier = LSoc 5.17

The World of learning. London.

For a full record of the Library's holdings apply to the Reference Desk or the Serial Division.

Latest = {RR 1515.6 / Catal. Rm.}
Earlier = AL 1.86.10

Who's who among North American authors. Los Angeles.

For a full record of the Library's holdings apply to the Reference Desk or the Serial Division.

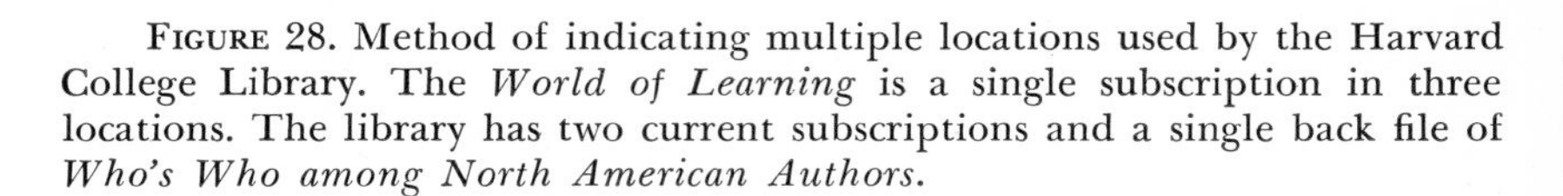

FIGURE 28. Method of indicating multiple locations used by the Harvard College Library. The *World of Learning* is a single subscription in three locations. The library has two current subscriptions and a single back file of *Who's Who among North American Authors.*

latest volume on the reference shelves. Likewise the regular shelf list should show the volumes located in the stacks, without regard to parts of the set in the reference room or elsewhere. Careful maintenance of the reference room shelf list is advised even in libraries which deemphasize the shelf list. Since relatively more items are lost from the reference shelves than from the stack collection, there is justification for taking repeated inventory of the reference books. In fact, a hard-worked reference collection should be inventoried every year.

Originally the United Nations Library followed another plan for divided sets, a plan which is not recommended. A charge was placed in the circulation file for parts of a set located semi-permanently in the reference room, a department library, or elsewhere. The system was given up because loans of this type needlessly complicate the day-to-day work at the charge file, and because readers and staff are inconvenienced when volumes they seek are not shelved according to the call number given on the catalog cards.

The catalog records should be marked in such a way as to make the division of a serial set clear. Double or triple call numbers may be necessary to show that the latest volume is in the reference room, the next-to-the-latest is in the catalog room, and the earlier volumes are in the stacks; or to show that the last ten years of a periodical file are in the reference collection or a department library, while the earlier volumes are in the general stacks (see Figure 28).

When volumes are susceptible of being transferred from one location to another after they have been superseded, the serial checkers can help by listing all the successive locations on the verso of the title page of the current volumes. This device permits reference librarians and others to tell at a glance where earlier volumes may be found, and it facilitates the transfer of items from one location to another. A specimen listing might be:

R 305.S8
Catalog room
305.S8

The former location is lined out as each transfer takes place.

Deposit-library holdings

A few American libraries have adopted a classification by size for the serials they house or intend to house in deposit libraries. The scheme in operation at Yale University Library is as follows:

WO up to 22.5 cm.
WP 22.5 to 26 cm.
WQ 26 to 32 cm.
WS 32 to 45 cm.
WT 45 cm. and over

At Harvard College Library a distinction has been made between current serials and back files. The current publications go in KS, which is an active classification. Volumes may be added to KS from year to year as they are acquired. Back files more commonly go into the size classification for monographs, even though the remainder of the set may likewise be transferred to the Deposit Library at some time in the future. An additional location among the monographs or in KS can be assigned if and when the second installment is relocated; and in a storage library there is no serious objection to the split as there might be in the regular bookstacks. The W material at Yale is shelved in the main stacks, ready to be moved to a storage library should occasion arise. At Harvard part of the material is in the New England Deposit Library and part is in the main stacks where it will remain pending the erection of a second unit of the Deposit Library. Experience has proved that there is a certain advantage in holding newly cataloged items for a year or so in the bookstacks before transferring them to the storage library. For instance, the catalogers themselves may want to refer to the publications while the records are still in process.

CHAPTER 10

Housing and Servicing Current Serials

WHENEVER THE SIZE of an institution or its serial collection warrants, separate reading and storage facilities are provided for several classes of current publications which must be assembled before they can be bound, and which, therefore, are not good stack material in the first instance. Periodicals are the first and most natural type of serial to be given a room of their own. This room may in some cases include current newspapers in its scope, especially in college and university libraries; and it may even assume some measure of responsibility for government serials. As more specialization sets in, especially in public libraries, a newspaper room may be established to care for both bound and unbound files; while in the largest institutions, the Library of Congress and the New York Public Library in particular, the periodical room is supplemented by both a newspaper and a document room.

The organization at the Library of Congress is particularly interesting because since 1944 periodicals, newspapers, and government publications have been for administrative purposes consolidated in a Serials Division, although each retains its own reading room in different parts of the library. While the name is reminiscent of the serials department which is the goal of some serial librarians, the Division is strictly a reference unit; processing duties are incidental. Its scope is somewhat unusual, as the concluding part of the following statement discloses:

> The function of the Division is to have custody of certain groups of materials "which require, or for reasons of conveniencee are given, reader and reference service prior to their addition to the general classified collections." Insofar as they are not allocated to other divisions, the following groups are included: periodicals and general serials, learned society publications, government serials, pamphlets, books in parts, and ephemera of various sorts.[1]

[1] Library of Congress *Departmental & Divisional Manuals* 9:7, 1950. This manual should be studied in detail, since it relates exclusively to the Serials Division.

The periodical room

In small libraries current periodicals are generally located and serviced in the reading room. If there is no separate reading room, they are commonly shelved near the circulation desk. Some small libraries have periodical rooms; they become quite common in middle-sized institutions, and they are the order of the day in large libraries. In the larger establishments there may be subject divisions which take the material in their fields away from the general periodical room.[2]

When current periodicals are in the reading room they naturally become the responsibility of the reference librarian. Then, when a periodical room emerges, it is just as naturally considered to be part of the reference service, even though the periodical librarian spends a major part of his time doing processing work: checking in current numbers, filling gaps, preparing volumes for binding, and so forth. The advantages of constituting the periodical room as a reference unit are: (1) reference services can be coordinated advantageously, (2) circulation procedures can be standardized, and (3) the processing departments are left desirably free of custodial duties.

The treatment accorded the current periodicals themselves varies greatly. Sometimes they are merely laid on shelves or on tables after the marks of library ownership have been added, or they may first be put in binders of one type or another. Springbacks and other patent binders, as well as a variety of less expensive covers, including manila rope, were commonly utilized in the past, and are still used in some libraries (for example, the Library of Congress puts some six hundred of the titles most in demand in springbacks). Perhaps the most pleasing of the older binders was one made in the local bindery, often with the name of the periodical stamped in gold on the front cover. These forms have quite generally been superseded by commercially made plastic covers which, being transparent, allow the cover of the periodical to display itself. These plastic covers are particularly desirable for periodicals that circulate, since they afford much-needed protection.

Some libraries favor periodical racks, because they allow a maximum of display. They are found mostly in smaller libraries where the total collection of current periodicals is small enough to fit into one or two units. However, no really satisfactory periodical rack has as yet been designed.[3] Even when the periodicals are first put in plastic

---

[2] The common organizational patterns in public libraries are described in *A Survey of Libraries in the United States* (Chicago: American Library Assn., 1926), v.2, p.145-49; the relevant passage for college and university libraries is v.2, p.217-20.

[3] A typical display rack is described in Joseph L. Wheeler and Alfred M. Githens, *The American Public Library Building, Its Planning and Design with Special Reference to Its Administration and Service* (New York: Scribner, 1941),

covers, they tend to look so disorderly standing up in a rack that the display value is reduced. To meet this objection, and at the same time to retain an element of display, the latest issues may be placed on sloping shelves. The effect is much neater, regardless of whether plastic covers are employed.

Obviously provision must be made not just for the latest issue, but for the balance of the current volume or year. Sometimes these back numbers are stored in any convenient spot: on regular shelves, in closets, or elsewhere. Sometimes they are put into containers with the rest of the set in the stacks. However, no open container, whether of cardboard or metal, is satisfactory if the unbound numbers must stand up in it unsupported, because the pieces gather dust and tend to be torn. The special library practice of housing some serials in vertical file cabinets gives adequate support to the items stored and does not expose them to dust. In general, however, unbound issues fare best when they are left lying flat, a desideratum which is overlooked in libraries which shelve the current issues of periodicals at the end of the bound set.

When sloping shelves are favored for the latest issues, it is possible to alternate them with regular shelves so that the rest of the file can be shelved immediately below the most recent number. Otherwise the earlier numbers may be laid flat on supplementary shelves elsewhere in the vicinity. In the Columbia University Library some of the latest issues are on display on counters with sloping tops, with the earlier issues on regular shelves below the counter. The rest of the latest issues with their back numbers are on flat shelves, because in a large collection it is difficult to supply enough space to display all of the latest issues.

In the Detroit Public Library a combination of sloping shelves and storage bins was specially designed and put to effective use. The latest number is on display; to secure an earlier number the reader simply raises the sloping shelf and selects the desired item. The plan affords a maximum of neatness for both current and earlier numbers. Equipment of this kind is illustrated by Wheeler and Githens in *The American Public Library Building.* Its chief drawback is its cost; for large installations space would also be a problem. A much less expensive form of bin storage was devised for the periodical room in the General Library at the University of Michigan where the display factor was completely disregarded. The periodicals are housed in pigeon holes,

---

p.462-63. This work should be consulted for other details relating to periodical and newspaper rooms and their equipment. In Great Britain an attractive table-model periodical rack has been installed in the Library of the Fuel Research Station of the Department of Scientific and Industrial Research. It has glass shelves. See N. E. Pettitt, "Display Rack for Periodicals," *Library Association Record* 55:397, 1953.

each with its own little door with a label bearing the name of the periodical.

When more than the latest issue is directly available to readers either the files are left in disarray or the staff must spend considerable time each day putting them in order, returning misshelved items to their proper place, and watching for issues that need minor repairs or have been mutilated. A larger measure of control can be gained by storing the unbound file except for the latest issues in areas where there is closed access. Readers must then fill out a call slip requesting the publications they want. The load of the periodical room staff is substantially increased when requests must be filled in this way.[4] The justification for servicing periodicals from closed shelves is that the pieces are better preserved, even though the call slip system is not an absolute guarantee against mutilation or theft.

All such factors must be taken into account in planning a new library building or in converting older quarters. They were reviewed, for instance, when Harvard's Lamont Library was being planned. There it was decided that a self-service system was desirable, a simple alphabetical arrangement on standard shelves, spaced a few inches apart and with a neat label for each title. Even with constant attention to the files, the appearance of the current periodicals in the Lamont Library leaves something to be desired, especially when the issues become worn. Thus the matter of shelving current periodicals boils down to a question of whether some amount of neatness is to be sacrificed or whether fairly expensive equipment should be installed.

Mutilation is a matter of constant concern to periodical room staffs, especially in libraries that preserve their files for binding. The ever-present threat of it is a major reason for collation before binding, with its heavy consumption of time.[5] As a precautionary measure, libraries sometimes withhold certain titles from current use. These become

[4] In the New York Public Library the burden of servicing current periodicals from behind a counter elicited this comment: "The work of bringing to the reader and reshelving promptly larger numbers of magazines which are briefly consulted has been a strain on the staff. On one day, 3,085 periodicals were used in the rooms. Under such pressure, with the rooms crowded to capacity, it has been difficult to maintain the usual standard of service." *Report* of the New York Public Library, 1931 (New York, 1932), p.41.

[5] At the Library of Congress it is estimated that a collator averages twenty completed volumes a day or about 4260 a year. For newspapers the rate is twelve volumes a day or about 2763 a year. "These assistants select the files of serials, periodicals and newspapers for binding, examine each issue to see that all pages, plates, maps, supplements, etc., are in place and are not mutilated, arrange the issues in order, with title-page at the front of each volume and index at the back; initiate want cards for missing issues; and remove duplicates which are not needed." *Annual Report* of the Librarian of Congress, 1946 (Washington, 1947), p.331.

available to readers only after they have been bound. In the case of some popular titles subject to an undue amount of wear and tear, duplicate subscriptions for binding purposes are at times necessary. When extra copies are so acquired they are set aside, possibly in locked closets, until the file is complete.

Many periodical rooms have been designed without anticipation or awareness of the tremendous expansion in the number of serial titles and holdings which the twentieth century has witnessed and whose end is not yet in sight. The periodical room in the Widener Library at Harvard University, a 1915 structure, was built to accommodate no more than a thousand periodicals. To provide more space, first the adjacent bookstacks and then the end of the reading room had to be pressed into service. And Columbia University's Butler Library, opened in 1935, allowed for only 1300 titles in the current periodical room. The New York Public Library with its great periodical collection has for many years overflowed into the bookstacks at some distance from the Periodicals Division. Examples like these can be multiplied. And if a periodical room is not large enough to house all a library's current periodicals, it certainly would be inadequate to house all the current serials. Yet one of the major tasks confronting administrators, most particularly in large general libraries, is to provide ample space for all current serials, without discrimination as to type.

In a large library a periodical room may be an extremely busy place. So busy had the Periodicals Division of the New York Public Library become in 1926 that it had to limit its scope by removing from circulation all magazines of a distinctly popular nature. This was done to provide seats for readers who came for current information, as well as for those who needed current material in connection with their research work.[6] The situation at the Library of Congress in 1945 was as follows:

> The Serials Division, broadly considered, is one of the busiest in our institution. Its custodial and service functions are exceedingly complex by nature of the material in its charge, and it is confronted by more than its share of problems. Into the Division's hands come all of the newspapers and almost all of the current periodicals, the main receipts of government publications, domestic and foreign, and all uncataloged pamphlets. For service it must bring order to this heterogeneous and refractory mass of printed products (many of which are of the highest importance) and make them available to the most variegated section of the public that visits the Library of Congress.
>
> The Division's three reading rooms last year served 390,768 items to about 75,000 readers. Only an approximation of the latter figure is given because of the impracticability of counting every visitant content with the daily papers on the reading room racks. It is known, however, that 93,791 of

[6] See the *Report* of the New York Public Library, 1926 (New York, 1927), p.37.

the items issued were government documents and were delivered to about 10,000 readers in a room where browsing can scarcely be indulged. No less than 46,284 volumes were loaned for use outside of the Library buildings, 26,183 telephone requests and orders were filled, and 614 letters were answered.

Serving the Congress, the Government and the public, the Division prepared reports on subjects as diverse as the following abbreviated list will indicate:

Admiral Farragut's capture of New Orleans.
Buddhist activities in southern California.
Business and finance.
Drugs and pharmaceuticals.
Farm machinery and tractors.
Horticulture.
Interior decorating.
Jewish newspapers and periodicals.
Lumber and woodworking.
Negro newspapers and periodicals.
Public speaking and lecturing.
Television.
Treaties with Switzerland.

Research scholars and students in the Library drew heavily upon the Division's resources as they explored subjects of equal diversity. Another brief sampling of their projects will bear this out.

Chinese newspaper editorials on the "Open Door" treaty.
Home conditions and the returning veteran—Civil War, World Wars I and II.
Early navigation on Maryland's Eastern Shore.
Life and death of John Dillinger.
Federal aid in education.
Editorial reaction to terms of the Versailles treaty.
Japan's plan of battle against the United States.
Evangelism of Billy Sunday.
Student youth movement in Southern colleges.
Vice in New York City, 1848.[7]

Reports for other years reflect the changing interests of the times. Similar values attach to the reports of other libraries, particularly the big-city institutions which reflect major concern with business affairs. Thus the New York Public Library reported:

The work in the Periodicals Division has continued to reflect the current thought and interest throughout the city. The tall office buildings which have closed in about the Library have increased largely the demands of the business world for a quick response to a pertinent question.

Such opening phrases as "The latest statistics of ——," "The new markets for ——," "The newest fashions in ——," "The effect of the recent

[7] *Annual Report* of the Librarian of Congress, 1945 (Washington, 1946), p.75-76.

tariff revision on ——," serve to illustrate the type of questions which range from bottle designs and metal tubing for modern furniture to the output of gasoline in Russia.

Illustrations of all phases of manufacturing have been much in demand. The predominance of such inquiries has made the trade papers of prime importance, and they have extended their interests far beyond the limits implied by their name.

During the year the "digest" magazines with their abbreviated presentation of material have been in constant use. The faster tempo of American life as it expresses itself in the economic and business world demands the magazine of concrete ideas and facts, and these magazines have become each year of greater value in giving concisely the information desired.

The searching for advertisements of employment has meant a continuous use of the latest issues of a great number of various types of magazines.[8]

If to the recorded interests of readers in the Library of Congress, the New York Public Library, and elsewhere, were added the untold story of quiet and patient study in research libraries of all kinds, the contribution of current periodicals to the advance of knowledge would be recognized as truly imposing.

Shelf arrangement

On closed shelves the arrangement of current periodicals is as a rule alphabetical. The purposes of this arrangement are to facilitate the work of the staff in fetching and reshelving material and to save readers the trouble of supplying class marks or call numbers for the periodicals they request. The arrangement of periodicals on open shelves, however, differs sharply among libraries. Some collections of current periodicals are arranged alphabetically, but others are arranged by subject, generally in broad subject groupings. The staff is helped by the alphabetical arrangement, both in shelving publications and in directing readers to a specific location. Readers who want to browse in a designated field are helped by the subject arrangement, which is favored in college and university libraries. A professor or a student can keep an eye on the economics or the philosophy shelves, for example, without having to make the rounds of the collection. But for the person who works from the periodical indexes, or whose interests are not narrowly defined, the subject arrangement may prove something of a handicap. The balance may be slightly in favor of alphabetical arrangement, all things considered.

When the periodicals are grouped by subject, their class should be recorded on the cover. The class can be designated by the letters in the Library of Congress classification scheme or by the first three figures of

---

[8] *Report* of the New York Public Library, 1931 (New York, 1932), p.40-41.

the Dewey number, or it can be a completely arbitrary and quite broad designation. The notation by which items are shelved in the periodical room should be specified on the visible index; it can then be added to the pieces at the time they are posted so that they can be shelved and reshelved readily.

The staff collection

Even in smaller institutions it is customary for libraries to subscribe to a number of library periodicals for the benefit of the staff. Such a staff collection is usually kept not in the periodical room but in a staff or work room. Multiple copies are acquired in the larger libraries, especially when the periodicals are circulated extensively among staff members. Some libraries debate whether it is proper for staff members to read professional literature while they are on duty. An informed staff, however, is an asset to any library, and the money spent on staff periodicals should be reckoned a wise investment. In any case, such a doubt can hardly relate to the typical librarian, who tends to be so conscientious that the library is not the loser for the privilege extended him of being able to keep up to date with library affairs. The periodicals in this collection should be housed in as satisfactory a place as possible for the staff to inspect and read and should be circulated for home use in a simple and convenient way, even in libraries which do not ordinarily circulate current periodicals.

Included in the collection should be a few periodicals that are not exclusively of library interest. The *Publishers' Weekly* and the *Saturday Review* (formerly the *Saturday Review of Literature)* are obvious cases. The Public Library Inquiry disclosed something of the periodical reading habits of librarians:

> Among the professional librarians, *Life* and *The Saturday Review of Literature* have the highest percentage of readers, 64 percent and 63 percent, respectively. *The New Yorker* and *Time* are next in popularity. Considerably lower in percentage of readers is the *Atlantic; Harpers, Newsweek,* and the *Saturday Evening Post* follow closely, about one fourth of the librarians being readers of each. One or more of the digest magazines are read by 46 percent of the professional librarians.
>
> The subprofessional librarians prefer to read much the same type of magazines as the professionals. The largest number, 70 percent, had read *Life*. Next in popularity were *Time* and *The New Yorker,* then *The Saturday Review of Literature* (read by 40 percent). About half of the subprofessionals read one or more of the digest magazines.[9]

---

[9] Alice I. Bryan, *The Public Librarian* (New York: Columbia Univ. Pr., 1952), p.48. In his *A Library Primer* (Boston: Library Bureau, [1920]), p.69, John Cotton Dana said: "Of all of a librarian's reading perhaps the most profitable to him in his work is that which he gives to periodicals."

The newspaper room

Although the periodical room seldom has custody of bound volumes, the newspaper room may service the bound volumes of newspapers as well as the current issues, especially in a public library. Format is the decisive factor in both the periodical and the newspaper room. Bound volumes of periodicals can be serviced and shelved like books, so they fit naturally in the classified stacks, even though they may form a group by themselves, with or without call numbers. Newspapers, on the contrary, are poor stack material. They require special shelving, by virtue of their bulk, and are very wasteful of space if they do not have it. Moreover, they are not suited to book conveyors. In the past they were often located in specially designed quarters adjacent to the newspaper reading area; but the picture is changing rapidly as bound volumes give way to photocopies or are transferred to storage libraries.

The Library of Congress, like many college and university libraries, locates its current newspapers not in its Newspapers Section but in the Periodicals Reading Room. The functions of the Newspapers Section are

> to receive, shelve, make available to readers and borrowers, and prepare for binding the Library's large collection of newspapers from all over the world; to provide a reader and reference service of the bound newspaper collections, and to prepare and keep current checklists of the Library's holdings. During the fiscal year 1949 the Section received 2,395,774 issues, prepared and submitted 3,685 volumes for binding, and assisted 17,334 readers in the use of 59,477 bound volumes. Readers using unbound issues are counted in the Periodicals Reading Room, and are not separately distinguished. However, statistics show that they used 189,411 unbound issues during the year. . .
>
> Historians and research students are becoming increasingly aware of the importance of newspapers as a basic source of information. It is only natural therefore that the Library's newspaper collections, unequalled by any other like collection, should be used as no other single collection in the Library is used. Last year reader demands resulted in a turn-over in the 128,878 volumes of the bound newspaper collection of 46 percent.[10]

Some periodical rooms take on a number of processing functions; newspaper rooms quite generally do so. One reason is that newspapers lend themselves to check-listing rather than cataloging. The Library of Congress has published several of its check lists,[11] and maintains supplements to them in its Newspapers Section. The check list for nine-

[10] Library of Congress *Departmental & Divisional Manuals* 9:21, 1950.

[11] *A Check List of American Eighteenth Century Newspapers in the Library of Congress* (New ed.; Washington, 1936). *A Check List of American Newspapers in the Library of Congress* (Washington, 1901). *A Check List of Foreign Newspapers in the Library of Congress* (Washington, 1929).

teenth and twentieth century American newspapers is in the form of a shelf list.[12]

One obvious advantage of the check list is that it does not have to occupy itself endlessly with changes of heading as serial cataloging traditionally does. The reason for this difference is that the basic listing is by place rather than by title, and is therefore not subject to numerous changes as title entries are. The arrangement in the Library of Congress is alphabetical by state if domestic or by country if foreign, then by city and title. This is also the natural way to arrange the newspapers on the shelves, and because of this natural scheme newspapers seldom receive class marks or call numbers.[13] Likewise entries for newspapers are often omitted from the general card catalog, since if they are included they would have to be cataloged twice, once by place for the newspaper room and once by title for the card catalog.[14] This omission from the card catalog may be somewhat puzzling to readers, especially when they find a listing of other publications issued by the newspaper, possibly its index.

The greatest problem the newspaper librarian has to face is the decay of the files later than 1870, due to the extensive use of wood pulp paper for newspapers after that date.[15] The rate of decay can be retarded by housing the newspaper collection in air-conditioned quarters, as in the annex of the Library of Congress. The New York Public Library made a valiant attack on the problem by having its bindery mount both sides of each sheet of newspaper with Japanese tissue. In 1921 it reported on this airproof covering as follows:

> Earlier reports have mentioned the progress of the Library's experiments toward the best method of preserving the paper stock of newspapers in bound files. The decision was that the covering of each sheet of the original with a thin sheet of Japanese tissue paper insured preservation for an indefinite period. Since June, 1916, the files of the New York "World" have been so treated, and the experience of five years has confirmed faith in the process. Little more need be said than that this year one of the volumes so treated came back to the bindery for rebinding. Under ordinary circumstances rebinding of a newspaper is impossible, the paper stock being so poor that

[12] At Harvard College Library the check lists are typewritten in loose-leaf volumes.

[13] Although the Library of Congress has a class AN for newspapers, it has not developed or applied that class in any way.

[14] A skeleton entry can be placed in the public catalog at comparatively small cost. As a minimum, this should be done for the principal papers in the library.

[15] The first pulp paper manufactured in the United States was produced in 1867. Studies conducted in the New York Public Library indicate that the first American newspaper to use wood pulp was the *New Yorker Staats-Zeitung* which first came out on wood pulp on January 7, 1868, and adopted it regularly in 1870. Cf. "When Did Newspapers Begin to Use Wood Pulp Stock?" *Bulletin* of the New York Public Library 33:743-49, 1929.

though it is possible to sew it once when the paper is fresh and new, it is impossible to get the thread to hold when it is a year or two old. With this volume of the "World" it was possible to resew it like a book printed on good book stock paper; the buckram back had worn because of the constant use, but the sheets were as strong as the day they were finished.[16]

Treatment with Japanese tissue is a slow, expensive process. It is not satisfactory when photostat or microfilm copies are wanted. It is, however, highly desirable whenever the original publications should be preserved. Two alternatives are in more common use. Microfilm, which is discussed in Chapter 13, is one answer to the problem. It has the great advantage of reducing the bulk of a newspaper collection. One bound volume of a newspaper may have upwards of a hundred times the cubic capacity of the corresponding microfilm. The other answer is the rag paper edition which a few papers print daily after the regular run on wood pulp stock has been completed. As microfilm becomes more popular fewer rag paper editions are available. The *New York Times* was issued in this form from 1927 to 1953.

Another expensive form of subscription is the air mail edition of foreign newspapers. Since the essence of a newspaper is its timeliness, an air mail subscription may be justified when it brings important material to the research worker a day or two, rather than weeks, after publication. The London *Times* and the Russian *Pravda* and *Izvestia* are not infrequently procured by air mail. The air mail edition of the London *Times* may be obtained in two ways. The full cost of an individual copy sent direct by air mail must be borne by the library that wants its copy with the least delay; but considerable savings are possible when somewhat less speed is required. When the lower rate is charged, bulk shipments are sent by air from London to New York, whence the individual copies are forwarded by surface mail. This procedure is satisfactory for most libraries within convenient distance of New York. Libraries subscribing to the air mail edition of the London *Times* often acquire the regular edition as well, since the index relates to the regular edition.

Newspaper bibliography is especially complicated by reason of the

---

[16] *Report* of the New York Public Library, 1921 (New York, 1922), p.53-54. For further details see "How Newspapers Are Preserved," *Report* of the New York Public Library, 1925 (New York, 1926), p.48-49. Cf. also Harry M. Lydenberg and John Archer, *The Care and Repair of Books* (3d ed.; New York: Bowker, 1945), p.37-40. More recently the New York Public Library has turned to microfilm to take care of the *New York Herald Tribune*, the *New York World-Telegram*, and other papers. For an account of the newspaper collection in the New York Public Library see Karl Brown, *A Guide to the Reference Collections of the New York Public Library* (New York, 1941), p.196-98. Figure 53 in Robert C. Binkley, *Manual on Methods of Reproducing Research Materials* (Ann Arbor, Mich., 1936), is a portion of a newspaper page covered on both sides with Japanese tissue.

number of editions that a paper may produce daily.[17] Matter may appear in one edition and not in another. Yet it is manifestly impossible for libraries to preserve files of all editions. Lack of knowledge of what constitutes a complete set makes it difficult to determine the completeness of many files. Extra issues, omitted issues, gaps in publishing due to Sundays and holidays, as well as frequent errors in numbering, all conspire to make newspaper bibliography uncertain.

Libraries, historical societies, and other local institutions have undertaken a large share of the responsibility both for preserving files of papers and for indexing them to make them more serviceable.[18] Because a network of institutions has divided much of the collecting responsibility for newspapers, most libraries can be highly selective, contenting themselves for the most part with current subscriptions and with microreproductions of indexed papers.

To some extent the indexes to national newspapers serve as a key to local papers. Since this cannot apply to local news, it is almost as important to index the distinctive parts of local newspapers as it is to preserve the files themselves. Here, then, is an area that should be covered. The outstanding example of newspaper indexing is to be found in the California State Library, which has a card index to California newspapers from 1846 to date.[19]

Research needs are far from being the only justification for newspapers in libraries. In so far as a library is a community intelligence center it must have newspapers on hand. News was listed by Learned as the first of the three types of knowledge which he distinguishes:

> The first type is essentially "news"—the flood of ephemeral print out of which is selected the limited group of facts that orients for each his daily life. The newspapers and periodicals possess this field, and furnish as excellent models of diffusion in their well-nigh universal contacts, as of qualitative bedlam in their ideas. Everything that possesses conceivable "news value" is pitched into the furnace of publicity. There public opinion treats and reduces it, drawing off at last for permanent use a product dependent upon the quality and acuteness of its own insight. . .

---

[17] On this problem, see Folke Dahl, "On Quoting Newspapers: a Problem and a Solution," *Journalism Quarterly* 25:331-38, 1948. For some years *Notes and Queries* sought an answer to the inquiry "What is a newspaper edition?" In this connection it cited a London newspaper which had three editions, the first called the Fifth Edition, the second the Early Special, and the third the Special Edition. In another case five editions were issued, starting with the Third Edition and proceeding to the Fifth Edition, the Early Special, the Five O'Clock, and the Special. See *Notes and Queries* 10th series 3:287, 1905, and 8:117, 1907.

[18] For a list of American newspapers which have been indexed in part or in full, see H. O. Brayer, "Preliminary Guide to Indexed Newspapers in the United States, 1850-1900," *Mississippi Valley Historical Review* 33:237-58, 1946.

[19] See Mabel R. Gillis, "The Union Catalog and the Newspaper Index as Means of Increasing Reference Resources of the State Library," *A. L. A. Bulletin* 25:644-45, 1931.

> The bulk of the town's new ideas are derived from newspapers and periodical literature that originate outside, that are subscribed for by a few interested minds, and that have no evident bearing upon the concerns of the locality.[20]

As if in support of Learned, the Newspaper Division of the New York Public Library reported in 1926 that "the seeker after news still constitutes about 75 per cent of the readers. Fully one-half of this number read out-of-town and foreign newspapers, difficult to obtain elsewhere."[21] When the Enoch Pratt Free Library was built, the primary purpose of the newspaper room was tacitly to provide for idle and transient readers. Consequently popular magazines were also kept in the room for the pleasure of these people.[22] Unfortunately, however, idle and transient readers, who tend to appear in greater numbers when the weather is bad or cold, may give rise to administrative problems, for which reason some librarians doubt the wisdom of having a newspaper room.

Most readers in public library newspaper rooms are men. In the New York Public Library, "according to a test count of readers made during the year, it was found that the Newspaper Division showed a higher percentage of men than any other division in the building, ninety-three out of every hundred readers being men."[23] Women may shun the newspaper room; they may even have newspapers brought to them in other parts of the library.

Sometimes newspapers are not circulated on the day of issue in an attempt at reducing the problem of discipline. This device may decrease the demand for papers, but it by no means solves all the problems. Sometimes the current newspapers are housed on chest-high sloping counters at which readers must stand. The aim here is to discourage loafing and to prevent sleeping.

The location of a newspaper room is to a large extent conditioned by its distinctive clientele in a public library and by the stack facilities for bound volumes in a research library. It may be given its own outside entrance to separate newspaper readers from other users of the library. It may be located in the basement to divorce it still further from other library activities; but when that plan is followed, care should be taken to see that the children's room is not contiguous.

Whenever popular use is great, special provision should be made, in an adjacent room if possible, for the research worker. The advent

---

[20] William S. Learned, *The American Public Library and the Diffusion of Knowledge* (New York: Harcourt, Brace, [1924]), p.5, 13.

[21] *Report* of the New York Public Library, 1926 (New York, 1927), p.39.

[22] For this philosophy and for other ideas on newspaper rooms, see Joseph L. Wheeler and Alfred M. Githens, *op. cit.*, p.126-27.

[23] *Report* of the New York Public Library, 1926 (New York, 1927), p.39.

of the reading machine for newspapers on microfilm has helped to point up this need.

By having no newspaper room, public libraries cannot altogether avoid the difficulties that go with such rooms. The loafer will still come for the sake of shelter, and will naturally be found throughout the building if he does not have a room he feels is more particularly suited to him. When there is no newspaper room, the current papers are usually housed in the reading room. On the other hand, some libraries place a ban on the reading of newspapers in a general reading room. The reason for the ban is that a newspaper makes an excellent cover behind or underneath which to carry on various antisocial practices, such as the theft of readers' handbags.

In a public library reading room or periodical room the latest issue of a newspaper is commonly put first on a stick which is placed on a rack. A tub rack is more attractive than the traditional wall rack, but takes up relatively more floor space because of its smaller capacity. In a college or university library the file for the current month is sometimes kept in a large binder which may be laid on a counter or table. This plan is followed to maintain a large measure of self-service, but it does restrict consultation of a title that is much in demand.

Several miscellaneous library aspects of newspapers may be noted. Newspaper contests give rise to problems of various kinds, not the least of which is undue wear and sometimes mutilation of reference volumes. Special libraries, in particular, may acquire newspapers for clipping purposes, and may make a feature of their clipping file. Reference librarians can at times anticipate questions by alert reading of their newspapers. On occasion, too, word of a new publication of consequence appears in the news columns, and may be a matter of concern to acquisition librarians and others because of the reader demand that may be set up. The publicity that attached to the State Department's *China White Paper* is a case in point, since readers asked for the report the morning it was reported in the newspapers, although publication did not take place until eleven o'clock that same morning in Washington. One last specialized library use is fortunately less frequent than it was. Catalogers have spent much time of a morning scanning the obituaries in the *New York Times* for death dates they could add to their authority cards and catalog entries.

The document room

The two American libraries that have outstanding document collections also have fine document rooms. The Government Publications Section in the Library of Congress and the Economics Division in the New York Public Library are two centers of intense document activity.

But elsewhere there are all too few document rooms, due in part, no doubt, to the circumstance that document functions may be widely scattered in university libraries which must collect government publications on a large scale.

Deficiencies in document collecting and servicing represent one of the most serious shortcomings in American library economy. Without question, some of the trouble stems from uncertainty over a wise collecting policy. It is easy for administrators to see that libraries could be flooded with documents if they were acquired on a wholesale basis, since national, state, and local government publications throughout the world comprise a vast quantity of material. Rather than be overwhelmed, there has been a tendency to temporize. The confusion surrounding document collecting programs can perhaps be dramatized by saying that in the Harvard University Library over a period of a dozen years or so there were no fewer than five surveys or special reports that proposed plans for developing and strengthening the document collections, none of which led to any course of action.

Some of the reluctance to come to grips with the problem of document collecting derives from the fact that the Library of Congress has undertaken tremendous responsibility in building up its resources in the field of government publications. It is, in a very real sense, a national document center, thanks in no small measure to the efforts of James B. Childs, Chief of the former Documents Division. Part of Childs' philosophy is expressed in the following terms:

> Government publications are of such importance for the Library of Congress that it is not a matter of selection but of ascertaining what has been and is being issued, of taking any necessary steps to secure copies, and of assisting in making them available . . .
>
> Owing to the intricacies of governments and their publication activities, the difficulty of adequately representing all such material in the public catalog is rapidly increasing. More and more reliance for the use of these materials has thus to be placed on such printed catalogs as exist as well as increasingly upon the assistants and records in the Division . . . While the Library of Congress has without doubt the most extensive collection of official documents in the United States and is regarded as a national document center, increasing demands seem to make it imperative for the Library to take all possible steps to establish and to maintain a much more nearly complete coverage for all current material, to survey and perfect the older materials, and to facilitate the use of these important publications.[24]

One of the most effective means that Childs devised for the expansion of the Library of Congress document collection was a series of bilateral agreements between the United States and other countries whereby federal documents would be exchanged on an inclusive basis for the

---

[24] *Annual Report* of the Librarian of Congress, 1940 (Washington, 1941), p.48-49.

publications of other countries. By 1951 there were 43 bilateral agreements in force. These have brought a wealth of documentary material to the Library of Congress, which as recorded should provide other libraries with an opportunity to restudy their collecting programs.

The functions of the Government Publications Section at the Library of Congress are

> to have custody of the Library's collections of unbound serial documents of the United States and foreign countries, to provide a reader and reference service in government publications generally and the bound classified collections in J 1-999 in particular, to prepare the unbound serials for binding when complete, and to recommend the acquisition of materials needed to complete or augment the Library's collections. During fiscal year 1949 this section received an estimated 728,000 pieces of material to be shelved and serviced, prepared and submitted 8,377 volumes for binding, and assisted 16,501 readers in the use of 111,413 items in its custody.[25]

Each of the reference assistants in the Government Publications Section is assigned certain geographic areas for which he has primary responsibility. In 1950 there were eight such areas, approximately as follows:

1. Latin America, the Philippine Republic, Portugal, Spain
2. Great Britain, the British Commonwealth (except Canada), the British colonies
3. Europe (except France and Great Britain)
4. International organizations
5. Asia, Canada, Egypt, France, Liberia, Near and Middle East
6. United States federal documents
7. United States state and municipal documents
8. Loose-leaf services[26]

The elaborateness of this organization gives some idea of what is involved in maintaining a large-scale document program, though in most libraries it is out of the question to detail the proportionate amount of manpower to a feature whose role has not been clearly defined.

The Library of Congress has been ably backed up by other federal libraries and by the New York Public Library. In the field of American state and local documents it has been seconded by a number of state and local libraries. Still further, there are many special libraries which concentrate on one or more phases of governmental activity.

Rather generally elsewhere—the great university libraries not excepted—collecting policies, service facilities, and the extent of the specialized staff leave much to be desired. The first steps towards improving the situation in any library must be (1) to clarify and define

---

[25] Library of Congress *Departmental & Divisional Manuals* 9:17, 1950.

[26] As a matter of local convenience at the Library of Congress, the Government Publications Section takes care of loose-leaf business services.

the role of government publications; (2) to develop a sound collecting program; and (3) to house and service current serial documents in the periodical room (except when the functions warrant parallel services, as in the Library of Congress).

McCamy, in his *Government Publications for the Citizen,* sought to define the role of government documents in public libraries. His findings, based on a survey of sixty libraries, show that in their document programs public libraries have generally lagged behind research libraries. Careful consideration of the values he attaches to government publications may help to improve the situation, in academic institutions as well as in the public libraries with which he was concerned. He developed four theses:

1. Governments are a reliable and impartial source of authoritative information which should be accessible to citizens through numerous outlets.
2. The government's position should be known whenever there is public discussion of foreign policy, public health, social security, etc.
3. Public libraries are charged with the responsibility for "making available to all citizens the more serious, more reliable and more permanent materials of all kinds."[27]
4. Because they are tax supported, public libraries have a natural interest in acquiring and disseminating those government documents which can help in bringing the citizen and his government closer to each other.

McCamy brings out seven reasons why library programs for government documents are not as effective as they might be.[28] In general they relate to accumulated practices, tradition, laws which should be revised, and inadequacies in government bibliographies. It is particularly unfortunate that the bibliographies tend to list documents by agency instead of subject, do not differentiate between routine publications and others which contain important information relating to broad public problems, and do not provide a sure way for the librarian to know which items will be of general interest. There is confusion in the distribution of documents, while some information is lost because it appears only in processed form and is neither cataloged nor distributed. Lastly, public libraries have not acquired as many established government best sellers as might be expected.

In addition, McCamy expresses himself strongly about the cataloging of government publications, or rather the failure to catalog them:

It is far from easy for an untrained person to find government documents and pamphlets in a typical library catalogue, where librarians tend to dupli-

---

[27] James L. McCamy, *Government Publications for the Citizen* (New York: Columbia Univ. Pr., 1949), p.x.

[28] *Ibid.,* p.74-77.

cate for their clientele the difficulties they themselves encounter in ordering from the government catalogues.

Relatively few libraries, and those chiefly in the largest cities, list all their government publications in their general catalogues so that any reader searching for all the publications available on any particular subject would find the government publications included. Only seven out of forty-two libraries list all government publications in their general catalogues. Of the seven, five are in cities of more than 500,000 population; one is in a city of between 250,000 and 500,000, and one is in a city of 25,000-50,000.

Of the libraries in our sample half list in the general catalogue only titles which they think will be of general interest. This is roughly true of all the libraries in cities of 25,000 up to 500,000. . . The other half do not list even the titles that might have general interest. In half the libraries, of various sizes above 25,000 and below the very largest libraries, government publications are apparently considered as "documents," to be classified for reference use, but not as publications that might be of interest to ordinary readers.

For example, a reader browsing in the catalogue for material on civil rights would not find *To Secure These Rights,* the report of the President's Committee on Civil Rights and a readable, popular book, because it would be classified as a "document." In half the libraries such a pamphlet would be in the same file with routine statistical reports from government agencies. The rule in these libraries seems to be: "If it's a government publication, bury it except for reference purposes!" In most libraries popular government publications have suffered because of their family connections. They belong to a category that is principally reference material and not expected to be interesting to anyone save specialized readers.[29]

There is undoubtedly a measure of truth in these strictures. Nevertheless, the library that attempted to catalog all its documents in full (that is, to analyze them), could easily find itself snowed under. The Library of Congress itself does not attempt really full coverage. While it prints numerous cards from copy supplied by the Department of Agriculture Library and others, it does not always put them in its own dictionary catalogs even though it may have the publications in question. It is true that document collections must, to a considerable extent, be self-cataloging, and that printed indexes and check lists must make up for deficiencies in the catalog records. Note, however, that it may be wise economy to analyze relatively few documents for the card catalog whereas it would be unwise economy to omit the serial entries.

[29] McCamy, *op. cit.,* p.64-65.

CHAPTER 11

Reference and Circulation

A GLANCE AT WINCHELL'S *Guide to Reference Books* will show that for reference work in the narrow sense of the term serials of all kinds are constantly in demand. Even for quick reference work they play their part through titles like the *Statesman's Year-book, Who's Who in America,* and the *World Almanac,* while for standard reference service, annuals, directories, government documents, periodical and newspaper indexes, trade and national bibliographies, who's whos, and a host of other serial publications are part of the regular stock-in-trade. Serials are also basic for reference work in the larger sense in which all the resources of an institution are exploited. Here the pendulum may, in research libraries, swing in favor of serials over monographs. "The larger the library," said Charles McCombs, "the greater the proportion of periodicals and pamphlets—those foundation stones of a research collection—and the more numerous the government publications from the far corners of the earth."[1]

As soon as a library aspires to be something more than a mere circulation agency, it must acquire and exploit serial publications. The Montclair Free Public Library learned this lesson from a survey one of whose recommendations was: "You should certainly largely increase the number and variety of the current periodicals taken by the library for your several reading rooms, main library and branches."[2] It responded by nearly doubling the budget for magazine subscriptions, developing a collection of 229 periodicals around the six outstanding periodical indexes, and emphasizing the purchase of yearbooks and other continuations.

For reference work in the larger sense librarians should be masters of the intricacies of serial publications. Fortunately there is an excel-

---

[1] Charles F. McCombs, "The Reference Function in the Large Public Library," in *The Reference Function of the Library; Papers Presented before the Library Institute at the University of Chicago, June 29 to July 10, 1942,* ed. by Pierce Butler (Chicago: Univ. of Chicago Pr., [1943]), p.18.

[2] Margery C. Quigley and William E. Marcus, *Portrait of a Library* (New York: Appleton-Century, [1936]), p.172.

lent textbook on reference work, Arthur Roberts' *Introduction to Reference Books,*[3] which covers much of the necessary ground. Among general manuals on librarianship this book is exceptional in that more than half of it is devoted to serial publications. It is particularly valuable because a number of competent judges believe that the typical librarian has much to learn about serials. Among them is Beatrice Simon, who has said:

> I am afraid that, though generally speaking, the average librarian knows a lot about books, she does not know how to extract the full reference value from serials, and I do not think it is an exaggeration to say that even librarians who make a specialty of reference work are not sufficiently familiar with this source of information unless they have served a stiff apprenticeship in some scientific research or business library.[4]

Louis Kaplan also expressed doubt about the ability of the average reference librarian to handle serial publications effectively:

> It is unfortunately true that the majority of reference workers do not possess a first-hand knowledge of periodicals. Instead, there is an almost exclusive reliance upon the indexing services. This is a deplorable situation because it means that much reference material goes to waste.
>
> The truth is that it is not even possible to use the indexes efficiently without intimate knowledge of the periodicals.[5]

Help to readers with serial problems is a major function in many reference departments, e.g., in university libraries. The reference librarian of such a library should have an intimate knowledge of serial cataloging in order to give adequate help. In the Harvard College Library the head of the reference service makes a point of telling new members of his staff that the most important preparation for their job is to become fully conversant with serial cataloging. It should be noted in this connection that the most troublesome element in reader use of serials is the corporate entry. They simply do not understand it. They also constantly need help in interpreting names of serials that have been cited in abbreviated form, official or unofficial, or names that have been translated or otherwise altered from the original. The following are examples encountered in the University of Chicago Bio-Medical Libraries which show the title presented by a reader and the catalog form the reference staff eventually uncovered. Similar cases are met with daily in interlibrary loan work.

---

[3] A. D. Roberts, *Introduction to Reference Books* (2d ed.; London: Library Assn., 1951). Because Roberts has made so notable a contribution, the present chapter is briefer than it otherwise might have been.

[4] Beatrice V. Simon, "Let's Consider Serials Realistically," *Library Journal* 71:1301, 1946.

[5] Louis Kaplan, "Reference Work with Periodicals: Recent Progress and Future Needs," *College and Research Libraries* 1:244, 1940.

Abbreviated Title	*Catalog Entry*
Acta horti botanici	Riga. Latvijas universitate. Botaniska darzs. Raksti
Acta soc. scien. fen.	Finska vetenskaps-societeten, Helsingfors. Acta
Arb. a. d. Reichsgesundheitsamt	Germany. Reichsgesundheitsamt. Arbeiten
Arb. neur. Inst. Wien Univ.	Vienna. Universität. Neurologisches Institut. Arbeiten
Arch. arg. ped.	Archivos argentinos de pediatría
Bol. inst. clin. quir.	Buenos Aires. Universidad nacional. Instituto de clínica quirúrgica. Boletin
Bul. Commonwealth bur. meteor.	Australia. Bureau of Meteorology. Bulletin
Jour. cons. perm. int. exp. mer	International Council for the Study of the Sea. Journal
Jour. de phys. U.R.S.S.	Fiziologicheskii zhurnal SSSR
Phys. jour. U.S.S.R.	Fiziologicheskii zhurnal SSSR
Pubb. del R. Ist. di studi sup. Firenze	Florence. Università. Sezione di scienze fisiche e naturali. Pubblicazioni
Rep. A. M. Gorky All-Union inst. exp. med.	Moscow. Vsesoiuznyi institut eksperimental'noi meditsiny imeni A. M. Gor'kogo. Otchet
Rep. pub. health and med. Stat. off.	Great Britain. Ministry of Health. Reports
Russian biochem. jour.	Vseukrains'ka akademiia nauk, Kiev. Instytut biokhimii. Biokhimichnyi zhurnal
Russian jour. biochem.	Biokhimiia
Russian jour. physiol.	Fiziologicheskii zhurnal SSSR
Zeit. Phys. Sov. Un.	Fiziologicheskii zhurnal SSSR

A special type of reference aid for incomplete or inaccurate citations is the chronological conspectus as found in *Poole's Index to Periodical Literature,* Beilstein's *Handbuch der organischen Chemie,* H. C. Bolton's *A Catalog of Scientific and Technical Periodicals* and several other sources. For reference work at the Oak Ridge National Laboratory Libraries Helen H. Mason in 1954 compiled *Synchronistic Tables of Selected Journals in the Oak Ridge National Laboratory Libraries, 1880-1950.* Her listing is intended in a limited way to dovetail with Bolton's chronological tables.

Cumulated indexes to individual periodicals are also of special significance to the reference librarian. Hence the New York Public Library's *Check List of Cumulative Indexes to Individual Periodicals* is a useful tool, just as for more specialized use a reference desk may keep the index to the *National Geographic Magazine* on hand for ready consultation about colored plates and other matters.

That all is not wrong on the reference front is shown in a simple way by the report of the Fort Wayne Public Library on how it answered numerous reference questions from serial documents.[6]

Request	*Where Answer Was Found*
Address of the All American Beauty Culture Schools Associated	Foreign and Domestic Commerce Bureau. Industrial series 3. Trade and professional associations of the United States.
Date of Arbor Day in Indiana	Agriculture Department. Farmers' bulletin 1492. Arbor Day, its purpose and observance.
How to use Bentonite in quick drying paints	Mines Bureau. Technical paper 609. Bentonite: its properties, mining, preparation, and utilization.
How to run a dry cleaning establishment	Foreign and Domestic Commerce Bureau. Industrial (small business) series 33. Establishing and operating a dry cleaning business.
Explanation of farm parity	Agriculture Department. Yearbook, 1940.
Copyright on the song "I Want To Be Your Sweetest Memory"	Copyright Office. Catalog of copyright entries, 1945.
Location of a large hydroelectric plant near Detroit	Federal Power Commission. Directory of electric generating plants, 1941.
An article on industrial fatigue	Labor Standards Division. Special bulletin 3. Protecting plant manpower.
The selective service bill	Congressional record, volume 94.
School bus transportation; safety statistics	Federal Coordinator of Transportation Bureau. Public aids to transportation, volume 4.
A book about motorcycling	War Department. Technical manual 10-515. Motorcycle.
Names of superintendents of public instruction for Indiana, Ohio, and Michigan	Education Office. Educational directory.

Exploitation of a collection in a manner such as this lends a touch of distinction to the humblest of libraries, opening up to it some of the

[6] These illustrations are drawn from Mary Armstrong, "Documents Please Fort Wayne Patrons," *Wilson Library Bulletin* 23:319, 1948.

resources of larger institutions.[7] It also brings a sense of satisfaction to the librarian who makes the most of all potentialities. Hence the importance of building up the bibliographical apparatus of a library, for hidden wealth can often be uncovered by means of specialized reference tools. On occasion the tool may be a local manuscript record; for example, an index to congressional hearings; a bibliography on a current or emerging topic, with references drawn to a considerable extent from periodicals; or a subject list of serials in local libraries. The enterprising reference librarian will provide for printed or locally prepared tools to open up the contents of serial publications to readers and staff alike.

Instruction in the use of serials

School and college students are taught how to use periodical indexes and other keys to serial publications; they are told of outstanding serials in the reference collection. The most difficult task of all, however, is to make them aware of the abundance of information latent in serial publications. Since the hope for the best utilization of library resources in the future lies with foundation instruction at the secondary school level, it is imperative that high school libraries be equipped with an adequate supply of serials, both document and non-document, as well as some of the tools for use with these publications. In the words of Dr. Bishop:

> We ought to be able to assume that freshmen have learned in their preparatory school days how to consult a card catalog, how to make out an intelligent call for books, how to use Poole's "Index," and what encyclopaedias and bibliographies are for. This is but little in the way of equipment for serious study in a university or research library, but the want of just such an equipment on the part of students, and of readers in a public research library, confines much of the work of assistance to most elementary first aid to the injured.[8]

Handbooks that explain to students how to use library facilities and resources have been developed and put to good use in school and college libraries. More of these aids should be prepared, and they should give full attention to serial publications. Of greater value to the research worker are guides to special collections, still all too few in

---

[7] Even in school and small public libraries steps should be taken to get worthwhile free and inexpensive government publications. In this connection, the price lists issued by the Superintendent of Documents should be checked regularly, as well as the latest edition of its *Representative Government Best Sellers.* Also of value is W. Philip Leidy, *A Popular Guide to Government Publications* (New York: Columbia Univ. Pr., 1953).

[8] William W. Bishop, *The Backs of Books, and Other Essays in Librarianship* (Baltimore: Williams & Wilkins, 1926), p.68-69.

number, and guides to the resources of a region or country.[9] The greatest possible value, of course, attaches to exhaustive studies such as Brown's *Guide to the Reference Collections of the New York Public Library*.[10]

Much spade work remains to be done to disclose the untold resources of research libraries generally. The United States has not produced handbooks of a monumental character similar to those compiled in Germany. This is due in part to American reliance on the dictionary catalog with its wealth of information, whereas scholars in Germany have had to create their own working tools in lieu of comparable subject catalogs. Is there a loss to American scholarship through overreliance on the card catalog? Should reference librarians be compiling more handbooks, both as working tools and as comprehensive studies? It is true that the United States is noted for its bibliographical undertakings; witness the contributions made by the Library of Congress and the New York Public Library. But more is possible in opening up areas of research, especially in view of the rich holdings—notably of serials—in American libraries.

Self-cataloging serials

Certain types of publications in the general reference collection lend themselves to economical handling through self-cataloging. Efficiency is in no wise impaired by judicious application of this device. The reference staff must assume a great deal of responsibility for the arrangement, maintenance, and servicing of self-cataloging collections, no matter where they are located. Otherwise these collections may not be truly effective, or may involve the catalog department in almost as much work as if they were cataloged.

Some self-cataloging material may be located in the bookstacks, some in the reference room, and some in vertical files. At times it is desirable to assign an over-all class mark to the self-cataloged material to facilitate circulation, shelving, reshelving, and general access. In some collections each item may carry a call number.

---

[9] Attention may be called to the *Guides to the Harvard Libraries;* for example, to the pamphlet by E. Louise Lucas which describes Harvard's resources in the field of fine arts. In the field of regional and national resources the outstanding work of Robert B. Downs should be noted, particularly his *American Library Resources, a Bibliographical Guide* (Chicago: American Library Assn., 1951); *Resources of New York City Libraries, a Survey of Facilities for Advanced Study and Research* (Chicago: American Library Assn., 1942); and *Resources of Southern Libraries, a Survey of Facilities for Research* (Chicago: American Library Assn., 1938). Special mention should be made too of the various contributions of the Special Libraries Association, notably its four-volume *Special Library Resources* (New York: Special Libraries Assn., [1941]-47).

[10] Karl Brown, *A Guide to the Reference Collections of the New York Public Library* (New York, 1941).

Types of self-cataloging material vary greatly, particularly in special libraries which make a feature of their vertical file systems. Apart from government documents, which have already been discussed, the more common types are art exhibition catalogs, auction catalogs, booksellers' catalogs, city directories, college catalogs, out-of-town telephone books, prospectuses of private schools, prospectuses of summer camps, and reprints of periodical articles. Not all of these are serials, even in a loose sense, but all of them can be put to good use without expensive cataloging and classification.

City directories are best check-listed because their coverage is not always systematic. A given place may be included in a certain directory one year, in another the next year, and again be omitted altogether. Apart from this factor, they can easily be found by anyone when they are grouped together and simply arranged by state and locality, ignoring the vagaries of their titles. The New York Public Library developed its shelf list specially so that it could serve as a check list of city directories. Form cards under the name of the city, followed by the subheading "Directories," can be a useful adjunct in the card catalog.

Required reading

Just as the librarian in general has a twofold task—to get publications used and at the same time to conserve them—so, too, the serial librarian is confronted with the problem of use versus conservation. A periodical may be consulted only a few times a year, but reckoned in terms of half-centuries—from 1900 to 1950, for instance—there is appreciable and steady wear on sets that all too often are well-nigh irreplaceable. How will sets that have been used steadily in the first half of the century stand up throughout the second half?

It is against this general background that the more intensive wear caused by the assignment of selected serials for required reading must be studied. On the one hand, serials are part of the working collection; they are not rare books for jealously guarded perusal; and libraries want readers to become familiar with serials and their potentialities. On the other hand, they are not expendable material like textbooks which can be replaced when worn out or which may be superseded by a later edition. Successive generations may want to refer to the same contribution—an article by William James, or Mencken, or Keynes—for there is a rich store of historical as well as current matter in the funded contents of serials. Plagued constantly by the dilemma of use versus conservation, library staffs have resorted to a number of devices to save their sets. When possible, extra copies of a particular issue are acquired and placed on the reserve reading shelves. Sometimes these must be stored away for a semester or so while they are not in demand, for which reason facilities must be developed for storing and recalling the items as needed. Occasionally reprints are forthcoming, especially when the assigned reading is the professor's own writing. And on occasion photostat copies may be made, with or without the permission of the publisher, depending on circumstances. Publishers are generally willing to give permission if their stock has been exhausted; and permission is not necessary when a single copy is made or when an article is no longer covered by copyright. Substitutes such as these take time and money, but they must be exploited as far as possible to preserve sets for future generations. A certain amount of library cooperation is desirable too, for a public library may find its files of a serial being used for assigned school or college reading. Unless information is passed on to it by the college library staff the public library files may suffer undue wear.

Mary Spalding has summarized the problem of conservation created by required reading and other causes as follows:

> The various devices for the protection of our magazines include: providing extra copies by microfilm, mimeograph, or photostat; duplicate or triplicate subscriptions for popular magazines or those on required reading lists; purchasing extra copies of single issues for class assignments; protecting unbound numbers with wrappers or covers; treating chemically those pages which are going to receive severe punishment; binding the serials regularly and as soon as possible; using books whenever possible for routine reference work; and restricting or forbidding altogether circulation of certain periodicals. We may not have solved the problem of the current use versus the permanent preservation of periodicals completely, but we have at least taken the initial step in recognizing and weighing its difficulties.[11]

Photoduplication

A library's photoduplication service tends to make heavy use of serials. In the New York Public Library, for instance, it was stated that "patents and papers from scientific and technical journals are the two predominant classes" handled by its Photostat Section.[12] Orders for photocopies frequently require verification, especially when they are received by mail; and at times reference librarians have to exercise all their ingenuity to determine precisely what is wanted. In the largest libraries, with thousands of photoduplication orders to fill each year, the burden on the stack service is considerable.

Copyright is the question that vexes photoduplication services most. By a gentleman's agreement between publishers and librarians, tacit approval is given to the making of a single copy, since that can hardly interfere with the normal sale of the published work itself.

---

[11] Mary L. Spalding, "Current Use Versus Permanent Preservation of Periodicals as Reflected in Organization," *A. L. A. Bulletin* 34:P-204, 1940.

[12] *Report* of the New York Public Library, 1931 (New York, 1932), p.27.

More formal arrangements have been made in a number of cases by the Library of Congress, which,

> being the home of the nation's Copyright Office, gives close attention to the presence of copyright restrictions in all of its photocopying activities. To make it possible to reproduce material from newspapers and periodicals without a specific request for permission from the copyright owner in each instance, a program has been instituted for securing general permissions from various newspaper and magazine publishers to copy within certain time limits.[13]

The Library of Congress refuses several hundred orders a year because of copyright restrictions. Here then is an area for clarification and redefinition in any new copyright law. The interest of publishers in seeing that files of their serials are preserved in libraries should make them sympathetic to the wider application of photoduplication as an aid in preservation, especially in cases where reference use is particularly heavy, as is true of items on reserve reading lists.

Circulation of bound volumes

Although a diversity of practices governs the circulation of bound volumes of serials, particularly of periodicals, the trend is away from out-of-the-building use. As Jennie Flexner said: "The fact that magazines are usually treated as reference books and held for use in most libraries adds to the reader's opportunity of finding what he wants when he wants it."[14] That there is no hard and fast rule on the subject is shown by her further observation:

> Maps, pamphlets, bound magazines and other volumes belonging to the reference collection may be allowed to circulate, usually for a limited period, on special request to registered borrowers. A *temporary book card,* incorporating sufficient information to identify the material lent, must be made to record the charge until the transaction is closed. In some libraries, material of this type circulates with enough regularity to warrant a permanent file of temporary book cards to be used over and over. Much used sets of bound periodicals may be circulated in this way, by inserting the year and volume number on the temporary book card when each volume is charged.[15]

No precise statement can be made about practices in college and university libraries. As a generalization it can be said that bound periodicals are lent to faculty members on a fairly liberal scale; to graduate students to a smaller extent; and rather infrequently to undergraduates. *Serial Slants* for July, 1950, briefly described the

[13] *Annual Report* of the Librarian of Congress, 1948 (Washington, 1949), p.46.

[14] Jennie M. Flexner, *Making Books Work; a Guide to the Use of Libraries* (New York: Simon and Schuster, 1943), p.125.

[15] Jennie M. Flexner, *Circulation Work in Public Libraries* (Chicago: American Library Assn., 1927), p.118-19.

practices in eight middle-western institutions. Only one of these allowed bound volumes of periodicals to circulate to faculty members on indefinite loan, subject to recall, though another had the same provision for other than general periodicals. The next most generous loan period was four weeks, with renewal privileges; and the next was two weeks, with some renewals. The other institutions allowed no better than short-term loans, either overnight or for two or three days, though special permission might occasionally be granted for longer periods. For graduate students one institution allowed four weeks subject to renewal; another allowed two weeks, with renewal privileges, for non-general periodicals; while the others limited circulation from overnight to three days. Four of the institutions did not lend periodicals to undergraduates. The most liberal period was one week; the others were overnight or one day.

In so far as any trend is discernible in college and university libraries, it is probably in the direction of restricting the loan of periodicals. Oddly enough, the motive is not to preserve the volumes but to make them of wider use, particularly to the person who wants to browse through a set on the shelves, to the professor who is checking references for a new book or article, or to the reader who wants a volume for in-the-building consultation.

The situation is no clearer in special libraries. Some types, a chemistry library, for instance, may be unwilling to circulate journals because they may be needed urgently almost at a moment's notice; and a law library would not think of permitting its law reports to circulate. In general, however, the special library will do its best to accommodate a reader on the score that "books have only potential value as they stand on the shelf; it is the use that is made of them that is the ultimate measure of their worth."[16] The Science-Technology Division of the Special Libraries Association applies this philosophy as follows:

> In a small, closely-knit organization it may be altogether practical to permit the circulation of bound periodical volumes without any special restrictions. However, complications arise where the group is large and much literature searching is done in the library. The absence of one volume, borrowed for only one paper, puts a hundred or so others out of reach. The character of the particular literature involved will have a determining influence on the desirability of circulating bound volumes. If a reference such as Beilstein's *Handbuch der organischen Chemie* is used to any extent it will be a serious inconvenience not to have volumes of the *Berichte* or the *Annalen* on the shelf. A compromise may be effected by having bound volumes subject to immediate recall when needed in the library. The whole question of the circulation of bound volumes should be studied by the librarian who can

[16] Special Libraries Association, Science-Technology Division, *Technical Libraries, Their Organization and Management,* ed. by Lucille Jackson (New York: Special Libraries Assn., [1951]), p.66.

then decide which procedure best fits the needs of the clientele. Inasmuch as the majority of science-technology libraries are research libraries, their most important resource, the bound periodical files, ought to be freely available. For this reason, it is the policy of some libraries not to circulate bound periodical volumes.[17]

Circulation of current issues

When serials are acquired primarily for permanent preservation, as in a university library, there is general reluctance to circulate current issues which must be kept in as good condition as possible for eventual binding. When preservation is not a major factor, as in a public library branch, the current issues may be circulated freely. In some instances, particularly in special libraries, extra subscriptions may be placed to provide service copies for current circulation, copies which for the most part are expendable.

In popular public libraries the custom—although practices vary—is to circulate the next-to-the-latest number, not the latest. In some libraries periodicals may circulate when they are three months old; in others, they do not circulate as long as they are in the periodical room. Some libraries permit reserves to be placed on current numbers available for circulation, but some do not. As a rule, the reserve may not be placed in anticipation of the receipt of an issue; it may be placed at any time after the latest issue has been put on display.

In popular libraries the reason for restricting the circulation of the latest numbers is to give readers an equal opportunity to browse among the new periodicals and to place their reserves for them.[18] The theory is somewhat akin to that for a new-book shelf. However, the argument is rather attenuated when periodicals do not circulate until they are three months old, which is the time that requests may start to come for them by way of the periodical indexes.

In college and university libraries the reason for prohibiting the circulation of current issues must be sought first in the oldest of all library functions—namely, conservation—and second in their close tie-in with the current periodical indexes. In most of these libraries items in the periodical room circulate only by exception. The life expectancy of current numbers would be curtailed if they circulated freely for out-of-the-building use, though this statement is not as convincing as it was before the advent of plastic covers, which give much of the protection of a regular binding. Some periodical rooms keep a supply of covers on hand for use with the periodicals that circulate by special permission.

---

[17] *Ibid.*, p.70-71.

[18] For an application of this principle in a special library, see Elsie L. Garvin, "The '3-Day' Shelf," *Wilson Library Bulletin* 14:775, 1940.

Current periodicals are generally subject to a shorter loan period than books. Three-day loan periods are not uncommon in college, university, and public libraries, but more commonly readers may borrow an issue for a week. The reasons for limiting the loan period are: first, that it takes relatively less time to read a periodical than a book; second, that since timeliness is of the essence of current periodicals, they should be available to readers without too much delay; and third, that the supply of periodicals in demand is not great. For much the same reasons loans are almost always restricted to one title at a time.

Routing of current issues

A widespread practice in special libraries is to circulate current issues of journals to members of the firm, laboratory, etc. The visible index is marked with the names of individuals who are to see each issue. Routing slips are commonly mimeographed or otherwise duplicated and attached to the issues as they start on their way. A similar practice holds to a small extent in general libraries, but there it is largely confined to publications checked for book selection or other official purposes.

Contributors to *Special Libraries* have been much exercised over the problems of routing current journals. As Gertrude Bloomer has said: "Of all the routine practices carried out in the administration of special libraries, probably none is more controversial, more varied in method, and at the same time more important in its aim and purpose than that of the circulation of current journals."[19] None will dispute the need for research workers to be kept abreast of developments in their field. The problem comes with what has been called "magazine hoarding,"[20] which Miss Bloomer analyzed as follows:

> Failure of persons receiving journals to pass the journals along within the specified time, or within a reasonable period of time if no limit is set, is mentioned most frequently as the cause of delay and inefficiency in circulation. It appears that no library has been able to set up a system in which journals may be circulated freely, while at the same time, each receiver of journals is motivated to read and send them on promptly. The next most frequently mentioned cause of dissatisfaction is the tendency on the parts of many individuals to loan journals in circulation to persons not on the circulation list. This is actually temporary loss of a journal, and may even result in costly delay if the journal is needed, or in permanent loss.[21]

In an attempt to remedy this situation and to keep the staff informed of the whereabouts of any issue some libraries go to the trouble

---

[19] Gertrude Bloomer, "The Circulation of Current Journals in Special Libraries," *Special Libraries* 39:46, 1948.

[20] "Wanted: a Table-of-Contents Reprint Service," *Special Libraries* 41:257, 1950.

[21] Bloomer, *op. cit.*, p.49.

and expense of routing an item to one person at a time, instead of indulging in wholesale routing. After each individual circulation the item is charged to the next person on the list. However, the amount of work entailed in this operation is considerable and prolongs the whole operation, as Cole and Rowley found. They reported: "One girl spent 50 percent of her time checking in and out the periodicals and frantically sending overdue notices. Some of the journals with the longest routing lists were seen by the requester a year after the date of issue."[22] Harvey Bumgardner's experience at the Detroit Edison Company was somewhat similar:

> The first change made in our magazine circulation procedure was to discontinue having copies of the magazines returned to the library after circulation to a single individual. They are now returned to the library only after the circulation of ten names has been completed. At present, it takes on the average approximately twenty working days to circulate one copy of a magazine to ten names. This compares with over forty-three days under the old system of back-to-the-library between each circulation to an individual. Thus, this change, besides reducing the amount of labor required, has speeded up considerably the service to employes.[23]

It is customary for periodicals to circulate directly from the checkers to the first person on the routing slip. The circulation desk, however, may come into play for later circulations, and some librarians prefer to have the circulation staff handle even the initial routing, at times utilizing a visible index for the purpose.[24] At the Detroit Edison Company the introduction of a punched card system was considered to be the biggest single labor-saving device in its program for reforming the routing system. As a consequence of this and other changes, Bumgardner reports that the time required for circulation of magazines dropped from a hundred man-hours per week to thirty.

A few special libraries have solved the problem in a radical way by giving up routing altogether, but in the Technical Division Library of the Rayon Department of E. I. du Pont de Nemours and Company the system was given up only after a number of substitute measures were undertaken. One was to acquire additional copies of the basic journals; the most significant was to route a weekly bulletin of abstracts of current journal articles on the basis of which the chemists could request any item they specially wanted to see.[25]

---

[22] Barbara R. Cole and Helen Rowley, "Current Journal Routing," *Special Libraries* 35:326, 1944.

[23] Harvey E. Bumgardner, "Labor-saving Methods Applied to Magazine Circulation," *Special Libraries* 43:92, 1952.

[24] For details on visible indexes for circulation work, see David Grenfell, *Periodicals and Serials, Their Treatment in Special Libraries* (London: Aslib, 1953), p.75-81.

[25] See Cole and Rowley, *op. cit.*, p.326-27.

The preparation of lists of current periodical articles, whether with abstracts or not, is a development to which much interest attaches since notable bibliographies, often of more than local value, have resulted. Saul Herner has described the origins of such a list in the Applied Physics Laboratory at Johns Hopkins University,[26] while the *Weekly Selected Reading List* issued by the Brookhaven National Laboratory Library is of inestimable value.

A somewhat similar reduction of the problem is achieved when librarians scan incoming journals and apprise readers of articles they may wish to see. As an extension of that plan, excellent results have been obtained by reproducing and circulating the tables of contents of current journals, whereby researchers may request items which specially appeal to them. At the Massachusetts Institute of Technology contents pages are multilithed in several series and circulated to divisional libraries, laboratories, and individuals. The Technical Information Branch of the Arnold Engineering Development Center, Tullahoma, Tennessee, has demonstrated that greater and more efficient use of current periodicals follows from the preliminary distribution of contents pages (in that library reproduced by Xerox).[27]

While there is a definite trend towards such practices, at least in the larger special libraries, the general picture remains very much as Gertrude Bloomer drew it:

> In a survey of 24 pharmaceutical libraries, it was found that all but one of them circulate current journals regularly to personnel in various departments throughout their organizations. In 50 per cent of the libraries there is some discrimination as to personnel eligible to receive journals, and in 66 per cent, only certain titles or types of journals are circulated. If any restriction is set up, it is usually made on scientific journals. More than half of the libraries receive duplicate copies of those journals most in demand; these are usually circulated while one copy is kept in the library.
>
> Most libraries assign the duties connected with circulation to one member of the staff. In the average library these duties occupy 25 per cent of the working day of one person, but in some libraries circulation is a full-time job. Only 6 libraries furnish special messengers to deliver journals; the remaining libraries depend on plant mail for the distribution of journals. If a limit is set on the length of time an individual may keep a journal, this limit is most frequently 24 hours; however, only 50 per cent of libraries set up any restriction on time.
>
> Approximately one-third of pharmaceutical libraries publish abstract bulletins to supplement circulation, and a few post photostats or typewritten copies of tables of contents of new journals on the bulletin boards, in order to keep their personnel informed of current literature.

---

[26] Saul Herner, "The Selected Reading List: a Means of Improving the Use of Periodical Literature," *Special Libraries* 41:324-26, 1950.

[27] Cf. G. E. Randall, "Journal Routing, Greater Efficiency at Lower Cost," *Special Libraries* 45:371-73, 1954.

The great majority of librarians (64 per cent) feel that their journal circulation systems are probably the best that could be devised for their particular libraries, while 25 per cent rate their procedures as very good. Comments volunteered by many librarians indicate that the development of a more efficient system than that in current use in most libraries is very desirable.[28]

Interlibrary loan

Since serials are basic to research and information, numerous requests are made for them on interlibrary loan. The existence of various union lists facilitates the location of sets. However, some libraries are unwilling to lend periodical and society publications, current numbers in particular. For example, among the items that the Library of Congress cannot ordinarily lend are

> books in constant use in Washington, the loan of which would be an inconvenience to Congress, or to other Government agencies, or to reference readers in the Library of Congress. These conditions would ordinarily exclude from this loan system many official documents, Congressional hearings, newspapers and periodicals, genealogies and local histories. Photostats or microfilm reproductions of materials in the Library's Collections are procurable at a relatively small charge, except that copyright material will not be copied without the signed authorization of the copyright owner.[29]

Commonly a serial is wanted on interlibrary loan because a reference to an article in it has been found in a periodical index, a footnote, or other bibliographical source. As a rule the article is no more than fifteen pages long, yet a volume of several hundred pages may be requested to satisfy the need. The service costs involved in locating, charging, and shipping the volume may easily amount to two or three dollars or more, whereas a photostat or microfilm of the article could be provided at a much smaller cost. Further, while photoduplication may lead to a certain amount of wear and tear, it is not as hard on a volume as shipping and returning it by mail or express; and the volume is out of the collection for a much shorter time.

In some cases photocopies leave a great deal to be desired. Manuscript additions should be checked from the original, not from a copy; and other details, such as cancels, can be detected only at first hand. Rarely, however, do these limitations apply to photocopies of serial material, and in any case photocopies are superior for the reproduction of complicated formulas, as in scientific and technical publications, and of drawings, as in patent specifications.

Thus photoduplication provides a generally satisfactory alternative to the interlibrary loan of serials. The interconnection in point of

---

[28] Bloomer, *op. cit.,* p.50.

[29] Library of Congress *Departmental & Divisional Manuals* 11:15, 1950.

theory was highlighted in 1943 when the Army Medical Library, as it was then called, began to provide microfilm copies free, except for postage, in place of interlibrary loan, not only for government establishments, but also for any individual connected with an accredited institution. The idea behind this development was expressed in a statement issued on September 1, 1943:

> The Library recognizes that microfilm copying is a service which publicly supported reference libraries may well perform on an equal basis with that provided for readers and by interlibrary loans. In the pursuance of such a policy, microfilms will be sent without charge in lieu of the loan of books to those who prefer them or where books or journals cannot be loaned.[30]

The Army Medical Library could make this gesture partly because to a large extent it avoided photostats and concentrated on microfilm for short and long runs alike. The free service would have been out of the question, because of the greater cost, if it had included photostats. The free service was available for only a few years, after which a nominal charge was made for the microfilms; nevertheless, the incident provides matter for thought.

Of more immediate practical concern is the question of the interlibrary loan of microreproductions. Libraries have been somewhat reluctant to extend this service. There does not seem to be any good reason why this should be so, as the Library of Congress recognized in 1950 when it began to lend microfilms. Only positive microfilms are lent by the Library of Congress, and for these the negatives must be on hand. The loan period was set at one month and the minimum unit was one reel. For shorter runs copies must be purchased.

Television facsimile reproduction

In course of production for commercial use, after a pilot installation had proved itself in the National Laboratory Library at Oak Ridge, Tennessee, are television facsimile reproduction machines which should have far-reaching influence on library service. A network of these machines will make the resources of any member library available to any other. To a large extent, interlibrary loan will become an affair of the past.

In a television facsimile reproduction machine a television camera reproduces a document whose image is transmitted over a high fidelity telephone line to a receiving unit at a distance. The receiving unit turns out, in a matter of seconds, a copy of the document ready for use. Operating costs are relatively low; the basic expenses are the cost of the machines, rental of the telephone wire, and the manpower for

[30] Keyes D. Metcalf and others, *The National Medical Library; Report of a Survey* (Chicago: American Library Assn., 1944), p.38.

transmission and reception. Unlike photostats, whose product is similar, these machines serve equally well for short and long runs, and the original copy can be either the publication itself or a microfilm, the latter providing the greatest speed in transmission.[31]

The possibilities of television facsimile reproduction are immense for library materials of all kinds and for libraries of all kinds. But for serials they present the most difficult and challenging problems, because serials are likely to be the type of material most in demand. Systematic collecting of serials by libraries will become a matter of prime importance. Somewhere in the facsimile network there should be complete files of all possible serials, either originals or copies. For a variety of reasons it would be well to have at least two sets in the United States and to designate one or two institutions as primarily responsible for the maintenance and development of master files, and hence of master records of holdings. An acquisition program far exceeding the scope of the Farmington Plan would be necessary as a foundation. Serial processing would have to be developed on a sure and rapid basis. Part of this processing would be the further development of bibliographical controls—abstracts, indexes, and union lists—so that the resources of member institutions could be exploited to the full. In many cases the reduction of originals to microfilm and possibly to other forms of microprint would be essential to ensure preservation and to complete sets.

One great contribution the television facsimile reproduction machine can offer lies in its ability to retard the growth of libraries. Except for newspaper files, microprint has had no marked effect on the size of libraries. But the new development can bring about very pronounced results, because it will no longer be necessary for libraries to build up enormous independent collections of serials. A dramatic era of controlled cooperative serial collecting would be realized.

---

[31] Microfilm was the medium employed when *Gone with the Wind* with its 1047 pages was transmitted by Ultrafax in 2 minutes and 21 seconds. Cf. Luther H. Evans, "Images from the Air: the Beginnings of Ultrafax," *Journal of Documentation* 4:248-50, 1949.

CHAPTER 12

Binding

THE LIBRARY ROUTINES connected with the binding of serials are more complex than those for the binding of monographs. Serial librarians or binding-records assistants generally maintain a card file of instructions for the treatment of each current title. The file is to enable a set to be bound with reasonable uniformity despite the fact that the component parts as a rule are sent to the bindery disjunctively over a period of years and even decades. The collation of serials is often quite intricate: at times provision may have to be made for guards or stubs to be inserted in place of missing numbers, and in general a variety of technical matters must receive attention. The routines are somewhat less complex in libraries that take advantage of standardized lettering, because they do not have to make and maintain a file of rubs to show the size and position of the lettering on earlier volumes of a set.[1] The supply of serials for binding has peak periods, because volumes tend to be completed in midyear and at the end of the calendar year; or they may be held to go to the bindery in summer when reader demand is relatively low. To satisfy readers, the staff may have to make frequent searches for titles on their way to or from the bindery.

Much desirable standardization has been achieved through the work of the Joint Committee of the American Library Association and the Library Binding Institute. Their recommendations have been embodied in Feipel and Browning's *Library Binding Manual,* the relevant passages of which should be studied by serial librarians.[2]

Library binding practices

It is customary for service units to prepare volumes in their custody for binding. They may write out the instructions that accompany a

[1] For an account of standardized lettering see Louis N. Feipel and Earl W. Browning, *Library Binding Manual,* prepared under the direction of the Joint Committee of the A. L. A. and L. B. I. (Chicago: American Library Assn., 1951), p.26-27.

[2] The principal passages relating to serials are on pages 3, 7-8, 25-29, 36, and 48-50.

serial to the bindery, or that function may be performed by a binding-records assistant. The catalog department may do the preparatory work for items that do not go to a service unit.

The assistant who prepares a volume for binding cannot be content with seeing that all issues are present; a closer check may disclose mutilated pages. Some types of publication are more susceptible to mutilation than others; for example, an art periodical should be checked through more carefully than a library journal. In some libraries there may even be a double check. At the Library of Congress, for instance, the Binding Division reviews serials for completeness after they have been prepared in a service division.[3] Most binderies also collate volumes faithfully, even though they know that the library has already performed a similar task. Yet bindery collation is expensive. One binder has expressed the opinion that "probably the most costly operation of any is the collating and arranging of the material that is to be bound."[4] In at least one library, the University of Oregon, procedures have been reorganized so collation at the bindery is no longer required:

> The Divisions remove the completed volumes from their shelves, collate them issue by issue and send them to the Bindery Unit, tied securely and with a notation of title, volume and dates. This is the only collation a volume receives in the whole process. We have eliminated further collation in the Library and at the Bindery knowing full well that an occasional volume will be imperfect. But it is cheaper to correct this error when it may be discovered than to give each volume a more exact inspection.[5]

Unquestionably there has been duplication of effort in collating volumes prior to binding; and unquestionably there is room for economy whenever librarians and binders jointly delimit their functions.

One of the recurrent questions of collation is whether the covers of serials should be discarded or whether they should be included in the bound volume. Some libraries preserve both front and back covers, others preserve only the front covers unless there is significant text on the back, while still others dispense with both as a general rule. Some bind the covers in place; some bind them as a group at the end of the volume. Frances Warner has made a good case for preserving covers and binding them in place, especially in research libraries:

> Some of our economies have been very irritating to scholars and scientists. Many of us have discarded the covers of scientific periodicals in order to reduce the size of the volumes. But on most of these covers, there is much information that is not found in the issue itself. Furthermore, covers serve to

---

[3] Library of Congress *Departmental & Divisional Manuals* 5:17, 1950.

[4] Ernst Hertzberg, "The Bindery Industry," *Serial Slants* v.1, July 1950, p.15.

[5] Emma G. Wright and E. B. Barnes, "Binding at the University of Oregon," *Serial Slants* v.2, Jan. 1952, p.2-3.

separate issues. When they are removed, a chemist, for example, who is running through the volumes of *Chemical Abstracts* to ascertain what is published in each number on the fundamentals of chemistry will have great difficulty in locating this section in the twenty-four issues published during the year. In one institution, during one month, over one dozen complaints were filed as a result of this rather common practice of librarians.[6]

Another moot point is the extent to which advertising matter should be included in the bound volume. Shires says "anything up to 80 per cent of a technical journal to-day consists of advertisements."[7] Thus, if everything is retained the issues of one bibliographical volume may have to be bound in two or three physical volumes. Some libraries feel that they must bind the whole work for the benefit of artists, the historian of a subject, or indeed anyone who wishes to study the advertisements of former times. Others are content with preserving the text and perhaps the advertising matter from a single issue each year. In 1935, as an attack on the problem, an informal committee of the Conference of Eastern College Librarians checked 34 libraries and published *A List of Periodicals Bound Complete with Advertising Pages in New England and New York City Libraries.* This list still serves to some extent as a guide to libraries that wish to economize by informing them that at least one recorded library has preserved the advertisements. At the University of Oregon an over-all decision was given in favor of retaining the advertising pages:

> All advertisements and covers are bound in, unless they might result in serious structural weakness in the finished volume. The practice of binding in all advertisements and covers has been adopted for a number of reasons. From the standpoint of binding economics, we may pay for more binding, but we do not pay for the labor spent in cutting them out. These two factors probably balance each other. In addition to these considerations, our practice avoids the danger of mutilated volumes (text accidentally removed when cutting out advertisements). Certain bibliographical information which is frequently unobtainable elsewhere is retained as well as items that are often of most practical immediate interest (e.g. prices of instruments) and may very well be of considerable sociological interest in the future.[8]

The binder is inclined to agree, judging by the following statement:

> Is it necessary in all cases to remove ALL advertising material? A librarian

---

[6] Frances Warner, "Current Binding Practices at Iowa State College," *Serial Slants* 3:40, 1952.

[7] G. A. Shires, "Information from the Advertisement Pages," *Aslib Proceedings* 2:23, 1950. A contributor to *Notes and Queries* (7th series 3:336, 1887) said: "I cannot agree . . . that in binding up magazines *any* advertisement sheets should be removed; I would rather say let the loose ones be carefully secured by the binder as insets. The most interesting available material for a yet-to-be-written history of English lotteries is the multitude of amusing handbills distributed in now almost forgotten magazines by Bish and other giants of the trade in lottery tickets."

[8] Wright and Barnes, *op. cit.,* p.4.

not so long ago asked me—"Why do that in every case, are not the ads a history of the times also?" If this were possible in some cases, the binder could leave the book fairly intact without going thru it page for page and eliminating all ads. A large part of the hand operation would be eliminated, and the saving passed on to the library. Probably those ads in the center could be left in each magazine and those on either end taken out, which would save the paging thru the text in the center to find the ads.[9]

Feipel and Browning urge librarians "not to remove pages of advertising but to instruct the binder whether to remove or retain them."[10]

The cost of binding has forced many economies on libraries. For the most part practices reminiscent of the old days of leather binding have long since been given up, particularly colored panels and gold lines to represent bands, although the latter may still be found.[11] Developments at the University of Oregon illustrate this trend:

The work at the Bindery has been greatly simplified. First . . . there is no rub file. The size of type used in lettering depends on the thickness of the volume. Vertical placement for the lettering is determined by the heights and measured from the bottom. Color and wording are stated on the Bindery Slip. Trimming is the one operation that is not controlled. Different volumes of a set may vary from one-quarter to one-eighth of an inch, but since the lettering is all measured from the bottom, the titles of the volumes standing on a shelf are even.

In addition to instructions for individual volumes, there are a number of standing specifications. The materials used in all our binding are the same. The cloth binding is all standard quality Library Buckram. The board used is a #1 book binding board. . .

In addition to standard cloth binding, the Press binds many items in what we call Board Binding. This consists of paper covered boards, of the same high quality used for cloth, with a vellum spine that is not lettered. Board Binding is specified in all cases where it appears the use will not be too heavy, where the paper is comparatively light and where other considerations make a cheaper binding advisable. Board bindings cost exactly 50 per cent of cloth bindings.[12]

This library realized that it must compromise between perfection and economic conditions. It was motivated by the philosophy that volumes are bound to make them serviceable and to preserve them for the

---

[9] Hertzberg, *op. cit.,* p.15-16.

[10] Feipel and Browning, *op. cit.,* p.26.

[11] Because morocco bindings decay unless they are carefully treated, American libraries in the early part of the twentieth century generally gave them up in favor of buckram; consequently part of a set may be in morocco and part in buckram (cf. Figure 29). To make the transition less abrupt, some libraries added colored panels and gold lines to the buckram. But while American libraries favor buckram for volumes in the working collection, Grenfell *(op. cit.,* p.114) recommends it for lightly used sets only. His advice is to use leather for heavily used sets; cloth or buckram for lightly used volumes; and quarter binding, with either cloth or buckram backs and paper or board sides, for volumes subject to the least wear and tear.

[12] Wright and Barnes, *op. cit.,* p.3-4.

FIGURE 29. Four styles of library binding. The 1909 volume is in morocco; the 1910 in buckram with leather panels. Six double lines were later employed to give the effect of panels; by 1947 the lines had also been given up.

future. With such a philosophy esthetics can still be regarded, but in a secondary way. This is a counsel of wisdom for the workaday serial.

Feipel and Browning take the attitude that "cheap binding, at best, is never cheap." Instead of resorting to it, they say, "it will usually be wiser for the librarian to determine what files must be preserved, bind them substantially according to Class 'A' Specifications and tie up the rest (or such parts as may not safely be discarded) into volumes."[13] This advice would never serve in the research library which preserves numerous government documents, annual reports, and other serials that should be bound for preservation and order on the shelves but do not warrant standard binding.

---

[13] Feipel and Browning, *op. cit.,* p.27-28.

Cost is a factor that must be taken into account quite seriously. As an illustration of the way the cost of binding has risen, the situation at the University of Illinois Library may be cited. There the annual appropriation for binding increased from $26,000 in 1946 to $50,000 in 1950. Even then—despite rigid selection of titles to be bound, reduction of duplicates, and other economies—the new figure was inadequate, so a supplementary appropriation had to be obtained to cover arrearages. The bindery was instructed "(1) to collate volumes only if specially requested by our Binding Department, (2) to leave pages containing advertising in all issues unless directed otherwise, and (3) to omit lettering on less important and little used serials as designated by the Binding Department."[14]

As in many other respects, the binding problem in the Library of Congress is far more serious than that in any other American library. In 1951 it reported arrearages of 435,000 volumes awaiting initial binding plus 259,000 volumes in need of rebinding, a large proportion of both groups being serials. The accumulation could monopolize the entire Library of Congress binding quota for ten years to come. A Binding Committee was therefore constituted to debate the possibility of reducing large quantities of material to photocopy form and of employing inexpensive types of binding. The following were among the points brought out by the Committee:

The Library should have in ink-print form at least one major newspaper from each foreign country.

No more than three, preferably two, newspapers from each foreign country should be bound, and these should be microfilmed when their physical condition warrants; all other foreign papers which are to be retained should be acquired in microfilm or be microfilmed and the originals discarded.

Prompt binding of serials is necessary for preservation and protection against loss, therefore serials should be given precedence in binding.

The greatest demand is for American serials listed in the standard indexes.

Large periodical volumes do not stand up well under heavy use; quarter binding single issues would probably cut down the need for rebinding certain periodicals; but in many cases quarter binding one or more issues of a periodical would be more expensive than full binding an annual volume, particularly if the more desirable oversewn quarter-binding style were adopted. Only those periodicals listed in the standard indexes would need to be considered for such special binding treatment.

Some lettering is desirable on the quarter binds. It would lessen deck-attendant error, help the attendants to correct reader error in call numbers, and make it easier to spot mislabeled volumes.

---

[14] Arnold H. Trotier, "Some Persistent Problems of Serials in Technical Processes," *Serial Slants* v.1, Jan. 1951, p.11.

Each volume sent to the Bindery for quarter binding will be accompanied by a prelettered buckram strip which will become the back of the book. The strip will be hand-lettered with a Leroy lettering set, using black ink on precut, light-colored buckrams.

Corporate authors will be condensed or abbreviated when necessary.

In view of the standardization of lettering panels, pattern volumes and dummies will no longer be used.

There are sets on public reference in mixed Library of Congress and publisher's bindings where even the substance of the lettering differs. All the contract binding for the Department of Agriculture Library is being done in red buckram with black ink lettering. When present stocks of buckram are exhausted, the standard color for full binding at the Library of Congress will be ruby, except that the Congressional Document series and all law material other than periodicals will be bound in law buckram, and United States bills will be bound in olive buckram.[15]

Clearly there is much hard thinking for libraries to do about the binding of serials and about their reduction to microcopy form. The problem is doubly serious when arrearages are involved. Frances Warner has this to say about arrearages of serial binding:

We have found that the practice of leaving unbound publications on the shelf, of tying up publications in brown paper or cardboard, only results in heavier costs later. In our experience, we have found no permanent economy in postponing binding or in placing unbound publications on the shelves for any considerable length of time. Issues of volumes of serials which are left unbound disappear. The cost of replacement is heavy both in time and money. Often missing numbers cannot be replaced. Deterioration of paper from age and infiltration of dust add to the damage. Binding is one item in the library budget which cannot be curtailed without serious loss.[16]

The problem of deferred serial binding is not new. It became acute during and after both the first and second World Wars. In 1919 the New York Public Library reported:

With our present funds for binding we can do nothing but adopt makeshifts which are expensive and unsatisfactory. They require the double handling of material, once when it is temporarily put into Manilla-rope paper, and once when it is to be bound in some permanent form. These makeshifts are expensive in time, since it takes longer to tie, untie, and retie a volume in Manilla-rope paper than to consult a bound volume. They are unsatisfactory, because the volumes so treated are difficult to handle on the shelves; because they suffer more from wear and tear; and because they lend themselves to slipshod, careless and inconsiderate treatment from readers and attendants. Work deferred is not avoided; it has to be done at a later day, and usually costs more than if done when the occasion arises.[17]

To a large extent the problem of serial binding costs is most

[15] Abstracted from the Minutes of the Library of Congress Binding Committee, 1952-53.

[16] Warner, *op. cit.*, p.39.

[17] *Report* of the New York Public Library, 1919 (New York, 1920), p.22.

acute in the historical-research type of library. Many a popular public library has ceased to bind its periodicals. The tendency is to tie up back files and shelve them in closed stacks; individual issues are then circulated when wanted.

Some special problems

Technicalities of all kinds must be faced in the binding of serials, and each special situation must be figured out as well as may be. Paged-in cumulative indexes may be left in place, but given special mention on the spine. Paged-in monographs are commonly removed, but if they are called for in the table of contents they may be left in place or the table of contents may be annotated to show the different location. Maps may sometimes be removed to go to the map collection. A typewritten slip may be inserted to show that a number is located elsewhere than in the set—or elsewhere in the set when continuity of text so dictates—or to specify that an issue of a document serial is restricted and therefore unavailable.

Change of format within a volume usually creates a binding problem. The best solution may be to bind the two sizes independently, especially when one of them is to go on the oversize shelves.[18] The British *Command Papers* have proved troublesome to bind and shelve because of changes in format.

Spearheaded by the Department of Agriculture Library and the Library of Congress, there is a growing tendency towards putting virtually all serials in a single color of buckram. This is an economy measure to which little objection can be raised, except possibly in the library that does not classify its serials. Most libraries have some mismatched bindings on their shelves: a mixture of publishers' and library binding, of morocco and buckram, or colors poorly matched during emergency periods. Some variations are simple errors in binding; others are caused by building up sets from a variety of sources.

There is a danger that serial volumes, like pamphlet volumes, may be made too thick from motives of economy. Such a policy should be followed only if the material will receive slight use over the years, and if it will not have to remain unbound for too long a period while the desired thickness is accumulating, otherwise it is shortsighted. As has been found with newspapers, bulk reduces the life expectancy of

---

[18] In the purely serial parts of the classification, folios are often neither distinguished nor segregated as monograph folios are. This is because there is not the same waste of space, since all volumes on a shelf tend to be of a size, with only occasional variations. It is a convenience to readers to have all the general serials in one sequence, particularly so when call numbers are avoided. Very large works may be treated differently; in fact, some of them may be classed with the newspapers.

a volume. Some newspapers are now bound two or three volumes to a month, but the lesson has not carried over as much as it should to other types of serials. On the contrary, two or three volumes are often bound together. For example, when three volumes of *College and Research Libraries* are bound in one (as was unfortunately done in the Harvard College Library) the bulk is too great in libraries where the work is consulted frequently. Such volumes are off the shelves more often than if they were bound in single volumes, and it is an annoyance to the reader to find three title pages and indexes scattered through a volume, if indeed he does find them; but the most serious trouble develops from keeping unbound files in the periodical room or elsewhere for several years instead of binding them on schedule and sending them to the bookstacks after the normal period of a year. Feipel and Browning point out that

> delay in binding results in heavy wear, and frequently in loss of numbers and parts. Unbound files are hard to shelve. Much time will be saved by the staff if it does not have to struggle with the job of keeping unbound magazines in order; and the public will be greatly pleased if it may have access to magazines which have been promptly bound.[19]

Binding units of less than a volume

A bibliographical volume of the *New York Times* is now bound in 24 physical volumes; the *Library Journal* has expanded so in recent years that one of its bibliographical volumes must now be bound in two physical ones. Thus libraries do at times take a smaller quantity than the bibliographical unit for serial binding. This principle needs to be thought through and perhaps extended. It is possible, for instance, that it should be applied to many an incomplete volume which, because of its incompleteness, is bundled in some fashion or other. When there are only one or two issues on hand it may be wise to put them in a cheap pamphlet binder. In that way they are protected, and by being stapled in can readily be removed later when they are to be incorporated in a larger volume. More commonly, however, only a few issues are missing. If guards are not provided so that the volume can be bound, it may be possible to bind the major part because it represents a straight run. The remainder can then perhaps be stapled into a cheap binder. By such devices the shelves can be kept in better order and the serials themselves will wear better than if they are left unbound.

Apparently Russian librarians have forsaken the bibliographical volume as the binding unit to a considerable extent. Klenov says that the two factors to be considered in binding periodicals are the use

---

[19] Feipel and Browning, *op. cit.*, p.3.

each individual title will get and the type of library in which it is located. In library parlance the terms "tonkie" (thin) journals and "tolstye" (thick) journals are used. Thin journals, such as *Ogonek, Krokodil,* and *Rabotnitsa,* which are widely read when they first appear but are less in demand later on, are bound by the quarter, half-year, or year. But thick journals of the type of *Novyi mir, Oktiabr',* and *Voprosy istorii,* where interest in the individual articles will persist over a number of years, are bound by separate issue and not by the year or half-year. A periodical such as *Pchelovodstvo,* which although not large in size will have value for scientists for years to come, can be treated in one of two ways. From the point of view of economy it would seem wise to bind two, three, or more numbers in one volume. But it can also be said that if each issue is bound separately circulation will be faster and fewer duplicate copies will have to be bought. Likewise, in a rural library the complete year of *Bibliotekar'* could be bound in two volumes, but in a large library, where library science students consult the file extensively, it is wise to bind each number separately to make it available to the fullest extent.[20]

The Wesleyan plan

The ever-resourceful Fremont Rider has developed a plan for serial binding that has points in common with Russian practice as described by Klenov. It is one that few will care to follow in its entirety; nevertheless, it deserves careful attention as an aid in clarifying some aspects of the theory of serials, and because of possible applications in limited respects. Rider suggests that each issue of a quarterly or monthly be put into an individual pamphlet binder, and that the four or twelve issues comprising a volume be placed in a box.[21] He tried out the plan in a small way at Wesleyan University Library. The faculty welcomed the innovation and wanted it extended. They discovered that when they had an article in a back file to read they could carry home an issue that weighed one pound as against a volume that weighed four pounds. Moreover, one professor did not inactivate all the issues comprising a volume when he borrowed only one of them; the remaining three or eleven issues were left in the box for other professors to consult or borrow. Thus the change in the binding program resulted in an increase in accessibility.

Binding costs were notably less. For a quarterly like the *Yale*

[20] See A. V. Klenov, *Bibliotechnaia tekhnika; uchebnoe posobie dlia bibliotechnykh tekhnikumov* (Izd. 4; Moskva: Gos. izd-vo kul'turno-prosvetitel'noi lit-ry, 1947), p.43, 48-49.

[21] For the details of Fremont Rider's plan see his *Compact Book Storage; Some Suggestions toward a New Methodology for the Shelving of Less Used Research Materials* (New York: Hadham Pr., 1949), p.86-90.

Review the cost per bibliographical volume dropped from $2.80 to $1; and for a monthly that was hitherto bound two volumes to the year the new figure was $2.40 instead of $5.60. Indirectly the Library of Congress cast doubt on these figures when it said that in many cases it would cost more to put the separate issues in quarter binding, particularly when oversewn, than to bind an annual volume in the regular way. Certainly reliance on a 20 or 25 cent binding is open to question.

Libraries may find Rider's idea of greatest practical value in the handling of annual reports and other low frequency publications whose issues are accumulated before they are bound. Even though flush binding does not give the same protection as regular binding, these publications might be preserved somewhat better if they were put in a pamphlet binder without delay.

Rider records three disadvantages to his scheme: issues are more easily lost; call numbers are longer; and there is no satisfactory way of dealing with the title page and index. Other factors should also be noted: the cost of extra lettering and boxes, and the facts that care and consultation of the shelves are more exacting processes and that the plan does not provide for high-frequency serials. As a final caution, the end processes may already be suffering from a surfeit of pamphlet binders. No preparation-for-shelves unit welcomes the sight of large quantities of pamphlet binders fresh from the bindery. A large addition to the number should be made only after careful consideration.

Title pages and indexes

Libraries go to considerable pains to procure title pages and indexes whenever they are printed. The index in particular is a valuable addition to a set, even though the set may be indexed in a standard source. The annual indexes to the *A. L. A. Bulletin* and the *Library Journal,* for instance, are most useful, even though both publications are well covered in *Library Literature*. They are useful because they may bring out more detail and because they facilitate consultation at the shelves. On this point research libraries will take exception to Feipel and Browning, who have said: "If the publisher's index is not easily available, and if the magazine is included in the *Readers' Guide* or other reliable compilation, the individual index to a bound volume becomes of little value, and is scarcely worth the effort frequently necessary to obtain or retain it."[22]

The title page naturally is bound in front of the issues to which it

[22] Feipel and Browning, *op. cit.,* p.26. In themselves the Stechert-Hafner check lists of title pages and indexes attest the value research libraries place on them.

relates. When the index constitutes a unit with the title page, as frequently is the case, it is also put in the front of the volume, even though monographs accustom a person to looking at the back for the index. Some libraries prefer to place the index at the back of a serial whenever possible. Feipel and Browning seem to imply that the index should always be bound at the front of a volume. Either convention is satisfactory as long as it is carried out systematically throughout a set.

Lettering

Care and restraint need to be exercised in selecting the information that the binder is to put on the spine. At approximately ten cents a line the lettering can add appreciably to the cost of binding, particularly for items cataloged under long corporate names. A hard-pressed binding budget can be made to go further by thoughtful saving on lettering. If two or three lines can be saved on each volume of a shipment of a hundred items, $20 or $30 is gained which can then be applied to the binding of other volumes.[23]

There has been a tendency to follow the catalog entry in determining the lettering. Up to a point this is a good policy, but on the shelves a finding title may suffice for practical purposes. So "Building Science Abstracts" may serve instead of "Gt. Brit. Dept. of Scientific and Industrial Research. Building Science Abstracts"; and "Airway Bulletin" may do instead of "U. S. Dept. of Commerce. Aeronautics Branch. Airway Bulletin." It is of course not difficult to find longer corporate names than these.

On the spine, as in all serial work, arabic numbers should be substituted for roman. Likewise the terms "volume," "tome," "Band," etc. may be omitted unless two related terms must be distinguished. Thus "1" can stand for "V.1," "Vol. 1," or any other such form; but if volume 1, part 1 must be brought out, then "Vol. 1, pt. 1" may be used, though some libraries adopt devices such as "72^2" to differentiate volumes and parts (see Figure 29).

The library name or seal appears on the spine less often than formerly. There is more than a sufficiency of library marks of ownership in most bound serials, since each issue is stamped as it is received. Some institutions, the Library of Congress, for example, are effectively utilizing end papers with the library's name or seal interwoven.

It is better to strike a happy medium, if possible, rather than have

---

[23] The 1948 "Guide of Fair Values" includes not more than five lines of lettering on the spine, plus head and tail gold lines, in the general cost of binding. Call numbers are an extra charge at seven cents for the first line and three cents for each additional line. See Feipel and Browning, *op. cit.*, p.55.

an excess of lettering on some sets and none except the call number on others. There is a growing tendency to shelve minor serials, especially those that are put in cheap bindings, without any lettering apart from the call number. Some of these items are hand-lettered in the preparation-for-shelves section; some have typewritten labels pasted on the spine or the side. Fewer of these substandard measures may be required if lettering is held down to bare essentials on all types of binding.

Newspapers

The Library of Congress specifications for newspapers and for journals that have newspaper format are as follows: "Back and corners of heavyweight buckram, No. 16 gray binders boards, marble paper sides turned in, tight back, visible silesia joints, backbone lettered in ink."[24]

Some of the history of newspaper binding is revealed by the following statement of New York Public Library practice:

> Newspaper volumes in the Library were bound with leather backs and cloth sides a generation ago. The leather decayed, and full canvas or heavy duck was then used. Newspapers make large, heavy volumes that are sometimes stored flat on the shelves. The rough canvas sides proved to be such excellent dust collectors that full buckram was next resorted to. Even buckram proved to have insufficient strength for the backs of such large volumes, and we are now using strong canvas backs with buckram sides.[25]

In some libraries one or more grips are included in the binding as an aid in pulling volumes off the shelves. There is no occasion for this device when the volumes rest on roller shelves, when several volumes are not piled one on top of the other, or when volumes are not made unduly large.

In the past the natural binding unit for a daily newspaper was taken to be the month, but now the unit may be two weeks or ten days to avoid the creation of volumes too large for convenient handling. Bibliographical volumes have generally been ignored, both in the binding unit and in lettering on the spine.

Substitutes for binding

Apart from reduction to microcopy, libraries must devise various ways of dealing with unbound serials. Some cannot be bound because

---

[24] Library of Congress *Departmental & Divisional Manuals* 5:7, 1950. The A. L. A. minimum specifications for Class A newspaper binding are given in Feipel and Browning, *op. cit.*, p.49-51. Cf. also p.28-30 for the authors' views on newspaper binding.

[25] *Report* of the New York Public Library, 1925 (New York, 1926), p.48.

the paper is too poor. Some must wait their turn until gaps have been filled. Others, such as college catalogs, may be given so low a priority that they are never bound. Items sent directly to a storage library may purposely be left in an unbound state. Substitutes for binding must generally be found for these types of material, as well as for items like annual reports that tend to be accumulated until enough are on hand to make a good-sized volume. The most common substitutes are manila-rope bundles tied with string, tape, or lawyers' "pink pulls"; boxes and containers of various kinds; and, in special libraries, vertical files. When manila rope is used, it is bought sometimes in precut sizes and sometimes in large rolls that must be cut to size each time it is wanted. Manila rope is usually lettered in india ink. For large bundles it may be necessary to add boards as supports.

With notable exceptions, there is a marked trend away from the binding of newspapers. The widespread acceptance of microfilm is responsible for this development. In the Harvard College Library, for instance, only one newspaper is now bound, the London *Times,* whereas formerly quite a number were bound regularly. For the rest the Harvard College Library is employing portfolios and even brown-paper bundles: indefinitely in some cases, and until the microfilm comes in others.

CHAPTER 13

Microreproductions

THE GREAT CONTRIBUTION that microphotography makes to research lies in its ability to provide copies of works which otherwise might be inaccessible, or relatively so, through scarcity or cost. Microreproductions are admittedly substitution mediums. As such they have their limitations, though they serve many purposes adequately. They have one noteworthy drawback from a reader point of view: they restrict freedom of operation through pinning consultation down to those locations where reading machines may be found. The multiplication of portable reading machines may eventually reduce this shortcoming. Because government research workers have less option in the matter, they accept microreproductions far more extensively than those who are engaged in private enterprise. In so far as they restrict freedom of operation microreproductions are in a class with certain other important mediums of research, notably reference books, rare books, and other non-circulating materials. In archival work, banking, and many other applications this fixation is inconsequential; in much scholarly research, however, it is a real handicap. The printed page conduces to the patient and quiet investigations carried on at home, in carrells, studies, laboratories, and elsewhere. Offset editions share this quality with the originals—for instance, the offset editions of European serials produced to complete sets at the end of World War II, editions which were so good that some libraries discarded the originals as unwanted duplicates when they were eventually received.

Microfilms of newspapers, on the other hand, have come to be valued over the original publications for most library research. Because of their bulk and weight, sometimes because of their fragile condition, bound volumes of newspapers are even less convenient to consult than microreproductions, and are not always welcomed by readers. Such was the experience in the Newspaper Division of the New York Public Library which withdrew its bound files from service once microfilms were on hand. It reported that many readers, who have used both, prefer the film to the volume. It is largely a matter of getting accustomed to reading from a screen instead of from a book. The average reader has no difficulty in operating the projector after the film has been inserted by a library attendant, although others who insist that they are not "mechanically-minded," or do not like machines, prefer to use bound volumes, heavy and cumbersome though they be.[1]

Five years later a gain in housekeeping was noted in addition to continued reader acceptance of the films and reading machines:

Readers seem to have come to prefer films to actual volumes. The use of film contributes in many ways to their comfort, for tables are no longer heaped high with huge volumes rendering it difficult to find working space. Tables and floor are not littered with showers of wood pulp. The disheveled appearance common to newspaper rooms is disappearing.[2]

Louis Fox, Chief of the Newspaper Division in the New York Public Library, analyzed the situation in the following terms:

The advantages to the reader of the newspaper film as contrasted with the bound file are first, that the print of the newspaper as it appears on the screen is enlarged approximately 50 per cent above the size of the print in the paper itself. Again, the definition of the letters and figures on the screen is much sharper and clearer. This is especially noticeable in the case of financial quotations on which so much research work in a newspaper division is done. Then, the reader does not have to crane his neck to read the top of the newspaper page on the screen as he must when the volume is laid flat on a table or, even, if it is placed on a sloping table or easel.[3]

Fox also reported improved service to readers, especially when more than one volume is consulted:

It was certainly much easier and quicker to take the film spool 3 11/16 inches in diameter and 1 3/8 inches in thickness from its box and insert this spool in the projector than to give a reader a seventeen-pound bound volume of the *New York Times*. The saving in time, when several volumes were wanted, was considerable.[4]

So successful was the transition from the bound volume to the microfilm that in 1941 the New York Public Library transferred its newspaper collection to a storage library. The microfilm collection of newspapers was all that remained in the main building, and is what readers have used since that time.

Apart from newspapers, and from other items on poor paper, libraries must generally plan to acquire and preserve the actual publi-

---

[1] *Report* of the New York Public Library, 1934 (New York, 1935) , p.44-45.

[2] *Report* of the New York Public Library, 1939 (New York, 1940), p.63.

[3] Louis H. Fox, "Films for Folios," *Library Journal* 62:364, 1937.

[4] *Ibid.*, p.363. Cf. also Fox's "Turn a Handle and Get Your Page," *Library Journal* 60:675-76, 1935. In this he says: "Handling the film is, of course, infinitely easier than carrying a bulky newspaper volume weighing from 17 to 25 pounds and this results in greatly accelerating service to the reader."

cations themselves in so far as they can. It may be entertaining to speak of the twilight of the printed book, but collection and dissemination of the publications themselves must be the primary objective of libraries as long as writers and research people are individuals who prefer to work with as little regimentation as possible. It is still true as Goethe said that talent develops in quietude, character in the stream of the world.

Microfilm

By far the most common form of microreproduction of serial files is microfilm. It has been notably successful for various serial projects, newspapers, periodicals, and government documents in particular. The microfilming of newspapers grew out of attempts to preserve wood pulp papers that disintegrated after a few years. The alternatives were expensive and little used: papers could be covered with Japanese tissue, as at the New York Public Library, or they might be published in miniature editions on rag paper.[5]

Microfilm runs of newspapers have already won wide acceptance. Consequently projects have been undertaken in a number of centers to record newspapers, especially those of a given region, by this method. In some cases the newspaper publishers have arranged for the microfilming of their papers; in others, associations and institutions have accepted the responsibility, among them the Boston Public Library, the Canadian Library Association, the Library of Congress, the New York Public Library, and the University of California Library. A union list of newspapers on microfilm has been published,[6] and in 1950 an attempt was made to set standards for the microfilming of newspapers.[7]

There is a large and constantly increasing number of newspaper files on microfilm. The Microfilm Clearing House (which is part of the Union Catalog Division in the Library of Congress), reflects the great activity in this field; in 1950 it could provide information about 255 film copies of newspapers;[8] by 1953 the figure had increased to about 3200. In addition the Union Catalog Division in 1953 had a record of about 2800 serials on microfilm, including some labor and

[5] For an account of the proposed miniature edition of the *New York Times* see Robert C. Binkley, *Manual of Methods of Reproducing Research Materials* (Ann Arbor, Mich.: Edwards Brothers, 1936), p.115-16. In Figure 54 of Binkley's book a sample page of the miniature edition is reproduced.

[6] George N. Schwegmann, *Newspapers on Microfilm* (2d ed.; Washington: Library of Congress, 1953).

[7] "A Proposed Standard for the Microphotographic Reproduction of Newspapers," *American Documentation* 1:46-50, 1950.

[8] *American Documentation* 1:164-65, 1950.

religious publications which might be considered newspapers. Amongst the notable titles on film are the *Christian Science Monitor, Izvestia,* the London *Times,* the *New York Herald Tribune,* the *New York Times, L'osservatore romano, Pravda,* and *Le temps.* Since 1938 Harvard College Library has microfilmed the current issues of the leading newspaper from some forty-four countries.[9]

University Microfilms has been responsible for several microfilm projects for periodicals. After it microfilmed all extant and available periodicals published in the United States from 1741 through 1799,[10] it added roughly five hundred American periodicals published between 1800 and 1825.[11] The value to research libraries of these undertakings can be gauged by the following statement which relates primarily to the nineteenth-century project:

> Good portions of the existing Americana must be had in the form of facsimiles if they are to be had at all; this is especially true of periodicals. Older libraries, fortunate enough to have the originals, control the supply; yet few can boast. It was necessary to use the resources of seventy-six libraries to complete the series under consideration. Except the Library of Congress, no single institution holds complete files of more than 30 per cent of the titles.[12]

A companion project undertook to microfilm approximately two hundred English literary periodicals of the seventeenth, eighteenth, and nineteenth centuries.[13]

In the scientific field both the American Documentation Institute[14] and University Microfilms[15] have microfilmed important works, and a

---

[9] "Newspapers Microfilmed by Harvard University," *American Documentation* 1:210-11, 1950, includes the list of titles as of January 1, 1951. Cf. also Laurence J. Kipp, "Microfilming Foreign Newspapers," *Harvard Library Bulletin* 2:410-12, 1948.

[10] See Eugene B. Power, "Source Materials for the Study of American Culture," *Journal of Documentary Reproduction* 3:192-97, 1940. For the full list of 91 titles see University Microfilms, *American Periodical Series, Eighteenth Century* (Ann Arbor, Mich., [194-]).

[11] See Robert E. Booth, "American Periodicals, 1800-1825; University Microfilms Commences a New Series," *Library Journal* 71:156-63, 179, 1946; also Benjamin M. Lewis, "The American Periodical Series, 1800-1809," *Serial Slants* 5:12-16, 1954. For the list of titles included in the series see University Microfilms, *American Periodical Series, 1800-1825* (Ann Arbor, Mich., 1947-50. 4 pts.). The termination date for the project has been extended to 1850.

[12] Booth, *op. cit.,* p.156.

[13] See "English Literary Periodicals on Microfilm," *American Documentation* 1:208, 1950.

[14] "ADI List of Periodicals on Microfilm, 1951," *American Documentation* 2:108-09, 1951.

[15] For this and other University Microfilms projects, see its *The Problem of Periodical Storage in Libraries* (Ann Arbor, Mich., 1954), which contains a list of films being made on a current basis as well as a list of back files of periodicals on microfilm. See also its *University Microfilms, a Microfilm Service Organization Devoted to Filling the Needs of Scholars and Libraries* (Ann Arbor, Mich., 1952).

scheme has been devised by University Microfilms for libraries to acquire microfilms in lieu of binding and preserving certain titles.[16] With the approval of the publishers, files of some nine hundred current periodicals are microfilmed after the completion of each volume. Libraries which subscribe to this service do not need to go to the expense of binding their files, but may discard them on receipt of the microfilm, or as soon as they are no longer needed as current periodicals.

Notable developments in the filming of government documents include the *Congressional Record,*[17] the Patent Office *Gazette,*[18] the legislative journals of the American states,[19] the congressional hearings and reports, and beginning in 1953 the congressional set through the seventieth Congress. The legislative journal project includes manuscript as well as printed material. The master negatives are in the Library of Congress. In some ways, the most notable project is that undertaken by the National Archives.[20] A considerable portion of the archival material it has microfilmed is serial in character.

There is no special list of non-newspaper serials on microfilm; however, the *Union List of Microfilms*[21] includes serials of all kinds, and the *Union List of Serials* employs the letters "mf" against the statement of a library's holdings to indicate that its file is on film.

Microcards

Most highly publicized of the methods of microreproduction is the microcard. Unfortunately it is at the same time the least satisfactory form for serials, which are workaday materials that should not have

---

[16] See Eugene B. Power, "Microfilm as a Substitute for Binding," *American Documentation* 2:33-39, 1951; also the first title cited in Footnote 15.

[17] See "Congressional Record to Be Available on Microfilm," *American Documentation* 1:52-53, 1950.

[18] See "Patent Office Gazette on Microfilm," *American Documentation* 1:52, 1950.

[19] The Library of Congress has issued *A Guide to the Microfilm Collection of Early State Records,* prepared by the Library of Congress in association with the University of North Carolina; collected and compiled under the direction of W. S. Jenkins; edited by Lillian A. Hamrick ([Washington], 1950); see also William S. Jenkins, "Peregrinations of an Itinerant Microphotographer—Microfilming the Journals of State Legislatures," *Journal of Documentary Reproduction* 5:177-97, 1942. This article is reproduced in Jenkins' *Some Selected Materials Relating to the Microfilm Collection of Early State Records, an Undertaking of the Library of Congress and the University of North Carolina* [n.p., 1953].

[20] For a list of microfilms made by the National Archives, copies of which are on sale consult the latest edition of its *List of File Microcopies;* for background on this undertaking see Vernon D. Tate, *Microphotography in Archives* (National Archives, *Staff Information Circulars* 8, 1940).

[21] *Union List of Microfilms* (2d ed.; Ann Arbor, Mich.: Edwards, 1951).

to be closely guarded as if they were rare books. Microcards do not lend themselves to the principle of self-service on which library economy must be based in most institutions. The card or cards wanted by a reader must be selected for him, and this is not a simple process like handing him a bound volume or a reel of microfilm. Close track must be kept of all cards issued to readers by setting up a charging system for microcards alone, for when cards are souvenired expensive files are broken. Finally, the staff must refile the cards carefully, a matter of such importance that Wilcox makes special mention of "the constant filing and refiling of 3 by 5 cards, and the tantalizing problem of misfiling."[22] Naturally all these operations place a burden on the reference staff.

One consumer, being concerned over these matters, suggested that sets of microcards might be tied together. The reaction of the Microcard Foundation was:

It is true that a single tiny card is more easily mislaid than a fat book. And, for that reason, we are inclined to advocate that one's "microcard library" be maintained on a "closed stack" basis, i.e. as a file from which cards may be removed, and into which cards may be filed, only by a trained staff member. But it is also true that, if a card *is* lost once in a while, the loss is relatively trivial and not irreparable.[23]

It must furthermore always be remembered that one of the great advantages of microcards is that they offer material for use in small units, just as it is one of the great disadvantages of conventional, thick, periodical volumes, and of long reels of periodical film, that they tie up with one user a lot of material which he is not using but which he is keeping other library patrons from using. In other words, the more "separable" we make our research materials, the more usable we make them. This means that the moment we "bind" microcards together in any way we tend to destroy this flexibility and so to cancel one of their advantages.

"Nevertheless and notwithstanding," if some library does want to "bind" its microcards together into "volumes," it is a perfectly simple matter for it to do so, and to do so without any change whatsoever in either the cards or the machines. Tie the cards together—loosely—with *thread,* and insert the cards in the reader one at a time, as now. With our Model 3 readers leave the unused cards of the "volume" dangling in front of the card holder; with

[22] Jerome K. Wilcox, "The Point of View of the Librarian," *American Documentation* 2:163, 1951. Since government agencies are less concerned over manpower, the objections listed above apply more to other types of library. The federal government is actually the largest consumer of microcards, especially in relation to technical reports literature.

[23] Part of the objection to microcards for serials would be offset if the Microcard Foundation could reassure users on this point. Individual cards can be bought by paying a "broken set surcharge," but the Microcard Foundation is not happy over that type of sale. It says that "the selling of even one odd card effectually 'spoils' a $1000 set." *(Microcard Bulletin* 7:5, 1951.) In any event, libraries may spend much time hunting for missing cards.

our Model 2 readers lay the unused cards of the tied-together "volume" tucked away on the flat shelf in front of the light hole. This last needs more thread "leeway" and a little practice, but it can be done if you feel you must tie the cards together. But still we say don't do it![24]

The serials, as well as the monographs, issued by the Microcard Foundation and other agencies are listed in the *Microcard Bulletin.* Among the monograph series reproduced on microcards the following are of special interest: Bell's *British Theatre,* the Chaucer Society *Publications, The Chronicles & Memorials of Great Britain and Ireland during the Middle Ages* published by the British Public Records Office, Dibdin's *London Theatre,* Dodsley's *Select Collection of Old English Plays,* and the publications of the Early English Text Society, the Hakluyt Society, and the Shakespeare Society. Important periodicals have been microcarded in a number of fields, among them botany, chemistry (basic German and Russian journals), geology, history (including the *Annual Register* and the *English Historical Review),* law (including a number of state law reports, the records and briefs of the United States Supreme Court, the *New York Law Journal,* and the *Yale Law Journal),* mathematics, medicine, physics, and psychology. In the field of business, corporation reports, beginning with reports of firms listed on the New York Stock Exchange, are being reproduced. Both the United States patent specifications and the Patent Office *Gazette* are on microcards. The list of serial titles is being added to steadily, but still the number amounts to less than a tenth of the number available on microfilm. Some publications are obtainable in both forms, so that libraries can choose whether they want microcard or microfilm copies of such works as the *Berichte der Deutschen chemischen Gesellschaft,* the *Library Journal,* or the *Saturday Review.*

For current serials microcards can be supplied more promptly than microfilm, the reason being that a single issue of a periodical may be microcarded while the microfilm is delayed until it can include a much longer run. Microcards for *Newsweek* are supplied weekly, for the Patent Office *Gazette* monthly, and for the *Federal Register* quarterly.

Microcards have proved themselves to be unsatisfactory for newspapers by actual test. The Louisville Free Public Library had the *Louisville Courier-Journal* microcarded from February 15, 1949, through February 15, 1953. Ralph Shoemaker, who is familiar with both the microcard and the microfilm edition of the *Louisville Courier-Journal,* has pointed out that there are ten newspaper pages on each microcard, compared with eight hundred on a reel of microfilm. For anyone who wants to go through the file of a paper, this means eighty loadings and unloadings for the microcards against one for the micro-

[24] "Keeping Microcards in 'Bound' 'Volumes'," *Microcard Bulletin* 7:8, 1951.

film. And a full page of newspaper may be seen on the microfilm reading-machine screen, whereas only a quarter page is seen on the microcard screen, thereby involving four moves per page instead of one. He concludes that microfilming is the best method known today for the preservation of newspaper files.[25] An additional point worth mentioning is that photocopies cannot be made from newspapers on microcards.

Readex microprints

The disadvantages of microcards for serial publications also apply to the Readex microprints, though to a somewhat lesser degree because the cards are larger so that there are fewer of them proportionately. Three important items of serial interest are on Readex microprint: the British House of Commons *Sessional Papers,*[26] beginning with 1953 the current non-depository United States documents, and the United Nations documents. In the case of the British parliamentary papers, libraries will generally prefer to retain their partial files in addition to the microreproduction. But in the other two cases, there is small reason for most libraries to keep—maybe even to acquire—files of less important documents, especially processed material, once they have the microprint edition. Since current serials must be accumulated before they can be microprinted, it may be necessary to acquire some, if not all, of the publications as they are issued, and then to discard the file when the microreproduction is on hand.[27]

Cataloging microreproductions

There is fairly general agreement in principle that microreproductions should be cataloged like the originals. All too often in actual practice technicalities have crept in to make the cataloging elaborate. The Library of Congress introduced a special form wherein the collation specifies the extent of the microreproduction, while the collation of the original is given in note form. It is possible to add a variety of special notes, such as a designation of the type of reproduction or a specification of the location of the work that has been copied. On the other hand, some libraries have been content with relatively simple

[25] Ralph J. Shoemaker, "Remarks on Microcards and Microfilm for Newspapers," *American Documentation* 1:207-08, 1950.

[26] Cf. Edgar L. Erickson, "The Sessional Papers," *Library Journal* 78:13-17, 1953; also his earlier article, "The Sessional Papers Project," *Journal of Documentary Reproduction* 4:83-93, 1941.

[27] For a study of Readex microprints see Albert Boni, "Microprint," *American Documentation* 2:150-52, 1951. For the attitude of the Superintendent of Documents, which led to the Readex program for current federal documents, see Roy Eastin, "The Point of View of the Division of Public Documents," *American Documentation* 2:160-62, 1951.

entries, regular Library of Congress cards, or additions to existing records.[28] The class mark "Film," "Microcard," etc., may in these libraries take the place of a note as to the type of reproduction; no special forms are required; and notes are held to a bare minimum.

Actually in cataloging microreproductions of runs of serials, the collation, changes of imprint, variations in size and numbering, etc., must to a large extent be glossed over. Much has to be taken on faith. It is out of the question to go through the file carefully, looking for all the technical details that are sought in the handling of originals. For this reason, the essential data, at least for bibliographical units, should be incorporated at the start of the microreproduction to simplify the task of the cataloger.[29] But the situation is not always as simple as this. The cataloger may have to dovetail the records for a broken set of the original with records of microreproductions that may fill some or all of the gaps and may overlap with the original. Obviously, very complicated cases should be brought out on the official serial records rather than in the card catalog.

Although Fremont Rider's first thought was that microcards would catalog themselves, it has generally been found necessary to catalog them.[30] But for the Readex microprints of non-depository United States documents and of United Nations documents, most libraries are advised to work through the *Monthly Catalog of United States Public Documents* and the *United Nations Documents Index* and to catalog only selected titles.

The classification of microreproductions offers few problems. Microcards and microprints are usually arranged alphabetically, and thereby dispense with classification. Microfilms are usually arranged in broad classes to correspond with form divisions, such as newspapers, periodicals, rarities, etc. The class designation is followed either by a running number or by a Cutter number. Jones and Hagan have recorded some of the variant practices.[31] Assigning the class mark and the running or book number are comparatively simple procedures, but problems may be encountered in accommodating new reels which must be added to established files.[32]

---

[28] Some differences in library practice can be observed from the four cards for serials that Maurice F. Tauber has reproduced in his "Cataloging and Classifying Microfilm," *Journal of Documentary Reproduction* 3:21-23, 1940.

[29] Cf. Ralph H. Carruthers, "Titling of Microfilm Editions," *American Documentation* 1:190-93, 1950.

[30] Cf. Evelyn M. Hensel, "Microcard Cataloging Being Solved at Penn State," *Library Journal* 75:344, 1950.

[31] Helen J. Jones and Jeannette Hagan, "Microfilm Cataloging Lacks System," *Library Journal* 72:505-07, 1947.

[32] Cf. Ralph H. Carruthers, "N.Y.P.L. Changes Treatment of Microfilm Serials," *Library Journal* 72:880-82, 1947.

Checking records

Some current microreproductions may be regarded as self-checking as well as self-cataloging, for example the Readex microprints of United States documents. The reference staff must be alert in watching for gaps and making claims for self-checking sets; but, in general, current microreproductions should be checked in as other serials are, since bills must be certified for payment and sets should be kept complete. On the checking records it may be wise to employ a color system to distinguish between originals and microreproductions. At the Linda Hall Library red indicates microfilm and green indicates microcard holdings.

Microfilm for newspaper clippings

The *New York Times* has solved the problem of the disintegration of newspaper clippings by resorting to microfilm and a special reading machine. The clippings are copied onto 70 mm. microfilm, as many as thirty or forty on a frame. The sheet film is then put in an acetate envelope from which it does not have to be removed when it goes in the reading machine.[33] The machine is expensive, but has potentialities for documentation as well as for newspaper clippings.

---

[33] Eugene B. Power, "The Use of Sheet Film for Newspaper Clippings," *Special Libraries* 45:111-14, 1954.

CHAPTER 14

Rarities and Archival Material

MANY SERIAL SETS possess the two conspicuous characteristics of rare books: scarcity and commercial value. Their scarcity can be determined by a study of the *Union List of Serials;* while their value can be tested against either a periodical dealer's catalog or a price list of serial microreproductions. A rough yardstick of value is $7.50 for each bound volume of a periodical, with the general range of prices running from two to fifteen dollars per volume. Naturally a complete file brings more per volume than an incomplete one.

Although a set of a hundred volumes may easily be worth $750, its place is still in the main stack collection, not with the rare books where a monograph of that value would belong. Some 1952 and 1953 prices for serial sets, not all of which are complete, are as follows:

Price	*Number of Volumes*	*Title*
$ 370	17	Physica, 1934-51
450	32	Isis, 1913-49
770	28	Inscriptiones graecae, 1873-1939
780	30	La revue blanche, 1891-1903
810	41	Mémoires de l'Académie royale des sciences de l'Institut de France, 1818-79
840	71	Analecta Bollandia, 1882-1950
990	34	The kokka, 1889-1923
1,060	115	Archief voor de Javasuikerindustrie, 1893-1934
1,115	66	Romania, recueil trimestriel, 1872-1939
1,944	236	Bulletin de l'Académie royale des sciences et belles-lettres de Bruxelles, 1832-1947
2,025	195	Publications of the Musée royal des sciences naturelles de Belgique, 1877-1949
2,120	52	Repertorium für Kunstwissenschaft, 1876-1931
2,125	53	Archivio storico dell'arte, 1888-1949
4,050	455	Publications of the Koninklijke Akademie van Wetenschappen te Amsterdam, 1854-1948
13,250	881	Publications of the Akademie der Wissenschaften, Wien, 1848-1944

Prices for microcards and microfilms can also be quite high, witness the following:

Price		*Volumes and Years*		*Title*
Microcard	*Microfilm*	*Microcard*	*Microfilm*	
$ 296	$ 700	100 1865–1915	167 1865–1948	The Nation
1,009	1,010	554 1832–1943	557 1832–1945	Annalen der Chemie
	1,111		49 1900–48	Saturday Evening Post
1,175	1,175	77 1868–1945	73 1868–1940	Berichte der Deutschen chemischen Gesellschaft
1,831		116 1830–1945		Chemisches Zentralblatt

Obviously, then, other criteria than scarcity and price must apply for the inclusion of serials in rare book collections. Mary Spalding has described some of these:

Magazines containing the first printing of well-known authors often sell at fancy prices. One finds the *New York Saturday Press* for 1865 and 1866 containing articles by Josh Billings, James Russell Lowell, Artemus Ward, and "Jim Smiley and His Jumping Frog" by Mark Twain, selling for $22; and the third and fifth volumes of the *New England Magazine* with contributions by Longfellow, Holmes, and Whittier, with Whittier's contributions corrected by himself in pencil bringing $190 for the two volumes! The *Godey's Lady's Book* and *Peterson's Magazine,* because of engraved fashion plates are often collectors' items. The first issue of most magazines is valuable. Collectors are on the outlook for these first issues, and competition in the market shoots their prices skyward. Los Angeles Public Library contained a complete file of the British aviation magazine, Flight, except for that valuable Volume 1, Number 1, and was glad to pay $50 for this issue.[1]

More systematically, the principal types of serials to be found in treasure rooms, apart from bibliographical tools, are—

Association copies

Early printed material; for example, almanacs, documents of the first fourteen Congresses, newspapers, statute laws, as well as items in check lists such as Beer,[2] Brigham,[3] or Crane and Kaye[4]

[1] Mary L. Spalding, "Current Use Versus Permanent Preservation of Periodicals as Reflected in Organization," *A.L.A. Bulletin* 34:P-201-02, 1940.

[2] William Beer, *Checklist of American Periodicals, 1741-1800* (Worcester, Mass.: American Antiquarian Soc., 1923).

[3] Clarence S. Brigham, *History and Bibliography of American Newspapers, 1690-1820* (Worcester, Mass.: American Antiquarian Soc., 1947). 2v.

[4] R. S. Crane and F. B. Kaye, *A Census of British Newspapers and Periodicals, 1620-1800* (Chapel Hill: Univ. of North Carolina Pr., 1927).

Little magazines[5]

Publications of special presses

Serials that contain the first printing of works of collected authors,[6] e.g., the *London Magazine* which contains original contributions by Keats and Lamb. The issues of these serials that are preserved in rare book rooms are often single numbers of ordinary magazines in their original wrappers. They are frequently classified, not as serials, but among the works of the particular collected author as though they were monographs. A rare book collection may well have parts of the same magazine scattered among the works of several different authors; but unless the serials are unusually significant in themselves no serial record should be made of them. Mention may be made of the Tauchnitz Edition among other types of serial publications which are of interest to rare book rooms because they contain the first appearance of an author's work. For example, the first edition, sometimes even the only edition, of some of the works of Anthony Trollope appeared in that series.

Wood pulp publications, sometimes with literary connections and sometimes with acquired value, e.g., the Beadle Dime Novels[7]

Of passing interest from a serial point of view are the issues of monographs in serial form, especially following the success of Dickens' *Pickwick Papers* (though the serialization of novels goes back much earlier, for example to some of the works of Daniel Defoe).[8] Strictly speaking, however, the part-issues are monographs, at least in retrospect, despite their original serial form.

The description of the *KS class for rare serials in Brown's *Guide to the Reference Collections of the New York Public Library* gives some idea of the kinds of serials collected as rarities:

Almanacs—about 2500 pieces—are a rich feature. The collection in-

[5] For a description and listing of little magazines see Frederick J. Hoffman, *The Little Magazine, a History and a Bibliography,* by F. J. Hoffman, Charles Allen, C. F. Ulrich (2d ed.; Princeton: Princeton Univ. Pr., 1947).

[6] For fiction writers see John Carter and Michael Sadleir, *Victorian Fiction, an Exhibition of Original Editions* ([London]: Cambridge Univ. Pr., 1947), especially pages 1-2 and 10-14 which relate to magazine serials and fiction series. See also the relevant passages in: John Carter, *Collecting Detective Fiction* (London: Constable, [1934]) ; Graham Pollard, *Serial Fiction* (London: Constable, [1934]) ; and Michael Sadleir, *Collecting "Yellowbacks"* (London: Constable, [1934]). These three pamphlets appeared originally in *New Paths in Book Collecting* (London: Constable, 1934).

[7] See Albert Johannsen, *The House of Beadle and Adams and Its Dime and Nickel Novels; the Story of a Vanished Literature* (Norman: Oklahoma Univ. Pr., [1950]), 2v.; also Frank P. O'Brien, *The Beadle Collection of Dime Novels Given to the New York Public Library* (New York, 1922).

[8] For example, *Robinson Crusoe* was first published in *The Original London Post, or Heathcot's Intelligence* from October 7, 1719, to October 19, 1720. Only three copies are known today, and like similar serial publications of literary classics, particularly in the eighteenth century, they are naturally valuable.

cludes, among the American through 1820, the only known copy of the 1649 edition of Danforth's *Almanack,* printed at Cambridge . . .

Directories in this collection include only the few printed in America before 1801 . . .

Newspapers constitute one of the important collections in the Library. Early files and rare issues are numerous, among them, Bradford's *New-York Gazette,* Zenger's *Weekly Journal* (best file known), Parker's *Post-Boy,* and excellent files of Holt's *Journal,* Gaine's *Mercury,* and of Farley's *American Chronicle* (the only known run; incomplete). Outside New York, the representation of Philadelphia newspapers includes the second-best known sets of Franklin's *Gazette* and Bradford's *Journal* . . .

The Library's collection of rare American periodicals is excellent. The representation of eighteenth-century sets is the third-best in existence . . . Only the very rare, irreplaceable material is actually kept in *K; the collection in this sub-class is therefore small.[9]

The collection at the Library of Congress is somewhat similar. Among the principal collections in its Rare Books Division are the following serial classes:

Almanacs, chiefly those printed in America between the 17th and early 19th century, together with some English and other foreign ones. 5019 pieces, arranged according to State, if United States, or by country of origin.

Dime novels, 19,543 volumes, arranged according to the "series" in which they were published.

Documents of the first fourteen Congresses of the United States, 20,532 pieces, arranged according to the order of their listing in A. W. Greely's *Public Documents of the First Fourteen Congresses* (Washington, 1900, 1904).

Harry Houdini Library of books, pamphlets, periodicals, and miscellany on magic and spiritualism. About 4350 titles arranged by L. C. classification, with unclassified pieces in appropriate groups at the end. The large assortment of periodicals on magic and the psychic includes such titles as *The Sphinx* (Chicago and Kansas City, 1902-19); *The Magic Circular* (London, 1906-24): *The Mahatma* (New York, 1895, 1898-1906); and *The Spiritualist Newspaper* (London, 1877-82).

Magazines, American and foreign, chiefly of the eighteenth and nineteenth centuries. 825 titles, arranged by L. C. classification.

Newspapers, American and foreign, down through the year 1800; 1637 volumes of American newspapers arranged according to the order given in the Ingram-Parsons *A Check List of American Eighteenth Century Newspapers in the Library of Congress* (Washington, 1936);

[9] Karl Brown, *A Guide to the Reference Collections of the New York Public Library* (New York, 1951), p.217-18.

> 492 volumes of foreign newspapers arranged by country and place; and about 3500 unbound issues, American and foreign.[10]

No special cataloging rules are required for those serials that are treated as serials in rare book collections. The features can be brought out in notes. On the other hand, the rare book cataloger qua bibliographer may be interested in check-listing some or all of the serials in the treasure room, thereby giving attention to variant issues and to issues with the original wrappers.[11] Much less attention is paid to such matters in everyday serial work.

Check lists which supplement the cataloging may in turn lead to the publication of significant bibliographies. This is true at the Library of Congress, where

> newspapers issued before 1801 are controlled by typed shelf-lists prepared by the Serials Division and by the *Check List of American Eighteenth Century Newspapers in the Library of Congress* (Washington, 1936) and *Check List of Foreign Newspapers in the Library of Congress* (Washington, 1929).[12]

Sometimes the rare book catalogs may have special sections of serial interest, as at the Library of Congress where there is a supplementary catalog of American almanacs. The almanac catalog has three different arrangements: by title, date, and place of publication.

Manuscripts and archives

There are many serials, a few of them in printed form and more of them in processed form, in collections of manuscripts and archives. They may not be treated as serials but rather as archives or in manuscript groups. For instance, the annual reports in the files of the American Board of Commissioners for Foreign Missions in the Houghton Library at Harvard University are not bound together in regular library style; instead, anyone looking for them must go through the file year by year, discovering each issue amid a mass of other material all bound together to reflect a year's over-all activities. And in the League of Nations Archives, the file copies of League documents were not held together as a set, but were distributed archivally.

Serials in manuscript, processed, and printed form are to be found in the archives of governments and other institutions, such as universities, and in the local history repositories of libraries and societies. These serials vary from the extremely important to the utterly trivial,

---

[10] Taken from the Library of Congress *Departmental & Divisional Manuals* 18:8-10, 1951, and from the Library of Congress Rare Books Division's *Guide to Its Collections and Services* (Washington, 1950), p.51.

[11] For this type of description see J. D. Cowley, *Bibliographical Description and Cataloguing* (London: Grafton, 1939), p.167-73.

[12] Library of Congress *Departmental & Divisional Manuals* 18:15, 1951.

with the emphasis to a large extent on the ephemera, even in public archives where there are documents of the utmost importance for the historian. They include: annual reports; club publications; court records; commencement, concert, football, and other programs; commercial catalogs; examination papers; minutes of meetings; notices of faculty meetings, town meetings, etc.; political pronouncements and records of all kinds; student magazines, yearbooks, etc.; trade union material; voting lists; and a host of other material. Serials in the National Archives include

> messages, proclamations, orders, rules, and regulations; . . . census schedules and scientific data; statistical tables and compilations; reports of departments, bureaus, commissions, and officials; treaties, conventions, and records of diplomatic negotiations; laws, legislative journals, and minutes and reports of committees; petitions and resolutions; and court records.[13]

Sometimes the ephemeral material is mounted in scrapbooks without regard to its serial or non-serial character. Sometimes the more substantial publications, such as municipal documents, are bound in yearly groupings to give a cross section of life and activities. But more commonly an archival scheme provides a place for each type of publication, in which case the classification may furnish the most important approach to the collection. In view of the trivial nature of much of the material and the relatively slight use to which it will be put, the catalog records should be simple and brief, despite the fact that they generally represent the primary or only listing for many of the items. Self-cataloging may suffice for large areas, and the shelf-listing can be held to a bare minimum except when normal procedures can be justified.

These shortcuts are similar to the ones a special library may employ; but vertical file systems are seldom adopted since the material does not have to be readily accessible. The objective is preservation rather than ready use or frequent service.

---

[13] National Archives, *Manual of Information about the National Archives for Government Officials* (Washington, 1941), p.1.

CHAPTER 15

Publications of the League of Nations, United Nations, and Organization of American States

THE PUBLICATIONS of international governmental organizations are predominantly serial in character. When they are not serials in their own right (i.e., periodicals, annuals, etc.), they are largely held together by symbols which serve as serial notation; and in the case of League of Nations and United Nations documents, when the symbol is lacking, the serial control element may be derived from the sales number. In fact, among United Nations documents the principal nonserials are the items issued in all manner of languages by the Department of Public Information for publicity purposes.

Almost all libraries experience difficulty in acquiring the publications of these organizations because numerous documents in a series are unavailable to them. Some documents, especially those pertaining to the Security Council, are classified as restricted and are not procurable until they have been declassified;[1] others may be reproduced in relatively small quantities and limited to official internal use. The distribution programs have never been thorough, so that one library may have a document which another lacks.[2] And sometimes differences in sets come about because of a personal connection. Thus, for

[1] The master microfilm file of United Nations documents maintained in the United Nations Archives includes all documents: restricted, limited, or not.

[2] Several times a year the World Peace Foundation and the Harvard College Library have occasion to compare their holdings. They often find that one library has a document which the other lacks.

example, a professor who has held an important post in an international governmental agency may turn over his files of documents to the library of the institution he is connected with, which thereupon comes into possession of some documents it could hardly acquire otherwise.[3]

The frequent issuance of revisions, corrigenda, and addenda is a major problem in collecting the publications of international governmental agencies. When these come after the relevant numbers have been bound, it is necessary to bind them up separately, commonly in pamphlet binders. The United Nations Library itself cannot avoid doing this. Even though the binding of a volume is postponed for a year or so to allow for the arrival of such additional material, the possibility that further items will appear that should go in a bound volume is ever present. The extent of the problem can be judged by studying the list of revisions, corrigenda, and addenda regularly given in the *United Nations Documents Index*.[4]

A large proportion of the documents issued by international governmental organizations appear in an English edition, either originally or in translation. Sometimes, however, the only edition is in French or Spanish. For instance, the publications of the Universal Postal Union appear chiefly only in French. A library which maintains files in several languages must at times check to see whether a document not available in English is present in the French or Spanish set. For the same reason, a library which desires to maintain only a file of the documents in English may occasionally find it necessary to insert a document in another language, or its collection will be defective.

League of Nations

Surprisingly enough there is no definitive set of League of Nations documents in existence. The League of Nations Library (now the United Nations Library at Geneva) did not compile a set as the documents were published; instead, the documents were officially preserved throughout the League of Nations archives. For some time the United Nations Library at Geneva has been attempting to repair the omission and to assemble a complete file. In view of these circumstances, the best existing set may well be the one in the United Nations Headquarters Library in New York, which was gathered by the Woodrow Wilson Foundation with much assiduity. Moreover, there is no official

---

[3] It was in large measure thanks to the enterprise of the Library of Congress staff members who were present that documents of the San Francisco Conference were run off and assembled for libraries.

[4] *United Nations Documents Index; United Nations and Specialized Agencies Documents and Publications* (New York, 1950-).

check list of League of Nations documents[5] comparable with the check lists and index produced by the United Nations, so there is no real way of determining the completeness of a set. The Library of Congress cards, which include thousands of entries supplied by the Woodrow Wilson Foundation Library, afford, in conjunction with Carroll's *Key to League of Nations Documents,* the best check.

The problems of assembling, cataloging, classifying, and binding League documents, which vexed librarians in the twenties and thirties,[6] are for the most part no longer a matter of active concern. There does remain, however, the serious question of the future of the bound files of League documents, since so many of the processed documents are disintegrating rapidly. Steps should therefore be taken to develop files for preservation, either through microreproduction or through offset printing.

In the transition from the League of Nations to the United Nations it was necessary for librarians to decide how to treat serial publications that carried over from one organization to the other.[7] Generally the wise course of action was to set up the serial in the United Nations collection, even though recataloging and reclassification were thereby involved. If some of the serials in question were classified apart from the main set of League publications, the procedure was to recatalog them. Thus the Library of Congress recataloged under "United Nations. Library, Geneva" the *Liste mensuelle d'ouvrages catalogués* which began publication in 1928. It was classified in Z, not in JX with the main set; at the same time, an added entry under "League of Nations. Library" was indicated.

Many libraries acquired a set of Library of Congress cards to go with their League collections. These cards were commonly not inter-

---

[5] The unofficial check list is Marie J. Carroll, *Key to League of Nations Documents Placed on Public Sale, 1920-1929* (Boston: World Peace Foundation, 1930); Supplement 1-4 (Boston, 1931-38). Of value too is A. C. von Breycha-Vauthier, *Sources of Information; a Handbook on the Publications of the League of Nations* (New York: Columbia Univ. Pr., 1939). A more recent work is Hans Aufricht, *Guide to League of Nations Publications; a Bibliographical Survey of the Work of the League, 1920-1947* (New York: Columbia Univ. Pr., 1951).

[6] See, among others: Clarence E. Walton, "Classifying, Cataloging, and Binding League of Nations Publications," *Library Journal* 55:155-59, 1930; also his "The Classification of the Documents of the League of Nations," *Proceedings* of the Catalog Section, American Library Association, 1929, p.70-86; and T. Franklin Currier, "The League of Nations Publications: a Simplified Treatment," *Catalogers' and Classifiers' Yearbook* 2:99-102, 1931.

[7] No such decision was necessary for publications of the International Labour Organisation which was carried over intact from the League of Nations to the United Nations—even to the spelling of its name. For the problem in general, see Marie J. Carroll, "League of Nations Documents Comparable with or Continued in United Nations Publications," *College and Research Libraries* 13:44-53, 1952.

filed in the public and official catalogs, but were housed in special files near the publications themselves. The League of Nations catalog so constituted consisted of four parts: main cards, added entries for symbols, title entries, and subject cards. Now that the League of Nations has gone out of existence most libraries are advised to transfer the cards to their regular catalogs, the symbols being treated as a supplementary file under League of Nations.

One reason for constituting the Library of Congress cards as a special League of Nations catalog was that the headings used on them were greatly simplified because of the difficulties encountered in determining the normal corporate heading. Walton found in this procedure

> a tacit admission that our usual cataloging principles have broken down, to which some would object. I suppose the most direct criticism of the Library of Congress cards for League material lies in their frequent ambiguity on the question of real authorship; yet on this point we must remember that the truth about authorship is often very hard to discover, even in Geneva.[8]

Actually, it was not so much a question of the breaking down of cataloging principles as of a large-scale misuse of library cataloging. The majority of League documents should have been check-listed rather than cataloged, a situation which was fortunately realized by the United Nations Library in time to see that adequate check lists of United Nations documents were provided. Consequently the cataloging of United Nations documents need not give rise to the problems encountered in recording League publications.

United Nations

Already United Nations documents are more numerous than League of Nations publications. They exist in English, French, Spanish, Russian, and Chinese editions in descending order of completeness. In addition, some publications issued by the Department of Public Information have an edition in almost every existing language; while unofficially some United Nations documents have been republished in various languages. Often the unofficial edition or translation is an independent monograph, although it may carry the symbol for the original, and sometimes it is part of a non-United Nations series.

Beginning in 1951 symbols have been assigned to United Nations documents generally. Prior to that date some publications lacked a symbol. The visible index entries for United Nations documents should utilize these symbols. They should not be made in the typical way by author or title. By means of the symbols it is comparatively easy to

[8] Clarence E. Walton, "Classifying, Cataloging, and Binding League of Nations Publications," *Library Journal* 55:158, 1930.

check each successive issue of the *United Nations Documents Index* against the visible index records to discover gaps among both the regular documents and the revisions, corrigenda, and addenda. This is an essential procedure because, unlike other serials, the serial notation represented by the symbols does not provide a control element. Consequently the ordinary routines for claiming missing numbers are a waste of time for United Nations documents, so many of them being classified as restricted or limited. An "R," an "L," or some other device should be added in the checking square on the visible index entry whenever it is discovered that a document is unprocurable. The documents that are not serials in their own right should generally be checked off like numbered series.

Prompt follow-up work based on the *United Nations Documents Index* is of great importance. The stock of some documents is exhausted rapidly, and the stock of processed material in general is held no longer than two years. The index discloses the publications available to depository and subscribing libraries; it omits restricted (that is, confidential) items and internal papers. Thus for follow-up work everything may be requested that is not marked "Limited."

The *United Nations Documents Index* is a valuable acquisition and reference tool, both for libraries that acquire the publications on a global basis and for those that wish to be selective. Information concerning the distribution and sale of the documents is given in each issue, preceding the actual list. An asterisk is added to the entry for documents which summarize the work of an organ of the United Nations, which represent the final results of international conferences or research projects, or which are works of reference such as bibliographies, handbooks, and yearbooks. Any library, by checking and acquiring these starred items regularly, can build up a basic working collection of United Nations publications.

In the United Nations Library, as in most libraries that acquire the documents on a global basis, comparatively few of the documents are cataloged or need to be cataloged:

> The vast mass of United Nations and Specialized Agency publications are now serviced through the monthly index UNDI. In addition, the cards prepared by the Documents Index Unit will provide the special floor catalogue for this material. The author and subject cards will be held for a five-year period, but the entries for document symbols will be held for one year only. This threefold catalogue (author, subject, and symbol) will be located in such a way as to provide a common tool for the United Nations collection and the Specialized Agency collection.
>
> Standard catalogue records for selected items may, however, be necessary or desirable to supplement UNDI and the special floor catalogue. This special treatment will be given only to a very small percentage of the documents, since we do not want to duplicate unnecessarily the functions of the

monthly index. Classes of material which may receive regular cataloguing treatment are: 1) important monographs; 2) unofficial editions and translations; and 3) the main series of documents. A main entry only will generally suffice, since the records will for the most part take the form of a finding list.[9]

It should be clear that the situation with regard to United Nations documents is completely different from that which prevailed in League of Nations days. Then there was no official check list or subject index. These do exist for United Nations publications, and they alter the picture radically. Accordingly, relatively few United Nations documents should be cataloged, and even those should be treated as simply as can be because the *United Nations Documents Index* and the various check lists are a better key than catalog records could provide, a key that should be utilized like the *Readers' Guide* and similar tools.

The Library of Congress has entered into an agreement with the United Nations Library whereby the latter indicates the publications which it thinks should be cataloged. So Library of Congress cards represent the extent to which United Nations documents should be cataloged in most libraries. The bulk of the documents can be organized as a self-cataloging collection, the approach to which is through the *United Nations Documents Index* and the various check lists that record the publications issued prior to its inception. Thus the cataloging of United Nations documents is vastly different from that for League of Nations publications.

Nixon and Chamberlin have questioned the catalog entries for United Nations documents made by most institutions, including the Library of Congress. They maintain that

the author entry for each United Nations document should follow the structure of the United Nations in as much detail as possible.

The reason for this proposal is, since the structure of the United Nations is functional, if the above procedure is followed, the United Nations organization itself provides extensive subject guidance. Experience in libraries maintaining large United Nations collections indicates increasingly the absolute need for a knowledge of structure. In addition, the wealth of bibliographical tools prepared by the United Nations Secretariat are arranged according to structure . . .

It is strongly advised that the author entries include the name of the ultimate organ or sub-organ responsible for the document. The single exception to this practice is the entry *United Nations. Charter,* which should be used for texts of the charter. For all other entries, there must be a subdivision naming one of the six principal organs mentioned in Article 7 of the Charter of the United Nations, and in most cases, the name of a suborgan should be provided . . .

---

[9] United Nations Library, *Manual of the Cataloguing Unit* (Lake Success, N.Y., 1950), p.34.

Since most of the users of the library, and many cataloguers, will not be familiar with the structure of the United Nations, it is necessary to use an extensive system of cross references from every variation of author under which the entries may be searched.[10]

The bulk of the pamphlet by Nixon and Chamberlin is devoted to a listing of United Nations headings as conceived along these lines. As examples of the indirect headings they recommend, the following may be cited:

United Nations. Economic and Social Council. Commission on Human Rights.

United Nations. Secretariat. Library.

United Nations. Security Council. United Nations Commission for India and Pakistan.

Some of the headings are unconscionably long and unsuited to catalog entries. Examples are:

United Nations. Economic and Social Council. Economic, Employment and Development Commission. Temporary Sub-Commission on Economic Reconstruction of Devastated Areas. Working Group for Europe and Africa. Sub-Committee III (Southern Europe and Africa).

United Nations. General Assembly. Committee to Assist the Secretary-General in Negotiations with the United States Government Regarding the Arrangements Necessary as a Result of the Establishment of the Seat of the United Nations in the United States of America.

United Nations. Security Council. Sub-Committee on the Palestinian Question, to Consider Amendments and Revisions to the Second Draft Resolution Submitted by China and the United Kingdom and to Prepare a Revised Draft in Consultation with the Acting Mediator in Palestine.

United Nations. Trusteeship Council. Committee to Join, with Respect to Clauses Concerning the Trusteeship Council, the Committee on Negotiations with the Inter-Governmental Agencies of the Economic and Social Council.

In addition to the length of the headings, note that this theory relies on official instead of customary forms of name. Thus the Library of Congress heading "United Nations. Secretary-General" is passed over in favor of either "United Nations. Executive Office of the Secretary-General" or "United Nations. Secretariat. Secretary-General, Executive Office of." It also tends to put material under corporate headings when a title entry would be better. So the *United Nations Bulletin* (which the Library of Congress enters under its title, with an added entry for the Department of Public Information which issues it)

---

[10] Emily O. Nixon and Waldo Chamberlin, *How to Catalogue United Nations Documents* ([New York, 1952]. New York University Conference on United Nations Documents, May 19, 1952, Paper no. 3), p.1-2.

is entered, according to Nixon and Chamberlin, under "United Nations. Secretariat. Dept. of Public Information."

Libraries are cautioned against following any such plan. Trouble and expense will inevitably follow the adoption of headings based on the structure of the organization and on long and involved official forms of name. The very fact that the Nixon-Chamberlin system requires an extensive system of cross references to become workable should be a warning in itself.

The battle over direct and indirect headings was fought many years ago, and the decision went in favor of the direct heading. Since libraries use "U. S. Bureau of Insular Affairs" and not "U. S. War Dept. Bureau of Insular Affairs," it is natural for them to prefer the direct form for United Nations headings. As in other organizations, functions are shifted in the United Nations. If a direct heading has been followed, no change in wording may be necessary when a unit is relocated, but if an indirect heading has been favored all entries must be changed. It should also be pointed out that the simple, direct approach in the catalog adds to the serviceability of the collection. The symbols and the *United Nations Documents Index* emphasize the structure; the catalog records should definitely take the reader's point of view, which is apt to be non-technical, inclining to headings like "United Nations. Secretary-General" without interposing the word "Secretariat" or anything else.

A desirable cataloging policy can be briefly summarized. There are comparatively few true serials, that is, periodicals, annuals, etc., among United Nations documents. These serials should be cataloged in the regular way. The great majority of the documents take on a serial character because of the symbols. The question then is whether these factitious serials should be analyzed as such. In most libraries analyzing must be held to a minimum, especially the analyzing of government documents. So it is with United Nations documents. The check lists and the *United Nations Documents Index* must serve as the detailed author and subject approach to most of the material. For the rest, the entries should be simple and direct; there is no occasion for a more elaborate scheme which would be expensive to follow and troublesome to all users, staff and readers alike.

Fortunately, the classification of United Nations documents can be just as simple as the cataloging. It should be based on the symbols, if it does not actually incorporate them. Thereby the collection becomes self-cataloging to a large extent. In order to curtail numbers, the base notation in the Dewey Decimal classification or the Library of Congress classification scheme can be reduced to the letters UN. This device is especially desirable in libraries that use Dewey and that have a fairly extensive collection of United Nations publications, otherwise the notation will become too long. The United Nations Library, which uses the abridged English edition of the Universal Decimal classification, has followed this plan. Under the letters UN (which stand for 341.13) it has developed a special scheme for the official and unofficial documents and for works about the United Nations. Since it preserves sets in the various working languages, it has added a letter denoting the language to the classification symbol. So UNF is the notation for the French documents, and parallels the scheme for the documents in English. Libraries that find it desirable to develop a special scheme for use under a class UN should consider adopting the one worked out for the United Nations Library.[11]

Walton found that 56 per cent of the libraries he investigated kept their League of Nations documents together as a unit.[12] There is a much stronger reason for keeping all United Nations publications together, namely, the existence of the *United Nations Documents Index* which is the key to them.

The documents which may be separated from the main collection are those of the specialized agencies, though it should be remembered that the *Index* is still the key to them. Libraries may well have the publications of the International Labour Organisation classified under labor as a carry-over from League of Nations days. Justification may be found, too, for detaching the publications of agencies like the World Health Organization and the World Meteorological Organization from the main library collection.

One reason why the *United Nations Documents Index* is so useful is that it employs the terminology found in the documents themselves. Library lists of subject headings are somewhat conservative, especially when confronted with new ideas like "trust territories" which are, and yet are not, the equivalent of subject headings for colonies and colonization. The United Nations Library has adjusted its list of subject headings to the new terminology—it could not, for instance, have "Civil rights" as a subject heading when everyone at the United Nations spoke of "Human rights."

Microreproductions of United Nations documents are on the market in two forms, microfilm and Readex microprint. The microfilm edition through 1951 may be procured from the World Peace Foundation, thereafter from the United Nations. The World Peace

---

[11] The United Nations Library scheme is outlined in Fernando Caballero-Marsal, Jorgen K. Nielsen, and Harry N. M. Winton, "United Nations Documents in the United Nations Library: Organization and Servicing," *Journal of Cataloging and Classification* 7:69-72, 1951.

[12] Walton, *op. cit.*, p.157.

Foundation maintains files of the processed documents for about three years; then it replaces them by microfilm copies.

Organization of American States

Since 1948 the Organization of American States has existed as an agency somewhat like a regional United Nations. Its secretariat is the Pan American Union, which retains its original name despite its change in functions. A number of serial publications have carried over into the new organization. Some reclassification was necessary to cope with the new situation, especially as the Inter-American conferences, beginning with the ninth, fall within the province of the Organization of American States as well as the Pan American Union.

Many libraries will prefer to classify the specialized organizations and conferences by subject, leaving under the Organization of American States such units as the Council, Secretary-General, Inter-American conferences, Meeting of Consultation of Foreign Ministers, Inter-American Economic and Social Council, and the Pan American Union with its various departments. Affiliated with the Organization of American States are various specialized organizations that likewise should be classified by subject.

CHAPTER 16

Reprints

SERIAL LIBRARIANS have comparatively little interest in reprints. These are for the most part the concern of the acquisition staff and the monograph catalogers.

In one way or another libraries manage to acquire considerable quantities of reprints, preprints, separates, etc. of material from journals. Scientific libraries in particular may accumulate them by the tens of thousands. Collections of such size are frequently arranged alphabetically by author in a self-cataloging file. McGrath, who describes the various ways of handling reprints, favors an alphabetical arrangement, at least for scientific libraries; and to it he would add a listing of the articles under the name of the journals. However, when the reprints are acquired for informational purposes, he favors a vertical-file arrangement by subject.[1]

A few reprints are worth cataloging individually, and some must be processed because of local interest or pressure.[2] In earlier years more reprints were cataloged than is the case now when material for cataloging tends to be screened more carefully. There is still somewhat of a tendency to give special consideration to a reprint when it is distributed in the form of a doctoral dissertation; but in most libraries there is no reason for treating such dissertations differently from other reprints, even when they contain a brief vita which the original lacks. The institution in which the dissertation originates is, of course, an exception.

Collections of reprints, particularly those of local faculty members, may be cataloged as such and bound up as a unit. The cataloging can often consist of a mere form card, stating that the library has a collection of reprints by this particular author and giving the call number. Collections about a person or subject can be treated similarly.

---

[1] N. E. McGrath, "Reprints," *South African Libraries* 17:167-70, 1950.

[2] For the Library of Congress rule for "detached copies," see *Rules for Descriptive Cataloging in the Library of Congress* (Washington, 1949), p.43-44. For a technicality relating to some dissertation reprints, see page 11 of that code.

In acquisition work it is a generally accepted convention that items bought from secondhand catalogs may be returned for credit if they prove on receipt to be reprints but were not designated as such in the bookseller's catalog. Also, in gift work a postal card as an acknowledgement to the author will suffice, and there need be no record of the gift in the donor file.

The serial staff may be asked to check some reprints to see if the library has the periodical in which the article appeared. If it has, the reprint can be the more safely discarded. If it does not have the periodical, there may be a presumptive case in favor of keeping and cataloging the reprint.

Only cataloged reprints should be counted in recording the size of a library. Special files of uncataloged reprints may be counted for the sake of the record, if desired, but the figures should be kept entirely independent.

Monographs in series

Replacement of the standard stock of monographs is one of the constant activities of acquisition librarians in school and public libraries. Orton's *Catalog of Reprints in Series*[3] facilitates the selection of replacement copies through listing the different publishers' series in which standard titles are issued. Librarians can predetermine which of these series they are ready to accept; thereafter it is a comparatively easy task to order replacement copies of standard publications. No series record should be made anywhere in the library for this type of publication.

A kept-together series tends to resist the addition of reprints and editions of a given monograph in the series, especially when a number of the monographs are bound together. Consequently it may be best to treat such reprints and new editions as independent monographs, and to insert a note in the original edition specifying that a later edition may be found elsewhere. This device is to help the person who makes a serial approach to an item; it is not necessary for extra copies kept for subject value, since readers and staff should always check the catalog to see if extra copies are available anywhere.[4]

---

[3] Robert M. Orton, *Catalog of Reprints in Series* (New York: Wilson, 1940-).

[4] At the searching stage, some monographs in series may best be treated serially while others should be checked as monographs. For less common items that are more likely to be in kept-together sets, it may be simpler to route the material through the serial checkers first. But for more common items there may be economy in having them searched as monographs. The analytical entry in the card catalog may give desirable information about the number of copies already in the library, information which will be an aid in deciding whether still another copy is needed. In general the serial records should not keep track of added copies.

In some libraries there is another reason why it is desirable to scatter the reprints and new editions of monographs in kept-together series. There may be duplicate sets of kept-together series. In that event all of copy 1 may be shelved as a unit, followed by all of copy 2, as duplicate sets of an author's works are arranged.[5] In these circumstances it is generally inadvisable to add the reprints and new editions to the sets, just as it is inadvisable to add multiple copies of any individual monograph in a kept-together series. Instead, each of these types should be classified by subject.

Sometimes part or all of a serial that is not a monograph series is reissued in such a way that catalogers may debate whether the resultant work is a serial or a non-serial. A number of Argentine periodicals have been reprinted in such a way as to raise this question. Each case must be decided on its own merits, but runs should generally be handled by the serial staff, partly because of the special serial records they may have to make. But when a single issue of a periodical or newspaper is republished in book form, it should generally be treated as a monograph, with no serial record whatsoever.

---

[5] Obviously this argument does not hold in a library which intercalates the individual volumes of duplicate kept-together sets. In such libraries it is easier to add multiple copies, reprints, and editions as integral parts of a kept-together series, provided, that is, the bound volumes do not comprise a number of titles.

CHAPTER 17

Abstracting and Indexing

IN THE SAME WAY that libraries consider serials as basic to their research and information programs, so too they regard the promotion of adequate abstracting and indexing services as of first importance in making the contents of serials more accessible to research workers. More than a thousand services abstract or index the contributions in journals of various kinds, according to a check list issued by the International Federation for Documentation,[1] yet countless titles are not covered at all, while others are covered by two or more services. The duplication of effort exists on a national basis as well as within subject fields. For instance, there is overlap between the British *Subject Index to Periodicals*[2] and the American *Readers' Guide* and *International Index to Periodicals;* and there is much duplication, for instance in the medical and biological fields. Some services are slow, and some are appreciably more difficult than others to consult. Bibliographical practices and standards vary greatly.

Dr. Bradford has on several occasions made known the extent of the problem. According to him:

It has been estimated that in one year as much as 15,000 useful scientific periodicals are published, and that these contain about 750,000 useful articles. Whilst some three hundred abstracting and indexing periodicals, which appear during a similar period, include together about the same number of references to useful articles, but cover less than half of these. It follows therefore that enough work is being done to abstract or index all the useful articles published, if only this energy were rightly directed. . .

Abstracting services concentrate upon the comparatively few periodicals where many articles on the subject may be expected and ignore the very large remainder, where the frequency of the articles is far less, but the aggre-

[1] *List of Current Abstracting and Indexing Services* (The Hague: International Federation for Documentation, 1949). The list relates mainly to the fields of pure and applied science.

[2] For the bibliography of this and other indexes mentioned the reader is referred to Constance M. Winchell, *Guide to Reference Books* (7th ed.; Chicago: American Library Assn., 1952).

gate of articles is greater. It would be impracticable for them to do otherwise. To pick out all the articles on a subject would involve the scrutiny of many thousand periodicals, most of which would certainly contain less than one article a year. The same periodicals would need to be scrutinized again from other points of view by other independent abstracting agencies: an obviously time wasting task, which they do not attempt. The result is that a majority of the useful articles is missed.[3]

Bradford's findings are borne out by Varossieau's systematic study. Varossieau found that the 42 largest abstracting and indexing services list 787,010 titles a year, while 402 services list 1,195,639 articles. These are truly impressive figures, but Varossieau goes on to point out that:

Further comparison of the numbers of periodicals abstracted on an average per service and the numbers of abstracts or titles produced on an average per service, leads to the conclusion that only 20% of the articles produced per periodical are abstracted on an average by one of the 402 services.[4]

Germany has produced the most comprehensive national indexes.[5] The monumental *Bibliographie der deutschen Zeitschriftenliteratur* has in the course of a year indexed more than 4500 publications in the German language in all fields of knowledge. It covers journals, transactions, *Festschriften,* and other collections. A complementary work, the *Bibliographie der fremdsprachigen Zeitschriftenliteratur,* indexes another 2000 publications in languages other than German. Still fur-

[3] S. C. Bradford, "A Plan for Complete Scientific Documentation," *Review of Documentation* 14:54, 1947. In commenting on the Bradford-Varossieau figures, F. Donker Duyvis said: "We may roughly estimate the amount of science abstracts and indexed titles to be one million and a half . . . Surely the estimate Ralph Shaw gave of the number of valuable articles in science and technology is more than twice as high as the number Bradford mentions and perhaps nearer the truth." ("Secretarial Report on the Survey of Abstracting Services," *Review of Documentation* 16:47, 1949.) He went on to say that the goal for indexing services is the complete registering of two million articles a year. Shaw's figures were developed about 1941 in connection with postwar planning for libraries. For a proposed international index to scientific and technical literature he estimated that 40,000 scientific journals and approximately 1,850,000 important, good, or fair articles are issued annually. The third edition of the *World List of Scientific Periodicals Published in the Years 1900-1950* (London: Butterworth, 1952) lists in the vicinity of 50,000 titles. With due allowance for the steady increase in the number of scientific periodicals from 1947 to date, these various estimates should be compared with Fry's estimate for 1950 of 50,000 scientific periodicals and 1,850,000 individual articles [Bernard M. Fry, *Library Organization and Management of Technical Reports Literature* (Washington: Catholic Univ. of America Pr., 1953), p.4.] and with Brummel's later statement that "there are more than 50,000 periodicals dealing with the exact sciences." (L. Brummel, "National and International Organization of Bibliography," *Das Antiquariat* 8:17, 1952.)

[4] W. W. Varossieau, "A Survey of Scientific Abstracting and Indexing Services," *Review of Documentation* 16:44, 1949.

[5] Russian services probably compare very favorably with the German, but since they have been unavailable to other countries for so long it is hard to compare them.

ther, the *Bibliographie der Rezensionen* and the *Halbmonatliches Verzeichnis von Aufsätzen aus deutschen Zeitungen,* which were wartime casualties, covered book reviews and newspaper articles respectively. Between the four the field of German newspapers and periodicals (plus many non-German titles) has been opened up in splendid fashion, but the resultant all-embracing works are not easy to use. Abbreviations are prevalent; titles of the publications indexed are identified only by number in the entries; and the mass of entries under many topics makes checking a matter of patient endeavor.

By contrast, the American plan has favored a clear, simple arrangement for a highly selective group of publications. The Wilson indexes are simple to check by comparison with the German. And since the general Wilson indexes at least are not intended to give extensive coverage of American periodicals, they tend to favor the more popular titles. In this the three general services offer a graded approach: the *Abridged Readers' Guide* covers 35 very popular titles; these are indexed afresh in the *Readers' Guide* along with 82 other popular titles; while the *International Index to Periodicals* inclines somewhat towards scholarly and research periodicals in its 175 titles. Among the three an insignificant number of titles is indexed in relation to total American output or by comparison with the German indexes.

In the *Canadian Periodical Index* with its 38 titles there is a small amount of duplication with the Wilson indexes. There is much more duplication in the British *Subject Index to Periodicals,* which covers some 300 titles but restricts itself to subject entries. (Through 1953 the *Subject Index to Periodicals* indexed 530 journals; in 1954 the local history items were left for a separate local history index to cover.) These general indexes are supplemented by a variety of special indexing and abstracting services, some of which in part duplicate the work of the general indexes, and some of which duplicate each other to a greater or smaller extent. Their scope can be seen from the *Index Bibliographicus.* They relate among other things to agriculture, art, bibliography, biography, biology, book reviews, Catholic publications, chemistry, dentistry, education, engineering, industrial arts, labor, law, library science, mathematics, medicine, nuclear science, photography, physics, physiology, psychology, public affairs, and United Nations documents.

The whole picture is impressive, but unfortunately over-all planning and coordination are lacking. Various associations, including the American Documentation Institute, have attempted to rationalize the indexing and abstracting program. Latterly Unesco has been the focal point for discussions of the problem, and in its deliberations the

Library of Congress has played an active part.[6] Unesco's interest in the matter stems from recommendations made in London in 1946 to the first session of the Preparatory Commission, at which time the Committee on Letters and Philosophy proposed a card index of references to articles in the world's philosophical journals; the Committee on Libraries, Museums, and Special Projects envisaged a world central library to concern itself in part with abstracting and standardization; the Natural Sciences Committee expressed interest in the production of abstracting and reviewing journals in fields not adequately covered; and the Social Science Committee urged the establishment of an abstracting and bibliographical service. All the deliberations and discussions serve to highlight the significance of serial publications for research and information, and thereby the need for adequate tools to disclose their contents.[7]

The abstracting and indexing problems with which Unesco is grappling are reflected in a small way in the Wilson indexes.[8] There is duplication between one and another of them, though the approach and the terminology may differ from index to index. Of the ten educational publications indexed in the *Readers' Guide,* for example, seven are also included in the *Education Index.* Lawler observes that "the *Abridged Readers' Guide* can list under 'education' virtually every relevant article in its thirty-odd magazines; but, of course, the *Education Index* needs hundreds of subdivisions to cover the same field."[9] Further, he points out:

> The *Industrial Arts* editors use "education of workers" in the belief that the education part is more important to their readers than the second part. On the other hand, the editors of *Education Index,* which is entirely concerned with education, stress the opposite thought by using "workers—education."[10]

With the exception of those in the *Readers' Guide,* the periodicals indexed in the Wilson publications are chosen by the subscribers.

---

[6] See, for example, *The Unesco Library of Congress Bibliographical Survey: 1. Bibliographical Services, Their Present State and Possibilities of Improvement* (Washington, 1950). *2. National Development and International Planning of Bibliographical Services* (Paris, 1950).

[7] The most valuable summary of the whole problem is Verner W. Clapp's "Indexing and Abstracting: Recent Past and Lines of Future Development," *College and Research Libraries* 11:197-206, 1950. It should be supplemented by the statistical analysis of W. W. Varossieau, "A Survey of Scientific Abstracting and Indexing Services," *Review of Documentation* 16:25-46, 1949. For a historical study see Verner W. Clapp, "Indexing and Abstracting Services for Serial Literature," *Library Trends* 2:509-21, 1954.

[8] John L. Lawler, *The H. W. Wilson Company; Half a Century of Bibliographic Publishing* (Minneapolis: Univ. of Minnesota Pr., [1950]), p.163-67, lists and describes the various Wilson indexes.

[9] *Ibid.,* p.105.

[10] *Ibid.,* p. 103.

Every publication sent to the company . . . is not automatically entered in an index. The chosen ones are selected, in accordance with long-standing policy, by a vote of the subscribers to each index. Polls are conducted at regular intervals to determine which periodicals, in the opinion of the subscribers, have the greatest reference value. Mere popularity is not enough to justify acceptance; some widely circulated magazines have relatively little worth as sources of research material. The voters also have to consider the problem of balance. Since the indexes are necessarily limited in size, the inclusion of too many journals in one field may mean the exclusion of some other field entirely.[11]

Since the *Readers' Guide* has about 9000 subscribers, the same plan of polling all the subscribers has not been followed. There is some concern, therefore, on the part of the editor to know whether the selection of periodicals for indexing in the *Readers' Guide* is the best possible.[12]

New York University has a valuable and extensive card index to early American periodicals that serves in a very real sense as a complement to Poole.

Some 339 titles of periodicals and a grand total of about 7,000 volumes are indexed more or less completely for the period 1728 to 1870. Few of these titles appear in Poole's Index or in its supplements. Fifty-two of the titles indexed were published before 1800. A limited number of periodicals are indexed from date of publication up to 1930. This work covers a virgin ground of early "Americana," preceding all known periodical indexes, and for the first time makes available to scholars and students a vast store of early periodical literature heretofore practically lost.[13]

Professor Pollard has highlighted the need for adequate abstracting and indexing services by giving several illustrations of advances in science and technology which passed relatively unnoticed for a generation.[14] The best known case is that of Mendel's laws governing the inheritance of characters in plants and animals which were published in the *Verhandlungen* of the Naturforschender Verein in Brünn in 1865 and 1869. There they remained comparatively unknown until

[11] *Ibid.*, p.100; cf. also p.118-19.

[12] See Sarita Robinson, "Are We Indexing the Right Magazines?" *Wilson Library Bulletin* 25:597-98, 1951. For a companion study of the *International Index* see Henry M. Fuller, "International Index under Study by Librarians," *Serial Slants* 5:82-88, 1954.

[13] Nouvart Tashjian, "Periodical Literature Index," *Library Journal* 64:918, 1939. For a more detailed account of this project, see her "New York University Index to Early American Periodical Literature, 1728-1870," *College and Research Libraries* 7:135-37, 1946. The list of periodicals indexed, as well as the entries relating to Emerson, Poe, Whitman, and French fiction, were issued under the title *Index to Early American Periodical Literature, 1728-1870* (New York: Pamphlet Distributing Co., 1941-43. 5 numbers).

[14] A. F. C. Pollard, "The Disordered State of Bibliography and Indications of Its Effect upon Scientific and Technical Progress," *Proceedings* of the British Society for International Bibliography 4:41-52, 1942.

1900 when they were rediscovered and confirmed. Professor Pollard says there is no doubt that the belated discovery of Mendel's work delayed the progress of biology by many years. He gives a parallel case in engineering. The modern airplane was fully described in a French patent granted in 1876, but it was not until 1916 that the French contribution came to light.

CHAPTER 18

Union Lists

THE TOOLS ESSENTIAL to the full utilization of serial publications are indexes and abstracts to disclose the individual contributions by author and subject, and union lists to help in locating sets wherever they may be. Creation and exploitation of these tools have become a feature of modern library economy, and there is evidence which suggests that the accomplishments of the future will dwarf those of the past. Such a prospect is attributable particularly to the planning that is being done at the Library of Congress and in Unesco, just as it is attributable in general to the continued interest of special and general libraries in the creation of more and more of these tools.

The most notable achievement in serial bibliography in the first half of the twentieth century was the publication of numerous union lists of national, local, and subject coverage. The American and Canadian *Union List of Serials* passed through two editions and a number of supplements. As is commonly the case in serial work, the term "serials" is employed in a loose sense in the title of this work. Actually the *Union List of Serials* includes little more than periodicals, periodical-type publications of societies and institutions, and numbered monograph series. For the most part it is concerned with non-governmental material, but it does include government documents when they are periodical in character; and it lists the periodical publications of museums, universities, etc., whether they are private or government establishments. On the other hand, it excludes most titles published in the so-called incunabula period, as well as house organs and a variety of other publications.

As a practical tool, the *Union List of Serials* must be judged on the basis of what it includes. Its outstanding accomplishment is to be found in its successful recording of the holdings of more than 110,000 titles in Canadian and American libraries. It had one unfulfilled hope, because large-scale consolidation of broken sets by contributing libraries did not follow its publication. The Midwest Inter-Library Center has, however, taken a step in this direction by instituting a "fragmentary sets program" whereby member libraries may deposit their partial holdings either unsolicited or in response to a request from the Center made on the basis of an entry in the *Union List of Serials.*

The second edition of the *Union List of Serials* is vastly more reliable than the first, but even so the work must not be taken as a definitive bibliography. A comparison of entries in the two editions will show the abundant occasions on which pronouncements, thought in the first edition to be final, were revised in the second; and there are numerous entries in the second edition that could be revised were more information forthcoming. But this does not detract from the immense contribution to research the *Union List of Serials* has made. It is simply a recognition of the fact that it should be regarded at all times as a working list based on actual holdings. As such it is a magnificent achievement, worth all the effort and cost its compilation entailed.

A counterpart to the *Union List of Serials* is the *List of the Serial Publications of Foreign Governments,* which however has had no supplements or second edition.[1] It was probably wise to keep the two lists separate in the first instance, but the separation has resulted in the comparative neglect of the records for government serials. Part of the success of the *Union List of Serials*—according to Grenfell "the greatest union list ever issued"[2]—came from demonstrating the very possibility of a national list. So extensive an undertaking might easily have been jeopardized if the scope had been enlarged to cover government serials as well. And the independent *List of the Serial Publications of Foreign Governments* has afforded an opportunity to study the deficiencies in the document-collecting program of research libraries generally.

The time is surely ripe, then, for the developments at the Library of Congress which aim at the conversion of the *Union List of Serials* into the comprehensive work its name implies.[3] The pioneer work of the early lists has laid a foundation on which the compiling of an inclusive union list can be undertaken with confidence. The new turn of events means that there will be no third edition of the *Union List of Serials* as such. Instead the basic records will be on punched cards and become the responsibility of the Serial Record Division at the Library of Congress to be developed in correlation with *New Serial Titles.* From these punched cards union lists of various kinds can be

---

[1] *List of the Serial Publications of Foreign Governments, 1815-1931* (New York: Wilson, 1932). This publication is far less reliable bibliographically than the *Union List of Serials.*

[2] David Grenfell, *Periodicals and Serials* (London: Aslib, 1953), p.141.

[3] See Andrew D. Osborn, "The Future of the *Union List of Serials,*" *College and Research Libraries* 15:26-28, 118, 1954.

run off as occasion warrants; in particular, local or regional lists, subject lists, and lists by country of origin. So a new era of union list activity, of greater intensity than ever before, is in sight: ready to serve the increasingly urgent research and informational needs of the second half of the twentieth century, and ready to respond to the unlimited demands for serial publications that the advent of television facsimile reproduction can create.

Part of the new program has been in operation since January, 1953, when *New Serial Titles,* which is essentially a current union list of serials, came into being. It is in the interests of all that as many libraries as possible should send a unit card to the Library of Congress for each serial they catalog which started publication on or after January 1, 1950. It is particularly desirable to report titles that are likely to be uncommon, such as are found in special libraries of all types. The supplying of a unit card is a comparatively simple matter. A certain amount of extra work may be entailed whenever a contributing library is the only institution to report a new title. In that event the Serial Record Division at the Library of Congress will ask it to supply somewhat fuller information than is given on the unit card so that a standard entry (with data about the publisher, subjects covered, etc.) may be included in *New Serial Titles.*

The years ahead may well come to be known as the serial era in library history. Even popular libraries will be touched by the movement as it becomes possible for them to extend their area of usefulness. Experience in the Montclair Free Public Library foreshadows this. In its reorganization it reported:

Recently reference purchases have taken cognizance of the library's ability to locate material in the immediate vicinity with a reasonable degree of speed. In consequence the library has been working to produce various substitutes for regional shelf lists. So far the Montclair Library has:

1. Catalogue cards in the main public catalogue of all books in the Montclair Art Museum, a half mile distant
2. A union list of some 680 magazines in 32 public and semi-public institutions of Montclair, and the terms under which these magazines will be loaned
3. A union list of newspapers on file in all libraries within a ten-cent fare of Montclair
4. A record of the holdings of the subscriptions of local banks to financial services, such as Moody's
5. The Granger and Granger supplement holdings of seven public libraries in the vicinity

A reader who is not adequately served at the Montclair Library, or who believes that all material at his local library has been studied, does not need to take the long trip to New York only to find that he may not borrow books in the city library to take home, or that the collection he really needs to examine is in another building perhaps several miles away. If given the opportunity, the information assistant will direct such an inquirer to the special library which best suits his need and equip him with time-saving bibliographic references.[4]

As the importance of union lists on the national level grows, so too it should increase on the local level; for local union lists can widen the horizon by bringing to light files of publications hitherto accessible only to a limited few. And like the national list, there should be a tendency to make the local coverage extend to serials of all types.

All the anticipated serial activity in the years that lie ahead implies that libraries must review their philosophy of collecting, processing, servicing, and preserving this perplexing, frustrating, at times elusive, but increasingly valuable type of publication. In the new philosophy the visible index and the union list should bulk large, and correspondingly cataloging should be de-emphasized. It is essential that acquisition policies become more systematic, alert, and inclusive, and cataloging processes more streamlined; and that republication programs be intensified and abstracting and indexing services promoted both nationally and internationally, with some modicum of local indexing. All this philosophy lies latent in the theory and achievement of *New Serial Titles* and the *Union List of Serials.*

---

[4] Margery C. Quigley and William E. Marcus, *Portrait of a Library* (New York: Appleton-Century, 1936), p.41-42.

Appendix

Six Case Studies of Serials

THE STATEMENT is made in several places in the text that only the experienced serial librarian has any real conception of the intransigent nature of serials. The complexities of this type of publication have to be known to be believed. In a sense there is a parallel between serials and medicine. Diseases and operations in a small hospital are often accounted rare, whereas in a big city hospital the identical situations are encountered sufficiently frequently for the staff to take them in stride. It is much the same with serial publications. Naturally the vast majority of periodicals, government documents, annual reports, etc. handled in the course of a day's work goes along without let or hindrance in the typical institution. But this does not mean that irregularities occur only by exception or are rare events. On the contrary, they are met with so persistently that serial specialists, especially in large research libraries, are quite accustomed to dealing with them.

The half-dozen case studies which follow are not intended for the specialist. Their aim is rather to give non-serial librarians some idea of the problems that continually arise. The titles cited are by no means the most troublesome that could be found. They have all been taken from the daily work in the Harvard College Library.

Archivio di filosofia. The Harvard College Library has volumes 1-11, published from 1931 to 1941, of this quarterly periodical. It lacks volumes 12-13. The S-card (see page . . .) says: "Beginning with anno 14 (?) ceased to be a quarterly periodical and became a monograph series with some volumes numbered, others unnumbered." Because of uncertainty over the nature of volumes 12-13, a manuscript note has been added which reads: "If 12-13 ever rec'd, give to Ser. Cat. If they are periodicals, add to cat. cards & remove ? after anno 14 on S cd note. If 12-13 are monographs, correct S cd note to read: Beg. with anno 12 (or 13)."

The bibliography, and hence the treatment, of wartime casualties is often uncertain. Naturally, the periodical part of this publication should be held together. Because of its antecedent, the monograph series probably would have been kept together also had it been numbered throughout. But with the mixture of numbered and unnumbered volumes, the only wise course of action is to scatter the monographs. At Harvard the decision was to remove the entry from the visible index and to record on the S-card that the monograph catalogers are to be instructed to call for added entries in both the official and public catalogs under *Archivio di filosofia* for each monograph. The added-entry cards are filed after the entry for the periodical, which reads: "anno 1-11 (1931-41), For later years, see separate cards following."

Canadian Journal of Research. Volumes 1-12 were published normally, and a cumulative index was issued for them. The Harvard sets are in the Chemistry and Farlow libraries. Volumes 13-21 were divided into four sections issued in two parts: Section A/B for the physical and chemical sciences, which is in the Chemistry Library; and Section C/D for the botanical and zoological sciences, which is in Farlow. The pattern changed again for volumes 22-28, each of which was issued in six parts. These parts, with their Harvard locations, were:

Section A, physical sciences	Chemistry Library
Section B, chemical sciences	Chemistry Library
Section C, botanical sciences	Farlow Library
Section D, zoological sciences	Zoological Museum Library
Section E, medical sciences	Medical School Library
Section F, technology	Widener

Then with volume 29 each section became an independent journal with a title of its own. However, each of the new journals began, not with volume 1, but with volume 29. The titles of the journals are:

Canadian journal of botany
Canadian journal of chemistry
Canadian journal of medical sciences
Canadian journal of physics
Canadian journal of technology
Canadian journal of zoology

Le disque vert. The Harvard holdings for this monthly literary review, from 1922 through 1941, are:

Année 1, no. 1-6 (mai-oct. 1922)
Année 1, sér. 2, no. 1-4/5/6 (nov. 1922-avril 1923), entitled Ecrits du nord (fusion du Disque vert et de la Lanterne sourde)
Année 2, no. 1-3 (oct.-déc. 1923)
Année 2, sér. 3, no. 4/5 (1924) and num. spécial (1924)
Année 3, sér. 4, no. 1-3 (1925) also unnumbered issue (1925) entitled Le cas Lautréamont
Unnumbered issue (1934) entitled Au disque vert
N. s. année 1, no. 1 (15 juillet 1941)

An issue "hors série" appeared in December, 1952, entitled *Hommage à Marcel Proust.* In October, 1952, the dealer reported: "Your set is complete." Then the periodical came to life once more with année 1, no. 1 (avril 1953). Because of the confusion in the periodical's numbering, the catalogers decided to give the issues beginning with April, 1953, a separate book number.

The binding of such a periodical presents considerable difficulties, all the more so since this particular title adopted three different formats during its short career. The Harvard solution—once the dealer's report had come—was to bind the numbered and unnumbered issues chronologically. There are now bound volumes for 1922-23, 1924, 1925, 1934, 1941, and 1953. The single issue for 1941 is in a pamphlet binder.

A number of the items had to be analyzed, among them whole issues devoted to Charlie Chaplin, Freud, and Max Jacob.

Internationale Zeitschrift für Erziehungswissenschaft. Harvard has volumes 1-13 Heft 4/5, April, 1931, to August, 1944, of this journal, plus volumes 4-6, 1947-[51]. Despite the gap in years and volume numbering, this is a complete set. Volumes 1-3, 1931-34, were published in Cologne under the editorship of Professor Friedrich Schneider. A Nazi editor took over with volume 4, 1935, and the place of publication was changed to Berlin. At the same time the title was modified to *Internationale Zeitschrift für Erziehung.* The work of the Nazi editor ended in August, 1944. In 1947 Professor Schneider resumed publication under the former title, this time in Salzburg; but because he did not recognize the Nazi volumes, he designated his revival volume 4, the fourth under his editorship, instead of volume 14. Thus there are two volumes numbered 4, 5, and 6.

Harvard decided to treat the set as one work, arranging the volumes on the shelves chronologically. The *Union List of Serials,* which entered the first thirteen volumes under the Nazi title, accorded the revival a separate entry but specified that volumes 1-3 were published in Cologne in 1931-34.

Bibliographical Bulletin of the Linda Hall Library. This series consists of mimeographed bibliographies, numbered consecutively. Many of the items belong in departmental libraries, yet if the whole set were scattered and each item cataloged separately the card catalog entries under Linda Hall Library would multiply at an undesirable rate.

Accordingly, a decision was made to keep all Widener Library issues together as a set. This set would be bound incomplete, with slips inserted at appropriate places specifying the department libraries where the missing numbers are located. A note has been added on the visible index telling the checkers to submit each issue as received for a decision on location and to arrange for the issues in the stacks to be bound when there are ten of them. Further, the note specifies that the set is to be indexed by subject only.

Oxfordshire Record Society. This monograph series represents a problem in binding and analyzing. Each part is numbered consecutively, which would be well and good if each monograph was complete in a single issue. Unfortunately the monographs may run through several issues, and not consecutively. For example, Sir Samuel Luke's *Journal,* volumes 1-3, appeared in volumes 29, 31, and 33 of the series; and volumes 1-4 of *The Church Bells of Oxfordshire* were published in volumes 28, 30, 32, and 34 of the series. Before this problem was realized, much of the set had been bound up consecutively in the order of the monograph series, several issues to the physical volume. Thereafter the monographs were bound together, with the same class mark but a separate book number. Incidentally, the Library of Congress call number for Sir Samuel Luke's *Journal* is "DA670.09A3 vol. 29, etc." This points up one difficulty in dealing with analyticals of this type, the fact that analytical entries for some subseries present impossibly long lists of numbers if all details are recorded. For this reason "etc." is employed in the series note and call number, although stack service may be hindered thereby.

Most libraries have erred in making volumes of serials too large. The difficulties with the Oxfordshire Record Society's publications were increased because each volume was not bound independently. If this had been done, the set could have been rationalized more readily. Since the multiple physical volumes were on the shelves, there was a natural reluctance to tear the bindings apart, even in a good cause.

Selected Bibliography

Bibliographies relating to serials

Bibliographic Index, a Cumulative Bibliography of Bibliographies (New York: Wilson, 1937-). See the entries under House organs, Newspapers, Periodicals, etc.

Downs, Robert B., *American Library Resources* (Chicago: American Library Assn., 1951). "Government publications," p.5-7; "Periodicals, newspapers, and journalism," p.21-34.

Fry, Bernard M., *Library Organization and Management of Technical Reports Literature* (Washington: Catholic Univ. of America Pr., 1953. Catholic University of America Studies in Library Science, 1). "Bibliography," p.118-26.

Grenfell, David, *Periodicals and Serials, Their Treatment in Special Libraries* (London: Aslib, 1953). "Bibliography," p.169-89; "National and international bibliographies and lists of house journals," p.144-56.

Library Literature (New York: Wilson, 1933-). See the entries under Cataloging—Documents, Cataloging—Serials, Exchange of books, periodicals, etc., Government publications, Newspapers, Periodicals, Photographic reproduction and projection, Serial publications, etc.

Markley, A. Ethelyn, *Library Records for Government Publications* (Berkeley: Univ. of California Pr., 1951). "Bibliography," p.33-58.

Public Affairs Information Service, *Bulletin* (New York, 1915-). See the entries under Government publications, House organs, Newspapers, Periodicals, etc.

Roberts, Arthur D., *Introduction to Reference Books* (2d ed. London: Library Assn., 1951). "Directories and other business publications," p.52-59; "Directories of societies, institutions, etc., and bibliographies of their publications," p.125-35; "Government publications," p.136-53; "Newspapers and other records of recent events, yearbooks," p.42-51; "Serials," p.84-101.

Winchell, Constance M., *Guide to Reference Books* (7th ed. Chicago: American Library Assn., 1951). "Government documents," p.105-10; "Periodicals and newspapers," p.87-104.

General works

Cabeen, Violet A., and Donald C. Cook, "Organization of Serials and Documents," *Library Trends* 2:199-216, 1953.

Clark, Pearl H., *The Problem Presented by Periodicals in College and University Libraries* ([Chicago]: Univ. of Chicago, 1930) . 39p.

Deutsch, Karl W., and others, *Is American Attention to Foreign Research Results Declining? A Tentative Attempt at Measurement for Selected Data from Seven Fields of Pure and Applied Science, 1889-1954* ([Boston: American Academy of Arts and Sciences, 1954]) . 39p.

Dickinson, Sarah S., "Idiosyncrasies of Periodicals," *Catalogers' and Classifiers' Yearbook* 2:93-98, 1930.

Ewald, Alice E., "Peculiarities, Perplexities, and Perversities of Periodicals, with Illustrations," *A. L. A. Bulletin* 30:730-36, 1936.

Fry, Bernard M., *Library Organization and Management of Technical Reports Literature* (Washington: Catholic Univ. of America Pr., 1953. Catholic University of America Studies in Library Science, 1). 140p.

Grenfell, David, *Periodicals and Serials, Their Treatment in Special Libraries* (London: Aslib, 1953) . 200p.

Jackson, Eugene B., *Unpublished Research Reports, a Problem in Bibliographical Control* ([Urbana], 1950. University of Illinois Library School Occasional Papers, 17) . 11p.

Kilpatrick, Norman L., "Serials Records in a University Library," *Journal of Cataloging and Classification* 6:33-35, 1950.

Kuhlman, Augustus F., "Administration of Serial and Document Acquisition and Preparation," in *The Acquisition and Cataloging of Books: Papers Presented before the Library Institute at the University of Chicago, July 29 to August 9, 1940,* ed. by William R. Randall (Chicago: Univ. of Chicago Pr., [1940]) , p.95-116.

Matthews, Sidney E., "The Ohio State University Library Serial Program," *Serial Slants* 5:101-07, 1954.

Munn, Ralph, "The Library Mission of Magazines," *Wilson Bulletin* 4:59-60, 1929.

Plant, Marjorie, "Periodicals Procedure in a University Library," *College and Research Libraries* 3:57-63, 1941.

Serial Slants, a Quarterly (Chicago, 1950-).

Simon, Beatrice V., "Let's Consider Serials Realistically," *Library Journal* 71:1296-301, 1946.

Simpkins, Edgar G., "A Study of Serials Processing," *Serial Slants* v.2, Jan. 1952, p.6-17.

Special Libraries Association. Public Business Librarians Group, *Business and the Public Library; Steps in Successful Cooperation,* ed. by Marian C. Manley. (New York: Special Libraries Assn., 1940) . 83p.

Special Libraries Association. Science-Technology Division, *Technical Libraries, Their Organization and Management,* Lucille Jackson, ed. (New York: Special Libraries Assn., [1951]) . 202p.

Special Libraries Association. Social Science Group, *Public Administration Libraries, a Manual of Practice* (Chicago: Public Administration Service, 1948). 91p.

Trotier, Arnold H., "Some Persistent Problems of Serials in Technical Processes," *Serial Slants* v.1, Jan. 1951, p.5-13.

U. S. Library of Congress, *Annual Report,* 1942- (Washington, 1943-).

Weil, H. B., ed., *The Technical Report, Its Preparation, Processing, and Use in Industry and Government* (New York: Reinhold, 1954). "Filing the Technical Report in Industry and Government," by H. Tovey and J. F. Smith, p.259-83; "Subject Classifying and Alphabetical Indexing of Technical Reports," by L. B. Poland, p.285-300; "Report Indexing by Hand-Sorted Punched Cards," by S. W. Dinwiddie and C. C. Conrad, p.303-16; "The Uniterm Coordinate Indexing of Reports," by M. Taube, p.319-32; "Cataloguing Government Technical Reports," by B. M. Fry, p.335-43; "Records and Control Procedures for Security-Classified Technical Reports," by B. M. Fry, p.345-52; "The Storage and Housing of Unpublished Technical Reports," by S. Herner, p.355-61; "Putting Technical-Report Files to Work," by L. B. Poland, p.371-88; "How to Locate and Obtain Government Information Reports," by P. L. Brown, p.391-409.

Abstracting and indexing

Bradford, S. C., "A Plan for Complete Scientific Documentation," *Review of Documentation* 14:54-56, 1947.

Clapp, Verner W., "Indexing and Abstracting: Recent Past and Lines of Future Development," *College and Research Libraries* 11:197-206, 1950.

——— "Indexing and Abstracting Services for Serial Literature," *Library Trends* 2:509-21, 1954.

Ditmas, E. M. R., "The Co-ordination of Abstracting Services, Unesco's Approach to the Problem," *Journal of Documentation* 4:67-83, 1948.

Fuller, Henry M., "International Index under Study by Librarians," *Serial Slants* 5:82-88, 1954.

Lawler, John L., *The H. W. Wilson Company; Half a Century of Bibliographic Publishing* (Minneapolis: Univ. of Minnesota Pr., [1950]). 207p.

Morton, Elizabeth H., "A Century of Periodical Indexing," *Canadian Library Association Bulletin* 4:78-81, 1947.

Plant, Marjorie, "A Project for a Periodicals Indexing Service," *Proceedings* of the British Society for International Bibliography 9:57-64, 1947.

"Present State of the Development of Indexing, Abstracting and Bibliographical Services by Unesco," *Library of Congress Information Bulletin* May 29, 1950, appendix p.1-3.

Robinson, Sarita, "Are We Indexing the Right Magazines?" *Wilson Library Bulletin* 25:597-98, 1951.

Tashjian, Nouvart, "New York University Index to Early American Periodical Literature, 1728-1870," *College and Research Libraries* 7:135-37, 1946.

——— "Periodical Literature Index," *Library Journal* 64:918-19, 1939.

Varossieau, W. W., "A Survey of Scientific Abstracting and Indexing Services," *Review of Documentation* 16:25-46, 1949.

Acquisition and selection

Abrahams, Jack, "A Forward Look at Back Periodicals," *Serial Slants* 4:7-11, 1953.

Anderson, Geraldine D., "Use of Short Cuts, Forms and Simplified Methods," *Special Libraries* 45:245-49, 1954.

Association of Research Libraries, "Cost of Serials; Report of the Serials Committee," *Serial Slants* v.2, April 1952, p.16-27.

Ball, Alice D., "Costs of Serial Acquisition through USBE," *Serial Slants* v.2, April 1952, p.11-15.

——— "Exchange Supermarket," *Library Journal* 78:2057-61, 1953.

——— "Serials Acquisition through the U. S. Book Exchange," *Serial Slants* v.2, July 1951, p.7-19.

Benson, Nettie L., "Acquisition of Serials from Latin America," *Serial Slants* 4:110-14, 1953.

Björkbom, Carl, "Bibliographical Tools for Control of Current Periodicals," *Review of Documentation* 20:19-24, 1953.

Brodman, Estelle, "Choosing Physiology Journals," *Medical Library Association Bulletin* 32:479-83, 1944.

——— *Methods of Choosing Physiology Journals* (New York, 1943). 39p. Thesis, Columbia University Library School.

Brown, Charles H., *Library Resources in Selected Scientific Subjects at Louisiana State University* (Baton Rouge: Louisiana State Univ. Library, 1950).

——— "Serial Costs in Relation to Other Library Expenditures and to Inflation," *Serial Slants* v.2, July 1951, p.20-24.

Colburn, Edwin B., "Mutual Problems of Serial Agents and Librarians," *Serial Slants* v.1, Oct. 1950, p.20-26.

Dane, Charles, "No Newspapers!" *Wilson Library Bulletin* 28:699-700, 1954. Discusses the need for newspapers in the school library.

Davis, Albert H., "The Subscription Agency and the Library; Responsibilities and Problems from the Dealer's Viewpoint," *Serial Slants* v.1, Oct. 1950, p.14-19.

Hallam, Bertha B., "Periodical and Book Selection and Ordering," in *A Handbook of Medical Library Practice* (Chicago: American Library Assn., 1943), p.65-84.

Holloway, A. H., "Acquisition of Reports," *Aslib Proceedings* 5:323-28, 1953.

Jackson, Eugene B., "How to Obtain Research and Development Reports from the Government," *Special Libraries* 44:101-08, 1953.

Lane, Alfred H., "The Economics of Exchange," *Serial Slants* 3:19-22, 1952.

——— "Exchange Materials Used in College and University Libraries," *College and Research Libraries* 8:44-49, 1947.

Lessing, Ralph, "Subscription Problems as Seen by an Agent," *Serial Slants* 4:5-7, 1953.

Logasa, Hannah, *Book Selection Handbook for Elementary and Secondary School* (Boston: Faxon, 1953). "Magazines," p.99-102; "Newspapers," p.107-09.

MacIver, Ivander, "The Exchange of Publications as a Medium for the Development of the Book Collection," *Library Quarterly* 8:491-502, 1938.

McLean, Philip T., "Acquisition of Serials from Eastern Europe," *Serial Slants* 4:115-23, 1953.

Matthews, Sidney E., "The Ohio State University Library Serial Program," *Serial Slants* 5:101-07, 1954.

Medical Library Association, "The Exchange and the Policies Underlying Its Administration," *Medical Library Association Bulletin* 33:357-59, 1945.

Miller, Robert A., *The Purchasing of Books and Journals in Europe* ([Urbana], 1953. University of Illinois Library School Occasional Papers, 36). 11p.

Naylor, Mildred V., "Exchange," *Medical Library Association Bulletin* 34:167-75, 1946.

Orne, Jerrold, "A Serials Information Clearing House," *Serial Slants* v.1, April 1951, p.10-17.

Postell, William D., "Further Comments on the Mathematical Analysis of Evaluating Scientific Journals," *Medical Library Association Bulletin* 34:107-09, 1946.

Poynter, F. N. L., "A Duplicate Exchange Service for Medical Libraries," *Library Association Record* 52:41-43, 1950.

Shaw, K. B., "Periodical Acquisition Policies," *Aslib Proceedings* 5:81-85, 1953.

Smith, L. Herman, and Eleanor H. Hidden, "Selection and Organization of Periodicals in the Junior College Library," *College and Research Libraries* 12:343-45, 1951.

Stevens, Rolland E., "Characteristics of Subject Literatures," *ACRL Monographs* 6, 1953.

——— *The Use of Library Materials in Doctoral Research; a Study of the Effect of Differences in Research Method* (Urbana, 1951). Ph.D. Thesis, University of Illinois Library School.

Thompson, Donald E., "Duplicate Exchange Union," *College and Research Libraries* 6:158-60, 1945.

U. S. Library of Congress, *Exchange and Gift Division* (Washington, 1950. Departmental & Divisional Manuals, 6). 25p.

——— *Order Division* (Washington, 1952. Departmental & Divisional Manuals, 20) . 63p.

Vickery, B. C., "Periodical Sets: What Should You Buy?" *Aslib Proceedings* 5:69-74, 1953.

Woolston, John E., "American Technical Reports, Their Importance and How to Obtain Them," *Journal of Documentation* 9:211-19, 1953.

Binding

Feipel, Louis N., and Earl W. Browning, *Library Binding Manual* (Chicago: American Library Assn., 1951) . 74p.

Hertzberg, Ernst, "The Binding Industry," *Serial Slants* v.1, July 1950, p.10-19.

Hughes, Margaret H., "Periodical Binding Schedules for Improved Reader Service in University and College Libraries," *College and Research Libraries* 13:223-26, 231, 1952.

Ort, J. George, "Standardization of Periodical Bindings," *Serial Slants* 4:12-14, 1953.

Stratton, John B., *Library Binding Practices in College and University Libraries* (New York, 1952). Thesis, Columbia University Library School.

Trotier, Arnold H., "Some Persistent Problems of Serials in Technical Processes," *Serial Slants* v.1, Jan. 1951, p.5-13.

U. S. Library of Congress, *Binding Division* (Washington, 1950. Departmental & Divisional Manuals, 5) . 30p.

Warner, Frances, "Current Binding Policies at Iowa State College," *Serial Slants* 3:39-42, 1952.

Wright, Emma G., and E. B. Barnes, "Binding at the University of Oregon," *Serial Slants* v.2, Jan. 1952, p.2-5.

Cataloging and classification

Bird, Nancy, "Title Cataloging of Periodicals at Florida State University," *Serial Slants* 4:19-20, 1953.

Black, Henry T., "Indexing Selected Periodicals Proves Sound Investment," *Library Journal* 74:1296, 1312, 1949.

Cameron, A. R., "Accessioning and Cataloguing of Reports," *Aslib Proceedings* 5:329-34, 1953.

Cresap, McCormick and Paget, *Survey of Preparation Procedures, Reference Department, New York Public Library* ([New York, 1951]) .

Flannery, Anne, "To Analyze or Not?" *Journal of Cataloging and Classification* 5:42-43, 1949.

Franck, Marga, "Some International Differences in the Cataloging and Bibliographical Listing of Serial Publications," *Serial Slants* v.2, Oct. 1951, p.1-10.

Goss, Edna L., "The Cataloging of Serials," *Catalogers' and Classifiers' Yearbook* 2:73-92, 1930.

Iskenderian, Y., *Extent and Possibilities for Co-operation in the Cataloging of Serial Publications, Based on a Survey of Libraries of over 350,000 Volumes* (New York, 1942). Thesis, Columbia University Library School.

Lubetzky, Seymour, "The Cataloging of Publications of Corporate Authors, a Rejoinder," *Library Quarterly* 21:1-12, 1951.

New York Public Library. Preparation Division, "Cataloging and Adding of Serials," Its *Technical Order* 53-83.

Pierson, Harriet W., "The Forest of Pencils; Adventures in Corporate Entry," *Library Quarterly* 4:306-13, 1934.

——— "The Gay Science—the Cataloguing of the Publications of Learned Societies," *Proceedings* of the Catalog Section, American Library Association, 1929, p.136-44.

Quartz, Beatrice M., Marian Harman, and Esther J. Piercy, "Policies for Analyzing Monograph Series—a Panel Discussion," *Serial Slants* 4:124-40, 1953.

Schilpp, Emily C., "Short-Cuts in Serials Cataloging?" *Serial Slants* v.1, April 1951, p.2-9.

Schley, Ruth, and Jane B. Davies, *Serials Notes Compiled from Library of Congress Cards Issued 1947-April 1951* ([New York]: Columbia Univ. Libraries, 1952). 27p.

Simon, Beatrice V., "Cataloguing of Periodicals," *Ontario Library Review* 33:237-45, 1949.

Taube, Mortimer, "The Cataloging of Publications of Corporate Authors," *Library Quarterly* 20:1-20, 1950.

U. S. Library of Congress, *Descriptive Cataloging Division* (Washington, 1950. Departmental & Divisional Manuals, 8). 88p.

——— *Subject Cataloging Division* (Washington, 1950. Departmental & Divisional Manuals, 3). 62p.

Walkins, P. S., "Filing and Storage of Reports," *Aslib Proceedings* 5:335-40, 1953.

Wimersberger, Evelyn G., "Methods of Indicating Serial Holdings in the Catalogs of College and University Libraries," *Catalogers' and Classifiers' Yearbook* 8:133-34, 1939.

Yale University Library, *Cataloging of Serials in the Yale University Library* (New Haven, 1951). 67p.

Circulation

Bloomer, Gertrude, "The Circulation of Current Journals in Special Libraries," *Special Libraries* 39:46-50, 1948.

Bray, Robert S., "Rapid Announcement of the Contents of Scientific Journals," *American Documentation* 2:213-16, 1951.

Bumgardner, Harvey E., "Labor-Saving Methods Applied to Magazine Circulation," *Special Libraries* 43:92-93, 102, 1952.

"Circulation of Bound Periodicals," *Serial Slants* v.1, July 1950, p.7-9.

Cole, Barbara R., and Helen Rowley, "Current Journal Routing," *Special Libraries* 35:324-27, 1944.

Garvin, Elsie L., "The '3-Day' Shelf," *Wilson Library Bulletin* 14:775, 1940.

Herner, Saul, "The Selected Reading List: a Means of Improving the Use of Periodical Literature," *Special Libraries* 41:324-26, 335-36, 1950.

Murch, E. H., and C. E. C. Hewetson, "A Scheme for Circulating Periodicals," *Aslib Proceedings* 5:131-36, 1953.

Price, Robert F., "A Man-Hour Analysis of Periodical Circulation," *Library Quarterly* 16:239-44, 1946.

Randall, G. E., "Journal Routing; Greater Efficiency at Lower Cost," *Special Libraries* 45:371-73, 1954.

Southern, Walter A., "Library Bulletins in American Industrial Libraries," *Aslib Proceedings* 5:320-21, 1953.

Spalding, Mary L., "Current Use versus Permanent Preservation of Periodicals as Reflected in Organization," *A. L. A. Bulletin* 34: P201-04, 1940.

"Wanted: a Table-of-Contents Reprint Service," *Special Libraries* 41:257-58, 1950.

Wright, Marie G., and Richard G. Gremling, "Abstract Bulletin Xerographic Short Cut," *Special Libraries* 45:250-51, 1954.

Government publications

Andriot, John L., "Government Serials at Mid-Century," *Serial Slants* v.2, April 1952, p.1-10.

Barr, William F., "Advantages and Disadvantages of a Superintendent of Documents Classification as a Key to a Depository Collection," *College and Research Libraries* 12:40-42, 1951.

Brown, Everett S., *Manual of Government Publications* (New York: Appleton-Century-Crofts, [1950]). 121p.

Caballero-Marsal, Fernando, Jorgen K. Nielsen, and Harry N. M. Winton, "United Nations Documents in the United Nations Library: Organization and Servicing," *Journal of Cataloging and Classification* 7:65-72, 1951.

Carroll, Marie J., "League of Nations Documents and Publications Comparable with or Continued in United Nations Publications," *College and Research Libraries* 13:44-52, 64, 1952.

Cassidy, Thomas R., "United Nations Documents in the Medium-Sized University—Nuisance or Necessity," *College and Research Libraries* 13:107-10, 1952.

Chamberlin, Waldo, and Carol C. Moor, "The United Nations Documents Collection at New York University," *College and Research Libraries* 12:52-61, 1951.

Eastin, R. B., "Documents Problems Will Be Solved," *Library Journal* 72:1069-73, 1947.

——— "Let's Use Public Documents!" *Library Journal* 73:1554-58, 1948.

Fleming, Thomas P., "The Organization of Work with Public Documents in University Libraries," in *Public Documents; Papers Presented at the 1935 Conference of the American Library Association* (Chicago: American Library Assn., 1936), p.101-27.

Hull, Jeanne E., "Obligations and Staff Requirements of a Complete Federal Depository," *College and Research Libraries* 12:37-39, 1951.

Humphrey, Mary B., "Obstacles and Opportunities in Specialized Treatment of Federal Depository Documents," *College and Research Libraries* 12:45-47, 51, 1951.

Jackson, Ellen P., "Administration of the Government Documents Collection," *ACRL Monographs* 5, 1953.

——— *A Brief Guide to Government Documents* ([Urbana], 1950. University of Illinois Library School Occasional Papers, 7). 11p.

Jackson, Isabel H., "Advantages and Disadvantages of a Subject System of Classification as Key to a Depository Collection," *College and Research Libraries* 12:42-45, 1951.

Kyle, Barbara, "Official Documents in a Special Library," *Aslib Proceedings* 1:262-66, 1949.

McCamy, James L., *Government Publications for the Citizen* (New York: Columbia Univ. Pr., 1949). 139p.

Mallaber, K. A., "Official Publications in Public Reference Libraries," *Aslib Proceedings* 1:257-61, 1949.

Markley, A. Ethelyn, *Library Records for Government Publications* (Berkeley: Univ. of California Pr., 1951). 66p.

Miller, Kathryn N., *Selection of United States Serial Documents for Liberal Arts Colleges* (New York: Wilson, 1937). 364p.

Moen, Blanche, "Care of Congressional Hearings and Reports," *Library Journal* 65:523-24, 1940.

Moor, Carol C., and Waldo Chamberlin, *How to Use United Nations Documents* ([New York, 1952]. New York University Conference on United Nations Documents, May 19, 1952, Paper no. 1). 38 leaves.

"Official Checklists and Indexes Versus Cataloging of Government Publications, a Symposium. Papers by Isabel H. Jackson, Ruth Hardin, Violet A. Cabeen, and Arthur D. Roberts, Presented at the Meeting of the A. L. A. Committee on Public Documents, July 19, 1950," *College and Research Libraries* 12:158-70, 1951.

Pierce, Catharine J., "The Care of United States Public Documents in a College Library," *Library Journal* 66:295-97, 1941.

Roberts, Arthur D., "The Documents and Publications of International Organizations," *Review of Documentation* 17:3-17, 1950.

Saunders, Janet F., "Libraries and the Publications of the UN Specialized Agencies," *Unesco Bulletin for Libraries* 8:E102-08, 1954.

Ward, Pauline, "Processing Government Documents," *College and Research Libraries* 12:48-51, 1951.

Wilcox, Jerome K., *Manual on the Use of State Publications* (Chicago: American Library Assn., 1940). 342p.

Microreproduction

Boni, Albert, "Microprint," *American Documentation* 2:150-52, 1951.
Booth, Robert E., "American Periodicals, 1800-1825. University Microfilms Commences a New Series," *Library Journal* 71:156-63, 179, 1946.
Carruthers, Ralph H., "N.Y.P.L. Changes Treatment of Microfilm Serials," *Library Journal* 72:880-82, 1947.
——— "Titling of Microfilm Editions," *American Documentation* 1:190-93, 1950.
Eastin, R. B., "The Point of View of the Division of Public Documents," *American Documentation* 2:160-62, 1951.
Erickson, Edgar L., "The Sessional Papers," *Library Journal* 78:13-17, 1953.
——— "The Sessional Papers Project," *Journal of Documentary Reproduction* 4:83-93, 1941.
Fox, Louis H., "Films for Folios," *Library Journal* 62:361-64, 1937.
——— "Turn a Handle and Get Your Page," *Library Journal* 60:675-76, 1935.
Jolley, Leonard, "The Use of Microfilm for Completing Sets," *Journal of Documentation* 4:41-44, 1948.
Kipp, Laurence J., "Microfilming Foreign Newspapers," *Harvard Library Bulletin* 2:410-12, 1948.
Lewis, Benjamin M., "The American Periodical Series, 1800-1809," *Serial Slants* 5:12-16, 1954.
Metcalf, Keyes D., "Newspapers and Microphotography," *Journal of Documentary Reproduction* 2:180-83, 1939.
Microcard Bulletin (Middletown, Conn., 1948-).
Micro-Photo Service Bureau, *A Program for the Microfilming of Newspaper Files; Earlier History and Modern Developments* (Cleveland, [195-]). 7p.
Power, Eugene B., "Microfilm as a Substitute for Binding," *American Documentation* 2:33-39, 1951.
——— "Source Materials for the Study of American Culture," *Journal of Documentary Reproduction* 3:192-97, 1940.
——— "Symposium on Microreproduction: Microfilm," *Serial Slants* 3:43-46, 1952.
——— "University Microfilms—a Microfilming Service for Scholars," *Journal of Documentation* 2:23-31, 1946.
——— "The Use of Sheet Film for Newspaper Clippings," *Special Libraries* 45:111-14, 1954.
Sale, Robert C., "Is Binding the Answer?" *Special Libraries* 42:380, 394, 1951. Experience in a library that decided to use microreproduction only as the very last resort. It planned therefore to continue binding its serials.
Shoemaker, Ralph J., "Remarks on Microcards and Microfilm for Newspapers," *American Documentation* 1:207-08, 1950.

Tate, Vernon D., "Microphotography in Archives," *National Archives Staff Information Circulars* 8, 1940.

University Microfilms, *The Problem of Periodical Storage in Libraries* (Ann Arbor, Mich., 1954). 17p.

Wilcox, Jerome K., "The Point of View of the Librarian," *American Documentation* 2:162-66, 1951.

Organization of serials work

Erlandson, Ruth M., "The Organization of Federal Government Publications in Depository Libraries," in Anne M. Boyd, *United States Government Publications* (3d ed. New York: Wilson, 1949), p.569-79.

Rothman, Fred B., "Pooh-bah of the Serials Division," *Library Journal* 62:457-59, 1937.

——— and Sidney Ditzion, "Prevailing Practices in Handling Serials," *College and Research Libraries* 1:165-69, 1940.

Reference

Armstrong, Mary, "Documents Please Fort Wayne Patrons," *Wilson Library Bulletin* 23:319, 327, 1948.

Barton, Mary N., "Serials: Bane and Blessing to the Reference Librarian," *Serial Slants* 4:14-17, 1953.

Cheney, Frances N., "Wilson Publications as Reference Tools," *Wilson Library Bulletin* 22:801-05, 1948.

Hoffman, Frederick J., "Research Value of the 'Little Magazine,'" *College and Research Libraries* 6:311-16, 1945.

Kaplan, Louis, "Reference Work with Periodicals: Recent Progress and Future Needs," *College and Research Libraries* 1:241-45, 1940.

Little, Gretchen D., "Locating Difficult Periodical References," *Special Libraries* 35:373-79, 1944.

Meyer, Ida M., "Government Publications as Sources of Information," *Special Libraries* 36:241-43, 1945.

Pfoutz, Daniel R., "Our Special Indexes Do Save Our Time," *Library Journal* 73:1638-41, 1948.

Smith, W. A., James D. Stewart, and Ursula E. Price, "Locating Periodicals," *Library Association Record* 55:245-52, 1953.

Spalding, Mary L., "Reference Work in a Periodical Room," *Wilson Bulletin* 11:602-03, 1937.

U. S. Library of Congress, *Serials Division* (Washington, 1950. Departmental & Divisional Manuals, 9). 26p.

Wright, R. C., "Exploiting Report Literature," *Aslib Proceedings* 5:341-44, 1953.

Regional cooperation

Hampshire Inter-Library Center, *Annual Report* (South Hadley, Mass., 1952-).

Midwest Inter-Library Center, *Annual Report* (Chicago, 1950-).
——— *Newsletter* (Chicago, 1949-).

The visible index and its rivals

Bennett, Fleming, "A Multi-Purpose Serials Record," *College and Research Libraries* 9:231-37, 1948.

Berry, Paul L., "Library of Congress Serial Record Techniques," *Serial Slants* 3:14-18, 1952.

Campbell, D. J., "The Control and Utilization of Periodicals; Technical Methods at the Royal Cancer Hospital, London," *Library Association Record* 54:7-11, 1952.

Hartje, George N., *Centralized Serial Records in University Libraries* ([Urbana, 1951]. University of Illinois Library School Occasional Papers, 24). 10p. Reprinted in part in *Serial Slants* v.1, Jan. 1951, p.14-22.

Jacobs, R. M., "Focal Point: a Composite Record for the Control of Periodicals Using a Visible Signalling Device," *Journal of Documentation* 6:213-28, 1950.

Keller, Alton H., "A Flexoline Record of Serial Holdings," *Library of Congress Information Bulletin* Jan. 16, 1950, p.21-23.

Litchfield, Dorothy H., "Paleolithic Practices in the Checking and Cataloging of Periodicals," *Library Journal* 60:58-61, 1935.

Los Angeles Public Library, *Work Book of Serials Procedure* (Los Angeles, 1932). 43 leaves.

McGaw, Howard F., *Marginal Punched Cards in College and Research Libraries* (Washington: Scarecrow Pr., 1952). "The serials department," p.151-55.

Moffit, Alexander, "Punched Card Records in Serials Acquisition," *College and Research Libraries* 7:10-13, 1946.

Moore, M. S., "Visible Indexing Techniques Applied to Library Records," *Library Association Record* 50:184-86, 1948.

Shachtman, Bella E., "Current Serial Records—an Experiment," *College and Research Libraries* 14:240-42, 248, 1953.

——— "Simplification of Serial Records Work," *Serial Slants* 3:6-13, 1952.

Shaw, Ralph R., "Photoclerical Routines at USDA," *Library Journal* 78:2064-70, 1953.

Skipper, James E., "Organizing Serial Records at the Ohio State University Libraries," *College and Research Libraries* 14:39-45, 1953.

Index